B형: 고3

파이널편

고득점 수능듣기

Listening Power Is in You

KB068597

RHK
알엔비컨텐츠

집필진

한소영
현) Target English Clinic 대표
전) 압구정 본원 파인만학원(주) 크라센어학원
　　고등부 수석팀장 및 특목중·고 입시담당
전) 목동 본원 서준어학원 특목중·고 입시담당

박명재
현) 메가스터디 외국어 듣기 전문강사
현) 경선식 에듀 듣기 대표강사
전) EBS 듣기 대표강사
전) 비타에듀 외국어 듣기 대표강사
전) 강남 영독학원 외국어 듣기 대표강사
전) 청평 비타 외국어 듣기 대표강사

감수

변성우
현) 인천고등학교 교사
전) 인천공항중학교 교사
숙명여자대학교 SMU-TESOL Diploma
인하대학교 영어영문학과

David Charlton
동원대학교 영어 회화 교수

검토진

유영욱
전) EZ어학원 교수부장

장지혜
현) Target English Clinic 팀장
전) 크라센어학원 iBT Final 강사

이윤선
전) Boston어학원 강사
전) Yes영도어학원 강사

서울권 대학생 및 고등학생 일동

고득점 수능듣기

B형: 고3 파이널편

Listening Power Is in You

1판 1쇄 **인쇄** 2013년 8월 19일
1판 1쇄 **발행** 2013년 8월 26일

지은이 한소영·박명재

발행인 양원석
총편집인 이헌상
편집장 오수민
책임편집 유정윤
편집진행 김진경
디자인 황선재
전산편집 함동춘
삽화 김태복
해외저작권 황지현, 지소연
제작 문태일, 김수진
영업마케팅 김경만, 임충진, 곽희은, 주상우, 장현기, 임우열, 정미진, 송기현, 우지연, 윤선미

펴낸 곳 ㈜알에이치코리아
주소 서울시 금천구 가산동 345-90 한라시그마밸리 20층
편집문의 02-6443-8800 **구입문의** 02-6443-8838
홈페이지 www.dobedobe.com
등록 2004년 1월 15일 제2-3726호

Contents

수능 10일 전   대학수학능력평가 대비 영어영역 듣기(B형)   008

수능 9일 전   대학수학능력평가 대비 영어영역 듣기(B형)   026

수능 8일 전   대학수학능력평가 대비 영어영역 듣기(B형)   044

수능 7일 전   대학수학능력평가 대비 영어영역 듣기(B형)   062

수능 6일 전   대학수학능력평가 대비 영어영역 듣기(B형)   080

수능 5일 전   대학수학능력평가 대비 영어영역 듣기(B형)   098

수능 4일 전   대학수학능력평가 대비 영어영역 듣기(B형)   116

수능 3일 전   대학수학능력평가 대비 영어영역 듣기(B형)   134

수능 2일 전   대학수학능력평가 대비 영어영역 듣기(B형)   152

수능 1일 전   대학수학능력평가 대비 영어영역 듣기(B형)   170

Answer Key   188

영어영역 듣기 답안지

이 책의 특징

수능 막바지 최종 정리 모의고사
"고득점 수능듣기 파이널편"이 해답입니다!

1. 정부 발표 연계 문제를 심층 분석했습니다.

정부에서 발표한 교육 방송 교재 연계 문제 분석하여
새로운 접근을 시도하는 수능의 입맛에 최대한 맞춘 파이널 교재입니다.
수능 직전, 이제 이 책으로 변별력을 높일 차례입니다.

2. 수능 10일을 앞두고 최종 점검하세요.

총 10회 구성으로 아쉽지도, 버겁지도 않도록 구성하였습니다.
수능 보기 한 달 전부터 최소 10일 전까지 활용할 수 있는 파이널 교재로
부담과 걱정 없이 외국어 영역 듣기를 정복하세요.

3. 이 책으로 여러분의 대학이 한 단계 높아집니다.

22문제로 늘어나 비중이 높아진 영어 듣기 시험 유형에 발맞추어
모든 문제마다 유형을 반복 연습하고 마무리할 수 있도록 구성하였습니다.
다양한 수준의 질문으로 간과했던 부분을 최종 정리하세요.

4. 현직 교사와 영어 전문가 및 수능 경험자들이 직접 검토하였습니다.

현 문제 출제 경향 및 연계 문제에 대한 검수를 현직 교사가 직접 검수하였습니다.
또한 여러 영어 전문가의 검토진 외에도 전 수능 세대인 대학생과 현 수능 세대인
고등학생이 직접 문제를 검토하여 문제의 실제성을 높였습니다.

- **대학생:** 송형주 (서강대 영어영문학과), 이승민 (연세대 언더우드 국제학부), 이예인 (연세대 언더우드 국제학부),
  윤현진 (연세대 노어노문학과), 김길중 (건국대 사학과), 김다은 (상명대 환경공학과),
  함형범 (상명대 경영학과), 성은지 (삼육대 식품영양학과)
- **고등학생:** 나다솜 (여의도여자고등학교), 이영기 (우신고등학교), 이한희 (신도림고등학교), 서은식 (장훈고등학교),
  송다현 (장훈고등학교), 이병헌 (우신고등학교), 김동현 (환일고등학교)

이 책의 구성

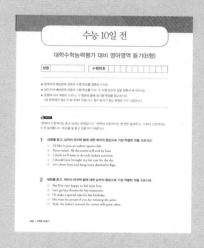

1. 수능 전 카운트 다운

수능 최소 10일 전부터 1일 전까지 카운트 다운을 하면서
영어 듣기로 조금 더 실전처럼 긴장감 있게
풀어볼 수 있도록 구성하였습니다.

2. 개별 받아쓰기

시험 전까지 정확히 짚고
넘어갈 수 있도록 구성하였습니다.
받아쓰기는 영어 듣기를 가장 효과적으로
잡아주는 도구입니다.

3. 지문별 MP3 수록

학습 시간 절약을 위해 모든 지문은 각각 나누어 MP3에 담았습니다.
부족한 부분을 단시간에 집중하여 학습할 수 있도록 구성하였습니다.

• 수능 10일 전

10일이면 10점은 올릴 수 있다!

내 속의 수많은 고통과 번뇌와 인내의 그 시간의 결실이 10일 남았다. 그렇다고 멘탈 붕괴? 안 되지. 10일이면 10점은 올릴 수 있다고! 10점이면 대학이 바뀌지. 이 책 저 책 막 뒤지지 말고 연계교재를 손에 잡자. 눈에 보이는 한 단어 한 문장 한 문제에 충실하자. 그러면 10점은 올릴 수 있어!

수능 10일 전

대학수학능력평가 대비
영어영역 듣기(B형)

수능 10일 전

대학수학능력평가 대비 영어영역 듣기(B형)

성명		수험번호										

- 문제지의 해당란에 성명과 수험 번호를 정확히 쓰시오.
- 답안지의 해당란에 성명과 수험 번호를 쓰고, 또 수험 번호와 답을 정확히 표시하시오.
- 문항에 따라 배점이 다르니, 각 물음의 끝에 표시된 배점을 참고하시오.
  3점 문항에만 점수가 표시되어 있습니다. 점수 표시가 없는 문항은 모두 2점입니다.

MP3 01

1번부터 22번까지는 듣고 답하는 문제입니다. 1번부터 20번까지는 한 번만 들려주고, 21부터 22번까지는 두 번 들려줍니다. 방송을 잘 듣고 답을 하기 바랍니다.

1 대화를 듣고, 남자의 마지막 말에 대한 여자의 응답으로 가장 적절한 것을 고르시오.

① I'd like to join an indoor sports club.
② Never mind. All the events will end by four.
③ I think we'll have to do only indoor activities.
④ I should have brought my fur coat for the day.
⑤ Let's draw lines and hang some decorative flags.

2 대화를 듣고, 여자의 마지막 말에 대한 남자의 응답으로 가장 적절한 것을 고르시오.

① She'll be very happy to feel your love.
② Let's go buy flowers for her tomorrow.
③ I'll make a special cake for her birthday.
④ She must be proud of you for winning the prize.
⑤ Yeah, the bakery around the corner sells great cakes.

3 대화를 듣고, 남자의 마지막 말에 대한 여자의 응답으로 가장 적절한 것을 고르시오.

① Yes, I go there twice a month.
② No, I usually go to the hospital by bicycle.
③ I worked in the hospital parking lot then.
④ If I don't have any other plans, I try to.
⑤ Yes, they're great singers and really enjoy that time.

4 다음을 듣고, 남자가 하는 말의 목적으로 가장 적절한 것을 고르시오.

① 천문학 강의 교수가 변경됨을 안내하려고
② 천문대 관측 프로그램에 대해 공지하려고
③ 날조된 천문학적 이론들에 대해 고발하려고
④ 천문대 관람 예약 시 주의사항을 당부하려고
⑤ 대학교에서 진행되는 천문학 특강을 소개하려고

5 대화를 듣고, 남자의 일기에 관한 여자의 충고로 가장 적절한 것을 고르시오.

① 원고를 몇 번 더 정리해야 한다.
② 시간의 흐름 순으로 써야 한다.
③ 사실에 기반을 둔 내용을 써야 한다.
④ 다른 사람의 의견을 반영해야 한다.
⑤ 구체적인 주제를 정해서 써야 한다.

6 다음을 듣고, 여자가 하는 말의 요지로 가장 적절한 것을 고르시오.

① 입 냄새가 나면 바로 치과에 가야 한다.
② 건강이 좋지 않은 사람들은 입 냄새가 난다.
③ 이를 규칙적으로 닦으면 입 냄새는 사라진다.
④ 입 냄새는 질병의 증상일 수 있어 주의가 필요하다.
⑤ 친구에게 입 냄새가 난다고 하는 것은 예의가 아니다.

7 대화를 듣고, 두 사람이 하는 말의 주제로 가장 적절한 것을 고르시오.

① 텃밭 가꾸기의 장점
② 텃밭을 가꾸는 방법
③ 유기농 채소를 먹어야 하는 이유
④ 텃밭에 심을 수 있는 식물의 종류
⑤ 채소 샐러드를 많이 먹어야 하는 이유

8 대화를 듣고, 두 사람의 관계를 가장 잘 나타낸 것을 고르시오.

① 작가 – 편집자   ② 면접관 – 꽃가게 주인
③ 사진작가 – 저널리스트   ④ 영화감독 – 관객
⑤ 기자 – 영화감독

9 대화를 듣고, 그림에서 주유소의 위치를 고르시오.

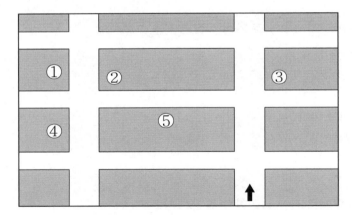

10 대화를 듣고, 남자가 할 일로 가장 적절한 것을 고르시오.

① 서점에 가서 추천 도서 사기
② 세계사 수업에 늦지 않게 도착하기
③ 국회 도서관에 가서 발표 자료 찾기
④ 발표 준비를 위해 선생님 찾아가기
⑤ 인터넷에서 대학살 관련 정보 찾기

11 대화를 듣고, 여자가 남자에게 부탁한 일로 가장 적절한 것을 고르시오.

① to plan a party schedule
② to text tennis club members
③ to book a restaurant on Sunday
④ to call Steven to explain a party
⑤ to put his name on a birthday card

12 대화를 듣고, 남자가 여자를 찾아온 이유를 고르시오.

① 경쟁팀에 대한 정보를 얻으려고
② 악기의 문제에 대해 보고하려고
③ 새로운 곡 선정을 제안하려고
④ 회의가 성공적이었음을 알리려고
⑤ 커피숍에서 들은 얘기를 확인하려고

13 대화를 듣고, Manni 필라테스 센터에 관해 두 사람이 언급하지 <u>않는</u> 것을 고르시오.

① 주차 시설   ② 강습비
③ 강습 시간   ④ 강사의 자질
⑤ 샤워 시설

14 대화를 듣고, 남자가 추가로 낼 금액을 고르시오.

① $10   ② $20
③ $30   ④ $40
⑤ $50

15 화요 조찬 모임에 관한 다음 내용을 듣고, 일치하지 <u>않는</u> 것을 고르시오.

① 오늘의 토론 주제는 '신화: 잃어버린 상상을 되찾다'이다.
② 오늘 토론은 지난 3월 이후 10번째로 맞은 토론이다.
③ 참가자가 원하는 대로 조를 정할 수 있다.
④ 다음 주 주제는 '차세대 사무 환경'이다.
⑤ 식사는 한식과 양식 중에서 선택할 수 있다.

16 다음을 듣고, 갤러리 정에 관한 내용과 일치하지 <u>않는</u> 것을 고르시오. [3점]

① 옛 시청 청사 내에서 개관될 예정이다.
② 전시실 대관 비용이 무료이다.
③ 예술 전공 학생들도 전시실을 대관할 수 있다.
④ 4월 18일부터 도자기 작품이 전시될 예정이다.
⑤ 개관일부터 전시실 대관 신청이 가능하다.

17 다음 표를 보면서 대화를 듣고, 여자가 사기로 한 체중계를 고르시오.

	Manufacturer	Price	Color
①	Hiksan	$17	Black
②	Jinkyung	$24	Green
③	Somina	$31	Red
④	Borad	$19	Yellow
⑤	Pole	$27	Orange

18 대화를 듣고, 여자의 마지막 말에 대한 남자의 응답으로 가장 적절한 것을 고르시오.

Man: _____

① I've already reserved a fancy restaurant.
② I know a great artist from there.
③ Sorry, I don't have your email address.
④ I'll send you an email with the information after work.
⑤ It takes such a long time to have a French dinner.

19 대화를 듣고, 남자의 마지막 말에 대한 여자의 응답으로 가장 적절한 것을 고르시오.

Woman: _____

① That's very nice. You are on a roll!
② Never, ever, give up. I believe you'll be the one.
③ I can't go to the movies tonight.
④ What a coincidence! I'm here for the movie.
⑤ Can you tell me what I have to do?

20 다음 상황 설명을 듣고, Joanne이 Ms. DeJesus에게 할 말로 가장 적절한 것을 고르시오.

Joanne: _____

① Let me show you my plan for the presentation.
② It's hard to arrange my schedule in detail.
③ Check your schedule closely in the future.
④ I'll try to write down a to-do list in my planner.
⑤ I'm so sorry but I can't follow the class schedule.

[21~22] 다음을 듣고, 물음에 답하시오.

21 담화의 제목으로 가장 적절한 것은?

① 예방 접종을 해야 하는 이유
② 당뇨병을 치료하는 예방 백신
③ 필수 예방 접종의 시기와 종류
④ 인슐린을 조절해야 하는 병: 당뇨병
⑤ 결핵과 당뇨병의 공통점과 차이점

22 다음 중, 소개된 실험의 결과에 어울리는 속담은 무엇인가?

① Out of the frying pan and into the fire.
② That's killing two birds with one stone.
③ Carry fire one hand and water in the other.
④ A good medicine tastes bitter.
⑤ A little learning is a dangerous thing.

Dictation

문제 지문을 다시 한 번 듣고 빈칸을 채워보세요. 잘 안 들리는 부분은 음성을 반복해서 익혀 보세요.

1 🔊 MP3 01-01

M: Hey, Eunice! Did you prepare for the _____ _____?

W: Not yet, but the weather forecast says it'll _____ _____ _____ _____ _____ on that day.

M: Oh, boy! What should we do?

2 🔊 MP3 01-02

W: Dad, Grandma's 60th _____ _____ _____ soon, isn't it?

M: Yes, it's May 2nd, a month from now.

W: Because the 60th birthday is so special, I want to _____ _____ _____.

3 🔊 MP3 01-03

M: Jennifer, what did you do last weekend?

W: I went to a _____ _____ to sing old pop songs. I do _____ _____ _____ _____.

M: Great! I know well you're a great singer. Do you _____ _____ _____ _____?

4 🔊 MP3 01-04

M: There are myriads of stars in the night sky. If the star-filled _____ _____ _____ _____, join the many amateur astronomers pursuing astronomy as a hobby. The David Frankel _____ _____ _____ _____ place to do this. From March 1st to October 31st, it is open Tuesday through Sunday. The activities for amateur astronomers _____ _____ Jupiter viewing and telescope displays. If you want, Professor Owen Wilson from University of Cunningham can guide you around the observatory. An early-bird program starting at 10 p.m. gives visitors _____ _____ _____ _____ the beautiful Cunningham sky.

5

W: Joss, I have _____ _____ _____ _____ _____ your homework–writing in your English diary.

M: What's that, Ms. Palicki?

W: Your English diary is not just for writing the sequence of events that happen to you each day. You are supposed to _____ _____ _____ _____ _____ and present supporting ideas or your thoughts or your experiences.

M: Okay, should I be more specific when I write in my diary?

W: Yes.

M: But there's _____ _____ _____ _____ _____. I just go to school and go back home, do some homework and watch TV.

W: What about _____ _____ _____ _____ TV program? You can think about the jobs of the people who made that program and the stage sets, etc.

M: Okay, I'll make sure to _____ _____ _____ my second draft.

6

W: Hello, students. I'm Doctor Elly Kim. I'm here to talk to you about bad breath today. What do you feel when your friend has bad breath? Whenever he talks, you sometimes _____ _____ _____, I think. Does he brush regularly and still have bad breath? If so, it's a kind of big deal. You should _____ _____ _____ _____ a doctor. Sometimes, bad breath can mean some serious health problems. It's not really common, but it could be chronic liver disease, diabetes, or stomach failure. After gargling, if his _____ _____ _____ _____ and it continues for more than several days, he should consult a doctor and make sure it is not _____ _____ _____ _____ _____.

7 MP3 01-07

M: Granny, why are you growing _____ _____ _____ _____?

W: When seeing these little creatures growing, I feel full of energy.

M: What do you usually do for them?

W: _____, _____, _____ into another pot, and so on.

M: Are those plants edible?

W: Yes. It's all organic and _____ _____. I'm so happy to give you fresh salad from the garden.

M: That's so nice. I _____ _____. I'll eat a lot, Granny.

W: Okay, and someday you can have your own garden. What would you want to grow?

M: My favorite: eggplants. And, your favorite: chili peppers, too.

W: How sweet you are! Probably, you can _____ _____ _____ _____ now.

M: I'd love to.

8 MP3 01-08

M: Hello, Ms. Liman.

W: Hi, Tom. Thank you for coming.

M: I appreciate _____ _____ _____ _____. This time your focus seems to be on the eternal cycle of _____, _____, _____ _____.

W: You're right. It was my first time working with samsara.

M: How did you like it?

W: It was very interesting and creative. I have studied a lot about _____ _____ _____ _____ and I am sure everyone will love it.

M: Sounds great. Where did you _____ _____ _____ for this?

W: It is from my neighbor, who runs a flower shop. She has an interesting view of life. I have had a lot of conversations with her and I _____ _____ _____ _____ _____.

M: I see. Would you do me a favor?

W: Sure, anything.

M: Could you pose in front of your poster? I'd like to include your photo in the newspaper article.

9 MP3 01-09

M: Excuse me. Is there a gas station near here?

W: Yes. There is one near Aran Bank.

M: I'm new to this area. I have no idea where Aran Bank is, either. Can you tell me how to get there?

W: Oh, yes. First, _____ _____ _____ _____ until you reach the second intersection.

M: Go down this street until I _____ _____ _____

_____ _____.

W: Yes. Then, make _____ _____ _____ _____.

M: All right, and then?

W: Keep going until you see Aran Bank on your right.

M: Aran Bank? Then, where is the gas station? You said it's near the bank.

W: Yes. It's not far from the bank. _____ _____ _____

_____ _____ _____ at the intersection. The oil station is

_____ _____ _____.

M: I think I can get there without any difficulty. Thanks for your help.

W: You're welcome.

10 MP3 01-10

M: Hi, Naomi! I need to buy some books for my presentation next Wednesday.

W: You mean the _____ _____ _____ _____?

M: Yes, I picked the subject of genocide.

W: That sounds very interesting. But, why are you _____ _____

_____ _____?

M: You mean why I don't search on the Internet? I know the Internet is so convenient and has so much information, but I need _____ _____ _____ _____ _____.

W: Sometimes, we can use books more properly than websites. But, _____ _____ _____ _____ the National Assembly Library?

M: No, not yet.

W: There are millions of books, and anyone can _____ _____ _____ _____. So I think you can get more information from there.

M: I should go there right away.

11 🔊 MP3 01-11

W: Hey, Daniel. I'm planning to _____ _____ _____ _____ for Scarlett this Sunday.

M: Sounds fun! Who is coming to the party?

W: I'm thinking about inviting our tennis club members. Is that okay with you?

M: Why not? What about her brother, Steven?

W: Of course, he is _____ _____ _____ in the party. Please call him and explain our plan. I'll _____ _____ _____ _____ my tennis club members.

M: Sure thing, and where are we going to _____ _____ _____?

W: Our favorite, Chris's Diner. I've booked it already.

M: Great! Scarlett likes it there without doubt. She's _____ _____ _____ _____.

W: Okay, I'll prepare a gift and write a card.

M: And write my name on it too, please.

12 🔊 MP3 01-12

M: Hello, Ms. Oliver. As you know, we chose _____ _____ _____ _____ for this Maduro Contest.

W: Yeah, I heard that all the club members liked them very much. Were there any problems?

M: Yes, the problem is our _____ _____ _____ _____ the same songs. They're the winners from last year.

W: You mean Kitsilano Secondary School?

M: Yes. I happened to _____ _____ _____ _____ some people's conversation at a coffee house near the school.

W: So, you're saying _____ _____ _____ _____ our songs, right?

M: Yes. We haven't practiced yet, so we can still change and _____ _____ _____ _____ _____.

W: I see. I'll talk about it with the president of our club and call a meeting.

M: Thank you.

13 MP3 01-13

M: Natalie, how is the Manni Pilates Center you're attending?

W: That place is really nice, you know. The instructors are _____ _____ _____ teaching and consulting about health.

M: That's good. How much is the monthly tuition fee?

W: $100 a month. That's a little _____ _____ _____ _____, but they have many kinds of physiotherapy exercise tools. They used to use them for patients getting physical therapy.

M: You know, I have _____ _____ _____, so it could be very helpful. Does it have a parking lot?

W: Yes, but _____ _____ _____. It's not really far from here. Why not walk there to help you warm-up?

M: I think I can walk around two bus stops. What about after class? Are there clean shower stalls?

W: They have _____ _____ _____ _____, and the fee is included in the tuition.

M: Sounds good.

14 🔘 MP3 01-14

W: May I help you, sir?

M: Yes. I bought this yellow tie here yesterday. I'd like to _____ _____ _____ another one.

W: Do you have the receipt?

M: Yes. Here you are.

W: You bought it for $250. Okay, _____ _____ _____ _____ _____ _____ exchange it for?

M: I like this blue-striped one.

W: That's $300. It's $50 _____ _____ _____ the previous one. Is that okay?

M: That's fine, but I saw a 10% discount sign in the show window. Does the _____ _____ _____ _____ _____ as well?

W: Oh, yes. We've just started a regular bargain sale from today. You're so lucky. With the discount, that'll be $270.

M: That is nice. I already paid $250.

W: Right, you can just _____ _____ _____, $20.

M: Okay. Here's my credit card.

15 🔘 MP3 01-15

W: Welcome to Tuesday's breakfast meeting. This will be our tenth discussion since last March. _____ _____ _____ _____ on the schedule before we start. Today, we are going to discuss the subject "Myths: Restoring Lost Imaginings". Please double check your name tag on your seat. Where your name tag is shows _____ _____ _____ _____ _____ for today. After the discussion, one member from each group will _____ _____ _____ _____. Next week, our subject will be "The Next Generation Office Environment". We have prepared and distributed some reading materials on that topic, so don't forget to _____ _____ _____ _____. After the speeches, breakfast will be served. You can choose between Korean and Western style breakfasts. Let the waiter or waitress _____ _____ _____. Now, enjoy your discussion!

16 🔘 MP3 01-16

M: I'm so happy to tell you this news. A newly-created arts space, the Gallery Jung, will be opening _____ _____ _____ _____ _____ _____. The gallery will provide a good opportunity for many young artists to _____ _____ _____ _____ _____. Individual and group exhibition applications are welcome from not only professionals _____ _____ _____ _____ _____ _____ in art departments. The gallery will be officially opened on April 18th, and a ceramic exhibition will show the works of a famous artisan of pottery, Sunho Lee _____ _____ _____ _____, April 18th, to April 26th. Applications to exhibit are _____ _____ _____ _____. For further information, please contact the Culture and Arts Department of Portsmouth City at 1464-2648 or visit our website www.portsmouthart.com.

17 🔘 MP3 01-17

M: Hi, Yuna. What are you looking for?

W: Oh, hi Michael! I'm _____ _____ _____ _____.

M: Then take a look at this chart. This shows information about scales.

W: Oh, thank you. Hmm... I _____ _____ _____ _____ anything over $25. In fact, I don't think a scale should be that expensive.

M: Yeah, I agree with you.

W: And I don't want _____ _____ _____ _____ _____.

M: I know what you mean. Then I think there are two options.

W: Right. Oh, Borad is a Japanese company. I don't want to buy anything _____ _____ _____ _____ _____. If it breaks, there could be a problem.

M: You're right. Then _____ _____ _____ _____ our answer.

W: Yes. Let's go and get one.

18 🔘 MP3 01-18

M: Jennifer, what are you going to do this vacation?

W: I want to go on _____ _____ _____ _____.

M: What a romantic city!

W: Have you been there?

M: Yeah, I went there around five months ago _____ _____

_____ _____.

W: You mean Pompidou Centre? That _____ _____ _____

_____.

M: Absolutely, it was beautiful. There were many _____ _____

_____ _____.

W: Oh, I'm eager to go soon.

M: _____ _____ _____ some beautiful places for you to visit.

W: Thank you, Jake. That'd be great.

19 🔘 MP3 01-19

W: Keunwoo. I haven't seen you in ages. How have you been?

M: Really good. Believe it or not, I _____ _____ _____ eight

months ago.

W: Really? What kind of book? I know you're so good at English.

M: Maybe _____ _____ _____ _____. It's *The Innovation*

of Cancer.

W: Did you really translate that book? I read it twice! In fact, my aunt has liver cancer.

M: Oh, poor her. I'm sorry to hear that.

W: No, it's okay. She will be better soon. She _____ _____ _____.

Anyhow, I heard the book is a bestseller, right?

M: Yeah, in the _____ _____ _____.

W: What are you working on now?

M: I'm translating _____ _____ _____ _____

Yoonkyung Cho.

20 🔘 MP3 01-20

W: Joanne is taking _____ _____ _____ _____

_____. On the first day of the class, Ms. DeJesus, her linguistics teacher,

said that every student should choose a foreign language they wanted to learn. And

she also wanted the students to submit a brief introduction about the language before

the start of the next class. Joanne understood what she had to do. However, on that

day, she came to class forgetting _____ _____ _____

_____ _____ _____. After class, Ms. DeJesus advised her

to _____ _____ _____, adding that it's helpful to make a

habit of _____ _____ _____ in her day planner. Joanne

_____ _____ _____ _____ to follow Ms. DeJesus's

advice. In this situation, what would Joanne most likely say to Ms. DeJesus?

21-22 🔘 MP3 01-21

M: One of the world's oldest vaccines now has a new use. BCG is an 80-year-old

_____ _____ _____ _____ tuberculosis. But it

has now been found effective in treating long-term type 1 diabetes, which is on the rise

worldwide. BCG has long been administered to children in developing countries to

guard against tuberculosis. But in a recent clinical trial, researchers at Harvard Medical

School found the vaccine was also able to _____ _____ _____

in patients with type 1 diabetes. Dr. Denise Faustman, the lead researcher, says the

team was able to cure type 1 diabetes in mice. And she said in a small clinical trial,

the _____ _____ _____ _____ _____

_____. What they saw was that even with two very tiny doses of vaccine, four

weeks apart, they could start to see the _____ _____ _____

_____ _____ _____. Also, to our astonishment the pancreas

started making small amounts of insulin again. Type 1 diabetes destroys insulin-

producing cells. People who have the disease must constantly monitor and manage their

blood glucose level. She expects that _____ _____ _____

_____ of BCG will be the major challenge in producing a sustained result for

type 1 diabetes patients.

• 수능 9일 전

9일 남았다…

수능 시험이 내일이건 한 달이 남았건 일 년이 남았건, 영어 듣기는 매일매일 하는 게 진리. 우리가 우리말을 매일매일 들어서 이렇게 잘하게 된 것처럼, 영어도 한 문제 한 문제 매일매일 꼼꼼하게 들어 보자. 영어는 다른 과목들과 다르게 우리 곁에 살아 숨 쉬는 언어잖아! 오늘도 한 문장도 놓치지 말고 꼼꼼하게 들어보자고.

수능 9일 전

대학수학능력평가 대비
영어영역 듣기(B형)

수능 9일 전

대학수학능력평가 대비 영어영역 듣기(B형)

성명		수험번호										

● 문제지의 해당란에 성명과 수험 번호를 정확히 쓰시오.

● 답안지의 해당란에 성명과 수험 번호를 쓰고, 또 수험 번호와 답을 정확히 표시하시오.

● 문항에 따라 배점이 다르니, 각 물음의 끝에 표시된 배점을 참고하시오.
  3점 문항에만 점수가 표시되어 있습니다. 점수 표시가 없는 문항은 모두 2점입니다.

🔘 MP3 02

1번부터 22번까지는 듣고 답하는 문제입니다. 1번부터 20번까지는 한 번만 들려주고, 21부터 22번까지는 두 번 들려줍니다. 방송을 잘 듣고 답을 하기 바랍니다.

1 대화를 듣고, 여자의 마지막 말에 대한 남자의 응답으로 가장 적절한 것을 고르시오.

① We are closed on every Wednesday.
② I'll help to find the books when I'm free.
③ I've just finished writing chemistry lab reports.
④ It seems someone has already checked out the book.
⑤ I forgot them completely. I should have checked the due dates.

2 대화를 듣고, 남자의 마지막 말에 대한 여자의 응답으로 가장 적절한 것을 고르시오.

① Didn't you say it was okay?
② No, this is too small for my living room.
③ Did you need some advice before buying new one?
④ You should have told me about this important decision.
⑤ I can help you move the old one near the door.

3 대화를 듣고, 여자의 마지막 말에 대한 남자의 응답으로 가장 적절한 것을 고르시오.

① I took them to the recycling agency yesterday.
② I'm going to throw away old boxes, cans, and plastics.
③ I'm thinking of making some toys for my son out of them.
④ Many people want to know how they get turned into new cans.
⑤ It's supposed to be on every Friday near the garbage dump.

4 다음을 듣고, 여자가 하는 말의 목적으로 가장 적절한 것을 고르시오.

① 학교 급식의 위생 상태를 조사하려고
② 학교 식당의 업체를 변경하도록 제안하려고
③ 학교 급식의 영양 불균형 상태에 이의를 제기하려고
④ 학교 식당의 시설과 평판 개선을 촉구하려고
⑤ 학교의 불만 사항들을 처리하려고

5 대화를 듣고, 여자의 의견으로 가장 적절한 것을 고르시오.

① 이어폰을 이용하는 것은 청력에 좋지 않다.
② 정신없이 길을 가면 교통사고의 위험에 노출된다.
③ 이어폰으로 음악을 크게 듣는 것은 위험하다.
④ 음악을 제대로 감상하려면 되도록 작게 들어야 한다.
⑤ 범죄의 표적이 되기 쉬운 곳에는 가지 않는 것이 좋다.

6 대화를 듣고, 두 사람이 하는 말의 주제로 가장 적절한 것을 고르시오.

① 빨래를 삶는 시간
② 삶아야 하는 세탁물들
③ 빨래를 깔끔하게 너는 방법
④ 빨래를 하얗게 하는 방법
⑤ 소금물에 빨래를 담가야 하는 이유

7 대화를 듣고, 두 사람이 하는 말의 주제로 가장 적절한 것을 고르시오.

① 스마트폰 변경에 따른 요금의 증가
② 학생에게 적합한 스마트폰 요금제 소개
③ 스마트폰 통화료와 데이터 요금의 차이
④ 학생들 사이에서 인기 있는 스마트폰 앱
⑤ 아동의 휴대폰 소지와 관련된 안전성 문제

8 대화를 듣고, 여자의 심정으로 가장 적절한 것을 고르시오.

① upset and disappointed
② hopeful and excited
③ relieved and thankful
④ confident and satisfied
⑤ concerned and anxious

9 대화를 듣고, 그림에서 대화의 내용과 일치하지 <u>않는</u> 것을 고르시오.

10 대화를 듣고, 남자가 여자를 위해 할 일로 가장 적절한 것을 고르시오.

① 설문지 만들기
② 점심 사기
③ 콘서트 함께 가기
④ 새 음반 구해주기
⑤ 축구 경기 표 구하기

11 대화를 듣고, 남자가 여자에게 부탁한 일로 가장 적절한 것을 고르시오.

① to be a judge in the speech contest
② to rearrange the contest schedule
③ to attend the conference of phonology
④ to recommend a native-speaker professor
⑤ to give a presentation for passionate teachers

12 대화를 듣고, 남자가 여행을 취소한 이유를 고르시오.

① 유럽 항공권을 살 수 없어서
② 실험실 연구직을 얻게 돼서
③ 암 연구 실험에 참여해야 해서
④ 물리학 강의를 재수강해야 해서
⑤ 예기치 못한 사고가 발생해서

13 대화를 듣고, 물건 배달에 관해 두 사람이 언급하지 **않은** 것을 고르시오.

① 발송지와 배송지　　　② 발송하는 사람의 이름
③ 소포의 내용물　　　　④ 배송 예정 시간
⑤ 배송료

14 대화를 듣고, 여자가 결제할 금액을 고르시오.

① $108　　　　　　② $110
③ $118　　　　　　④ $120
⑤ $132

15 미니 마라톤 경기에 관한 다음 내용을 듣고, 일치하지 **않는** 것을 고르시오.

① 10, 15, 20km로 이루어져 있다.
② 상을 받는 사람은 총 9명이다.
③ 티셔츠를 받으려면 7월 31일까지 등록해야 한다.
④ 경기 당일에는 등록할 수 없다.
⑤ 참가 번호표와 티셔츠는 경기 전날 받는다.

16 다음을 듣고, 집의 상태와 일치하지 <u>않는</u> 것을 고르시오.

① 최신식 설비가 갖춰져 있다.
② 냉장고 문이 고장 났다.
③ 욕조가 막혔다.
④ 샤워실에 타일이 깨졌다.
⑤ 창틀이 고장 났다.

17 다음 표를 보면서 대화를 듣고, 여자가 갈 세탁소를 고르시오.

	Laundry	Cleaning Price (per suit)	Location
①	Smith	$5	Glory Avenue
②	Tommy	$5	Cape Street
③	Candy	$5	Cape Street
④	Chapman	$4	Glory Avenue
⑤	Iris	$4	Cape Street

18 대화를 듣고, 여자의 마지막 말에 대한 남자의 응답으로 가장 적절한 것을 고르시오.

Man: _____

① To get in shape, you should have persistence.
② It's not as difficult as you think it is. Just try it, now.
③ Riding a bike is also helpful for the environment.
④ That's why I gave up the change in my diet.
⑤ It's like a long journey, but you'll be in shape after the Pilates course.

19 대화를 듣고, 남자의 마지막 말에 대한 여자의 응답으로 가장 적절한 것을 고르시오.

Woman: _____

① Why don't you book an appointment at the clinic on your way back home?
② Keep your eyes open when you cross the road.
③ Mobile phones always adversely affect you.
④ Cell phones will keep you from focusing on your studies.
⑤ If you want to protect your eyes, stop doing it while on the bus.

20 다음 상황 설명을 듣고, Andy가 Marielle에게 할 말로 가장 적절한 것을 고르시오. [3점]

Andy: Marielle, _____

① can I borrow your umbrella?
② let's share your umbrella. Mine is broken.
③ would you mind taking me home in your car?
④ don't go out now. It could be really hot and humid.
⑤ you can take my umbrella. If I were free, I would give you a ride.

[21~22] 다음을 듣고, 물음에 답하시오.

21 여자가 하는 말의 목적으로 가장 적절한 것은?

① to list the agenda for this week's meeting
② to let the team know their new boss
③ to encourage their high performance
④ to thank team members for their team work
⑤ to announce the joining of a new team member

22 다음 중 여자가 하는 말의 내용과 일치하지 <u>않는</u> 것은?

① 새 직원은 소비자서비스 부서의 공석을 채우려고 합류했다.
② 새 직원은 6월 20일 수요일부터 일을 시작할 것이다.
③ 새 직원 환영 파티가 있을 예정이다.
④ 새 직원은 소비자서비스 분야에서 수년간 일해왔다.
⑤ 새 직원에 조언을 해주는 역할은 Nick Holmes 씨가 담당한다.

해답/해설 195p

Dictation

문제 지문을 다시 한 번 듣고 빈칸을 채워보세요. 잘 안 들리는 부분은 음성을 반복해서 익혀 보세요.

1 MP3 02-01

W: I'm afraid _____ _____ _____ to check out any books until next Wednesday.

M: Oh, no! But Ms. Hong, I really need this book for my chemistry lab report.

W: Why didn't you notice that you have _____ _____?

2 MP3 02-02

M: Jihye, did you buy this new TV?

W: Yes. Don't you remember _____ _____ _____ _____ a better one with a full HD screen?

M: Yes, but I can't believe you bought it on your own _____ _____ _____ _____.

3 MP3 02-03

W: Are you going to _____ _____ those plastic bottles?

M: No. I'm _____ _____ _____ to choose the ones I can reuse.

W: Sounds great. What is your plan for them? Anything in mind?

4 MP3 02-04

W: Hi, I'm Paula Patton. Did you enjoy lunch? I'm pretty sure you guys will say 'yes'. Then what do you think of the school cafeteria? Are you satisfied with all of its food? Are you happy enough with the service? I'm not sure you will say 'yes' about this. These days, I've heard that many of us are complaining about the _____ _____ and service. I heard an _____ _____ _____ the crew's service. We students are speaking, but do you think the school is listening? I'm so sure that our school already has a _____ _____ for its cafeteria. But, why do they remain spectators? For the students, the school should make the cafeteria better.

5 MP3 02-05

W: Oh, Hyunsun, it's too loud. Do you usually listen to music at this volume with your earphones on?

M: Sure thing. It _____ _____ _____.

W: But you know, it's not good for your ears.

M: Yeah, but there's no problem _____ _____ _____.

W: That's good. But, loud music with earphones on is dangerous.

M: What do you mean?

W: Some people get lost in music and stop paying attention to what's going on around them. For instance, one of my friends, Sachi, got into a car accident last year.

M: Oh, that could be dangerous. I should be more careful.

W: Also, I saw on the TV news that people using earphones can be _____ _____ _____ _____.

M: Uh oh. I really should be more careful then.

6 MP3 02-06

W: Robert, did you wash this laundry?

M: Yeah, Mom.

W: Well, it doesn't look clean.

M: I didn't think so, either. It's not really white, so I washed it several times.

W: If you want to have white towels, underwear, and socks, you should _____ _____ _____.

M: You know what, I already did that. I thought you didn't want me to do it that way, so I didn't tell you.

W: Why _____ _____ _____ _____? If you have boiled it already, you should put salt in the water while doing laundry.

M: Really? I'm curious if that really helps.

W: Trust me, son. A teaspoon of salt _____ _____ _____ _____.

M: Oh, that's very funny. But I'll try it next time.

7 🔘 MP3 02-07

W: Hi, Brandon. What are you reading? Anything new?

M: Hi, Lisa. I'm reading my smart-phone bill. It cost me more than 100,000 won this month.

W: What? Why was it so expensive?

M: Last month, I bought a new smart phone.

W: Ahh, so _____ _____ _____ for the smart phone is included in your bill.

M: Yes. And also the data usage allotment is included. It's much more expensive than my 2G cell phone.

W: That's true. When I used a 2G cell phone, I selected a 'pay as you go' program, and I paid _____ _____ _____ $20 a month.

M: If there is something similar to a 'pay as you go' program for data usage, I'd definitely _____ _____ _____.

8 🔘 MP3 02-08

M: Hi, Emily. Finally, you're going on a business trip to Tokyo the day after tomorrow, aren't you?

W: Yes, but I really wish _____ _____ _____ _____.

M: What? Why? You said you were excited about this trip because you could visit your dream city.

W: I was, but not anymore. _____ _____ _____ _____ _____ _____, I have to give a presentation in a big meeting, and I am really nervous.

M: Don't worry so much. You're one of the best presenters in this field.

W: It's really kind of you to say so, but I have to do it in Japanese. I'm afraid I might mess up.

M: Try to be yourself when you are giving the presentation, _____ _____ _____ _____. Imagine you're in Tokyo on vacation.

W: Well, I'm not sure I can.

9 🔘 **MP3 02-09**

W: Welcome back home, Lucas!

M: Home, sweet home, Mom. I'm so happy to be back here. The Italian homestay parents were really good people, but I missed you and Dad so much.

W: Anyhow, you've got your _____ _____ _____ _____ from Italy. I'm so proud of you. Anyway, what do you think of this room? I rearranged some things yesterday.

M: Oh, is this the new laptop for me?

W: I said you'd get one. It's a _____ _____ from your grandparents.

M: Ah, yes. I'll call them.

W: Do you like the photos on the board? I found some while cleaning your room, so I pinned them up.

M: I love them. Did you change my chair?

W: It looks like a new one, but _____ _____ _____
_____.

M: Wow, that's cool. I feel sleepy seeing my own bed. Mom, where is my photo with the frame?

W: Oh, it's under the bed. Its leg was broken the other day.

10 🔘 **MP3 02-10**

M: Hanhee, did you hear there's a 'Dream Concert' at the World Cup Stadium tomorrow? A lot of famous singers will be singing. Why don't you _____ _____
_____?

W: My schedule is hectic these days as I'm trying to _____ _____
_____. The deadline is this weekend. I have to go to the library to search for more information.

M: I think I can help you search for information on the Internet.

W: Really? But, _____ _____ _____ _____
_____, I should go to the library. I also have to make a list of questionnaires to ask to potential customers.

M: Do you mean questionnaires for the library users? If so, then I can make the list. I took a class on library and information last semester.

W: Sounds wonderful. _____ _____ _____ _____ _____. Let's go.

11 🔘 MP3 02-11

M: Long time no see, Ms. Jung. I thought I might meet you at this forum.

W: Oh, Mr. Song. How have you been? _____ _____ _____ _____ _____?

M: No, I don't have your personal contact information, so I looked for you.

W: What can I do for you?

M: Our school is planning to hold an English speech contest. We _____ _____ _____ to be a special school in English. So, our teachers are _____ _____ _____.

W: It could be a great opportunity for not only teaching speech strategy but also managing English projects of expertise.

M: If _____ _____ _____, we want to have you as a judge of the contest. There will be three judges: a native professor teaching phonology, an English teacher from Seyoung Girls' High School, and you, I hope.

W: It should be no problem, but let me check my schedule first.

M: Of course. The contest _____ _____ _____ on the 26th of September.

12 🔘 MP3 02-12

W: Ryan? I thought you would be in Europe by now.

M: Hi, Penny. I was planning to go, but I canceled the tickets to Europe.

W: Why? You were really _____ _____ _____ this trip.

M: I was, but you know what? Sometimes in life, _____ _____ _____ things happen.

W: What's that? _____ _____ _____ give up your dream trip?

M: Do you know Dr. Dave, the physics professor? He gave me the chance to be one of his staff in his lab. Since I got so excited and thought it would be the most important chance in my life, I just canceled the trip.

W: I am really happy for you! So, how's it going?

M: _____ _____, _____ _____.

13 MP3 02-13

W: First Courier Services. How may I help you?

M: I'd like to have a small _____ _____.

W: Where to?

M: To 444-448 Brighton Road.

W: Where's _____ _____ _____?

M: 11, Leeds Avenue, Worcester.

W: Okay. What does _____ _____ _____?

M: There are four books.

W: All right. A mailman will call you _____ _____ _____ _____ and come to pick it up. Did you pack it?

M: Yes, I did. How much will it be to Brighton Road?

W: It will cost $17, and your books _____ _____ _____ by 5 o'clock this afternoon.

M: Do you have a cheaper service?

W: We charge $20 for that kind of parcel, but we have a special discount for shipping books right now. So the total is 17.

M: I see. I'll pay with my credit card.

14 MP3 02-14

M: What are you looking at, Daeun?

W: Dad, check this necklace out. _____ _____ _____?

M: You're shopping online? It's really pretty. Is it your mom's birthday present?

W: Actually, I saw this at the department store this afternoon. But it's 10% cheaper online.

M: Do they sell it for $120 at the mall? You're _____ _____ _____ _____ _____ it at the mall but surf the Internet instead.

W: I'm buying this. Oh, something's wrong.

M: What?

W: I thought the delivery charge was included. They charge an extra $10.

M: Let me see. But that's still $2 cheaper than at the department store.

W: You're right. I'll just _____ _____ _____ _____. Oh, look at this. I can have this cute card and _____ _____ _____.

15 MP3 02-15

M: Athletes, may I have your attention please? Princes Park has _____ _____ _____ a mini-marathons event on September 20th. These mini-marathons _____ _____ three categories: a 10-km run, 15-km run and 20-km run. The top three finishers in each category will be awarded. If you register by the last day of July, you will receive a T-shirt sponsored by Newhaven Sports Club. There will be no _____ _____ on the day of the race, so make sure to sign up before the due date. On that day, you will receive your entry number label and _____ _____ _____ _____ _____ that can record your running time automatically, along with your T-shirt. For more specific information, please visit our website or the Princes Park office in person. Thank you.

16 MP3 02-16

W: This is Chaeyoung Lim, the tenant of the apartment in Sindorim-dong. I'm calling to inform you of the problems I'm _____ _____ in your apartment. Your apartment is _____ _____ with the latest appliances, but the refrigerator door is broken. I'm improvising by pushing a box against it to keep it shut. The broken tile in the balcony needs to be replaced. The window frame was also broken, so I've put up _____ _____ _____ _____ to keep out the rain and snow. The bathtub is clogged and the sink has a few leaks. I don't know how long I can survive under these conditions. I'm waiting for you to call back _____ _____ _____ _____ _____ this message. Bye.

17 🔘 MP3 02-17

W: My new clothes need washing. They have become too dirty.

M: Do you have a favorite laundry?

W: No. Can you _____ _____?

M: If you do an online search, there's a list of laundries in this town. Let's see. Do you need dry cleaning?

W: Yes. And I think it shouldn't be _____ _____ _____ _____.

M: Cape Street takes about an hour to get to from here. Glory Avenue is in this area. It'll probably take about 20 minutes to get there. How about the price? Chapman _____ _____ than Smith. But I heard Smith has _____ _____ _____.

W: I think price is more important. Thanks for your help.

18 🔘 MP3 02-18

W: Hey, Jinkyu! Do you _____ _____ _____?

M: Hi, Yura. Yes, to lose weight, I commute by bike and _____ _____ _____ _____ _____.

W: I've also worked out at the gym and taken the Pilates class. But my weight is the same, and I can't feel any change in my body shape.

M: You haven't lost any weight at all?

W: No. I also ride a bike along the beach on weekends, and I am careful about my diet.

M: How long have you been doing all that?

W: Well, _____ _____ _____ a month, I guess.

M: You have done a great job. But it's a little too soon to expect a noticeable body change.

W: Really? But I should have lost _____ _____ one or two kilograms I think.

19 🔘 MP3 02-19

M: Mom, I think I need to change my glasses.

W: Why? Has something happened?

M: No, just my _____ _____ _____ these days.

W: Oh, can't you read the words on the board?

M: I can read them, but sometimes the light seems dim.

W: You don't have any plans today, do you? Let's have your eyes checked at the clinic.

M: Yes. I'll _____ _____ _____.

W: Good. Now go wash your hands. And Minjun, you should _____ _____ _____ that harm your eyes.

M: What do you mean?

W: On the school bus, don't use your mobile phone and don't read books. I think those _____ _____ _____.

M: But, Mom, I would be _____ _____.

20 🔘 MP3 02-20

M: Marielle and Andy are seniors at university. They are preparing their _____ _____ _____. They have lots of experiments, surveys, and summaries. From the beginning of this month, sometimes they stay _____ _____ _____ _____ at the lab. Today, Marielle wants some rest, so she _____ _____ _____ _____ for a comfortable sleep. When she says good-bye to Andy, suddenly it starts raining cats and dogs. She doesn't have an umbrella, but Andy has a big one. Also, Andy's car is parked in the _____ _____ _____ of the same building. So, Andy doesn't mind lending her his umbrella. In this situation, what would Andy most likely say to Marielle?

21-22 🎵 MP3 02-21

W: Thank you for being here on time, everyone. The first item on the agenda from last week's meeting was the fact we should _____ _____ _____ to meet growing needs. So we will have Mia Foster with us from next week. Ms. Foster is joining Preacher Insurance to _____ _____ _____ _____ in customer service. Her first day will be Wednesday, June 20. Ms. Foster has worked for many years in customer service, and we are delighted to welcome her to the Preacher team. She will _____ _____ _____ employee welcoming activities for her first couple of weeks on the job. Ms. Foster's new employee mentor is Nick Holmes, so if you have questions for or need to meet with Ms. Foster, you can talk with Mr. Holmes before she begins. Ms. Foster will work closely with the customers. She will work in the west wing. _____ _____ _____ to stop by and welcome her to the company. This will _____ _____ _____ _____ _____ and improve job efficiency. Next, tell us what is second on the agenda, Henry.

해답/해설 195p

• 수능 8일 전

8일 남았다…

열심히 듣고 있었지? 틀린 문제는 어떻게 했어? 당연히 받아쓰기도 해 보고 해설 읽으면서 확인했지?
몰랐던 표현들은 열심히 암기해두자고. 연계교재들의 어휘와 표현들이 잘 녹아 있는 문제들이니까!
다 맞았다고? 그래도 지문 한 번 읽어보고 해설과 표현들 봐두자. 영어는 꼼꼼하게 챙기는 사람이 진정한
승리자가 되는 법이거든.

수능 8일 전

대학수학능력평가 대비
영어영역 듣기(B형)

수능 8일 전

대학수학능력평가 대비 영어영역 듣기(B형)

성명 [   ]   수험번호 [| | | | | | | | | |]

- 문제지의 해당란에 성명과 수험 번호를 정확히 쓰시오.
- 답안지의 해당란에 성명과 수험 번호를 쓰고, 또 수험 번호와 답을 정확히 표시하시오.
- 문항에 따라 배점이 다르니, 각 물음의 끝에 표시된 배점을 참고하시오.
  3점 문항에만 점수가 표시되어 있습니다. 점수 표시가 없는 문항은 모두 2점입니다.

🔘 **MP3 03**

1번부터 22번까지는 듣고 답하는 문제입니다. 1번부터 20번까지는 한 번만 들려주고, 21부터 22번까지는 두 번 들려줍니다. 방송을 잘 듣고 답을 하기 바랍니다.

1 대화를 듣고, 여자의 마지막 말에 대한 남자의 응답으로 가장 적절한 것을 고르시오.

① I hope you get over it soon, and come back quickly.
② There's no excuse. You can't make up the test.
③ No way, you have to see the doctor immediately.
④ She's going to be all right. Thank you for your helping.
⑤ Yes, she is okay. And now my sister's looking after her.

2 대화를 듣고, 남자의 마지막 말에 대한 여자의 응답으로 가장 적절한 것을 고르시오. [3점]

① So sign up early if you are interested.
② My brother, Tom, strongly recommended it.
③ Those are some friends of mine over there. Let's join them.
④ Thank you for letting me know about camping tips.
⑤ The children were looking forward to this summer camp.

3 대화를 듣고, 여자의 마지막 말에 대한 남자의 응답으로 가장 적절한 것을 고르시오.

① I don't think I like playing football.
② I'm sorry, but I can't take part in the competition.
③ You had better practice a lot to win the competition.
④ No, I haven't decided yet. My muscles are cramping.
⑤ Yes, I think the competition will help me become a better kicker.

4 다음을 듣고, 남자가 하는 말의 목적으로 가장 적절한 것을 고르시오.

① 잡지 박람회에 초대하려고
② 수상 작가의 소감을 전달하려고
③ 책 사인회가 취소된 것을 안내하려고
④ 교통에 관한 신간 소설을 홍보하려고
⑤ 저자와의 대화 시간이 변경된 것을 사과하려고

5 대화를 듣고, 여자의 주장으로 가장 적절한 것을 고르시오.

① 스마트폰은 현대인의 필수품이다.
② 최신 유행에 무분별하게 휩쓸리지 마라.
③ 시험 볼 때에 친구들에게 의존하지 마라.
④ 전화기는 통화 외의 기능이 꼭 필요한 것은 아니다.
⑤ 약속한 시간에 맞춰서 도착하지 않는 것은 무례하다.

6 다음을 듣고, 여자가 하는 말의 주제로 가장 적절한 것을 고르시오.

① Your emotion is affected by the weather.
② People feel happier in summer than in winter.
③ People can easily get upset when feeling hot and humid.
④ People are the only animals who don't care about weather.
⑤ Summer is the most energetic season according to the biorhythm of humans.

7 대화를 듣고, 두 사람이 하는 말의 주제로 가장 적절한 것을 고르시오.

① 한국인들의 민간 신앙
② 돌잔치에 참석할 때의 예절
③ 한국의 독특한 돌잔치 전통
④ 상업화된 한국 돌잔치 문화
⑤ 자녀에 대한 부모의 지극한 사랑

8 대화를 듣고, 남자의 심정으로 가장 적절한 것을 고르시오.

① frustrated   ② bored
③ excited   ④ nervous
⑤ disappointed

9 대화를 듣고, 그림에서 대화의 내용과 일치하지 <u>않는</u> 것을 고르시오.

10 대화를 듣고, 남자가 할 일로 가장 적절한 것을 고르시오.

① 여행 준비하기
② 렌터카 예약하기
③ 자동차 수리하기
④ 여행 계획 세우기
⑤ 여행 가방 싸기

11 대화를 듣고, 남자가 여자에게 부탁한 일로 가장 적절한 것을 고르시오.

① to publish his thesis
② to send him his documents
③ to discuss publishing a book
④ to send his colleagues his thesis
⑤ to keep in touch with his colleagues abroad

12 대화를 듣고, John Urban이 한국에 오지 <u>못한</u> 이유를 고르시오.

① 일정이 한꺼번에 겹쳐서
② 무리하게 식단 조절을 해서
③ 성대수술을 받고 회복 중이어서
④ 콘서트 준비를 하며 체력이 다해서
⑤ 과도한 노래 연습으로 성대를 다쳐서

13 대화를 듣고, 남자가 목이 쉰 이유를 고르시오.

① 감기 때문에　　　　　　② 자원봉사 활동 때문에
③ 가게 개업 홍보 때문에　　④ 교내 연설 연습 때문에
⑤ 가족과 함께 노래 불러서

14 대화를 듣고, 남자가 낼 금액을 고르시오.

① $100　　　　　　② $104
③ $130　　　　　　④ $136
⑤ $170

15 다음을 듣고, 흰돌고래에 관해 여자가 하는 말의 내용과 일치하지 <u>않는</u> 것을 고르시오.

① 유선형의 흰색 수생 포유류이다.
② 번식기에는 대략 200마리가 떼 지어 다닌다.
③ 이빨이 평평하다.
④ 등지느러미가 삼각형 모양이다.
⑤ 개체마다 고유의 휘파람 소리를 낸다.

16 다음을 듣고, 창조과학캠프에 관해 남자가 하는 말의 내용과 일치하지 <u>않는</u> 것을 고르시오.

① 열흘간 엑스포 공원에서 열린다.
② 다양한 과학 실험을 해볼 수 있다.
③ 참가자는 후원사에서 캠프 비용을 지원받는다.
④ 과학 성적 증명서가 있어야만 신청할 수 있다.
⑤ 오늘부터 인터넷으로 참가 신청을 할 수 있다.

17 다음 표를 보면서 대화를 듣고, 두 사람이 예약할 숙소를 고르시오.

Guest Houses in Chicago

	Name	Rate per Night	Breakfast	Location
①	Windy City House	$26	○	Downtown
②	Bravo CCH	$27	×	Downtown
③	Southern Mansion	$22	○	Southern Beach
④	Park View Pension	$29	×	Alice Park
⑤	Shiela de Maison	$29	○	Russian Hills

18 대화를 듣고, 여자의 마지막 말에 대한 남자의 응답으로 가장 적절한 것을 고르시오.

Man: _____

① I'm fed up with such talk.
② Sure. I'll make my essay more persuasive.
③ Of course! They are pieces of stylized reportage.
④ Definitely. I'd like to write an essay about reading.
⑤ Yes. The essay is comparable to a scattered puzzle.

19 대화를 듣고, 여자의 마지막 말에 대한 남자의 응답으로 가장 적절한 것을 고르시오.

Man: _____

① I really wanted to go out of the theater.
② I complained, but he didn't switch it off.
③ I asked him to be quiet, but it didn't work.
④ It was extremely boring and irritating. I don't recommend it.
⑤ How can you do that? Just go home and watch TV.

20 다음 상황 설명을 듣고, Jessie가 Logan에게 할 말로 가장 적절한 것을 고르시오.

Jessie: _____

① How about calling my father to pick us up?
② What about taking a taxi instead of the bus?
③ The queue is really long, so we could be late.
④ If it is okay, can you give me a ride home, please?
⑤ How long do you think we will have to wait for the bus?

[21~22] 다음을 듣고, 물음에 답하시오.

21 대화의 주제로 가장 적절한 것을 고르시오.

① 고대 중국 유물 발굴 과정
② 고대 중국 공예품의 가치
③ 고대 중국 인형의 특징과 아이들의 놀이
④ 고대 중국 왕족의 취미 활동
⑤ 고대 중국의 어린이 교육용 도구

22 고대 중국에서 인형에 사용한 재료로 언급되지 <u>않은</u> 것을 고르시오.

① straw   ② clay
③ ivory   ④ stone
⑤ ceramics

Dictation

문제 지문을 다시 한 번 듣고 빈칸을 채워보세요. 잘 안 들리는 부분은 음성을 반복해서 익혀 보세요.

1 MP3 03-01

W: Danny, why _____ _____ _____ yesterday?

M: My mom was so sick that I _____ _____ _____ _____ _____ her. My dad's out of town at the moment.

W: I was so worried about you. Is she all right now?

2 MP3 03-02

M: Hi, Christina. Are you in this camp?

W: Thank God, Hyungbum. You're here. It's _____ _____ _____ _____ _____ here.

M: _____ _____ _____ Kenny. Anyhow, what made you join this camp?

3 MP3 03-03

W: You _____ _____ _____, Greg. Are you coming back from your football club?

M: Yes. _____ _____ _____ a lot of free kicks for the competition.

W: Oh, have you been _____ _____ _____?

4 MP3 03-04

M: Good evening. This is _____ _____ _____ for those who came to the book signing in the Cornwell Book Center. It was supposed to be held by the best-seller author Virginia Madsen at four o'clock. However, _____ _____ _____ _____ _____, Ms. Madsen will not be arriving here today. So the book signing is postponed indefinitely. We _____ _____ _____ _____ to those who have been waiting. Also, we hope Ms. Madsen will be safe. The 2014 Magazine Fair is being held at the Main Hall. There are new magazines and journals there. Please visit the magazine fair while you're here. We're sorry to have to deliver this kind of message and thank you for your understanding.

5 MP3 03-05

M: Mom, I got an A⁺ on the English test today.

W: You really did a good job. I have to _____ _____ _____ _____. What do you want to have?

M: I want to have a smart phone.

W: Honey, you changed your new cell phone just three months ago.

M: But, Mom, _____ _____ _____ _____ have smart phones except Shane and me.

W: Billy, your phone doesn't have any problems and the function of a phone is to send and receive calls.

M: These days a cell phone is for more than just making phone calls. I can access the Internet anytime, communicate with all of my friends, and study with some specific apps.

W: Smart phones _____ _____ _____, but you can easily waste time with them _____ _____ _____ _____ _____.

6 MP3 03-06

W: How do you feel when _____ _____ _____ _____ has ended and spring has arrived? To some of you, just the thought of it probably makes your heart flutter. Changing weather can influence what we can do and where we can go, but it can also _____ _____ _____ _____ in affecting how we feel. In cold and rainy weather, people are often _____ _____, _____ _____ in their work, and feel less energetic. On the other hand, in warm, sunny weather, people usually have more energy, feel happier, work better, and seem to be _____ _____ _____. You probably see happier faces in summer than you do in winter, right?

7 🔘 MP3 03-07

W: Jeremy, here's _____ _____ _____ my daughter's first
  birthday party. Will you be able to come?

M: Sure. You must be working very hard to prepare the party.

W: No. There are _____ _____ _____ _____
  _____ who specialize in a baby's first birthday party.

M: That sounds interesting. What do they prepare for the party?

W: They prepare everything for the party!

M: Wow, that _____ _____ _____ _____.

W: Yes, indeed. People tend to have fewer babies nowadays, so they spend lots of money on
  babycare. So, the babycare business is one of the fastest growing businesses in Korea.

M: Very interesting. But it's quite strange to me. It sounds like a baby's first birthday party in
  Korea has _____ _____ _____.

8 🔘 MP3 03-08

M: Mom, how far is Aunt Kelly's house from here?

W: It's _____ _____ _____ _____ _____ away.

M: I'm dying to see her.

W: Which do you miss more, your aunt or your aunt's food?

M: Actually, both, but I really miss Aunt Kelly's delicious home-made cakes and cookies.

W: I called her last night, and she said that she would _____ _____
  _____. She's baking a chocolate cake for you now.

M: That's wonderful! I _____ _____ _____ _____
  _____. I'm really happy that we're spending this holiday there with her.

W: Same here. Oh, one more thing. Her dog had ten little puppies yesterday.

M: Ten puppies? I'm sure it's going to be a great holiday!

9

M: Hi, Hyerin. What photo _____ _____ _____ in the frame?

W: Hi, Brad. It's our family trip photo.

M: Let me see it. The tent looks so nice.

W: Yeah. My dad likes to go camping, so we travel once or twice a month.

M: So your dad bought a great tent.

W: Yeah, my mom can't sleep in _____ _____ _____.

M: What did you eat?

W: We had fish that my dad caught.

M: Camping, fishing, _____ _____ _____ _____ for family, playing the guitar... You have an excellent dad.

W: Yes. I love him so much. Look at this. Have you ever eaten sausages cooked like this? They're amazing.

M: I know your mom is an excellent cook.

10

W: I'm supposed to take a trip to Sapporo next week.

M: Did you _____ _____ _____ the place you are staying at?

W: I'm working on it. I'm considering a small hotel. But it's not easy to find the right one.

M: Do you want me to help you?

W: No, _____ _____ _____ _____. I'd like to choose the place on my own.

M: Just tell me what I can do for you.

W: Okay, _____ _____ _____ rent a car for me?

M: Sure. No problem. What kind of vehicle do you want?

W: The same kind as I have now, _____ _____. I want a vehicle that I'm used to.

M: I know what you mean.

11 🔘 MP3 03-11

W: Hello? Do Be Publishing House, Rachel Kim speaking.

M: Hello, Rachel. This is Jacob Anderson.

W: Hello, Doctor Anderson. Did you get the documents?

M: What do you mean?

W: I _____ _____ _____ _____ your office. You left them here yesterday in the meeting room.

M: Did I? I hadn't even _____ _____ yet. Thank you so much.

W: My pleasure. And what can I do for you today? Do you have any questions about the thesis?

M: I was wondering if there will be some copies left after you publish my thesis. I'd like to send some _____ _____ _____ _____.

W: How many copies do you need?

M: Around forty.

W: We will send them to your colleagues directly from our company.

M: _____ _____ _____ _____.

12 🔘 MP3 03-12

M: What are you listening to, Sunny?

W: I'm listening to John Urban's latest album. _____ _____ _____ all of his songs.

M: I was really hoping he'd visit Korea on tour, but it seems unlikely for the time being.

W: Why is that?

M: I heard that he _____ _____ _____ _____ two tours due to a vocal-cord injury.

W: In John's case, with his latest album, he put a horrible strain on his voice. I read in an article that he practiced songs for eight hours per day.

M: He's amazing. Singers usually have a lack of sleep, a poor diet, and drinking and smoking habits. That's terrible _____ _____ _____ _____, I guess.

W: It's possible to get a quick operation on the vocal cords. I think many singers
_____ _____ _____ _____.

13 🔘 MP3 03-13

W: Dan, _____ _____ _____ _____ today. Did you
catch a cold?

M: No, I'm perfectly fine. It's just my voice.

W: Hmm... Let me see. Did you practice _____ _____ _____ for
a school campaign?

M: Nope, it _____ _____ _____ _____ my family.

W: Oh, I got it! Your family had a good time singing together!

M: No. Actually, my mom opened a cosmetics store yesterday.

W: Okay, but what does that have to do with your voice? What did you do at the store?

M: I helped her with the opening sale. I distributed flyers to people, continuously shouting
_____ _____ _____ _____.

W: You're such a nice son. So, was it successful?

M: Yes. We had quite successful sales. It cost me my voice, though.

14 🔘 MP3 03-14

W: Welcome to DEF Mart. How can I help you?

M: I would like to buy that _____ _____ _____ over there. Is
there any discount for a display item?

W: Yes, we give a 20% _____ _____ _____ _____
_____.

M: Then, how much is the list price?

W: It's originally $170.

M: Wow, that's so expensive. What about the jogging shoes?

W: The blue ones are $100, and the blue ones with silver lining are $130.

M: _____ _____ _____ the first sneakers.

W: Okay. Anything else?

M: Hold on. I have a coupon from this store. Can I use it?

W: Let me see. You could have gotten a 10% discount, but _____ _____ _____.

M: Oh, okay.

15 🔘 MP3 03-15

W: You may have seen a white whale on TV, in an animated movie, or at a zoo. It is called a Beluga or Belukha whale. It's white like snow and is a sleek, streamlined, aquatic mammal. During breeding season, approximately two hundred Belugas _____ _____ _____ _____. It's found in and around the Arctic areas of Canada and Greenland. Some people continually get confused about the difference between belugas and dolphins. Dolphins have _____ _____ and a curved dorsal fin, while belugas have flat teeth and a _____ _____ _____. Belugas sing like canaries, but each dolphin learns from its mom its own signature whistle. Also, belugas are generally _____ _____ _____ _____.

16 🔘 MP3 03-16

M: The Creation Science Camp is a _____ _____ for all high school students who are into science. This camp will be held in the Brighton Expo Park from the 1st to 10th of March. Participants will enjoy _____ _____ _____ _____ _____ _____ during the event. There is no fee for the camp because our supporting electronic company, Canjin, will help financially. Students who want to join must register on the Canjin Internet registration site, starting from today. Only the first one hundred students who have _____ _____ _____ from their science teacher can participate. Your science teacher can visit www.canjin.com and _____ _____ _____. We expect the science lovers among our high school students to be highly interested in this camp.

17 🔘 MP3 03-17

M: Let's _____ _____ _____ _____. We need to book our rooms.

W: All right. The Chicago options. Well, I surfed the Internet and wrote down some choices.

M: Oh, it's a guesthouse list. What do you prefer?

W: _____ _____ _____ _____ where we stay in Chicago. I just picked places with lots of rooms because there are six of us.

M: Good idea. I really want to have breakfast. It could be much better for our trips.

W: Okay, what about the location?

M: Probably downtown is convenient to go anywhere, but I think near the beach would be nice.

W: Then, what about the price?

M: I don't expect it to be expensive. But _____ _____ we spend, _____ _____ opportunities we can have to do what we want.

18 🔘 MP3 03-18

W: Hello, Yongjae, come on in.

M: I'm here because of my essay, Ms. Han.

W: I've already read yours.

M: Would you _____ _____ _____ _____?

W: Well, it's _____ _____ _____ _____, but there's one thing to point out. I think you're good at structuring an essay, but yours is short of supporting ideas.

M: You mean, things that support the topic sentence?

W: Exactly. _____ _____ _____ help your readers accept what you're saying. This subject is very original, but your supporting ideas are kind of old-fashioned. Can you think differently and _____ _____ _____ _____?

19 🔘 MP3 03-19

W: Hi, Rupert. Did you enjoy the new movie yesterday? How was it?

M: It was great, but I didn't really enjoy it that much.

W: What do you mean?

M: I really _____ _____ _____ _____ the movie, but I argued with a man sitting in front of me.

W: What happened?

M: During the movie, he didn't _____ _____ _____ _____ _____, which had a big screen. His phone kept getting messages and bothering everyone.

W: You mean it made sounds constantly? That's terrible.

M: No sounds, actually. But _____ _____ _____ _____ the movie because of the light. You know, the phone light looks really bright in the dark theater.

W: That _____ _____ _____ _____. So what did you do?

20 🔘 MP3 03-20

W: Logan has a date with his girlfriend, Jessie, and now it's time to go home. They _____ _____ _____ _____ _____. As usual, Logan is going to escort her home. But Jessie realizes that the bus stop is _____ _____ _____. Logan must feel tired and sleepy because he played soccer before the date. She thinks if they take a bus, they will have to stand and _____ _____ _____ _____ _____. Suddenly, Jessie remembers that her father is near there, so she wants her father _____ _____ _____ _____ _____ _____. In this situation, what would Jessie most likely say to Logan?

21-22 🔘 MP3 03-21

W: Jake. What are you reading? You _____ _____ _____ on it.

M: Hi, Helen! It's a post about ancient Chinese. Look here! These are pictures of the dolls that Chinese children played with.

W: The dolls were made of stone and clay, right?

M: Yes. According to this post, ivory and ceramics were also used.

W: Those _____ _____ _____ _____ rich people. Ivory has always been valuable.

M: Exactly. They were for the royal family in China. Playing with marbles was also quite popular, especially with the children of the Chinese royal family. I think marbles were valuable, too.

W: Why do all the photos show dolls with soldiers' features?

M: That's an interesting point. The kings of the age, I guess, wanted to protect their honor and wealth, so they needed many soldiers. _____ _____ _____ _____ in their choice of dolls and other routine things.

W: _____ _____ _____. Have you heard about what "Cupak" is? It says here that it's the name of a game that was widely popular with ancient Chinese children.

M: Yeah, I already read that part. The player would hit a small piece of wood with a bat while the wood was in the air. Sounds like baseball or cricket.

W: Interesting! I think I should read that article myself.

일주일 남았다…

남은 동안 이제부터 매일 챙길 일은 오후 1시 10분에 영어 듣기 풀기. 점심 먹고 나른한 시간, 수험생
이라 더 힘들고 축축 처지는 몸이지만, 1시 10분에는 꼭 수능 영어 듣기를 풀자. 뒤에 독해 23문제를
연결해서 총 70분간 문제를 풀면서 실전감각을 키우면 더 좋겠지? 이제 곧 너의 실력을 증명할 날이
온다. 진.검.승.부. 한번 해보자!

수능 7일 전

대학수학능력평가 대비
영어영역 듣기(B형)

대학수학능력평가 대비 영어영역 듣기(B형)

성명		수험번호										

- 문제지의 해당란에 성명과 수험 번호를 정확히 쓰시오.
- 답안지의 해당란에 성명과 수험 번호를 쓰고, 또 수험 번호와 답을 정확히 표시하시오.
- 문항에 따라 배점이 다르니, 각 물음의 끝에 표시된 배점을 참고하시오.
  3점 문항에만 점수가 표시되어 있습니다. 점수 표시가 없는 문항은 모두 2점입니다.

🔘 MP3 04

1번부터 22번까지는 듣고 답하는 문제입니다. 1번부터 20번까지는 한 번만 들려주고, 21부터 22번까지는
두 번 들려줍니다. 방송을 잘 듣고 답을 하기 바랍니다.

1 대화를 듣고, 여자의 마지막 말에 대한 남자의 응답으로 가장 적절한 것을 고르시오.

① How did the boss react to the news?
② You are unable to attend the meeting.
③ We should advise Jane about being late.
④ Director Lee will preside over the meeting.
⑤ Why didn't you call me? I was so worried.

2 대화를 듣고, 여자의 마지막 말에 대한 남자의 응답으로 가장 적절한 것을 고르시오.

① I'm so happy to hear that.
② Of course, I bought it in person.
③ Well, but I paid the shipping charge, also.
④ I can offer you a 10% discount.
⑤ Do you guarantee the price gap?

3 대화를 듣고, 남자의 마지막 말에 대한 여자의 응답으로 가장 적절한 것을 고르시오.

① Do you have a cavity?
② All right then, maybe next time.
③ I like your bracelet. It's so cute.
④ But sorry I have a prior engagement.
⑤ I'd love to see him, too. I'm a big fan of his.

4 다음을 듣고, 남자가 하는 말의 목적으로 가장 적절한 것을 고르시오.

① 아파트 관리소장을 선출하기 위해서
② 각 엘리베이터의 게시판을 홍보하기 위해서
③ 아파트 부녀회의 대표 임기를 연장하기 위해서
④ 아파트 내 부대 시설의 확충을 안내하기 위해서
⑤ 아파트 내 주민들의 운동 시간을 조정하기 위해서

5 대화를 듣고, 남자가 주장하는 것으로 가장 적절한 것을 고르시오.

① 교통 법규 위반 감시 카메라를 설치해야 한다.
② 교차로 신호등을 정기적으로 점검해야 한다.
③ 정기적으로 차량 점검 교육을 받아야 한다.
④ 시민의 건의 사항에 바로 출동해야 한다.
⑤ 불법 유턴을 하는 운전자에게 벌점을 줘야 한다.

6 다음을 듣고, 여자가 하는 말의 주제로 가장 적절한 것을 고르시오.

① It's important to have a job that suits you.
② To achieve the goals you want, you should work harder.
③ Sacrificing your time by volunteering is highly respected.
④ Government social programs should care for the sick and poor.
⑤ You can get rewards when you do risky and difficult jobs.

7 대화를 듣고, 두 사람이 하는 말의 주제로 가장 적절한 것을 고르시오.

① 아이의 연령대에 맞는 장난감 선정
② 아이가 장난감으로 표현하는 감정을 읽기
③ 아이의 두뇌 발달에 좋은 장난감 종류
④ 아이의 창의력을 키울 수 있는 장난감
⑤ 다양한 장난감의 다양한 매력

8 대화를 듣고, 두 사람의 관계를 가장 잘 나타낸 것을 고르시오.

① 학부모 – 체육 교사
② 부동산 중개업자 – 고객
③ 방문객 – 가게 주인
④ 투자자 – 농부
⑤ 세입자 – 집주인

9 다음을 듣고, 여행 지도에서 네 번째로 방문하게 될 곳을 고르시오.

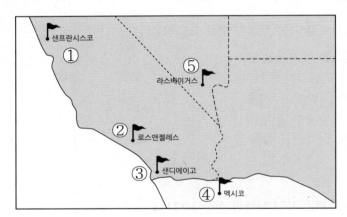

10 대화를 듣고, 남자가 할 일로 가장 적절한 것을 고르시오.

① 여학생에게 답장 쓰기
② 즉석커피 선물을 준비하기
③ 둘의 사진을 찍어서 보내기
④ 여학생의 교장 선생님께 전화하기
⑤ 학교 주변에서 운전 시 속도 줄이기

11 대화를 듣고, 여자가 남자에게 부탁한 일로 가장 적절한 것을 고르시오.

① to type some documents
② to reserve a camp site
③ to re-organize many files
④ to buy her a cup of coffee
⑤ to help her make up with her boss

12 대화를 듣고, 남자가 테니스 클럽에 나가지 <u>못하는</u> 이유를 고르시오.

① 입사한 지 얼마 안 되었기 때문에
② 곧 있을 승진 시험을 준비해야 해서
③ 일이 너무 바빠서
④ 새 업무에 적응할 시간이 필요해서
⑤ 승진 시험에서 떨어져 마음이 불편해서

13 대화를 듣고, 아이 돌보기와 관련하여 남자가 언급하지 <u>않은</u> 것을 고르시오.

① 샤워하는 시간 ② 숙제 과목
③ 편식 제재 ④ 컴퓨터 게임 시간
⑤ 저녁 식사 메뉴

14 대화를 듣고, 여자가 낼 금액을 고르시오.

① $180 ② $200
③ $220 ④ $320
⑤ $360

15 다음을 듣고, Valley Point 리조트에 관한 내용과 일치하지 <u>않는</u> 것을 고르시오.

① 주 단위로 바뀌는 다양한 여가 활동 프로그램을 즐길 수 있다.
② 풍광이 아름다운 곳에 자리 잡고 있다.
③ 멧돼지 사냥이나 번지 점프를 할 수 있다.
④ 아이 돌보미 서비스를 제공한다.
⑤ 무료로 물놀이를 즐길 수 있다.

16 다음을 듣고, 광고의 내용과 일치하지 <u>않는</u> 것을 고르시오.

① 항공사의 지상 근무자를 구한다.
② 28세 이상의 신입과 경력자가 지원할 수 있다.
③ 스페인어가 가능한 사람을 우대한다.
④ 일주일에 3일 유동적인 일정으로 근무하게 된다.
⑤ 보험과 숙소가 제공된다.

17 다음 표를 보면서 대화를 듣고, 두 사람이 선택할 정수기 모델을 고르시오.

		Ice Maker	Hot Water	Double Filter	Rental Fee per Month
①	Aisis	○	○	○	$45
②	Kireen	○	×	○	$35
③	Saem	○	○	×	$28
④	Cool	○	○	○	$38
⑤	Minerals	×	○	○	$25

18 대화를 듣고, 여자의 마지막 말에 대한 남자의 응답으로 가장 적절한 것을 고르시오.

Man: _____

① Can I have this for my health?
② In that case, I can feed some pupae.
③ Okay, Mom. I'll try.
④ That's why you like raisins.
⑤ Thanks, I really enjoyed the delicious meal.

19 대화를 듣고, 남자의 마지막 말에 대한 여자의 응답으로 가장 적절한 것을 고르시오. [3점]

Woman: _____

① Yes, there are three stations near the stadium.
② No, I mean the station where we've always met before.
③ You mean the ball park? Usually I just call it park.
④ I like the player, too. But again the uniform?
⑤ Sure. I'll call right back. Just be there.

20 다음 상황 설명을 듣고, Grace가 Anthony에게 할 말로 가장 적절한 것을 고르시오.

Grace: You need to take time off. _____

① I just kicked back at home.
② Why are you so focused on studying?
③ What do you feel like when you don't study?
④ There's nothing more important than your health.
⑤ The more you study, the better the university you will get into.

[21~22] 다음을 듣고, 물음에 답하시오.

21 태풍 매미에 관한 설명 중 일치하지 <u>않는</u> 것을 고르시오.

① 한반도에 상륙한 최악의 태풍 중 하나로 기록되었다.
② 열대성 저기압에서 태풍으로 급속도로 발달했다.
③ 오키나와를 통과할 때 풍속은 초속 74.1미터였다.
④ 2003년 9월 12일에 제주도를 통과했다.
⑤ 9월 14일, 홋카이도 부근에서 온대저기압으로 세력이 약화됐다.

22 태풍의 이름으로 '무지개'가 쓰이게 된 이유를 고르시오.

① The 'rainbow' stands for hope in general.
② The ship 'Mujigae' was badly damaged by Typhoon Maemi.
③ Typhoon Mujigae was much larger and mightier than Typhoon Maemi.
④ Typhoon Maemi caused huge damage in Korea, so the name was replaced.
⑤ The countries should submit some native language name of typhoons.

Dictation

문제 지문을 다시 한 번 듣고 빈칸을 채워보세요. 잘 안 들리는 부분은 음성을 반복해서 익혀 보세요.

1 `MP3 04-01`

W: Inkyu, I'm terribly sorry. I'm late.

M: Clare! _____ _____ _____ _____ you for almost an hour!

W: I'm so sorry. The meeting _____ _____ _____ _____ _____.

2 `MP3 04-02`

W: Where did you buy this smart-phone case? How much did you pay for it?

M: I bought it _____ _____ _____ _____ _____ _____. It was $25.

W: Really? I paid $50 _____ _____ _____ _____.

3 `MP3 04-03`

M: The final is over! I feel so relieved.

W: Yeah, _____ _____ _____ _____ _____ _____. What about going window shopping in Churchill Square?

M: I'd love to, but I'm going to _____ _____ _____ _____ _____, first.

4 `MP3 04-04`

M: Good morning, residents of McKibben Apartments. This is John Platt, the manager _____ _____ _____ _____ _____, speaking. As the bulletin on each elevator has said, the _____ _____ _____ _____ will start to move in around noon. The women's association of the apartment community has already bought the equipment, and it's going to be placed _____ _____ _____ _____ to create the second gym. For more details, please visit our apartments' web community or the office in person. Thank you for your cooperation.

5 🔘 MP3 04-05

W: Officer Ploddy. Thanks for coming.

M: You're welcome. After reading your opinion on the Internet, I thought I should come here earlier.

W: Thank you. Here is the road _____ _____. Traffic signs and signals are fine, but there are so many security risks.

M: You're right. We had one incident last month, in which we lost a 12-year-old girl from an illegal U-turn. It was _____ _____ _____.

W: Yes, it was so sad. But, there are some drivers still doing illegal U-turns every day. We need to _____ _____ _____ _____ _____ to stop this.

M: On this kind of road, a surveillance camera is needed. Nowadays, they're installed _____ _____ _____ speed and parking traps _____ _____ _____ security reasons.

W: That would be good. I think we need to raise awareness that U-turns here are illegal and very dangerous.

6 🔘 MP3 04-06

W: Nowadays, many people only think about having _____ _____ _____ _____ _____, a big house, an expensive car, and fashionable clothes, etc. _____ _____ _____ _____ _____ _____ to achieve these goals. But there are some people who give their time and energy to help those who can't help themselves. These volunteers do so without receiving any payment. They help the poor, the hopeless, the sick, and the dying, and they never look for anything in return. Volunteers may work in their own town or city or may even travel to another country or continent in order to help _____ _____ _____ _____ _____. It's these volunteers, who often work in dangerous and difficult situations, that _____ _____ _____ for their selfless acts.

7 🔘 **MP3 04-07**

M: How many toys did you buy for your son?

W: My son Jeremy is four now. He always wants to have _____ _____ _____ _____. But, you should know, it's not good for children to buy those fancy toys.

M: Really? There are so many items with pretty colors and cute cartoon characters.

W: They look beautiful, but they are _____ _____ _____. For our children, just some colored crayons and white paper is good. A few colored wood blocks can be fun, too. With around three hundred blocks, they can make anything they want.

M: Oh, that's really impressive. Sometimes, my daughter _____ _____ _____ very creative ideas when she plays with her blocks.

W: Yeah, simple things can spark creativity.

8 🔘 **MP3 04-08**

W: Hello, Mr. Roger. So did you _____ _____ _____ on which one to choose?

M: Yes. My wife and I like the one on 5th Avenue.

W: Oh, the three-story house with five bedrooms? You have made the perfect decision. It's _____ _____ _____ _____ _____ that we could suggest now.

M: It's _____ _____ _____ _____ _____. But we decided on it because it has a lovely backyard. I think my children will be happy to play there.

W: Yes, the yard is unbelievable. You are going to be happy having the yard.

M: Exactly. Is it possible to grow some vegetables in the yard? Could you ask the owner about it?

W: Sure. I've been _____ _____ _____ _____ for many years, and she never minds how the tenants use the yard.

M: That sounds good. Then I'm ready to sign the lease.

9 🔘 **MP3 04-09**

M: I'm your tour guide, Hajin. Before boarding, _____ _____ _____ _____ _____ about our trip. We are going to visit four cities in the western US. After a 13-hour flight, we'll arrive in San Francisco, where you can _____ _____ _____ and enjoy curved hills. Next, we'll go to Las Vegas, Sin City. You can be a millionaire or _____ _____. It could be a lot of fun, but I suggest you only gamble a little. Next, we can experience the combination of Mexican and American culture in San Diego. San Diego is _____ _____ _____ _____, so you can experience Mexican influence everywhere. And last but not least is Los Angeles. It's so hard to explain. So much fun, so much activity, and so much variety.

10 🔘 **MP3 04-10**

M: Christina, what are you looking at?

W: It's a letter from a girl in the second grade of Leeds Elementary School where you work.

M: Oh! There are some photos, and what's this? A bag of instant coffee?

W: Yes, near the school, there's a crosswalk that _____ _____ _____ _____. So I patrol the area every morning.

M: _____ _____ _____ _____ _____ thank-you gift?

W: Yes, it is. She saved her pocket money for this.

M: Oh, she is so kind and cute. But I also want to do something for that cute girl.

W: Right. So I'll _____ _____ _____ _____.

M: She deserves to be praised. I'll call the principal of the school.

W: That's a great idea. She will _____ _____ _____ from her teachers.

11 🔘 MP3 04-11

M: Hi, Eunmi. I booked the camp site for this weekend.

W: God, is it this weekend? I'd love to go, but I can't. I have to prepare my presentation by Monday.

M: What? Did you forget our plans?

W: No, it's just that _____ _____ _____ _____ my boss, so he gave me a lot of files, I guess.

M: What are they? Can you go camping if I help you to _____ _____ _____ _____ _____?

W: Absolutely. By tomorrow, I have to organize and re-categorize _____ _____ _____ _____ about statements of profit and loss from the last quarter. Would you type these paragraphs on the word documents?

M: Sure thing. After that?

W: I don't know. I could do with coffee. How about you?

M: No, I'm okay. I'll _____ _____ _____ for you.

W: That's sweet of you. Thanks!

12 🔘 MP3 04-12

W: Long time no see. Why do you miss so many tennis lessons?

M: _____ _____ _____ _____ _____ a promotion.

W: So did you get promoted?

M: No, I didn't.

W: Really? I'm sorry to hear that. You will _____ _____ _____ in the future. Cheer up. By the way, will you be able to play tennis with us again?

M: I'm afraid I can't.

W: Why not? We really need you. You are _____ _____ _____ _____ _____, and we have a tournament next week.

M: I know. But I really need some time to get myself together. _____ _____ _____ _____ to accept the result.

W: I'm sorry. I don't know what to say.

13 🎵 MP3 04-13

M: Although you already know it, _____ _____ _____
_____ a few things, again.

W: Okay.

M: Woody has to finish his homework before dinner.

W: Absolutely, I'll help him to finish it.

M: In the refrigerator, there's pasta and salad I made. Warm up the pasta in the microwave.
Please check whether Woody eats his cucumber or not. _____ _____
_____.

W: No problem.

M: After dinner, computer games _____ _____ _____ just one
hour. No more, never!

W: Absolutely.

M: I think I'll come back around that time, but _____ _____
_____ _____ _____ at eight thirty, Woody should take a
shower.

W: Okay, it's not really hard. I've been excited to spend time with him.

M: Thanks.

14 🎵 MP3 04-14

M: May I help you? We're having an _____ _____.

W: I'm looking for a windbreaker jacket. Can I have a look around?

M: Yes. The windbreaker corner is here. Take your time.

W: Let me see... _____ _____ _____ looks nice. How much is it?

M: It's $200. But it's not part of the sale.

W: I see. It must be a new arrival, then.

M: Yes. What about _____ _____ _____ _____
_____?

W: Oh, this trench coat is so chic. How much is it?

M: It's $400. But it's 20 percent off now.

W: The price of the trench coat is quite attractive. But I _____ _____
_____. I'll take it.

M: All right, if you have a membership card, you can get an additional 10 percent discount.

W: That's great. Here's my card.

15 MP3 04-15

M: Valley Point Resort provides so many activities to our guests _____
_____ _____ _____. Do your friends want to do something
more than scuba diving or sunbathing? Does your family seek thrills beyond just camping?
Then why don't you recommend trying wild boar hunting or bungee jumping off our
suspension bridge? Valley Point Resort _____ _____ _____ so
much fun all around that we guarantee you leave us relaxed and refreshed. If your child
is under seven, we will take care of him or her while you relax. We are located around
the most beautiful scenery in the world. Don't forget you can enjoy a wonderful summer
vacation with _____ _____ _____ _____ of Valley
Point Resort, which is _____ _____ _____.

16 MP3 04-16

W: The Boston branch of Lancer Airline _____ _____ _____
_____ _____ with at least three years' experience. Anyone aged
twenty eight and over with eligible experience and qualifications can _____
_____ _____ _____. If you can speak Spanish or Portuguese,
you'll be more welcomed because the Boston branch has many Latin customers.
But it's not _____ _____ _____. If you are chosen for this job,
you'll work three days per week. But the date and work time are flexible _____
_____ _____ _____ _____. You'll be paid $5,000
per month. All meals during working days, major insurance, and accommodation in
Boston will be provided. Applications will be accepted until December 26th. Thank you
_____ _____ for your interest in the position.

17 🔘 MP3 04-17

W: Honey, what are you looking at? Is it a brochure?

M: It's about different _____ _____ _____.

W: I heard they make it really _____ _____ _____ to make hot water and ice.

M: Right. Do you want to get one?

W: I think Sean would like to have one. He always eats ice _____ _____ _____.

M: I think they're good for making coffee early in the morning.

W: Right, it would be good for you, too. How much do they cost?

M: Hmm... I think under $30 per month is suitable. Do we need a double filter?

W: That could be nice, but it increases the cost.

M: _____ _____ _____ _____ the chart, then.

W: This one should be perfect for us.

18 🔘 MP3 04-18

W: Jemin, let's have salad.

M: Oh, Mom. What's this?

W: _____ _____ _____ _____ the plate? They are raisins.

M: They look like pupae. I won't eat this, never, ever.

W: Honey, they're not pupae. They're raisins. They _____ _____ _____ _____ and are very sweet.

M: Nope. I hate the shape and color. _____ _____ _____ _____ eat this, Mom? I can be strong and healthy without this disgusting food.

W: Jemin, don't be so picky. If you eat these raisins, you may change your mind. I am sure _____ _____ _____ _____.

19 🔘 MP3 03-19

M: Are you ready to go to see the baseball game?

W: Hey, Young. It is only 2 o'clock. Didn't you say it starts at 6?

M: Yes, I did, but we have to get there early because we haven't bought tickets yet.

W: Why don't you use your _____ _____?

M: They're not available to book reservations on the same day as the game. I _____ _____ _____ _____ yesterday. Sorry.

W: No problem. Then let's get tickets in advance, and before the game, let's look around the baseball shop.

M: That sounds nice. Do you think the _____ _____ _____ _____ _____?

W: Sure, nowadays baseball is really popular.

M: Yes, it seems everyone is going to the games these days. So, do you want to buy something?

W: I'd like to buy a summer jersey of the Bears. I'll get my favorite player's name _____ _____ _____, too. Let's meet at Gate 3 at the station.

M: You mean at the station near the stadium?

20 🔘 MP3 04-20

M: Grace has a son, Anthony, and _____ _____ _____ his health all the time. He's a senior in high school, and he is studying for the university entrance exam. She thinks that _____ _____ _____ his grades. She sees him studying for such a long time at his desk without any breaks. She never worries about his grades, but Anthony is _____ _____ _____ his bad grades or failures. He looks so exhausted and stressed, too. Plus, his nose bleeds before breakfast. Grace thinks he needs to rest and take some dietary supplements. So she suggests he should _____ _____ _____ for a while. In this situation, what would Grace most likely say to Anthony?

21-22 🔊 MP3 04-21

W: Typhoon Maemi was the strongest typhoon of 2003 and still stands as one of
_____ _____ _____ _____ to hit the Korean
peninsula. Though it developed slowly from a tropical atmospheric pressure to a typhoon,
it became a destructive typhoon near Sakishima Islands with 910 hectopascals of pressure
at its center, with maximum wind speed hitting 55m/s. When it passed through Okinawa,
_____ _____ _____ _____ _____ 74.1m/s.
After that, it headed north and passed through Jeju Island on the 12th of September,
and at 8:30 p.m. on the same day it arrived in Goseong-gun, Gyeongsangnam-do
and _____ _____ _____. When it landed on the Korean
peninsula, its central pressure and maximum wind speed had decreased a little to 950
hectopascals and 40m/s, but it was still one of the strongest typhoons to ever hit Korea.
Typhoon Maemi was downgraded to an extra-tropical cyclone near Hokkaido on the 14th
of September and then disappeared. After Typhoon Maemi occurred, the name 'Maemi'
has _____ _____ _____ _____ for typhoons because
of the extensive damage it caused. Instead, 'Mujigae' _____ _____
_____ _____.

해답/해설 208p

- 수능 6일 전

6일 남은 오늘의 할 일은?

입 열기. 듣기 문제를 다 풀고 나면, 받아쓰기와 틀린 문제 해설 보고 몰랐거나 헷갈리는 단어, 표현들 암기하기. 그동안 지나칠 만큼 정말 잘해왔잖아~ 긴장된 마음 풀기에는 집중만큼 좋은 게 없지. 소리를 들으면서 문장들을 원어민처럼 따라 읽어봐. 집중도 되고 머릿속에도 쏙쏙!

수능 6일 전

대학수학능력평가 대비
영어영역 듣기(B형)

대학수학능력평가 대비 영어영역 듣기(B형)

성명		수험번호									

- 문제지의 해당란에 성명과 수험 번호를 정확히 쓰시오.
- 답안지의 해당란에 성명과 수험 번호를 쓰고, 또 수험 번호와 답을 정확히 표시하시오.
- 문항에 따라 배점이 다르니, 각 물음의 끝에 표시된 배점을 참고하시오.
  3점 문항에만 점수가 표시되어 있습니다. 점수 표시가 없는 문항은 모두 2점입니다.

🔘 **MP3 05**

1번부터 22번까지는 듣고 답하는 문제입니다. 1번부터 20번까지는 한 번만 들려주고, 21부터 22번까지는
두 번 들려줍니다. 방송을 잘 듣고 답을 하기 바랍니다.

1 대화를 듣고, 남자의 마지막 말에 대한 여자의 응답으로 가장 적절한 것을 고르시오.

① But what if there is a connection?
② No problem. Let me do it at once.
③ How about using the flash for this shot.
④ Of course, you can buy postcards in the gallery shop instead.
⑤ No exceptions. Any photos are strictly prohibited.

2 대화를 듣고, 여자의 마지막 말에 대한 남자의 응답으로 가장 적절한 것을 고르시오.

① I did it on my own authority.
② I'm sorry, but I don't have the authority to do that.
③ The subject is mandatory for graduation.
④ Students are listed on the attendance sheet.
⑤ Could you enlarge that a little?

3 대화를 듣고, 남자의 마지막 말에 대한 여자의 응답으로 가장 적절한 것을 고르시오.

① It's an honor to have you here in San Diego.
② Was I? I didn't notice that you looked at me.
③ My pleasure. I'm so happy for you to go there.
④ That's okay. I can go soon after I finish this task.
⑤ You're welcome. I'm glad that I can help with your job.

4 다음을 듣고, 남자가 하는 말의 목적으로 가장 적절한 것을 고르시오.

① 걷기 운동의 중요성을 강조하려고
② 하이킹의 장단점을 설명하려고
③ 건강을 위한 영양제 보충을 권장하려고
④ 건강을 위해 하이킹을 해볼 것을 권유하려고
⑤ 하이킹 시, 자연의 소리를 듣는 법을 안내하려고

5 대화를 듣고, 영어 교육에 관한 여자의 의견으로 가장 적절한 것을 고르시오.

① 교재 선정이 중요하다.
② 독해 학습이 결국 가장 중요하다.
③ 모국어와 외국어 학습법은 다르다.
④ 듣기와 말하기가 가장 기본이 되어야 한다.
⑤ 어릴 땐 발음을 중심으로 공부해야 한다.

6 다음을 듣고, 남자가 하는 말의 목적으로 가장 적절한 것을 고르시오. [3점]

① 강연자를 소개하려고
② 여론 조사 결과를 발표하려고
③ 경기 침체 해결 방안을 토론하려고
④ 새로운 고용 정책에 대해 안내하려고
⑤ 청년 취업 준비 시 유의 사항을 알리려고

7 대화를 듣고, 두 사람이 하는 말의 주제로 가장 적절한 것을 고르시오.

① 지하철 이용의 어려움
② 지하철 내의 전화 예절
③ 노약자 우대석 증가의 필요성
④ 지하철 내 세대 갈등 해결의 필요성
⑤ 지하철 예절 교육의 중요성

8 대화를 듣고, 두 사람이 대화하고 있는 장소로 가장 적절한 곳을 고르시오.

① 기차역
② 공항
③ 버스 터미널
④ 영화관
⑤ 공연장

9 대화를 듣고, 그림에서 대화의 내용과 일치하지 <u>않는</u> 것을 고르시오.

10 대화를 듣고, 남자가 여자를 위해 할 일로 가장 적절한 것을 고르시오.

① 휴대폰 수리 센터에 함께 가기
② 새 휴대폰을 골라주기
③ 이동 통신사에 전화하기
④ 할인을 많이 해주는 이동 통신사 찾기
⑤ 자신의 휴대폰 빌려주기

11 대화를 듣고, 남자가 여자에게 부탁한 일로 가장 적절한 것을 고르시오.

① to get permission from grandmother
② to do the house chores
③ to go buy the puppy's food
④ to bath the puppy and brush its hair
⑤ to bring the puppy back to Jihye

12 대화를 듣고, 남자가 오늘 강의 시간에 일찍 온 이유를 고르시오.

① 지난 수업에 빠졌기 때문에
② 보고서를 작성해야 해서
③ 오늘 해야 할 발표 연습 때문에
④ 강의 시간 변경 소식을 못 들었기 때문에
⑤ 교수님의 세미나 준비를 도와야 해서

13 대화를 듣고, 여자가 출산 축하 파티에 가지 <u>못하는</u> 이유를 고르시오.

① 숙제를 끝내지 못해서   ② 선물을 준비하지 못해서
③ 장학금을 위해 더 공부해야 해서   ④ 마을 축제에 참가해야 해서
⑤ 동아리 모임에 참석해야 해서

14 대화를 듣고, 여자가 낼 총 금액을 고르시오.

① $75   ② $135
③ $150   ④ $210
⑤ $300

15 다음을 듣고, 숲 체험 프로그램에 관한 내용과 일치하지 <u>않는</u> 것을 고르시오.

① 오감을 통해 자연과 교감하는 것이 목적이다.
② 운영 시간은 7월 15일부터 8월 25일이다.
③ 7세 이상의 어린이가 있는 가족이 이용할 수 있다.
④ 날씨에 따라 일정이 변경 또는 취소될 수 있다.
⑤ 전화나 직접 방문을 통해 신청할 수 있다.

16 다음을 듣고, 베냉공화국에 관한 내용과 일치하지 <u>않는</u> 것을 고르시오.

① 프랑스 사람들이 베냉에 식민지를 건설했다.
② 1975년에 베냉공화국으로 이름을 바꿨다.
③ 프랑스어 사용을 배척하고 있다.
④ 연간 4%대의 경제 성장률을 기록 중이다.
⑤ 나이지리아에 인접한 아프리카 국가이다.

17 다음 표를 보면서 대화를 듣고, 여자가 보러 갈 아파트를 고르시오.

World Assets Real Estate Agency

	Unit	Bedrooms	Floor	Rent per Month
①	801	4	20	$390
②	802	3	16	$450
③	803	3	7	$440
④	804	2	2	$350
⑤	805	2	9	$380

18 대화를 듣고, 여자의 마지막 말에 대한 남자의 응답으로 가장 적절한 것을 고르시오.

Man: _____

① I'm going to donate money for disabled kids like my son.
② I'm in a publishing company. My fellow workers helped me a lot.
③ Many people support my family, so I really want to say "Thank you."
④ I suggest you enter the university to learn "Construction for the disabled".
⑤ My son enjoys making furniture, so we're changing the garage into a workshop.

19 대화를 듣고, 여자의 마지막 말에 대한 남자의 응답으로 가장 적절한 것을 고르시오.

Man: _____

① Don't worry. I will work on it and correct any mistakes.
② The contest is delayed, so you can have a lot of time.
③ I know how considerate you are to others.
④ Just try to practice English every day.
⑤ Then, I can't give you any good comments.

20 다음 상황 설명을 듣고, 주희가 Kenny에게 할 말로 가장 적절한 것을 고르시오.

Juhee: _____

① Can I have the old one for John?
② Is it okay if I have a look at this new one?
③ Why don't you fix this and use it more?
④ Why don't you donate the old one to the poor?
⑤ You have an eye for choosing a camera.

[21~22] 다음을 듣고, 물음에 답하시오.

21 세팍타크로에 관한 설명 중 일치하지 <u>않는</u> 것을 고르시오.
① 동남아시아에서 유래했고, 세계적으로 인기가 많다.
② 명칭은 말레이시아어와 태국어를 합쳐서 만들었다.
③ 15점을 따야 한 세트를 이긴다.
④ 공의 탄성을 위해 합성 섬유는 사용하지 않는다.
⑤ 공은 무릎, 발, 가슴, 머리에만 닿을 수 있다.

22 다음 중, 세팍타크로가 전 세계적으로 인기 있는 이유를 고르시오.
① 축구처럼 손을 사용하지 않는 경기여서
② 배구처럼 선수들이 높이 점프하는 경기여서
③ 무술 동작과도 같은 화려한 킥 동작이 볼거리라서
④ 경기 진행 속도가 빨라서
⑤ 공의 재질이 부드러워 부상의 위험이 적어서

해답/해설 215p

Dictation

문제 지문을 다시 한 번 듣고 빈칸을 채워보세요. 잘 안 들리는 부분은 음성을 반복해서 익혀 보세요.

1 ◉ MP3 05-01

M: Excuse me. May I ＿＿＿＿＿＿＿＿ ＿＿＿＿＿＿＿ in this gallery?

W: No, taking photos ＿＿＿＿＿＿ ＿＿＿＿＿＿ ＿＿＿＿＿＿.

M: What about if I ＿＿＿＿＿＿＿ ＿＿＿＿＿＿＿ the flash?

2 ◉ MP3 05-02

W: Mr. Cruise, can I ＿＿＿＿＿＿＿ ＿＿＿＿＿＿＿ ＿＿＿＿＿＿＿ your spring vacation class?

M: Oh, it's already full.

W: But I really need to take your class ＿＿＿＿＿＿＿ ＿＿＿＿＿＿. Could you increase the number of students?

3 ◉ MP3 05-03

M: Irene, what happened? Didn't you say that you would be in San Diego this week?

W: I canceled my holidays ＿＿＿＿＿＿ ＿＿＿＿＿＿ ＿＿＿＿＿＿ ＿＿＿＿＿＿＿ ＿＿＿＿＿＿.

M: That's too bad. I know how much you were ＿＿＿＿＿＿＿ ＿＿＿＿＿＿ ＿＿＿＿＿＿ ＿＿＿＿＿＿ ＿＿＿＿＿＿.

4 ◉ MP3 05-04

M: What are you doing for your health? Are you ＿＿＿＿＿＿＿ ＿＿＿＿＿＿＿ ＿＿＿＿＿＿ every day? What about hiking? Did you know hiking is very ＿＿＿＿＿＿ ＿＿＿＿＿＿ ＿＿＿＿＿＿ ＿＿＿＿＿＿? Some think hiking is just walking around in nature. That's not wrong, but hiking is great for your health. The more you walk, ＿＿＿＿＿＿＿ ＿＿＿＿＿＿ ＿＿＿＿＿＿ ＿＿＿＿＿＿ ＿＿＿＿＿＿. Additionally, hiking is an outdoor activity in natural environments, often in mountainous or other scenic terrain. ＿＿＿＿＿＿ ＿＿＿＿＿＿ ＿＿＿＿＿＿, you can put all your focus on what you're doing: your stride, your arms swinging, your breath, the sounds of an awakening neighborhood, or the sounds of bushes, wind, and birds.

5 🔘 MP3 05-05

M: My daughter, Kathy, has started to learn English, so I want some interesting books in English.

W: Well, I think she _____ _____ _____ _____ now.

M: Yes. She is just _____ _____ _____ _____ CDs and repeating them.

W: That is a good way! I think there's no need to buy English books yet. Just have fun with her _____ _____ _____ _____ and following them.

M: But, I think reading books is important, too.

W: All babies learn their own language by listening to and speaking with their parents and babysitters. Reading is the next step.

6 🔘 MP3 05-06

M: I'm Dwayne Johnson. As you know, we do an annual survey on the 100 most _____ _____ in this city. The person _____ _____ _____ _____ _____ has always been a successful politician or entrepreneur. However, this year's person on top was a surprise to many. Students have selected Brett Ratner, an instructor talking about vision and the future. He has _____ _____ _____ for college students about a positive survival strategy for these difficult times. Opportunities for employment are getting scarcer. Brett said that in this economic recession, the youth are in a plight to find jobs, to get married, and to have children. He's been preparing some special strategies for these people. Now, it's time to meet this person who _____ _____ _____ _____ for a bright future.

7 🔘 MP3 05-07

M: Hi, Linda. What's up?

W: I'm _____ _____ _____ about a young lady who yelled at an old woman on the subway.

M: I heard that story, too. They were arguing over a subway seat.

W: That's right. The young lady sat in a senior's seat. And the old woman scolded her about that.

M: So she yelled at _____ _____ _____?

W: Yes. That happens frequently on the subway.

M: Why don't they simply increase the number of senior's seats on the subway?

W: I don't think that should be a solution. _____ _____ _____ _____ between the young and senior citizens could make the situation worse.

M: You're right. Finding a fundamental _____ _____ _____ _____ _____ between the young and the old is more critical than any other physical measures in order to make the subway experience more pleasant for all of us.

W: You can say that again.

8 🔘 MP3 05-08

M: Hi, Sally. I'm so sorry I'm late. The _____ _____ _____ _____.

W: You know it's rush hour. You should have hurried.

M: You're right. I'm sorry. How much time is left?

W: About five minutes. Let's go inside. The train is already here.

M: Wait! Can I go buy some snacks? I haven't eaten anything yet. It _____ _____ _____ _____.

W: There's _____ _____ _____ _____ _____. You can get snacks there.

M: Sounds great. _____ _____ _____, your bag looks very heavy. What did you pack?

W: Some books and music to help relax on the train.

M: You seem to know how to enjoy traveling. Did you get the tickets?

W: Sure, I have them in my wallet. We have to go to Gate 1. I think we should hurry.

9 🔘 **MP3 05-09**

M: Oh, it's Jun and Minseo in the photo. Where have you and Jun been today?

W: We saw the musical *Cloud Candy*. It's a hit among the children of Jun's age.

M: Are those the main characters behind Jun and Minseo?

W: Yes, they are. They are two _____ _____ _____. When they eat cloud candy, they can fly. So the siblings—the two cats—fly around their town and help people in need.

M: That sounds interesting. What are Jun and Minseo eating, by the way?

W: After the musical, the actors and actresses came down from the stage and _____ _____ _____ to the children in attendance.

M: But, candy is not good for Jun's teeth.

W: Right. So I said _____ _____ _____ _____, "Jun, if you fly away, I will be so sad. And it's going to be very difficult to find you once you are gone!"

M: _____ _____ _____ _____.

W: So, Jun ate a small piece of bagel.

10 🔘 **MP3 05-10**

W: I can't see anything _____ _____ _____ _____ _____.

M: You mean, nothing is coming on the screen?

W: Nothing at all. I'll have to send it to the service center.

M: How long have you been using it?

W: Almost three years.

M: Quite a long time. I think _____ _____ _____ _____ _____ for a new one.

W: Well, sometimes, my telecommunication firm calls me to change my phone.

M: _____ _____ _____ a suitable one for you. These days, smart appliances are in.

W: Now that you mention it, let's go phone shopping. _____ _____ _____ _____ about smart phones. I should see what's available.

11 🔘 MP3 05-11

W: Oh, _____ _____ _____ _____! Jake, where did you

get it?

M: My friend, Jihye, is on vacation. She went to Guam for ten days.

W: So you are taking care of her dog during her vacation?

M: Yes. Is it okay, Mom?

W: Well... You _____ _____ _____ _____

_____ _____.

M: Sorry. It's really cute, so I had no time to think about anything else.

W: Yeah, it's really sweet, but I'm worried about your grandmother. She doesn't like having

pets inside the house.

M: _____ _____ _____. I want to ask you to convince Granny.

W: Oh, Jake, that could be hard.

M: Mom, please! Granny listens to you even more than to me. I'll do the dishes and

_____ _____ _____ the whole ten days.

W: That's a good deal.

12 🔘 MP3 05-12

M: Hi, Catherine. Where is everyone? Is the class canceled?

W: No. Class will begin at 11:30 a.m. today.

M: No way! I didn't know that. _____ _____ you and everyone else knew

about it except me?

W: I guess you didn't attend the last class. The professor said that since he would be late today

because of his seminar, he would change the class time.

M: I _____ _____ the last class, but I didn't hear that. When did he say

that?

W: He said it at the beginning of class.

M: That's why I didn't hear him say it. I arrived late last time _____ _____

_____. Well, what made you come here so early?

W: I have to finish my report that's due today. I _____ _____

_____ _____ _____ here for almost three hours.

13 🔘 MP3 05-13

M: Hyerin, did you finish your homework? You should _____ _____ _____ _____.

W: I've already finished and submitted it this morning. I really want to have A this term.

M: Then you can go to the party tonight?

W: What party? You mean Aunt Jane's _____ _____?

M: Yes, your mom and I prepared some gorgeous baby products. Don't you want to check them out?

W: _____ _____ _____ _____ _____ and want to hug the little prince, but I'm afraid I can't go.

M: What's wrong? Do you want to study more to try to get the scholarship this term?

W: No, Dad. I should attend _____ _____ _____ to organize a festival in the fall. I couldn't make it for last week, so the members are mad at me.

M: Oh, that's not a good situation. Were you absent from the meeting _____ _____ _____?

W: Yes, that's right. I should go there tonight to apologize and to contribute my ideas.

M: I see. I hope you're not in trouble, honey.

14 🔘 MP3 05-14

W: Okay, thank you for your explanation. So, I have _____ _____ _____ for this program. How much is the monthly fee?

M: It costs $50 a month.

W: That's not so cheap. It's just thirty minutes a day.

M: It _____ _____ _____ if you add _____ _____ _____ times.

W: You're right, but is there any discount?

M: If you pay for three months, we offer 10% off the total fee for the class.

W: That's good. Anything else?

M: I recommend that course. We have 30% off for six months and 50% off for a year.

W: That's good. Ah, do _____ _____ _____ _____ for using the parking lot?

M: Yes, you do. But only if you stay over two hours. And then it's only $2 a day.

W: Okay, I don't think I'll need it then. I'll pay the three-month fee as you suggested.

M: Okay. Please _____ _____ _____ _____ first.

15 MP3 05-15

M: I'm here to announce a forest-experience program for young children in Mount Dorking. _____ _____ _____ the program is to allow kids, by appealing to their five senses, _____ _____ _____ nature. The program is open to families with children younger than seven years. The program runs from July 15th to August 25th, from 10 a.m. to 4 p.m. You can register _____ _____ _____ _____ _____ when using the Mount Dorking facilities. Please note that the program schedule might change or be canceled, _____ _____ _____ _____. If you have any questions, please call our toll-free number: 094-973-1853.

16 MP3 05-16

W: The Republic of Benin is one of the African countries located on the Gulf of Guinea bordered by Nigeria. It became a protectorate in 1851. _____ _____ constructed the Dahomey colony in Benin, and then Dahomey was incorporated into West Africa in 1904. After it _____ _____ as the Republic of Dahomey in 1960, the country changed its name to the Republic of Benin in 1975. Benin still uses French _____ _____ _____ _____, though it also has its own local language. The Beninese economy has maintained _____ _____ _____ _____ of about four percent each year, but its GDP is only around $1,500, so it is still one of the poorest countries in the world.

17 🔘 MP3 05-17

M: Hello, ma'am. How can I help you?

W: I'm looking for an apartment near here. I don't know much about this area.

M: Okay, I can help you. Here, Main is _____ _____ _____ _____. How many people will be living in the apartment?

W: Four: my husband and I and our two daughters. So, we'd like two or three rooms.

M: And do you have _____ _____ _____ _____?

W: Not too high, not too low, I think the 10th through 20th would be nice.

M: What about the 7th or 9th floor?

W: Not too bad. Do you have anything good?

M: Yeah, you have three choices. _____ _____ _____ are you looking to pay?

W: Oh, under $400 per month would be okay.

M: Then we have one apartment that's _____ _____ _____. Let's go see it.

18 🔘 MP3 05-18

W: Well, I'm _____ _____. What made you start making these?

M: Several years ago, my son, Rubin, was in an accident and lost his legs. I've made all the renovations by myself so my son could move around more easily in the house.

W: I think it _____ _____ _____ a lot of skills. How did you learn them?

M: I went to a school to learn cabinetmaking and electrical wiring. My wife, Jihyun, joined me there later to learn plumbing.

W: What kinds of changes did you make in your house?

M: We widened the entrance hall and made a big bathroom for my son. We wanted him to _____ _____ _____ _____ in our house.

W: So what are you working on now?

19 🔘 MP3 05-19

M: Hi, Dawon. What brought you here?

W: Mr. Kim, here's my English speaking contest _____ _____ _____. Thank you again for extending the deadline for me.

M: Don't mention it. You were in hospital then. I always think health comes before anything else. How are you now?

W: I feel much better. Thanks for asking. And I'm more confident about my script now than I was the last time.

M: What do you mean?

W: For this task, I didn't need to use the _____ _____ _____ on my computer. I could just write what I wanted to say.

M: I know your English has improved a lot.

W: This is all thanks to you. I have _____ _____ _____ _____ _____ in English.

M: It's _____ _____ _____ _____ to say so.

W: But, I may have made some mistakes in this script, I think.

20 🔘 MP3 05-20

W: Juhee visits her cousin Kenny's home. While she's talking to him, she sees an old digital camera on the floor and a new one on his desk. Kenny tells her he needs a lighter _____ _____ _____ _____ _____ to handle more photography for his job. He says he bought the brand-new digital camera last week, and that he's going to _____ _____ _____ _____ tomorrow. Juhee thinks the old one still works well. And she remembers that her brother John needs a digital camera _____ _____ _____ _____. She thinks throwing the old camera away is wasteful, and she wants to _____ _____ _____ _____. In this situation, what would Juhee most likely say to Kenny?

M: Sepaktakraw is one of the most popular sports in Southeast Asia. Sepaktakraw is _____ _____ _____ combining Sepak from Bahasa Malaysia and Takraw from Thai, and it means 'kick the ball with the foot.' It is a kind of kick volleyball that is native to the Malay-Thai peninsula. Sepaktakraw differs from volleyball in its use of a rattan ball. It is made of synthetic fiber or soft durable material _____ _____ _____ _____ softening the impact when players touch the ball. Three players are _____ _____ _____. The players are allowed to touch the ball only with their knees, feet, chests, and heads. Any team that _____ _____ _____ _____ _____ in their court gives one point to the opponent. When a team reaches 15 points, it wins a 'set'. A match is won when a team wins three sets. The net is 1.55 meters high, so martial-arts-like kicks are frequently observed to _____ _____ _____ _____ the opponent's court. These spectacular actions have helped make this sport popular around the world. Now, more than 120 countries worldwide enjoy Sepaktakraw.

5일 남은 이 시점에서 "독해 문제 미리 보기" 있기 없기?

없기! 연계교재가 수능에 출제된 이후 좋은 점은 독해 문제가 눈에 익숙해서 시간이 모자라는 일이
별로 없다는 거야. 굳이 한정된 시간에 문제지 앞뒤로 들춰대지 말고, 한 문제 풀고 시간이 좀 남으면?
당연히 다음 문제를 읽어두고 생각해야지. 다시 말하지만 듣기는 다시 들을 수 없어. 초.집.중!

수능 5일 전
대학수학능력평가 대비
영어영역 듣기(B형)

수능 5일 전

대학수학능력평가 대비 영어영역 듣기(B형)

성명 [   ]　　수험번호 [| | | | | | | | | |]

- 문제지의 해당란에 성명과 수험 번호를 정확히 쓰시오.
- 답안지의 해당란에 성명과 수험 번호를 쓰고, 또 수험 번호와 답을 정확히 표시하시오.
- 문항에 따라 배점이 다르니, 각 물음의 끝에 표시된 배점을 참고하시오.
  3점 문항에만 점수가 표시되어 있습니다. 점수 표시가 없는 문항은 모두 2점입니다.

🔘 MP3 06

1번부터 22번까지는 듣고 답하는 문제입니다. 1번부터 20번까지는 한 번만 들려주고, 21부터 22번까지는 두 번 들려줍니다. 방송을 잘 듣고 답을 하기 바랍니다.

1 대화를 듣고, 여자의 마지막 말에 대한 남자의 응답으로 가장 적절한 것을 고르시오.

① Excellent. That serves two ends.
② What do you mean? Are you a performer?
③ I've seen a green river on St. Patrick's Day.
④ How can I get a certificate for volunteering?
⑤ I love the Irish dance festival. How can I enter it?

2 대화를 듣고, 여자의 마지막 말에 대한 남자의 응답으로 가장 적절한 것을 고르시오.

① Don't worry. They found it in the car.
② Where did you put it? You're careless.
③ I'm sorry. I lost your key in the garden.
④ I'll help you look for it. It must be around here somewhere.
⑤ Which floor did you park on? Do you remember?

3 대화를 듣고, 남자의 마지막 말에 대한 여자의 응답으로 가장 적절한 것을 고르시오.

① I think the content is lacking.
② I don't like the book that much.
③ I prefer operas to musicals.
④ This article is worth reading.
⑤ Me, too. After seeing the musical, I started reading.

4 다음을 듣고, 남자가 하는 말의 목적으로 가장 적절한 것을 고르시오.

① 새 쇼핑센터 준공 계획을 반대하려고
② 새 쇼핑센터의 개장 소식을 알리려고
③ 공원의 장점과 활용에 대해 설명하려고
④ 공원의 쓰임새를 다양화하는 의견을 제시하려고
⑤ 공유지가 사적인 용도로 쓰이고 있음을 신고하려고

5 대화를 듣고, 여자의 의견으로 가장 적절한 것을 고르시오.

① 현장에서 표를 사면 더 좋은 좌석을 얻을 수 있다.
② 비행기 표를 미리 사면 더 저렴할 수 있다.
③ 행사 기간에는 투숙객이 많이 몰려 호텔 숙박비가 비싸진다.
④ 숙박 시설을 일찍 예약하면 할인을 받을 수도 있다.
⑤ 여행 전에 필요한 목록을 만들어서 점검하는 것이 좋다.

6 대화를 듣고, 여자의 조언으로 가장 적절한 것을 고르시오.

① 문제 해결을 위해 상대와 면담해라.
② 시간 약속을 잘 지켜라.
③ 기분 전환을 위해 명상을 해라.
④ 선입견을 품는 것은 나쁘다.
⑤ 철자를 바르게 쓰는 연습을 해라.

7 대화를 듣고, 기사의 주제로 가장 적절한 것을 고르시오.

① 회사에서 원하는 인재상
② 멀티 태스킹을 하는 방법
③ 멀티 태스킹에 대한 통념과 실제
④ 동시에 여러 일을 수행하는 사람의 필요성
⑤ 직장 내 고충 해결 시설을 확대하는 현재 추세

8 대화를 듣고, 두 사람이 대화하고 있는 장소로 가장 적절한 곳을 고르시오.

① Cafe   ② Guest house
③ Herb garden   ④ Interior shop
⑤ Korean folk village

9 다음을 듣고, 그림에서 음악강당 건물을 고르시오.

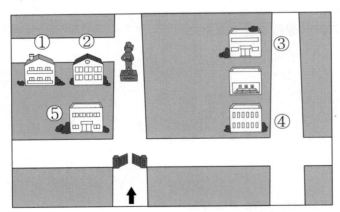

10 대화를 듣고, 여자가 할 일로 가장 적절한 것을 고르시오.

① 의사에게 진료받기
② 발표 준비 도와주기
③ 처방받은 약을 가져다주기
④ 같이 차 마실 시간 내기
⑤ 허브차를 가져다주기

11 대화를 듣고, 여자가 남자에게 부탁한 일로 가장 적절한 것을 고르시오.

① to tell many people he knows to help the zoo
② to donate some money for buying animals
③ to introduce new animals in the zoo
④ to volunteer for the zoo
⑤ to make survey question items

12 대화를 듣고, 여자가 가게를 방문한 이유를 고르시오.

① 신제품을 홍보하려고
② 매장 서비스를 점검하려고
③ 영업 사원의 교체를 알리려고
④ 상품에 관한 설문 조사를 하려고
⑤ 새 상품을 개발하기 위한 자료를 모으려고

13 대화를 듣고, 보고서에 대해 여자가 언급한 문제점을 고르시오.

① 색 지정 오류   ② 잘못된 핵심 내용
③ 수치의 부정확성   ④ 세부 자료 부족
⑤ 그래프 누락

14 대화를 듣고, 여자가 한 달에 벌게 될 총 금액을 고르시오.

① $15   ② $180
③ $360   ④ $1260
⑤ $1440

15 다음을 듣고, 코네 폭포에 관한 내용과 일치하지 <u>않는</u> 것을 고르시오.

① 세상에서 가장 긴 폭포 중 하나이다.
② 라오스 북부를 따라 흐르며, 국경에 인접해있다.
③ 메콩 강의 본류에 있다.
④ 높이는 21미터이지만 길이는 10킬로미터가 넘는다.
⑤ 우기에는 초당 4만 톤 이상의 물을 방류한다.

16 다음을 듣고, 강연에 대해 남자가 하는 말의 내용과 일치하지 <u>않는</u> 것을 고르시오.

① 주제는 면접을 준비하는 방법이다.
② 이번 주 수요일 저녁에 강당에서 1시간 정도 진행된다.
③ 강당에는 2, 3, 4학년 학생 모두를 수용할 좌석이 없다.
④ 원하는 학생들은 모두 개별 상담을 받게 된다.
⑤ 강연은 도서관에서 TV로도 시청할 수 있다.

17 다음 표를 표를 보면서 대화를 듣고, 일치하지 <u>않는</u> 내용을 고르시오.

RESERVATION FORM	
NAME	① Dominic Burgi
DATE	② September 24th
PERSONS	③ 2
OPTIONS	④ non-smoking room, great view
PRICE	⑤ $110
SURIN HOTEL	

18 대화를 듣고, 남자의 마지막 말에 대한 여자의 응답으로 가장 적절한 것을 고르시오. [3점]

Woman: _____

① Then, you don't have free time this week.
② Okay, I'll call Ms. Yang and say yes.
③ You should take a rain check on the breakfast meeting.
④ I think the marketing team prepared everything for the meeting.
⑤ You can call the Sussex Hotel directly. Do you know the number?

19 대화를 듣고, 여자의 마지막 말에 대한 남자의 응답으로 가장 적절한 것을 고르시오.

Man: _____

① Yes, they want to be vets.
② I can join a certain big company.
③ No, they're opposed to my plan.
④ They really want me to go study abroad.
⑤ I can't understand why you want to be a florist.

20 다음 상황 설명을 듣고, 농부가 할 말로 가장 적절한 것을 고르시오.

Farmer: _____

① More haste, less speed.
② It's never too late to learn.
③ A sound mind in a sound body.
④ Empty vessels make the most sound.
⑤ Birds of a feather flock together.

[21~22] 다음을 듣고, 물음에 답하시오.

21 두 사람이 들은 강의의 제목으로 가장 적절한 것은?

① Sales and marketing
② Competitive strategy
③ Business administration
④ Difficulty of management
⑤ Insights for executive officers

22 5대 경쟁 요인 중, 여자가 생각하는 가장 중요한 요소는?

① 통찰력
② 경쟁 조성
③ 진입 장벽
④ 구매자의 교섭력
⑤ 현 경쟁자들 간의 경쟁

Dictation

문제 지문을 다시 한 번 듣고 빈칸을 채워보세요. 잘 안 들리는 부분은 음성을 반복해서 익혀 보세요.

1 MP3 06-01

W: Donghyun, _____ _____ _____ at the St. Patrick's Day
    festival with me?

M: That _____ _____. I'm in.

W: Also, we can enjoy Irish dance performances in the free time.

2 MP3 06-02

W: Honey, _____ _____ _____ the car key on the table?

M: No, I haven't. But I saw you had it when you _____ _____
    _____ this morning.

W: I know, but I can't find it anywhere in the house.

3 MP3 06-03

M: Cathy, what do you read? You _____ _____ _____.

W: I'm reading *Les Miserables*. I like it, but it's a little difficult to read.

M: _____ _____ _____ the musical instead? When I saw that
    performance, I was so impressed.

4 MP3 06-04

M: Hello, I'm Justin Reardon, and I'm here to speak about the city's plan to build a
    shopping center at Bradley Park. As you know, Bradley Park is a wonderful place for
    every citizen to relax. Whenever I go there, I can see children playing together and
    families _____ _____ the grass or under the trees. We have two huge
    shopping centers in the neighborhood already. When another shopping center is built,
    you _____ _____ _____ _____ see these peaceful
    scenes anymore. Instead, every weekend, the park _____ _____
    _____ _____ cars. Do you think it'll improve our quality of life?
    Absolutely not!

5 MP3 06-05

W: What are you looking at, Robert?

M: I'm checking _____ _____ _____ my trip to Detroit next week.

W: Oh, you are finally going to the motor show.

M: Yeah, I've always been _____ _____ _____ the show. I'm so excited that I can see and touch my dream cars in person.

W: Great for you. So, did you book your flight and hotel?

M: Flight? Yes. A long time ago. But no hotel yet. I'm thinking of searching for one when I get there.

W: You'd better not do that. Due to the motor show, there are plenty of people. Hotels won't _____ _____ _____, I think.

M: You mean there might not be an empty room?

W: Right. Search for accommodations right now, and there could be a discount for _____ _____ _____.

M: What?

W: Some hotels give discounts if you book in advance.

M: That's good to know. Thanks.

6 MP3 06-06

M: I was scolded by Mr. Gwen for _____ _____ again.

W: Again? Why didn't you check the report more closely?

M: I reviewed it again and again, but he still found some mistakes. I think he hates me, and he just looks really carefully for my mistakes.

W: Why do you think that?

M: My first year here, I made a big spelling mistake in a very important meeting presentation. Since then, I think, he has had _____ _____ _____ of me.

W: Oh, that's too bad. I think you need to meet Mr. Gwen and talk to him about that. You can't _____ _____ _____ like this, can you?

M: You're right. I should talk to him about _____ _____ _____ I am from this.

7

W: There is a very interesting article about _____ _____ _____.

M: Multitasking? You mean somebody doing a number of jobs at the same time? Isn't that what most companies want from their employees?

W: That's right. But the interesting thing is that multitasking is _____. They followed the timelines of two workers, one who changed focus relatively few times and one who constantly shifted between activities.

M: So the one who shifted _____ _____ had less productive results?

W: That's right. It showed that the worker who shifted less frequently between activities spent only 40 minutes on _____ _____ compared to 5 hours on unproductive tasks for the worker who shifted more frequently.

M: Wow, so the paradox of multitasking means that while somebody is shifting between tasks, that person becomes unfocused and unproductive.

8

M: Why is the line so long here?

W: It is because this shop is very popular. _____ _____ _____ _____ _____ their own beans but they also have the best teas.

M: I see. Oh, the interior looks very special. It looks like a traditional Korean house.

W: It was not a shop at first, but originally a traditional Korean house. They just _____ _____ _____ the business.

M: Hmm, that's interesting. By the way, the garden over there is so beautiful!

W: Yes, it is. They also _____ _____ _____ _____ in their garden by themselves.

M: That's awesome. Do they _____ _____ _____ those rooms, too? If so, it would be a really special experience.

W: No, unfortunately, they don't. They just sell drinks.

M: That's a shame.

9 🔘 MP3 06-09

W: Welcome, everybody! I'm Professor Emily Choi, and _____ _____ _____ you Introduction to Music History. I'll let you know the location of the music hall where we have class this semester. On entering the main gate, you can choose paths going in three directions. Please take the one on the right and follow it until you see _____ _____ _____. Take a left and you can see the engineering college first. But _____ _____. Then, you can see a building with a big swimming pool on the first floor. The building _____ _____ _____ is the music hall. Also, if you want to see me in person visit me in my office from 9 to 11 a.m. every Tuesday. If you go _____ _____ _____ _____, you can see a statue. The building to the left of the statue is my office building. Find me on the second floor.

10 🔘 MP3 06-10

W: So, how are you feeling, Steve?

M: I thought I'd get better, but I feel _____ _____ _____.

W: That's too bad. You are scheduled to give a presentation at work on Friday, right?

M: Yeah, so I have to be better by then. I thought I had the flu, but the doctor said it was just a bad cold. He gave me some cold medicine, but it doesn't seem to help.

W: You know, my _____ _____ _____ _____ this herbal tea, and she and I use it for colds. Would you like to try it?

M: No thanks.

W: Come on! _____ _____ _____ _____. Drink it four times a day, and, believe me, it works. I can bring more to you after work, if you want.

M: Well, I guess it wouldn't hurt to _____ _____ _____ _____ since nothing else seems to be doing the job.

W: Great. I'll _____ _____ _____ _____ at 7:30. See you then.

11 🔘 MP3 06-11

M: Hello?

W: Good afternoon. I'm calling from Songhyung Zoo. _____ _____ _____ _____ _____ to talk?

M: I guess so. What can I do for you?

W: Songhyung Zoo _____ _____ _____ two chimpanzees from Africa. As you know, chimpanzees live far from here, so the shipment is very expensive.

M: Yes, I've heard about it.

W: Also, we want to buy one male and one female and _____ _____ _____.

M: I think that's a great idea. But why are you calling me?

W: Because the price is so high, we're asking people who have visited our zoo to send us money to _____ _____ _____ _____. Can you help us?

M: That sounds good, but I'll have to give it some more thought.

12 🔘 MP3 06-12

W: Hello, I'm Carla Jones from Dowon F&B Company.

M: Ms. Jones, so what is this visit about?

W: I'm a salesperson _____ _____ _____, and I am the one who designed and developed the Blue Shoes.

M: The Blue Shoes! Wow! They're really popular _____ _____ _____ these days.

W: I'm pleased to hear that. Now that you mention it, I'm here _____ _____ _____ _____ on the Blue Shoes. Could you give me a hand with that?

M: Sure. How can I help you?

W: Could you _____ _____ _____ _____? We'd like to know how shop owners feel about the Blue Shoes.

M: Okay. Would you like to have some tea while I'm _____ _____ _____?

W: That's really nice of you.

13 🔘 MP3 06-13

W: Greg, here is the report that you wrote _____ _____ _____.
   You did a good job. It's so helpful for our school.

M: Thank you, Kate. I worked hard on it.

W: I think it's one of the best, but there are some minor problems.

M: Could you explain what kind of problems it has?

W: It is _____, and has good content, but there are a few errors in the analyzing graph.
   Accuracy is important in figures. I marked the _____ _____ in red.

M: During the time I was writing and analyzing the figures, I got LASIK surgery. So I had
   blurry vision. I _____ _____ _____ _____.

W: But you still did great work. Just fix that part.

M: Okay, I'll go and correct right away what you've pointed out.

14 🔘 MP3 06-14

M: Hayun, how's your part-time job?

W: It's good, James.

M: Can I ask _____ _____ _____ _____ _____
   an hour?

W: The pay went up last month. I get $15 an hour.

M: Wow, that's really good. Did the Labor Department increase minimum wage or did your
   boss increase the pay rate?

W: _____ _____ _____ _____ _____.
   I'm satisfied with the position and pay now.

M: Great for you! How many days do you work?

W: Around twelve a month. I work on every Friday, Saturday, and Sunday.

M: How many hours do you work a day?

W: I have to work eight hours _____ _____ _____.

M: You work quite long. What about lunch?

W: The company doesn't cover it, but usually my boss or senior colleagues take care of me.
   So, I _____ _____ _____ on lunch.

M: It couldn't be better.

15 💿 MP3 06-15

W: Khone Falls is one of the longest waterfalls in the world. _____ _____ _____ _____ the southern part of Laos and runs through the border between Laos and Cambodia. It is _____ _____ _____ _____ of the Mekong River, which is also one of the longest rivers in the world. Though Khone Falls is only 21-meters high, its length is more than 10 kilometers because it _____ _____ _____ _____ _____ small falls such as Khong Phapheng Falls and Somphamit Falls. Approximately 11,000 tons per second of water flow through these waterfalls _____ _____ _____ and more than 40,000 tons per second in the rainy season.

16 💿 MP3 06-16

M: On this Wednesday evening, students will get together for a lecture about _____ _____ _____ _____ job interviews. The lecture will _____ _____ in the auditorium and last about an hour. We expect that most seniors will participate. Interested _____ _____ _____ will be there as well, so we cannot guarantee enough seats for everyone. Therefore, at 6 o'clock on the nose, we will close the doors. Latecomers can go to the library and watch the lecture on TV screens there. After the lecture, students will have _____ _____ _____ _____ _____ experts one-on-one. These consultations, however, are only open to seniors. The lecturer will be Jieun Kim, the HR manager from KW recruiting company.

17 💿 MP3 06-17

W: Hello. Surin Hotel. How can I help you?

M: I'd like to _____ _____ _____ for two people on the 25th of September. Are you all booked that night?

W: Well, no... We do have _____ _____ _____ and the view of the city is great. It's $250, plus 10% tax.

M: That's too expensive. What about either on the 24th or the 26th?

W: Well, would you like a smoking or a non-smoking room?

M: Non-smoking, please.

W: Okay, we do have _____ _____ _____ _____ on the 24th... The view is not good, though. And _____ _____ on the 26th.

M: Well, how much is _____ _____ _____ on the 24th?

W: $100, plus 10% room tax.

M: Okay, great. My name is Dominic Burgi. B-U-R-G-I.

18 MP3 06-18

M: Hello, I'm back. Ami, any messages for me?

W: Yes, Mr. Min. There were _____ _____ _____ _____ from Ms. Yang, the human resources consultant, about an hour ago.

M: Why did she call?

W: She asked to _____ _____ _____ to tomorrow morning.

M: Don't I have the breakfast meeting with JAU MBA members?

W: That's _____ _____ _____ _____, Friday morning, sir. You're not scheduled for anything tomorrow morning.

M: Oh, yeah. Where is the MBA meeting?

W: The 48th floor of the Sussex Hotel.

M: I got it. I remember that place. Ami, call the leader of the marketing team and ask him if it's okay to change the meeting time to tomorrow morning. _____ _____ _____ _____ with it, please call Ms. Yang and tell her that we have confirmed the change.

W: Yeah, and you are also _____ _____ _____ _____.

M: No, I should go to my son's soccer game that evening.

19 🔘 MP3 06-19

M: Hyeyoung, do you have plans for after college?

W: I'm thinking about going to England to study flowers.

M: That sounds great. _____ _____ _____ _____ graduate school?

W: No, it's a course in a private school. What about you?

M: I think I'm going to change my major.

W: Oh, Peter. You're already a senior. I don't think it's a good idea.

M: But I believe it's _____ _____ _____ _____ _____ _____ what I really want to do since it's still before graduation.

W: You're majoring in technical engineering. That could _____ _____ _____ _____ more easily than other majors.

M: I know, but I'd like to study veterinary science. I want to be Schweitzer for animals.

W: I think _____ _____ _____ _____ your student adviser.

M: Before that, I have to persuade my parents.

W: Don't your parents like the idea?

20 🔘 MP3 06-20

W: A farmer wished to buy a strong horse and _____ _____ _____ _____ _____ it was the right one before he bought it. He told the owner that he'd like to try out the horse for a day, and the owner agreed. The farmer took the horse home and _____ _____ _____ _____ _____ with his other horses. The next day, the new horse _____ _____ _____ the strong horses and sat beside the laziest and weakest one. Seeing this, the farmer decided not to buy the horse and _____ _____ _____ _____ its owner. Its owner asked how he knew it was not good in just one day. In this situation, what would the farmer most likely say to the owner?

M: Helen, have you listened to Mr. Porter's lecture this week? It was great!

W: Yes. It was really insightful. I _____ _____ _____ _____ how companies try to ease their competitiveness in the market.

M: Companies used to avoid the problems caused by other competing companies in the marketplace. But the focus of this lecture was how companies have to make their own competition environment. Basically, most companies now _____ _____ to make it difficult for other companies to step into the same business.

W: That way, the company can enjoy its strength in that business for a long time without competition.

M: I was also impressed with the five competitive forces that reflect the intensity of industry competition and profitability. When companies choose a business _____ _____ _____ _____ start with, these five forces are something they must consider in advance.

W: That's right. Among them, I think entry wall is the most important thing because it will make the company more profitable once it starts _____ _____ _____ _____ in the market.

M: I agree with you. Anyway, this lecture totally changed my way of thinking and broadened my point of view.

● 수능 4일 전

시험 당일 점심은 얼마나 먹으면 좋을까?

이것까지 생각해 봤니? 오늘부터 실험해보자. 너는 점심은 반만 먹었고, 혹시나 뇌운동이 활발해지지 않거나 졸릴까 봐 카페인이 들어있는 커피와 초콜릿을 먹었어. 커피는 이뇨작용으로 화장실을 가게 될지도 모르고, 시중의 카페인 음료는 몸에 안 맞는 경우도 있으니까 식사량과 간식들을 생각해두자고. 박태환 선수나 김연아 선수처럼 바로 그 타이밍을 위해 내 몸과 뇌가 어떻게 움직여줄지 예민하게 계산해두는 거야.

수능 4일 전

대학수학능력평가 대비
영어영역 듣기(B형)

수능 4일 전

대학수학능력평가 대비 영어영역 듣기(B형)

성명 [   ]   수험번호 [ ][ ][ ][ ][ ][ ][ ][ ][ ]

- 문제지의 해당란에 성명과 수험 번호를 정확히 쓰시오.
- 답안지의 해당란에 성명과 수험 번호를 쓰고, 또 수험 번호와 답을 정확히 표시하시오.
- 문항에 따라 배점이 다르니, 각 물음의 끝에 표시된 배점을 참고하시오.
  3점 문항에만 점수가 표시되어 있습니다. 점수 표시가 없는 문항은 모두 2점입니다.

MP3 07

1번부터 22번까지는 듣고 답하는 문제입니다. 1번부터 20번까지는 한 번만 들려주고, 21부터 22번까지는 두 번 들려줍니다. 방송을 잘 듣고 답을 하기 바랍니다.

1 대화를 듣고, 남자의 마지막 말에 대한 여자의 응답으로 가장 적절한 것을 고르시오.

① Yes, I went there to read books for the kids.
② Great! You're such a good man.
③ Do you do volunteer work every Saturday?
④ I went to a senior's hospital to do volunteer work.
⑤ Yes, I need some support and help from you.

2 대화를 듣고, 여자의 마지막 말에 대한 남자의 응답으로 가장 적절한 것을 고르시오.

① I really need the DVDs for my research work.
② You mean I've got three overdue books?
③ Someone already checked them out.
④ Oh, no! I should have checked the due date.
⑤ So, I can borrow a maximum of 3 items. That's neat.

3 대화를 듣고, 남자의 마지막 말에 대한 여자의 응답으로 가장 적절한 것을 고르시오.

① Thanks a lot, but I just need some rest.
② We don't need it. Just bring your textbook.
③ Yes, you should do it. Math is a core subject.
④ Do you really think the lab is closed?
⑤ Sure, you can bring anything you want for the party.

4 다음을 듣고, 여자가 하는 말의 목적으로 가장 적절한 것을 고르시오.

① 학교 교육 위원회의 구성원을 소개하려고
② 변경된 도서관 규정을 공지하려고
③ 도서관 임시 휴관일을 안내하려고
④ 도서관 이용 불만사항 접수 방법을 공지하려고
⑤ 열람실과 토론실 확충 공사가 곧 시작됨을 알리려고

5 대화를 듣고, 매출 증가를 위한 여자의 제안으로 가장 적절한 것을 고르시오.

① 중국 시장을 공략하는 것이 우선이다.
② 다양한 메뉴를 홍보해야 한다.
③ 전단 광고보다는 SNS를 활용해야 한다.
④ 특선 요리에 집중해야 한다.
⑤ 근처 식당들과 협력하여 홍보해야 한다.

6 다음을 듣고, 남자가 하는 말의 목적으로 가장 적절한 것을 고르시오.

① 위급상황을 보고하려고
② 수업 시간 변경에 대해 공지하려고
③ 에너지 절약 운동 참석을 권유하려고
④ 국가적 행사의 모금 운동을 알리려고
⑤ 정전 사태 발생 대비 비상 훈련을 안내하려고

7 대화를 듣고, 두 사람이 하는 말의 요지로 가장 적절한 것을 고르시오.

① 귀 건강을 위해서는 신형 이어폰을 사는 게 낫다.
② 음악을 큰 소리로 듣는 것은 예의에 어긋나는 일이다.
③ 이어폰 제작 기술이 점차 발달하고 있다.
④ 소음 공해는 심각한 사회 문제이다.
⑤ 비싼 이어폰일수록 그 값을 한다.

8 대화를 듣고, 두 사람이 대화하고 있는 장소로 가장 적절한 곳을 고르시오.

① 학교　　　　　　　　② 공항
③ 도서관　　　　　　　④ 서점
⑤ 놀이방

9 대화를 듣고, 그림에서 대화의 내용과 일치하지 <u>않는</u> 것을 고르시오.

10 대화를 듣고, 남자가 할 일로 가장 적절한 것을 고르시오.

① 동료와 친해질 계기를 만들기　　② 친구에게 전화하기
③ 뮤지컬 표 환불하기　　　　　　④ 아기를 돌봐줄 사람 찾기
⑤ 뮤지컬 관람 일을 다른 날로 바꾸기

11 대화를 듣고, 여자가 남자에게 부탁한 일로 가장 적절한 것을 고르시오.

① to advise her on portrait rights
② to introduce his friend Chloe to her
③ to visit her photography exhibition
④ to invite his friends to the exhibition
⑤ to post an article for marketing

12 대화를 듣고, 여자가 도서관에 늦게까지 남아있는 이유를 고르시오.

① 다양한 책을 읽고 싶어서
② 이사한 집이 맘에 안 들기 때문에
③ 이사한 집이 아직 정리가 안 됐기 때문에
④ 일찍 출발하면 교통 체증을 겪어야 해서
⑤ 늦은 시간에 보는 강의 경치가 더 아름다워서

13 대화를 듣고, 남자가 자신의 일상생활 중 언급하지 <u>않은</u> 시간을 고르시오.

① 기상 시간   ② 출근 버스 시간
③ TV 시청 시간   ④ 취침 시간
⑤ 독서 시간

14 대화를 듣고, 남자가 낼 총 금액을 고르시오.

① $24   ② $36
③ $58   ④ $60
⑤ $64

15 다음을 듣고, 베타카로틴에 대해 여자가 하는 말의 내용과 일치하지 <u>않는</u> 것을 고르시오.

① 간과 장에서 비타민 A를 활성화한다.
② 암, 성인병, 관절염 등을 예방한다.
③ 항산화 물질로 활성산소를 막는다.
④ 당근을 기름으로 조리하면 비타민 흡수율이 높아진다.
⑤ 베타카로틴이 많은 당근은 날것보다 주스로 먹는 것이 좋다.

16 다음을 듣고, 에티오피아 커피에 대해 남자가 하는 말의 내용과 일치하지 <u>않는</u> 것을 고르시오.

① 전 세계적으로 인기있는 에티오피아 커피는 예가체프이다.
② 커피는 에티오피아에서 처음 발견되었다.
③ 커피는 에티오피아 전체 수출품의 3 분의 1을 차지한다.
④ 예가체프 원두는 야생에서 자란다.
⑤ 예가체프는 꽃향기가 나는 달고 신 맛으로 묘사되는 커피다.

17 다음 표를 보면서 대화를 듣고, 남자가 살 가방을 고르시오.

	PRICE	COLOR	INNER POCKETS
①	$815	pink	4
②	$535	black	2
③	$696	blue	6
④	$682	pink	4
⑤	$758	brown	6

18 대화를 듣고, 여자의 마지막 말에 대한 남자의 응답으로 가장 적절한 것을 고르시오.

Man: _____

① Not really, it was the first day. I won't spend so much time on it anymore.
② The phone takes a shorter time to download them than others do.
③ Nowadays, it's the most popular item, so it can't be helpful.
④ We will be punished by my mom. I'm sorry.
⑤ You're right. I think I have to change the payment system.

19 대화를 듣고, 남자의 마지막 말에 대한 여자의 응답으로 가장 적절한 것을 고르시오.

Woman: _____

① Sure. I treated him to breakfast.
② Yes. I got it on my uniform!
③ Of course, I play catch with him.
④ No, he turned down my application.
⑤ I took him to the ball park for fun.

20 다음 상황 설명을 듣고, Murphy 선생님이 Ryan에게 할 말로 가장 적절한 것을 고르시오.

Mr. Murphy: _____

① You should study harder, and you'll get good grades.
② What do you think about learning the Korean language?
③ Remember that spelling is not that important for the tests.
④ You should make an effort to reduce mistakes in your spelling.
⑤ In the Korean language, there are spaces between the written words.

[21~22] 다음을 듣고, 물음에 답하시오.

21 두 사람의 대화 주제로 가장 적절한 것을 고르시오.

① When is the right time to criticize?
② How can people effectively persuade others?
③ How can people achieve what they want?
④ How can people effectively communicate?
⑤ What is the main factor for explaining ideas?

22 두 사람의 대화에서 다음 중, 비판 시 적절하지 않은 말을 고르시오. [3점]

① I am really disappointed with our performance last night.
② I am really angry that our sales decreased last month.
③ I don't believe you'll get better this year, and you underperformed last year.
④ I am not happy that our competitor won the bidding this time.
⑤ I understand your point, but it is not appropriate within our business environment.

Dictation

문제 지문을 다시 한 번 듣고 빈칸을 채워보세요. 잘 안 들리는 부분은 음성을 반복해서 익혀 보세요.

1 `MP3 07-01`

M: Sandra, what did you do last Saturday? I _____ _____ _____ somewhere.

W: Did you? I was _____ _____ _____ _____ the 'House of Love'.

M: The organization for orphans? For volunteer work?

2 `MP3 07-02`

W: Jason Park, I'm afraid you are not allowed to borrow any DVDs now.

M: What? I need these movies. I have _____ _____ _____ _____ them tonight with my friends. Why can't I borrow them?

W: You have _____ _____ _____.

3 `MP3 07-03`

M: Jiyoung, _____ _____ _____ _____ _____ help me with my English after dinner?

W: Why not? Let's meet in the language lab.

M: Okay. _____ _____ _____ my electronic dictionary?

4 `MP3 07-04`

W: Attention, please. Last Wednesday, the school board, _____ _____ _____ _____ and teachers, decided to revise some library rules to _____ _____ _____ of the students. First, the number of books you can borrow will increase from 4 to 5, and you can have them for 2 weeks, not just 1 week. Also, since most students come to school on Saturdays, our library will be open then from now on. But, _____ _____ _____ related to managing library personnel, only the reading room and the discussion room will be open. Its opening hours are from 9 a.m. to 7 p.m. I'm sure we'll use the library more effectively and comfortably even on Saturdays. These new rules will _____ _____ from this coming Wednesday.

5

MP3 07-05

M: Jennifer, _____ _____ _____ this month have dropped considerably.

W: You're right. And a new Chinese restaurant just opened nearby. We are _____ _____ _____.

M: But I don't have any good ideas to get our customers back.

W: I've thought about it. What about focusing on our special dishes?

M: You mean dishes we serve that other restaurants don't?

W: Exactly, focusing on and professionalizing that will save us.

M: Which dishes did you _____ _____ _____?

W: Of course, our best-sellers: curries.

M: Okay, then I'll promote our restaurant more.

W: Yeah, I'll use SNS for ads. You can check out the flyers. _____ _____ _____ from our last advertising campaign.

M: Okay. Let's do it.

6

MP3 07-06

M: Good morning, students. I'm Daniel Minahan, your vice-principal. Today after lunch, we're going to _____ _____ emergency drills to prepare for a possible major blackout. This afternoon, the drills will take place _____ _____ _____. When the siren goes off at 2 p.m., all of you should act according to your homeroom teachers' instructions. _____ _____ _____ _____ for about fifteen minutes. I ask all students of Timothy High School for your _____ _____ _____ _____. Thank you for your attention.

7

MP3 07-07

W: Jason, are you listening to Queen?

M: Did I interrupt you?

W: No. That's okay. But are you okay _____ _____ _____ _____?

M: I know. But if I listen to the music quietly, I can't enjoy the music properly. This drum and guitar.

W: _____ _____ _____ _____ _____. How about buying new earphones? Nowadays, there are a number of earphones with noise-canceling technology. With those earphones, you can enjoy the music _____ _____ _____ _____.

M: Well, yes. But it sounds a bit expensive.

W: It's better to spend some money now rather than to have _____ _____ _____ _____ later.

M: You're right. I'm going to buy new earphones this Saturday. Let's go together.

W: Okay. I know some good models.

8 MP3 07-08

M: I'm terribly sorry to keep you waiting for so long.

W: I was getting really _____ _____ _____, David. What happened?

M: My parents went out tonight, so a babysitter for my little brother _____ _____ _____ _____. But she arrived late.

W: I see. By the way, where's Amy?

M: Oh, she said she couldn't be with us today because she had to go to the airport to see her elder sister off.

W: Oh, no! I can't borrow books here _____ _____ _____ because of unpaid overdue charges. Besides, she has the book list we need to refer to for that report!

M: Well, I can check out the books instead. And why don't we ask her to give us the list and collect the data ourselves? She can type it up and _____ _____ _____ for us.

W: That sounds good. Let's start checking the reference books here.

M: Right. Okay.

9 🔘 MP3 07-09

W: Hello.

M: Hi, Ms. Hong. How is my campaign poster going?

W: Mr. Kensary. It's almost finished. I put _____ _____ _____ in the center and the election slogan at the bottom of the poster.

M: That's good. What about the candidate number?

W: It's _____ _____ _____ _____ _____. And I drew our party logo in the background. You'll like it.

M: Okay, good. What photo did you put in?

W: You prefer the one without glasses, but the image consultant, Ms. Timothy insists on the one with glasses.

M: So, you followed her, right?

W: Yes, I did. It looks _____ _____.

M: I think she would be right. That's why she's a professional. Thank you.

W: This is going to be really nice. I think there's _____ _____ _____ _____.

M: Thank you for your effort, again.

W: My pleasure.

10 🔘 MP3 07-10

M: _____ _____ _____ _____ _____ for the musical?

W: I'm sorry. I remember you mentioned it a few days ago, but it slipped my mind. So I forgot to call the babysitter. Why don't you just go by yourself?

M: I hate going to _____ _____ _____ _____ without you. And these tickets cost a bundle. I really don't want to waste them.

W: Well, there must be someone else who'd like to go.

M: Who am I going to call? It's pretty short notice.

W: Well, _____ _____ _____. What about Kyungmin?

M: Kyungmin's out of town.

W: Hmm. I'm trying to remember who likes musicals. What about Byunghyun?

M: Well... We don't _____ _____ _____ _____.

W: Give him a call. I think he might be free because he quit his job not long ago.

M: It's really short notice, but... All right.

11 🔘 MP3 07-11

W: Hi, Billy. This is Serena. I'm calling you to see if you know someone who can _____ _____ _____ portrait rights.

M: Portrait rights? Is there a problem with your photo exhibition?

W: No, not really. _____ _____ _____ publish a book using exhibited photos.

M: Do you want to know if you have to pay portrait rights fees or not?

W: Exactly, and more information.

M: Then, I know the perfect person for that. One of my friends, Chloe, _____ _____ _____ _____ portrait right protection.

W: That's perfect. So, can I have her phone number or email address?

M: Sure. But first _____ _____ _____ _____ her whether she can help you or not. Don't worry, she's generous and will be happy to help. But I think it's polite to ask first.

W: You're right. I'll wait for your call.

12 🔘 MP3 07-12

M: Shanon, what are you doing here? Why didn't you go home?

W: Well, I don't want to go home early.

M: Why not?

W: Do you remember my family just _____ _____ _____ _____ _____?

M: Yes. You said your apartment building has _____ _____ _____ _____ _____.

W: Right, the view is great.

M: Then what is the problem? Why do you stay out late?

W: The problem is it is located in the middle of downtown. So, many cars _____ _____ _____ at the time I finish school.

M: So that's why you stay here at the library till late.

W: Yes. It's much better to be here reading than to go home early _____ _____ _____ _____.

13 🔘 MP3 07-13

W: So, what's your usual day like? You always seem so busy.

M: I usually get up around 5 a.m. I _____ _____ _____ _____ at twenty to seven so I can catch a bus at 7 o'clock.

W: And what time do you get to work?

M: The subway _____ _____ an hour to get there, but the station is right in front of my office.

W: So, when do you work on your website? You said one time that _____ _____ _____ at home?

M: Well, my wife and I often watch TV or talk until 10 o'clock. She then often reads while I work on my site, and I sometimes _____ _____ until the early hours of the morning, but I try to finish everything by one.

14 🔘 MP3 07-14

W: Good morning, Mr. Choi. Thank you for coming every day.

M: Hello. _____ _____, I'd like to have a cup of iced coffee, please.

W: Sure, no onion bagel for you this morning?

M: No, thanks. Oh, _____ _____ _____ _____, please.

W: All right. It's $3.60, and the shot is ₡40. And here is your coffee.

M: Thank you. Is this that new French-roast coffee?

W: That's right. Do you like it?

M: I can smell the aroma of the freshly-brewed coffee. Do you sell these beans?

W: We sell the coffee _____ _____ _____. They were originally
   $3 per ounce, but now we're offering them at a 10-percent discount.

M: That's great! I'll take twenty ounces.

W: All right. Let me _____ _____ _____ _____
   _____.

M: How much is the total of my iced coffee and the beans?

15 MP3 07-15

W: Have you ever heard about beta-carotene? As people become more and more interested
   in health and well-being, _____ _____ _____ of beta-
   carotene keeps increasing. Beta-carotene is a nutrient that activates Vitamin A in the
   liver and intestine. Appropriate beta-carotene levels keep our bodies _____
   _____ _____, adult diseases, arthritis, etc. As an antioxidant, it
   maintains smooth skin and health and prevents free radicals. Carrots are one food high
   in beta-carotene. Many people _____ _____ _____ or drink
   them in juice, but it's much better for the body to consume them after cooking. Because
   beta-carotene is _____ _____, carrots cooked in oil allow for much
   higher vitamin absorption.

16 MP3 07-16

M: As people love coffee more and more, the preference in various coffee beans has been
   _____ _____ _____ _____. Coffee was first
   found in Ethiopia, and it still grows wild there throughout the country. In fact, coffee
   is _____ _____ _____ the Ethiopian economy, making
   up more than half of total exports. In the whole country, there are over 320,000 small
   farms. Among the various beans growing in Ethiopia, Yirgacheffe has become popular
   _____ _____ _____ _____. All Yirgacheffe beans
   grow wild as well. The coffee brewed from these beans is ranked as a great and refined
   coffee. Yirgacheffe beans are described as soft with a strong floral aroma, sweet and sour
   taste, and sweetness like chocolate.

17 🔘 **MP3 07-17**

M : I'm looking for a bag. But, in fact, I've never shopped _____ _____ _____ _____ before, so I'm very confused.

W : I'll help you. It's not that difficult.

M : Than you.

W: First of all, what price range are you looking at? There seems to be _____ _____ _____.

M : Around $500 through $700.

W: Is it for a special birthday?

M: It is for our 40th wedding anniversary.

W: Congratulations! _____ _____ _____ _____?

M: I think my wife has many black and brown bags, so she might appreciate something unique.

W: Then, how about this one? It's a pink bag _____ _____ _____ _____. What do you think?

M: It's gorgeous! I'll take it.

W: Okay, click here and type in your credit card number.

18 🔘 **MP3 07-18**

W: Sungmo, wow, what's this? Did you buy a _____ mobile phone?

M: My mom bought it for me yesterday. Doesn't it look cool?

W: Can I see it a little? Wow, it feels nice. How do I _____ _____ _____ _____?

M: Just push the button on the side of the phone.

W: _____ _____ _____ is really good. You already have so many apps.

M: Yes. In fact, yesterday I didn't do anything but download the applications.

W: Did your mom let you do that?

M: At first, she was _____ _____ _____, but then she yelled at me in the end. I spent almost 10 hours focusing on the new phone.

W: Don't you think that's too much?

19 🔘 MP3 07-19

M: Saeko, I heard you went to the baseball park yesterday. How was it?

W: It was one of the best days of my life.

M: The game ended _____ _____ _____ _____. It's good for your team, but I think, fans in the ball park were not very excited.

W: The game was okay, but _____ _____ _____ happened after the game.

M: What do you mean?

W: I got Dahyun Song's autograph. I still _____ _____ _____!

M: How did you get it?

W: After the game, I dropped by a snack bar near the ball park to get something to drink, and I saw him _____ _____ _____ _____!

M: Really? What was he doing there?

W: He was having a bottle of water after the game.

M: So, you got his autograph there?

20 🔘 MP3 07-20

M: Ryan is a middle school student. He gets good grades in every subject except in Korean. He decides to _____ _____ his Korean teacher, Mr. Murphy, about the matter. Although he is a Canadian, Ryan studies Korean really hard. So he speaks Korean very fluently _____ _____ _____ _____. However, the problem is that he never _____ _____ _____ his Korean spelling. Mr. Murphy figures out that Ryan's problem is that he knows how to read sentences but _____ _____ _____ on written tests. Mr. Murphy wants to tell Ryan that correct spelling is another important factor, especially in Korean. In this situation, what would Mr. Murphy most likely say to Ryan?

21-22 🔘 MP3 07-21

W: Dave, what did you do last weekend?

M: I _____ _____ a writer's lecture about effective communication skills.

W: That sounds great. So what are some important factors in effective communication?

M: It is quite difficult to define in just a few words, but _____ _____ is definitely one of the most important things in the communication.

W: But being assertive can easily fall into being aggressive. Once your partner _____ _____ _____ _____ _____, communication ends and you cannot achieve your goal.

M: I know. So being assertive without slipping over the line into being passive or aggressive is the key, but it's also _____ _____ _____.

W: Then, how can we become assertive without being passive or aggressive?

M: The writer said it is better to use "I messages" instead of "You messages" because people often receive "You messages" as blaming. For example, say "I am really disappointed that we lost the bidding" instead of saying "You didn't try hard enough to win the bidding."

W: I see. That means finger-pointing behavior easily _____ _____ _____. Right?

M: Right. Also, phrases like "Yes, I understand that", "I can see why you think that", "Yes, I think I've got your point", and "You may be right" can deflect criticism.

W: I will use them when I have to criticize.

M: Remember that avoiding criticism cannot help. When criticism is necessary, you have to do it; just try to be sensitive when you do.

듣는다는 건 참 흥미로운 일이야.

사람들은 대부분 의사소통을 엄마 뱃속에서 엄마 목소리를 들으면서 시작한다고 해. 그리고 죽음 직전까지 가장 끝까지 인지하는 게 바로 듣는 거래. 그만큼 듣는다는 건 중요한 일이야. 우리가 서로의 이야기를 듣는 거잖아. 부담 갖지 말고 원어민들의 대화에 귀를 기울여봐. 수능은 잠시 잊고 우리가 살면서 하는 이야기들을 담아둔 내용을 편안한 마음으로 듣고 답해보자고.

수능 3일 전

대학수학능력평가 대비
영어영역 듣기(B형)

대학수학능력평가 대비 영어영역 듣기(B형)

성명		수험번호									

- 문제지의 해당란에 성명과 수험 번호를 정확히 쓰시오.
- 답안지의 해당란에 성명과 수험 번호를 쓰고, 또 수험 번호와 답을 정확히 표시하시오.
- 문항에 따라 배점이 다르니, 각 물음의 끝에 표시된 배점을 참고하시오.
  3점 문항에만 점수가 표시되어 있습니다. 점수 표시가 없는 문항은 모두 2점입니다.

🔘 MP3 08

1번부터 22번까지는 듣고 답하는 문제입니다. 1번부터 20번까지는 한 번만 들려주고, 21부터 22번까지는 두 번 들려줍니다. 방송을 잘 듣고 답을 하기 바랍니다.

1 대화를 듣고, 여자의 마지막 말에 대한 남자의 응답으로 가장 적절한 것을 고르시오.

① I'm running my own store.
② That is none of your business.
③ You've always been so sporty. I envy you.
④ It seems the latter one is more suitable for you.
⑤ Did you tell your boss that you are leaving?

2 대화를 듣고, 남자의 마지막 말에 대한 여자의 응답으로 가장 적절한 것을 고르시오.

① I've never studied it before.
② That sounds like an excellent opportunity.
③ Italy has great programs about linguistics.
④ Never mind. You can go anywhere you want.
⑤ Look for some language program on the Internet, first.

3 대화를 듣고, 여자의 마지막 말에 대한 남자의 응답으로 가장 적절한 것을 고르시오.

① You can even write some music.
② There are so many audition programs.
③ I didn't realize you liked music that much.
④ That would be too stressful. I just play to relax.
⑤ Nowadays, many people make bands just for fun.

4 다음을 듣고, 여자가 하는 말의 목적으로 가장 적절한 것을 고르시오.

① 연극 토론 주제를 변경하려고
② 연극 동아리 가입을 권유하려고
③ 전통이 깊은 학교를 홍보하려고
④ 독일어 동아리 가입 방법을 안내하려고
⑤ 신입생의 고충 해결 방법을 설명하려고

5 대화를 듣고, 여자의 의견으로 가장 적절한 것을 고르시오.

① 약속은 반드시 지켜야 한다.
② 패스트 푸드는 자제해야 한다.
③ 무슨 일이든 엄마와 상의해야 한다.
④ 이번 수학 시험에서 성적을 향상해야 한다.
⑤ 집에서 음식을 만들어 먹는 것이 건강에 좋다.

6 대화를 듣고, 두 사람이 하는 말의 주제로 가장 적절한 것을 고르시오.

① 좋은 가구를 장만하는 방법
② 온라인 상거래 이용의 급속한 증가
③ 안전한 온라인 상거래를 위한 유의 사항
④ 온라인 매장 이용 시 개인 정보 유출
⑤ 가구 배송 시 유의 사항

7 대화를 듣고, 두 사람이 하는 말의 주제로 가장 적절한 것을 고르시오.

① 교통사고 발생 후 처치 요령
② 운전 중 전방 주시의 중요성
③ 급정거가 자동차에 미치는 영향
④ 올바른 도로 교통 문화의 정착
⑤ 정기적인 차량 점검의 중요성

8 대화를 듣고, 두 사람의 관계를 가장 잘 나타낸 것을 고르시오.

① 전화상담실 직원 – 고객
② 여행사 광고주 – 신문 편집자
③ 관광 안내원 – 여행객
④ 여행사 직원 – 고객
⑤ 승무원 – 탑승객

9 대화를 듣고, 그림에서 여자의 집 위치를 고르시오.

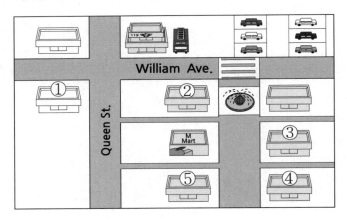

10 대화를 듣고, 남자가 할 일로 가장 적절한 것을 고르시오.

① 보관함 확인하기
② 시계 찾으러 가기
③ 택배 받으러 가기
④ 귀중품 보관함 이용하기
⑤ 분실물 센터에 전화하기

11 대화를 듣고, 여자가 남자에게 부탁한 일로 가장 적절한 것을 고르시오.

① to help her surf the Internet materials
② to expand the topic range of the report
③ to make a call to her parents
④ to introduce some parents to her
⑤ to discuss more about the nursery process

12 대화를 듣고, 남자가 여자를 찾아간 이유로 가장 적절한 것을 고르시오.

① 감독을 소개해 달라고
② 연기를 가르쳐 달라고
③ 방송에 출연해 달라고
④ 음반을 내게 해 달라고
⑤ 뮤지컬에 출연시켜 달라고

13 대화를 듣고, 남자가 여자를 위해 한 일이 <u>아닌</u> 것을 고르시오.

① 전기세 내기
② 화분에 물 주기
③ 세탁물 찾아오기
④ 앵무새 먹이 주기
⑤ 요가수업 결석 통보하기

14 대화를 듣고, 여자가 낼 총 금액을 고르시오.

① $250
② $495
③ $540
④ $630
⑤ $700

15 다음을 듣고, 갯장어에 관해 남자가 하는 말의 내용과 일치하지 <u>않는</u> 것을 고르시오.

① 심해에 살며, 길이는 보통 1.5미터이다.
② 일본에서는 전통 요리로 인기가 많다.
③ 중국인은 과거에 갯장어를 많이 먹었다.
④ 단백질이 풍부한 건강식품이다.
⑤ 혈액을 깨끗하게 하는 성분이 들어있어 심장 질환 예방에 좋다.

16 다음을 듣고, 플뢰르 드 셀 드 게랑드 소금에 관해 여자가 하는 말의 내용과 일치하지 <u>않는</u> 것을 고르시오. [3점]

① 염분이 풍부해 프랑스인들의 필수 요리 재료로 주목받는다.
② 알갱이가 있는 굵은 회색 소금이다.
③ 태양열로 증발시키는 염전에서 수확된다.
④ 프랑스 또는 켈트 해에서 채취된다.
⑤ 독특한 수확 과정을 통해 미네랄 함량이 풍부해진다.

17 다음 표를 보면서 대화를 듣고, 남자가 선택한 자전거를 고르시오.

	TYPE	NUMBER OF SPEED GEARS	AGES
①	Mountain	41	Adult
②	Mountain	35	The elderly
③	Cruising	18	Adult
④	Cruising	12	The elderly
⑤	Cruising	9	Children

18 대화를 듣고, 여자의 마지막 말에 대한 남자의 응답으로 가장 적절한 것을 고르시오.

Man: _____

① How can you say that mean thing?
② I think you can do it better next semester.
③ Thank you. I'm so lucky to have you as a friend.
④ In that case, you can give it up. There's nothing we can do.
⑤ Thank you so much. I know you're very talented at drawing.

19 대화를 듣고, 남자의 마지막 말에 대한 여자의 응답으로 가장 적절한 것을 고르시오.

Woman: _____

① This is the perfect house for us.
② Another family wants to see this house.
③ The furniture is included in the rental fee.
④ Within a five-mile radius, you can find a hospital and market, too.
⑤ Oh, this house is really well-lit owing to facing south.

20 다음 상황 설명을 듣고, 유미가 소년에게 할 말로 가장 적절한 것을 고르시오.

Yumi: _____

① Why don't you listen to me?
② Follow the rules, or you'll be hurt.
③ You must not use your earphones while cycling.
④ Don't take earphones on the road while driving.
⑤ Any idea to go to hospital? Don't you know the direction?

[21~22] 다음을 듣고, 물음에 답하시오.

21 다음 중, '스칸디나비안 플릭'에 대한 설명으로 맞는 것을 고르시오.

① 유명한 카레이서의 별명이다.
② 핀란드에서 자동차 면허증을 부르는 애칭이다.
③ 미끄러운 도로에서 코너를 도는 기술이다.
④ 핀란드의 필수 운전 교육 과정을 부르는 이름이다.
⑤ 스칸디나비아 지역에서 사고로 악명 높은 도로 이름이다.

22 다음 중, 핀란드에서 운전면허를 따기 어려운 이유로 적절한 것을 고르시오.

① They try to make competition-winning drivers.
② They want to make the world's largest car company.
③ They are traditionally proud of their driving skills.
④ Their driving school teaches some of the best driving skills.
⑤ Their road condition is bad due to their severe weather conditions.

해답/해설 237p

Dictation

문제 지문을 다시 한 번 듣고 빈칸을 채워보세요. 잘 안 들리는 부분은 음성을 반복해서 익혀 보세요.

1 🔘 MP3 08-01

W: Leon, I'd like to start _____ _____ _____.

M: What kind of business are you interested in?

W: Something to do with sports, but I'm not sure if I should open a sports equipment store

or _____ _____ _____ _____.

2 🔘 MP3 08-02

M: I want to go to Italy next semester. _____ _____ _____

_____ before?

W: I've been to Rome and Venice for summer vacation. Why do you want to go?

M: I'm interested in the language. But I don't know _____ _____

_____ to learn it.

3 🔘 MP3 08-03

W: Jinsu, I heard you play the drums very well.

M: Not really. _____ _____ _____ _____ as a kind of

hobby.

W: Do you have _____ _____ _____ _____ a band or

anything like that?

4 🔘 MP3 08-04

W: Hello, Luke students. I'm Laura Dern, _____ _____ in the Department

of German Language and Literature. It has already been a month since you entered

Luke College _____ _____. How's everything going? Is it as exciting

as you expected? If not, why don't you join the college's theater group? The club has a

40-year-old tradition, and it is one of the most popular clubs among students. If you

_____ _____ _____ of the club, you'll make friends with

many other members, and you can perform in a play every semester. I'm sure it'll make

your college life _____ _____. Even if you're only interested in

watching plays, join our theater group. You can also discuss your favorite plays.

5 🔘 MP3 08-05

W: Kevin! What is this _____ _____?

M: What? Ah, I ate a hamburger.

W: I told you lots of times, Kevin. Fast food is _____ _____

_____.

M: I know, Mom. But you kind of promised.

W: What do you mean?

M: You said if I got an A⁺ on the math exam, you'd _____ _____

_____.

W: Did you get an A⁺ in math?

M: Yes, so I bought and ate the hamburger. I love hamburgers.

W: You _____ _____ _____ _____ on the exam. But,

you should have called and asked me about the hamburger, first.

M: I'm sorry, Mom. But I was really hungry.

W: Okay, but again, fast food is not healthy. You should try not to eat it so often.

6 🔘 MP3 08-06

M: Hi, how are the wedding preparations going?

W: They're going well, thanks. I'm going to buy furniture this weekend.

M: Are you going to buy it in _____ _____ _____?

W: Well, I am planning to have a look in some offline shops first. Then, if I see anything

I like, I will try to find something _____ _____ _____

_____. I'll go for the cheapest offer.

M: That's a brilliant idea. But be careful with online shopping. You should research the online

seller before you give them your credit card information.

W: Of course. I always _____ _____ _____ _____ of

the company first.

M: Also, using credit cards can be safer than transferring money.

W: You're right. Online shopping is one good way to buy cheap products, but people should

always keep in mind that _____ _____ _____ _____.

7 MP3 08-07

M: Maria, I heard _____ _____ _____ just now. Can you step on the brake lightly?

W: Okay. Is that enough?

M: A little bit harder. Okay. There it is. When did you last change the brake pads?

W: I don't know. I haven't actually changed the brake pads for a few years.

M: Usually, people _____ _____ _____ _____ every 25,000 kilometers. Otherwise, you could have a serious car accident, especially when you _____ _____ _____.

W: Really? I didn't know that.

M: Oh, boy. Not only brake pads. There are a number of things you should periodically check in the car.

W: For example?

M: Engine oil level, timing belt, tire air pressure... There are many of them. I think it's better to go to the garage to check the brake pads. Then we can get some information about _____ _____ _____ _____ for a car.

W: That sounds great.

8 MP3 08-08

W: Good morning. What can I help you with?

M: I'm here to ask about some information _____ _____ _____ in today's paper.

W: You mean the Paris-Venice tour package?

M: That's right. _____ _____ _____ _____ some more details about it?

W: Of course. This one includes tours of the Eiffel Tower and the Louvre Museum and the wonderful scenery of water city from a boat, and you can enjoy original French and Italian cuisine.

M: Sounds fascinating. How about the flight? Can I _____ _____ _____ _____ ?

W: Of course.

M: Okay, then, how much is the package?

W: _____ _____ _____ is $3,500, but if you book it today, you can have a 25% discount.

M: That sounds great! I'd like to reserve it right away.

9 🔘 MP3 08-09

W: Hi, Eunsik. I'm Cathy. I just called to tell you how to get to my place.

M: Oh, thanks. I can _____ _____ _____ now.

W: Do you know the fire station between Queen Street and William Avenue?

M: Yes. Oh, I can use the parking lot near the fire station, right?

W: Right. _____ _____ _____ _____ _____ to William Avenue. Then you'll see a crosswalk.

M: Okay, I know that area a bit. Should I _____ _____ _____ there?

W: Yeah. Then you can see Italian Square and a fountain. Walk through the square until you get to an M-Mart on the right.

M: Okay, the M-Mart. Go on.

W: Then, you can see my place across from the M-Mart.

M: Across from the M-Mart? Which side do you mean? Across the square or beside the M-Mart building?

W: Oh, _____ _____ _____ _____. Just go to the next building. That's it.

M: Okay, I got it.

10 🔘 MP3 08-10

W: Harvia Sauna. How can I help you?

M: I left my watch there.

W: Did you use a safe deposit box or just leave it in _____ _____ _____?

M: It's not really an expensive watch, so I didn't use a safe deposit.

W: Okay, let me check... Hmm... *[Pause]* I checked our _____ _____. What color is your watch?

M: It's just white with a round-shaped face and a black strap. It's a very common kind of watch, but it has the initials "RB" on _____ _____ _____ _____ _____.

W: I can see it. Right, we have your watch.

M: Oh, thank you.

W: It's my pleasure. _____ _____ _____ _____ to have it delivered?

M: No, thanks. I'll stop by this evening on my way back home. Thank you so much.

11 MP3 08-11

M: Okhee, what are you doing?

W: I'm writing a social science report about a _____ _____.

M: What is the focus of the report?

W: _____ _____ my survey, there are so many children near my area and some of them can't go to the nursery.

M: I heard a lot of news that there's a nursery crisis.

W: Right. I didn't expect to find that the _____ _____ _____ _____, so one mother even quit her job. On the other hand, in the country, nurseries are closing because student numbers are too low.

M: That's true. Why don't you include an interview with a couple whose children go to a nursery in the report?

W: If possible, could you _____ _____ _____ _____ some parents so that I could talk to them?

M: I'll ask my neighbors.

12 🔘 MP3 08-12

M: Hello, Ms. Parker? My name is Dongkyun Lim. I was a student in your drama class last year.

W: Oh, you're a student at Yerin Art Institute! You sang _____ _____ _____ _____ of my class!

M: Yes, that was me. I released an album though it didn't sell very well.

W: Don't be disappointed. You are young and have so much potential.

M: Thanks. I heard that you _____ _____ _____ the musical, *The Romantic Holiday*. I was wondering if there was _____ _____ _____ _____ you with.

W: What can you do?

M: I can sing, act, and even dance. Would there be _____ _____ _____ _____ _____?

W: Hmm, why don't you audition first? That is the best I can do.

M: I know I won't disappoint you. Thank you so much!

13 🔘 MP3 08-13

M: Hello.

W: Hi, Roberto. It's me. _____ _____ _____ _____ to the hotel room.

M: Hey, how are you? Did you enjoy the flight?

W: It was okay. It is really nice here. The weather is cool and the wind is sweet.

M: You really like Rome, huh. I _____ _____ _____ and watered the plants.

W: Thank you. Are they okay?

M: Sure, and I _____ _____ _____ _____ from the dry cleaner's.

W: Oh, I should have done that before leaving. Thank you so much for that.

M: No problem. Also, I told our yoga teacher about your absence for two weeks. The _____ _____ _____, but the due date is far enough away. You can cover it when you get back.

W: Sure. Once again, thanks so much for everything! You are the best!

14 🔊 MP3 08-14

M: Good morning, ma'am. May I help you?

W: I'm from Dream and Love Kindergarten.

M: Ahh. Two hundred flowers, right?

W: Right. Which flowers _____ _____ _____ for this fall?

M: In fall, chrysanthemums are the most popular choice.

W: Is there _____ _____ _____ _____ between pink and yellow?

M: Not at all. They're both $3 each.

W: Then, I'll have 50 of each. _____ _____ this beautiful lotus?

M: Children will love it. You have a big pond, so it will be really good. They're $4 each.

W: Then I'll take 100 lotuses, too.

M: You've ordered over 100, so I can _____ _____ _____ _____ _____ on the total price.

W: Oh! Thank you.

15 🔊 MP3 08-15

M: A pike conger is _____ _____ _____ _____. They normally reach 1.5 meters in length and sometimes reach more than 2 meters. This species is caught in deep seas. It is popular in Japan for a _____ _____ named Hamo. In the past, people in China and Korea did not eat this because the fish look like snakes. So whenever they caught pike congers, they sold them to Japanese people. This eel _____ _____ _____ _____ _____, so it is also known to be a healthy food. It is especially rich in EPA and DHA, _____ _____ _____ effective to clean blood, so eating a lot of pike conger can help prevent heart disease.

16 🔘 MP3 08-16

W: Fleur de Sel de Guérande, this is a French or Celtic sea salt that takes on a gray color. It is a coarse, granular sea salt popularized by the French. As French cuisine _____ _____ worldwide, this gray salt is also becoming famous because it is one of the most important and basic ingredients in French cuisine. _____ _____ _____ _____ in solar evaporation salt pans, and the harvesters deliberately _____ _____ _____ _____ contact with the silt beneath it. This harvesting process may seem a bit dirty, but it is known that this process _____ _____ _____ _____ of the gray salt.

17 🔘 MP3 08-17

W: What type of bike do you want? Will you bike _____ _____ _____ _____ or just cruise downtown or along the river?

M: For cruising is good enough for me. My girlfriend rides so well, so I want to ride with her _____ _____ _____.

W: That sounds romantic. Actually, bikes are really fun and make your life so much easier.

M: What do you mean?

W: _____ _____, or going to a shop or library, there are some distances that make it difficult to decide whether to take a bus or to go on foot. _____ _____ _____, bikes are perfect.

M: Oh, yes. I see what you mean. Do you recommend a bike with high gears?

W: Well, in your case, _____ _____ _____ would be enough. Under ten is for the elderly and children.

18 🔘 MP3 08-18

W: What's wrong with you, Jaewon? You look down.

M: I'm in trouble, Hyunjoo. The science homework _____ _____ _____.

W: What, you mean for Mr. Han's class?

M: Yeah, _____ _____ _____ dissect a fish, and sketch the internal organs. I think it's too cruel. I don't want to do this assignment.

W: Jaewon, but you eat fish. Eating is much crueler, don't you think?

M: No, it's different. But when you put it like that, I think I want to _____ _____ _____.

W: Come on, Jaewon, don't be so silly! When do you _____ _____ _____ _____ _____?

M: By Wednesday. Do you think I can do it?

W: You can do it well, of course. Just do it.

19 🔘 MP3 08-19

M: This apartment is located near the subway station, so it's very convenient to _____ _____ _____ or anywhere else.

W: Yes, you're right. And to our family, that's an important option. Especially, my daughter is a freshman in University of Aran.

M: In that case, this town is _____ _____ _____ her. Okay, look around this house.

W: How many rooms are there? We need at least three rooms and two bathrooms.

M: This is just what you need. How old are your kids?

W: My daughter is a freshman as I said, and the boy is fifteen.

M: Near here, there's a middle school. It's _____ _____ _____ _____ with a long history and tradition.

W: That sounds so nice. _____ _____ _____ _____ _____ to get there?

M: Around fifteen minutes on foot.

20 🔘 MP3 08-20

W: Yumi is driving her car to go to her mother's place. When she's almost there, a boy suddenly comes out from _____ _____ _____. He is cycling with earphones on. She stops the car as soon as she can and honks at him. But he _____ _____ _____ due to the earphones. He's not really cycling fast, but Yumi feels he's going _____ _____ _____ any pedestrians. She is really astonished, but he doesn't know what happened. Yumi thinks about what to do. _____ _____ _____ _____ or listening to music with earphones while riding a bike is really dangerous. So she wants to warn the boy of this dangerous behavior. In this situation, what would Yumi most likely say to the boy?

21-22 🔘 MP3 08-21

M: Finland has probably the hardest and the most challenging drivers' tests in the world. It is known to have 36 months of _____ _____ _____, and the course includes theory and practical driving skills. One interesting thing is that this snow-covered country requests all drivers learn how to save a car in critical situations such as spinouts, _____ _____, and flat tires. So basically, all Finns who have a driver's license are familiar with drifting a car. It is indeed not a strange thing to request such a difficult driving skill to the drivers in Finland because Finland _____ _____ _____ _____ its severe weather conditions. Finland's roads are normally covered with snow and ice, so it is basically always slippery. There is a famous term describing their driving skills: the 'Scandinavian flick,' which is included in the practical driving skills learned at the driving school. The Scandinavian flick is the way Finnish people _____ _____ _____ on slippery roads, which is simply turning a corner by allowing the rear wheels to slide on the road. So it is no wonder Finns become champions in many driving competitions.

해답/해설 237p

● 수능 2일 전

내일은 예비 소집일이야.

내일은 내가 어떤 곳에서 시험을 보게 될지 가보게 되지? 아, 이런 곳이구나 하면서 장소에도 익숙해지고 내가 시험 치는 모습을 머릿속에 이미지로 그려봐. 그리고 오후 1시 10분에는 여지없이 뭘 하면 돼? 영어 듣기! 소집이 늦어지면 좀 안타깝지만 소집 전후에 바로 시작할 것! 이 과목 저 과목 많은 교재를 들추고 혼란스러워하지 마, 현실도피용 수면도 금물! 차분히 마음을 다스리면서 한 문장이라도 꼼꼼하게 읽자.

수능 2일 전
대학수학능력평가 대비
영어영역 듣기(B형)

대학수학능력평가 대비 영어영역 듣기(B형)

성명		수험번호										

- 문제지의 해당란에 성명과 수험 번호를 정확히 쓰시오.
- 답안지의 해당란에 성명과 수험 번호를 쓰고, 또 수험 번호와 답을 정확히 표시하시오.
- 문항에 따라 배점이 다르니, 각 물음의 끝에 표시된 배점을 참고하시오.
  3점 문항에만 점수가 표시되어 있습니다. 점수 표시가 없는 문항은 모두 2점입니다.

MP3 09

1번부터 22번까지는 듣고 답하는 문제입니다. 1번부터 20번까지는 한 번만 들려주고, 21부터 22번까지는 두 번 들려줍니다. 방송을 잘 듣고 답을 하기 바랍니다.

1 대화를 듣고, 여자의 마지막 말에 대한 남자의 응답으로 가장 적절한 것을 고르시오.

① It's a relief to hear that news.
② Nowadays, baseball is so popular.
③ I like playing baseball rather than watching it.
④ I just bought two tickets online. How can I get an extra one?
⑤ I'm sorry. I promise we will go there next Saturday.

2 대화를 듣고, 남자의 마지막 말에 대한 여자의 응답으로 가장 적절한 것을 고르시오.

① Their whole menu has changed totally.
② Did you order your food? Just make it two.
③ The air's so fresh and cool. I feel much better.
④ Then you go first. I'm supposed to prepare materials for the meeting.
⑤ A little rest and fresh air make you focus on the job better.

3 대화를 듣고, 남자의 마지막 말에 대한 여자의 응답으로 가장 적절한 것을 고르시오.

① Why don't you tune the flute to the violin?
② I'm glad you like the same music as me.
③ I was so happy to take flute lessons for 2 weeks.
④ But you've played soccer for 2 years, haven't you?
⑤ As everyone does, you just have to start as a beginner.

4 다음을 듣고, 남자가 하는 말의 목적으로 가장 적절한 것을 고르시오.

① 학생회장의 연임을 지지하려고
② 학생회장 직에서 사임하려고
③ 학생회의 불만 사항들을 전달하려고
④ 학생회장 투표 참여를 권고하려고
⑤ 지난해와 올해의 투표율을 비교 및 분석하려고

5 대화를 듣고, 남자의 의견으로 가장 적절한 것을 고르시오.

① 집에 일찍 귀가해야 걱정이 덜 된다.
② 버스를 좀 더 일찍 탈 필요가 있다.
③ 가까운 거리는 걸어 다녀야 한다.
④ 친구들과 함께 토론하면서 공부해야 한다.
⑤ 집에 돌아올 때는 항상 지하철을 타는 것이 좋다.

6 다음을 듣고, 여자가 하는 말의 주제로 가장 적절한 것을 고르시오.

① 칭찬은 고래도 춤추게 한다.
② 믿음과 칭찬을 통해 교육해야 한다.
③ 칭찬할 때는 구체적으로 해야 한다.
④ 운동선수에게는 격려가 제일 중요하다.
⑤ 선수의 신기록은 최고의 응원에서 비롯된다.

7 대화를 듣고, 두 사람이 Bilon 부족에 관해 이야기하는 주제로 적절한 것을 고르시오.

① 역사   ② 장례 문화
③ 결혼 문화   ④ 예술성
⑤ 독창성

8 대화를 듣고, 두 사람이 대화하고 있는 장소로 가장 적절한 곳을 고르시오.

① cable car   ② ship
③ aquarium   ④ airplane
⑤ mountain

9 대화를 듣고, 그림에서 여자가 사는 곳을 고르시오.

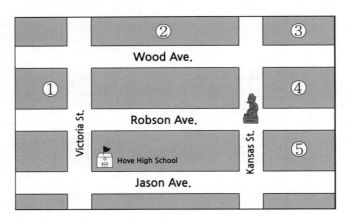

10 대화를 듣고, 대화 직후 여자가 할 일로 가장 적절한 것을 고르시오.

① 커피 만들기   ② 커피 사기
③ 표 사기   ④ 주차 공간 찾아보기
⑤ 입구 위치 알려주기

11 대화를 듣고, 여자가 남자에게 부탁한 일로 가장 적절한 것을 고르시오.

① 30분 정도 기다리기
② 여권과 항공권 준비하기
③ 준비를 서두르기
④ 친구에게 전화하기
⑤ 집 안을 살펴보기

12 대화를 듣고, 여자가 전화를 받지 **못한** 이유를 고르시오.

① 회의 중이어서
② 휴대폰이 고장 나서
③ 휴대폰의 배터리가 방전되어서
④ 일하느라 바빠서
⑤ 식당에서 식사 중이어서

13 대화를 듣고, 도서 구매 시 고려사항으로 남자가 언급하지 <u>않은</u> 것을 고르시오.

① 표지
② 작가
③ 주제
④ 출판사
⑤ 출판연도

14 대화를 듣고, Kingsley 다리 이용 시 단축될 시간과 터널 이용 요금을 바르게 짝지은 것을 고르시오.

단축될 시간 – 터널 이용 요금
① 약 30분 – $2
② 약 30분 – $4
③ 약 45분 – $2
④ 약 45분 – $4
⑤ 약 50분 – $2

15 다음을 듣고, 전시회에 관한 내용과 일치하지 <u>않는</u> 것을 고르시오.

① 8월 9일부터 9월 8일까지 국립 미술관에서 열린다.
② 다이아몬드, 유색 보석, 왕관 등이 전시된다.
③ 전시 시간은 화요일에서 일요일 오전 10시부터 오후 6시까지이다.
④ 20명 이상 관람하면 단체 할인이 적용된다.
⑤ 입장료는 성인 10달러, 고등학교 학생까지는 8달러이다.

16 다음을 듣고, 수족구병에 관한 내용과 일치하지 <u>않는</u> 것을 고르시오.

① 여름과 가을에 아이들에게 흔히 발생한다.
② 대부분의 경우 심한 고열을 동반하는 질병이다.
③ 구강, 입술, 손, 발과 다른 부위에 물집이 생긴다.
④ 보통 7~10일이 지나면 자연스레 낫는다.
⑤ 감염된 사람의 침, 코와 목 분비물에 의해 전염될 수 있다.

17 다음 표를 보면서 대화를 듣고, 남자가 예약할 시간을 고르시오.

DANTE BOARD ROOM BOOKING

	Mon	Tue	Wed	Thu	Fri
Morning Time (9-12)	Booked	①	Booked	②	Booked
Afternoon Time (13-17)	③	Booked	④	⑤	Booked

18 대화를 듣고, 남자의 마지막 말에 대한 여자의 응답으로 가장 적절한 것을 고르시오.

Woman: _____

① I'll adopt another dog from there if you want to.
② Would you take care of my cat during summer vacation?
③ I'll ask my boss to write a recommendation letter for you.
④ It is not difficult. You can visit the website and follow the directions there.
⑤ My work is so rewarding. I'm so happy that I can do something for them.

19 대화를 듣고, 여자의 마지막 말에 대한 남자의 응답으로 가장 적절한 것을 고르시오.

Man: _____

① They're celebrating their 10th anniversary.
② Then, I can recommend the Prince Hotel.
③ I was really satisfied with the hotel, so I recommend it.
④ Sorry, all the rooms are reserved already.
⑤ Because they have a gorgeous golf course.

20 다음 상황 설명을 듣고, 선생님이 Mark에게 할 말로 가장 적절한 것을 고르시오.

Teacher: _____

① Art will make your life beautiful.
② Art is either plagiarism or revolution.
③ You'd better not join the drawing club.
④ Art and engineering are closely related to each other.
⑤ Choose what you like, not what you have to do.

[21~22] 다음을 듣고, 물음에 답하시오.

21 다음 중, Robert Walpole 경에 관한 내용과 일치하지 <u>않는</u> 것을 고르시오.

① 재임 기간은 1721년부터 1742년까지였다.
② 나이가 든 후에도 강력한 군사 지휘력을 발휘했다.
③ 영국 정계에 미친 영향력이 막강한 인물이었다.
④ 60대 중반에 스페인과의 전투에서 패배한 후 사임했다.
⑤ 미국에는 경의 이름을 딴 도시가 있다.

22 Robert Walpole 경이 공식적이 아닌 통상적 의미의 영국 초대 국무총리로 알려져 있다고 말하는 이유는 무엇인가?

① 내각의 권한은 줄고 왕의 권한은 늘어나서
② 영국 왕실의 계속되는 전쟁 패배를 극복해서
③ 영국의 평화와 번영에 공화정이 큰 기여를 해서
④ 그 당시 도시 이름은 보통 국무총리 이름을 따라 지어서
⑤ 그 당시 내각에서 큰 영향력을 발휘해서

해답/해설 244p

Dictation

문제 지문을 다시 한 번 듣고 빈칸을 채워보세요. 잘 안 들리는 부분은 음성을 반복해서 익혀 보세요.

1 🔘 MP3 09-01

W: Honey, did you book the tickets for the baseball game?

M: Oh, God. I _____ _____ that. I'll do it right now.

W: How could you forget that? They're _____ _____ _____
_____. Jason will be so disappointed.

2 🔘 MP3 09-02

M: It's already noon. Let's go and have lunch. I'm starving.

W: Tommy, wait. I just _____ _____ _____ _____
_____ to finish this.

M: We can work on it more after lunch. Let's _____ _____ _____
_____ for a while.

3 🔘 MP3 09-03

M: Jina, _____ _____ _____ _____ playing the flute.

W: Thanks. Do you want to try it? It's easier than you think.

M: I'd love to, but I'm not a _____ _____ _____.

4 🔘 MP3 09-04

M: Good afternoon, everyone. I'm Steve Pink, _____ _____
_____ the student union, and I'm a senior in the Department of Arts Business
Administration. The reason I'm standing here is to talk about the _____
_____ for the student president. Nearly 80 percent of voters went to the polls
for last year's election, one of the college's _____ _____ ever. This
year, we have many improvements to talk about such as the school cafeteria, the beverage
vending machines, and the library's facilities. Please _____ _____
_____ _____ you should vote for a better school to improve your
school life. The election day is the 28th of February.

5 🔘 MP3 09-05

M: Eva, what time are you coming home today?

W: I don't know, Dad. It ＿＿＿＿＿＿ ＿＿＿＿＿＿ the traffic situation.

M: These days, I ＿＿＿＿＿＿ ＿＿＿＿＿＿ ＿＿＿＿＿＿ ＿＿＿＿＿＿ how late you've been coming home.

W: I have been studying at the library and coming home by subway, but it comes really late.

M: Yes, at night, ＿＿＿＿＿＿ ＿＿＿＿＿＿ ＿＿＿＿＿＿ ＿＿＿＿＿＿ ＿＿＿＿＿＿.

W: Right. And the bus going to the subway station is usually held up by traffic.

M: I think it would be better to come home early. You can study at home, too.

W: You know I can study better at school, but I don't want you to worry about me.

M: If it's okay with your friends, you can all study at our house. And I can drive them home when you're done.

W: Thanks, Dad. I'll tell Chris and Jun about it.

6 🔘 MP3 09-06

W: Everyone here has seen football or baseball games. Suppose a player makes a final touchdown or a batter hits a home run ＿＿＿＿＿＿ ＿＿＿＿＿＿ ＿＿＿＿＿＿ ＿＿＿＿＿＿ the ninth inning. What is about to happen? The crowd goes crazy and the stadium bursts with the sound of wild cheering, right? Then the player and teammates will be more motivated and try to do a better job. Likewise, I think ＿＿＿＿＿＿ ＿＿＿＿＿＿ ＿＿＿＿＿＿ ＿＿＿＿＿＿ should be formed when you are at work, home, or school. It's a well known fact that when people ＿＿＿＿＿＿ ＿＿＿＿＿＿ ＿＿＿＿＿＿ ＿＿＿＿＿＿, they will try their hardest. Rewarding one's efforts could be the best motivation.

7

MP3 09-07

M: Jihye, what pictures are you looking at?

W: It's about the Bilon people. These pictures are about their wedding ceremony.

M: Who is the bride?

W: The bride is the one _____ _____ _____ _____.
Nobody can see her. She looks like a ghost, doesn't she?

M: Yes. Also, it looks like a modern bridal veil. Does that originate from the Bilon people?

W: That sounds right, but I don't know _____ _____ _____
_____ _____.

M: What about the paintings? What are they for?

W: It's a sand painting. Making a sand painting on the ground is part of the ritual. They
believe the marks of the painting can _____ _____ _____
_____ have many children.

M: I like the designs, and they use a lot of white.

W: White means a new beginning.

M: Really? _____ _____ a wedding ceremony.

8

MP3 09-08

M: Sunny, hurry up! Everyone has already _____ _____ _____.

W: I'm doing my best. Just go ahead.

M: We can get fresh air and appreciate the fascinating scenery up there.

W: [Pause] Wow! It's really nice! It is definitely _____ _____
_____ here!

M: I told you so. Look! The water is clean and has an unbelievably beautiful color.

W: It really is beautiful! Hey, look! Seagulls!

M: Quick! Give me some chips. Do you know what happens if we throw some food to them?
They'll catch and eat it.

W: I am not sure if it is permitted for us to feed them, though.

M: It's okay. As you can see, other people are feeding them, too.

W: All right. Here you are, but you should be careful _____ _____
_____ _____ the ocean.

M: Where are you going? You don't want to try feeding them?

W: No, thanks. I'll just _____ _____ _____ _____.
I think I'm getting seasick. I have to sit down and rest for a while.

M: Oh, really? Then I'll come with you.

9 MP3 09-09

M: Congratulations! You finally _____ _____ _____ Harvard!

W: Thank you. Are you coming to my _____ _____ on Saturday?

M: Sure, I am planning to. I don't know where your new home is, though.

W: Do you know where Hove High School is?

M: Yes, it's _____ _____ _____ of Jason and Victoria, isn't it?

W: Yeah, from there, continue on Victoria and take a right at Robson. Go one block and
you'll see the statue in the middle of the intersection. Do you follow me so far?

M: Yes. Please go on.

W: Turn left when you see the statue. That's Kansas Street. _____ _____
_____ on Kansas until you reach another intersection. Turn right, and it will be
on your left.

M: Thanks for the directions. I'll see you there.

10 MP3 09-10

M: Sally, there's a sign that says "Cherry Blossom Festival" over there. Wow! There are a lot of
cars.

W: Yeah, parking will be _____ _____ _____.

M: We should park somewhere and grab a cup of coffee.

W: Oh, the "_____ _____ _____" sign is out on all these parking
lots.

M: I hope we can find a parking space.

W: Hey, I think we can park in the coffee house building parking lot.

M: Great idea! You go buy the tickets. I will park and come back to you. People are lined up
over there already.

W: Okay. Let's _____ _____ the entrance gate.

M: All right. What kind of coffee do you want? I'm getting a latte as usual.

W: Make it two.

11 MP3 09-11

M: Honey, are you ready?

W: Almost done. I'm just looking for my passport.

M: I'm carrying both our passports, don't you remember?

W: Oh, right. I totally forgot that. I guess I'm too excited about our trip to Milan!

M: I know it's your _____ _____ to see a fashion show in Milan. It will be at last accomplished. But, can't you hurry?

W: Okay, sorry. Do you also have our flight tickets?

M: I saved them on my cell phone.

W: That's good. And have our mail and newspapers been _____ _____ _____?

M: I've asked Alvin to get them while we're away.

W: Your friend Alvin? But he has become more and _____ _____ like me. Call him again and remind him.

M: I will. And please _____ _____ _____ call my parents.

W: No problem. I'll check the gas and electric cords. Then we can hit the road.

12 MP3 09-12

W: Hello, Andrea Anderson speaking.

M: Andrea, this is Gale. Where have you been? I have been _____ _____ _____ _____ for hours.

W: Really? Sorry. Why were you calling me?

M: I found a great restaurant on 10th Avenue.

W: Wow, that's great. _____ _____ _____ tonight?

M: I wish we could. But while I was trying to call you, it was booked up for tonight.

W: Oh, that's too bad. _____ _____ _____ _____ _____ the phone. My cell phone was completely dead.

M: What happened to it?

W: Unfortunately I dropped it into the toilet. Though I was trying to save it, I failed. So I had to buy another one.

M: _____ _____ you didn't answer the phone all morning.

13 MP3 09-13

W: Did you buy out the whole bookstore? One wall of the room is fully packed!

M: Yes, there are more than 800 books here.

W: Amazing! And _____ _____ _____ all these books?

M: Sure thing. I read books in the library or book stores, and if I find a book I like, I just buy it.

W: Wow, so those books seem to be entirely new. What do you _____ _____ _____ when you buy a book?

M: I consider who wrote the book, _____ _____ _____ _____ and whether its cover is unique.

W: Yeah, those are important things. Anything else?

M: I collect books from certain publishing companies.

W: Oh, you have collected books from only Random Publishing in this corner. Do you _____ _____ _____ _____ the company?

M: Not at all. I just happen to like the publisher.

14 MP3 09-14

W: Honey, let's go to the Emerson Museum today.

M: It's too far, darling. _____ _____ _____ an hour and half. I don't want to drive that far on a Sunday.

W: You know the Kingsley Bridge _____ _____ _____ _____. Let's take the road across the bridge.

M: Was the construction done? I guess we could get to the museum in half the time, then.

W: Right. You will have to pay money to cross the bridge, though.

M: I'll check it from my smart phone. Oh, it _____ _____. We have to pay $2.

W: Every crossing makes the government $2? That's too much, I think.

M: No, it's not _____ _____ _____. The original charge is $4. $2 is for local residents like us.

W: Oh, okay. Is it based on just the car or on the number of passengers?

M: Just on the car.

15 🔘 MP3 09-15

W: _____ _____ _____ _____ about the accessories of the French queen, Marie Antoinette? There will be an exhibition _____ _____ _____ _____ and fantastic accessories from August 9 to September 8 at the National Gallery. The exhibition will show the most expensive diamond in the world, some fabulous colored jewels, and the King's and Queen's crowns. It may be _____ _____ _____ _____ you to see these priceless jewels. The exhibition will be open Tuesday through Sunday, 10 a.m. to 6 p.m. The admission fee is $10 for adults and $8 for students up to high school. There is _____ _____ _____ groups of over 20 people.

16 🔘 MP3 09-16

M: Have you ever heard about 'hand-foot-and-mouth disease'? If you are a parent whose baby is under five, or if you have a baby sibling, you probably have. It's a common _____ _____ in summer and autumn for infants. It's usually a mild illness, sometimes _____ _____ a fever. The tongue and the inside of the mouth can become reddish, and there could be some blisters in the oral cavity, on lips, hands, feet, and other parts. Most patients recover spontaneously after seven through ten days. _____ _____ _____, patients will receive proper treatment. It's possible to spread this disease by saliva, nose and throat secretions, or the stool of the infected. Make sure to wash hands well after _____ _____ _____.

17 🔘 MP3 09-17

W: Hello, Facilities Management Team. This is Jungeun Bae speaking.

M: Hello, this is Cooper. _____ _____ _____ reserve the Dante board room next week.

W: Are you going to have a presentation?

M: Yeah, I will need a projector system and some refreshments during the meeting.

W: Don't worry. What time would you prefer? Morning or afternoon?

M: Afternoon _____ _____ _____ for us.

W: Then, three days are available. Monday, Wednesday, or Thursday.

M: Monday's so busy for everyone. I'd like to book Wednesday afternoon.

W: Okay. Oh, sorry! On Wednesday, _____ _____ to clean all the air conditioning system in the whole building.

M: Oh, you're right. I'll book _____ _____ _____ _____, then.

18 🔘 MP3 09-18

M: Woojin, where did you get this cute little kitty?

W: I adopted him from an animal shelter _____ _____ _____. His name is Nabi.

M: You did a good thing. I heard that some people abandon their pets when they go on vacation in the summer just because _____ _____ _____ to take care of them.

W: I am so mad at those people. And that's why I volunteer at the animal shelter.

M: Those poor animals, they all _____ _____ _____ _____. And you're such a good person.

W: I just do it since I like it.

M: _____ _____ _____ volunteer, too. How can I do it?

19 🔘 MP3 09-19

M: Dawa Travel Agency. How may I help you?

W: Hi, I'm calling to _____ _____ _____ _____ to Guam. There are 4 people including me, and we'd like to leave on July 5th.

M: Sure. And _____ _____ _____?

W: We're going to stay for 5 nights. Which hotels are available?

M: _____ _____ _____ _____ the Balijian Hotel. It's located near a beautiful beach and is well known for its great seafood.

W: Sounds lovely.

M: Oh, and I've just found out that they are having a special promotion. You will get a free round of golf on Monday.

W: That's great! What is the _____ _____?

20 🔘 MP3 09-20

M: Mark is a freshman at Ruffalo Secondary School. As the new semester starts, all the clubs in the school are _____ _____ _____. There are various clubs and Mark _____ _____ _____ _____ the drawing club called 'Terminals'. Mark is having _____ _____ _____ his counselor. He asks her whether he should join the club or not. Mark wants to be an engineer, so he thinks the drawing club is not really helpful for his university entrance. But, the teacher doesn't agree with him since he has joined a lot of _____ _____ already. In this situation, what would the teacher most likely say to Mark?

21-22 🔘 MP3 09-21

W: Sir Robert Walpole is known to be the first prime minister of Great Britain. Although the position was not precisely 'Prime Minister' at that time since there was no law acknowledging the position of a prime minister or _____ _____ _____ for it, there is no doubt that Walpole was the first prime minister because of his influence in the cabinet. His premiership was between 1721 and 1742, when the power of the king was _____ _____ and the power of the cabinet was gradually increasing. The French Revolution started in 1789, and a republic was proclaimed in 1792, so the British premiership was a little bit ahead of the rest of Europe. Walpole's _____ _____ _____ _____ of Great Britain was tremendous. He also contributed to his country's peace and prosperity. But in the year 1742, when he was in his mid-sixties, many politicians thought _____ _____ _____ _____ could not lead a military campaign. At that time, the British military was not as strong as it had previously been, and he finally resigned after a disastrous _____ _____ _____ _____ _____ Spain. The town of Walpole in Massachusetts, USA was founded in the same year when he started his premiership and named after Sir Robert Walpole, and Walpole Street in Wolverhampton is also named after him.

하루 전, 드디어 왔구나! 이 수능 녀석.

그동안 날 그렇게 괴롭히더니… 이제 너에게 내 실력을 제대로 보여주겠어! 자신감으로 무장하고 마인드 컨트롤하자. 실력이 모자란 것 같아 불안하다고? 노노노~ 그동안 수많은 선생님들의 강의 내용과 수많은 교재들이 차곡차곡, 네가 보고 듣다가 너도 모르게 알게 된 엄청난 지식이 네 머릿속에 쌓여 있어. 내일 그 지식을 살살 풀어내면 되는 거야. 하나하나 차근차근, 다른 날과 다르지 않게 오늘도 꼼꼼하게 풀어내자고!

수능 1일 전
대학수학능력평가 대비
영어영역 듣기(B형)

수능 1일 전

대학수학능력평가 대비 영어영역 듣기(B형)

성명	

수험번호										

- 문제지의 해당란에 성명과 수험 번호를 정확히 쓰시오.
- 답안지의 해당란에 성명과 수험 번호를 쓰고, 또 수험 번호와 답을 정확히 표시하시오.
- 문항에 따라 배점이 다르니, 각 물음의 끝에 표시된 배점을 참고하시오.
  3점 문항에만 점수가 표시되어 있습니다. 점수 표시가 없는 문항은 모두 2점입니다.

MP3 10

1번부터 22번까지는 듣고 답하는 문제입니다. 1번부터 20번까지는 한 번만 들려주고, 21부터 22번까지는 두 번 들려줍니다. 방송을 잘 듣고 답을 하기 바랍니다.

1 대화를 듣고, 여자의 마지막 말에 대한 남자의 응답으로 가장 적절한 것을 고르시오.

① I love your house. It's so cozy.
② I prefer the veranda for listening to music.
③ This symphony was really inspiring.
④ Oh, good for you. Mine is an orchestra seat.
⑤ So did I. I'm so happy to hear that news.

2 대화를 듣고, 여자의 마지막 말에 대한 남자의 응답으로 가장 적절한 것을 고르시오.

① Right, there are so many coaches.
② Well done. Remember your rehearsal.
③ Yes, they are excellent guys. Look at that.
④ I won't take this program. It takes so long to register for it.
⑤ Don't compare yourself with those around you. Just relax.

3 대화를 듣고, 남자의 마지막 말에 대한 여자의 응답으로 가장 적절한 것을 고르시오.

① I think the presentation was awful.
② Both are impossible. Take substitutes.
③ I look forward to hearing your presentation.
④ Always, family affairs belong at the top of the to-do list.
⑤ What about putting off graduation until the spring semester?

4 다음을 듣고, 여자가 하는 말의 목적으로 가장 적절한 것을 고르시오.

① 폐전자제품의 심각성을 알리려고
② 전자제품 업그레이드 방법을 알려주려고
③ 폐전자제품 수거 업체에서 하는 일을 소개하려고
④ 전자장치가 인체에 미치는 영향을 조사하려고
⑤ 전자제품을 이용한 환경 문제 해결책을 소개하려고

5 대화를 듣고, 여자의 의견으로 가장 적절한 것을 고르시오.

① 규칙적으로 건강 검진을 받아야 한다.
② 내장 비만을 방지하기 위해 운동을 해야 한다.
③ 성인병을 치료하기 위해 식단을 조절해야 한다.
④ 매일 채소와 비타민제를 섭취해야 한다.
⑤ 건강을 위해서 천천히 식단을 조절해야 한다.

6 다음을 듣고, 남자가 하는 말의 주제로 가장 적절한 것을 고르시오.

① 걱정을 어느 정도 하는 것은 유용하다.
② 걱정은 긍정적, 부정적 효과를 모두 가지고 있다.
③ 걱정은 우리 몸에 치명적인 문제를 초래하기도 한다.
④ 심한 걱정은 문제 해결에 필요한 집중력을 떨어뜨린다.
⑤ 다른 생각들로 걱정을 무마시킬 수 있는 능력이 필요하다.

7 대화를 듣고, 두 사람이 말하고 있는 신문 기사의 제목으로 가장 적절한 것을 고르시오.

① An Eective Way to Use Annual Budget
② Why Do ey Spend Lots of Money for the Border?
③ Educational Benets of Reading Newspapers
④ The Increase in Military Spending: Pros and Cons
⑤ How Can the Two Koreas Be Together?

8 대화를 듣고, 두 사람의 관계를 가장 잘 나타낸 것을 고르시오.

① 종업원 – 손님   ② 승무원 – 탑승객
③ 약사 – 환자   ④ 간호사 – 입원 환자
⑤ 호텔 직원 – 투숙객

9 대화를 듣고, 그림에서 대화의 내용과 일치하지 <u>않는</u> 것을 고르시오.

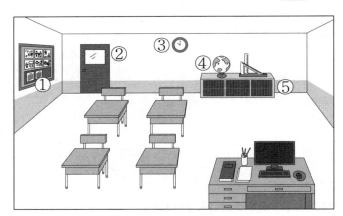

10 대화를 듣고, 남자가 할 일로 가장 적절한 것을 고르시오.

① 가족들과 제주도 가기
② 여행에 대한 더 많은 정보 찾기
③ 여행을 같이 갈 친구들을 모으기
④ 여행 비용 마련하는 방법에 대해 알아보기
⑤ 여행지에 대해 가족들과 상의하기

11 대화를 듣고, 남자가 여자에게 부탁한 일로 가장 적절한 것을 고르시오.

① 대신 콘서트 표 예매하기
② 쇼핑센터에서 물건 사오기
③ 사무실에 들러 컴퓨터 가져오기
④ 결혼기념일 선물로 노트북 고르기
⑤ 엄마에게 콘서트 표 예매를 부탁하기

12 대화를 듣고, 남자의 친구에게 자동차 사고가 난 이유를 고르시오.

① 졸음운전 때문에
② 운전 미숙 때문에
③ 앞차가 후진했기 때문에
④ 과속 운전을 했기 때문에
⑤ 눈길에 미끄러졌기 때문에

13 대화를 듣고, 남자가 딸에게 주는 용돈과 관련해 언급하지 <u>않은</u> 것을 고르시오.

① 용돈의 액수
② 용돈의 쓰임새
③ 처음 용돈을 주기 시작한 때
④ 용돈 제외 항목
⑤ 용돈 벌이를 위해 딸이 하는 일

14 대화를 듣고, 여자가 낼 금액을 고르시오. [3점]

① $28.8
② $30.6
③ $32
④ $34
⑤ $36

15 다음을 듣고, 대상 포진에 대한 정보와 일치하지 <u>않는</u> 것을 고르시오.

① 대상 포진 바이러스에 의해 발병한다.
② 초기 증상은 단순히 두통과 열이 나는 것이다.
③ 발병한 환자 모두 오랜 시간 극심한 통증에 시달린다.
④ 심한 통증은 몇 주간 지속되는 것이 보통이다.
⑤ 바이러스가 잠복 상태로 존재해 재발할 수 있다.

16 다음을 듣고, 황토 천연 염색 체험에 관한 내용과 일치하지 <u>않는</u> 것을 고르시오.

① 학생과 어른 참가비 모두 5달러이다.
② 황토에서는 공기 정화와 습기 제거 기능이 있는 원적외선이 나온다.
③ 황토와 함께 감귤, 대나무 숯을 재료로 한다.
④ 한시적으로 이번 주 수요일에만 체험 행사를 진행한다.
⑤ 20명 이상인 경우 단체 할인을 받을 수 있다.

17 대화를 듣고, 여자의 일정표를 보면서 여자와 남자가 함께 선생을 방문할 요일을 고르시오.

ARIN'S WEEKLY SCHEDULE	
① Mon	Meeting (Literature Project)
② Tue	Yoga Class
③ Wed	Meeting (Dance Club)
④ Thu	Volunteer Work
⑤ Fri	Movie with Mom
Sat	Preparation for the Pop Quiz

18 대화를 듣고, 여자의 마지막 말에 대한 남자의 응답으로 가장 적절한 것을 고르시오.

Man: _____

① That's why I'm sharing some information on the Internet.
② My father sometimes cooks instant food, though.
③ I hope so. I'll call you next time for sharing.
④ Your painting is really touching. I'm moved.
⑤ I like cooking, too. Let's cook something special together.

19 대화를 듣고, 남자의 마지막 말에 대한 여자의 응답으로 가장 적절한 것을 고르시오. [3점]

Woman: _____

① Thanks a lot. It was all great.
② Well, I'd like to have some coffee.
③ No thanks. Just iced water, please.
④ Okay. I'd like to pay in traveler's checks.
⑤ All together. And I need the receipt as well.

20 다음 상황 설명을 듣고, Natalie가 Gavin에게 할 말로 가장 적절한 것을 고르시오.

Natalie: _____

① A company dinner is an extension of work.
② Regular checkups are really helpful. Don't be stubborn.
③ You should take care of yourself. Let's play tennis after work.
④ Get up early. You should ride a bicycle to save money.
⑤ Let's go to the hospital. I can help you. Don't be afraid.

[21~22] 다음을 듣고, 물음에 답하시오.

21 다음 중, 호박을 크게 기르는 방법으로 바르지 <u>않은</u> 것은?

① 기르는데 140일 정도 걸린다.
② 충분한 양의 비료를 사용해야 한다.
③ 초반에는 실내에서 기르는 것이 좋다.
④ 액상 칼슘을 사용하는 것도 중요하다.
⑤ 시장에서는 구하기 힘든 희귀 종자가 필요하다.

22 다음 중, 현재까지 가장 무거운 호박으로 기록된 호박은 몇 파운드인가?

① 140   ② 900
③ 2009   ④ 2012
⑤ 2090

Dictation

문제 지문을 다시 한 번 듣고 빈칸을 채워보세요. 잘 안 들리는 부분은 음성을 반복해서 익혀 보세요.

1 MP3 10-01

W: You love Michael Nicolas's music. Do you know his cello _____ _____ _____ _____?

M: Of course, I do. I've got my ticket already.

W: Me, too. I've got _____ _____ _____. What about you?

2 MP3 10-02

W: Coach, it's my turn.

M: Don't be nervous. You've practiced this program _____ _____ _____ _____ _____.

W: Right. But there are so many _____ _____ _____ _____.

3 MP3 10-03

M: Bell, my daughter is going to graduate from high school tomorrow, but I have _____ _____ _____, too.

W: But it's impossible that you can do both.

M: I know. Which do you think is _____ _____?

4 MP3 10-04

W: Hello. I'm Lisa Smith from Green Efron Company. Have you ever heard about electronic waste? It means _____ _____ such as mobile phones, laptops, computers and televisions thrown away by people after they use them. It's said that every year more than 20 million tons of electronic devices _____ _____ _____. People nowadays upgrade their electronic equipment more frequently than ever before. So electronic waste is _____ _____ _____ _____, and there's not a good solution yet. Soon, it will be a more serious problem than any other kind of waste.

5 🔘 MP3 10-05

W: Honey, I think I have to go on a diet.

M: Why? You look great all the time. I've never thought of you as fat.

W: I know I'm not fat. But _____ _____ _____ my regular checkup said I'm likely to get an excessive accumulation of fat in the abdominal area.

M: That can't be right. Your belly is in fine shape.

W: Honey, it's called intra-abdominal fat accumulated obesity. In the future, when I'm in middle age, it could _____ _____ _____ _____.

M: All right. What are you going to do?

W: I need to be careful about my diet. I eat too many carbohydrates. I should instead eat carrots, tomatoes, and so on.

M: It could be really hard to change _____ _____ _____ _____. Slow and steady wins the race.

W: You can say that again.

6 🔘 MP3 10-06

M: There's no person who hasn't worried at one time or another. It's a part of our life. We all worry about family events, _____ _____ _____, financial problems, and so on. However, according to experts, worrying is not always bad. Some worry is necessary for concentrating on a problem and finding solutions or as a way to deal with a problem. Some worry is inspiring. It can _____ _____ _____ _____ better work or complete tasks on time. In other cases, however, our worries can _____ _____ our problem-solving abilities. We worry so much that it prevents us from taking steps needed to solve a problem. If it continues, worrying can _____ _____ _____ _____ and lead to even physical problems such as fatigue, headaches, muscle pain, or insomnia.

7 MP3 10-07

M: Jane, what are you reading?

W: Hi, Taejun. I'm reading the newspaper article Mr. McBryde _____ _____ yesterday.

M: I think we should spend more money on the military. Considering the situation on the Korean peninsula, we need to _____ _____ _____ _____.

W: But I think once we _____ _____ _____ the military to build a stronger army, then North Korea will also spend more money on their military and the tension between the two will never end.

M: You have a point, but it's quite difficult to say it's wrong to spend more money on the military when there is another country threatening us.

W: It might be a _____ _____, but I believe increasing military budget will make the situation worse.

8 MP3 10-08

W: Hi. Did you _____ _____ _____ _____, sir?

M: Yes, I did. Thank you for coming so quickly.

W: My pleasure, sir. How may I help you?

M: It's a little bit cold here, so I would like to get a blanket.

W: Of course. _____ _____ _____ for you right away. Is there anything else you need?

M: Yes. I am a bit thirsty. Can I have something to drink?

W: Sure. We have coke and water. Which one would you prefer?

M: Just water will be fine with me.

W: Okay. It is going to be _____ _____ _____. You should get some sleep.

M: Good idea. Do you know when we arrive?

W: _____ _____ _____ _____ at 11 p.m., local time.

M: Thank you very much.

9 🎧 MP3 10-09

W: How have you been? Wow, the room is really clean and neat. I'm so glad you arranged it well for my son to concentrate on studying.

M: Thank you. Actually, I study the relationship between study performance and surroundings.

W: I like _____ _____ _____. Children can reach any books they want. And I like the globe as well. Some people think that's not really a big deal, but _____ _____ _____ _____ always be able to see the globe.

M: You're right. When they want to know something about the world, a globe can satisfy their curiosity. And there's a bulletin board on which you can see Jay's drawing. He's good at fine art.

W: Thank you. Since the clock is behind the classroom, they can't always _____ _____ _____. It can be helpful for the class to remain focused on the lesson.

M: Right, but the door is _____ _____ _____ _____. When someone is late for the class, every student can see.

10 🎧 MP3 10-10

M: I want to get some information on package tours for Jeju or perhaps Hong Kong.

W: We have some very good _____ _____ _____ _____ 4 days and 3 nights.

M: How much do they cost?

W: To Jeju it is $500 and to Hong Kong it is a little more.

M: Which would you recommend?

W: It depends on your company. If you intend to _____ _____ _____ with your parents, Jeju is better, but with your friends, Hong Kong is preferable.

M: Is there _____ _____ about the two areas?

W: You can visit lots of attractive natural places in Jeju, and Hong Kong is one of the most popular places for shopping. You can get any item you want _____ _____ _____ _____.

M: It seems both places are so attractive. I need to talk with my family, and I'll let you know later. Thank you.

11 MP3 10-11

M: Hyeyeon, I'm _____ _____ _____ _____ on business today. But I left my laptop at the office.

W: Didn't you say you wanted to buy the concert tickets today?

M: Yeah, you know how much _____ _____ _____ _____ for that show.

W: Of course, it's your tradition for your wedding anniversary. So you want me to book the tickets for you and Mom, right?

M: That's right, honey. Can you do it?

W: Actually, I'm shopping at the mall with Jessie. What time _____ _____ _____ the tickets?

M: It's on a first-come-first-served basis. And tickets are _____ _____ from 5 p.m. You should go back home by quarter before five, I think.

W: Okay, Dad.

12 MP3 10-12

M: Hey, slow down, please.

W: Oh, sorry. I _____ _____ _____ _____ of driving too fast.

M: It's a relief that you know that, but you have to try to change it. You must always be careful when you're driving.

W: I know, but it's not that easy.

M: Do you remember my friend, Samantha? She was _____ _____ _____ _____ last week.

W: Really? Was she seriously injured?

M: Fortunately, she only broke one rib, and _____ _____ _____ now.

W: What a relief! How did she get into the accident?

M: While she was driving to work, she bumped into a car in front of hers.

W: Oh, that's terrible.

M: She told me that her car slid _____ _____ a lot of snow on the road from last week.

13 🔘 MP3 10-13

W: Stephen, do you usually give your daughter an allowance?

M: Yeah, I've been _____ _____ _____ _____ since she entered elementary school.

W: How much money do you think is _____ _____ my son?

M: Well, I give my daughter five bucks a week.

W: Is it enough for her?

M: I think so. And I buy her anything she needs for school. If she needs more money, she _____ _____ _____ around the house.

W: What does she do?

M: She washes the dishes, _____ _____ _____, helps her brother to do his homework and sweeps out the porch.

W: She must be learning the value of work and money.

14 🔘 MP3 10-14

W: I'd like to have a family-size hot chicken pizza to go.

M: Okay, ma'am. _____ _____ _____ our 50th anniversary and offering family-size pizzas _____ _____ _____ _____ large pizzas. So, that will only be $18.

W: That's great. Also, I want a mushroom pasta with cream sauce and a salad pack.

M: The pasta is $9, and the salad is $7.

W: Okay. I have a 10% discount coupon.

M: I'm afraid you can't use it as _____ _____ _____ a special promotion that gives you a bigger discount.

W: Okay. _____ _____ my loyalty card? I have $2 worth of discounts on my loyalty card.

M: You can use that.

15 MP3 10-15

W: Herpes Zoster comes with a painful skin rash. Herpes Zoster or simply 'zona' is a viral disease caused by the zoster virus. _____ _____ _____ of zona are simply headache and fever, which are quite non-specific, so they may result in a wrong diagnosis. Sometime later, those early symptoms _____ _____ by sensational burning pain. Zona in children is commonly painless, but older people are more likely to experience severe pain for a longer period of time. Severe pain normally lasts _____ _____ _____ _____ weeks, and the treatment is only to reduce the severity and duration of the pain. After the patient is up and about, the virus is still present _____ _____ _____ _____ and zona may occur again.

16 MP3 10-16

M: Have you ever heard about natural dyeing with ocher soil? Natural dyeing uses various materials from fruits, leaves of trees and grasses, and ocher soil. Ocher soil is red-and-ocher colored, and emits far-infrared radiation. This radiation has an amazing ability to clean, decompose, detoxify, _____ _____ _____ to heal a hangover, relieve pain, purify the air, and dehumidify. This campsite allows campers to _____ _____ every Wednesday from 9 a.m. to 4 p.m. You can try natural dyeing with ocher soil, tangerines, and bamboo charcoal. The field study fee is $5 for adults and students. If you are _____ _____ _____ with over 20 members, contact us to make a reservation and _____ _____ _____.

17 🔘 MP3 10-17

M: I will visit Mr. Miller, the calligrapher. _____ _____ _____ _____, Arin?

W: Sure, why not? It would be an honor to meet him. How do you know him?

M: He's my professor this semester.

W: Oh, that's fantastic. Let's see. I'm scheduled to go to the yoga class with Bella tomorrow. What about Wednesday? I have a meeting late in the afternoon, but _____ _____ in the morning.

M: I have to study on Wednesday because I have an achievement test on Thursday. What about Thursday afternoon or Friday?

W: I'm _____ _____ _____ at the library on Thursday. I was planning to watch a movie with Mom on Friday, but I should be able to reschedule it.

M: Then, I'll _____ _____ _____ of Mr. Miller now.

18 🔘 MP3 10-18

M: Misook, what do you usually do in your free time?

W: I paint and _____ _____ _____ _____ sometimes. I'm learning about coffee, nowadays. What about you, Hyunwoo?

M: I like cooking.

W: Really? I _____ _____ _____ _____ who enjoys cooking.

M: I know not many men do, but you see, the most famous chefs and lots of cooks in famous hotels are men.

W: You're right. I don't know why I didn't _____ _____ _____.

M: Usually, fathers don't cook, and mothers do. That's the reason. After cooking, I share my food with my friends and family. I love that moment.

W: Oh, you really _____ _____ _____ with food.

19 🔘 MP3 10-19

M: I hope that everything is satisfactory. How was your steak?

W: Perfect. We're all very _____ _____ our meals.

M: I'm glad to hear that. Would you care for dessert?

W: No, thank you. Just _____ _____ _____, please.

M: Certainly, ma'am.

W: By the way, I'd like to take the rest home. Could you _____ _____ _____, please?

M: Sure, no problem. Do you have our steakhouse membership card? If you do, you can get a 10% discount.

W: No, I don't. May I get a membership now? And the bill, please.

M: _____ _____ a new membership card for you. Is this all on one bill or on separate checks, ma'am?

20 🔘 MP3 10-20

W: Natalie and Gavin are really close siblings. They went to movies and played tennis together when they were young. _____ _____ _____ _____ and they grow up, they can't hang out together as much as before. Natalie gets up every morning and rides a bicycle to her office. _____ _____ _____ _____, Gavin favors after-work dining and drinking with his co-workers. Also he hardly does any exercise and is becoming more and more overweight. He recently _____ _____ _____ at the hospital and was told that he has a fatty liver. So, Natalie wants her brother to take care of himself and _____ _____ _____. In this situation, what would Natalie most likely say to Gavin?

M: The heaviest pumpkin ever recorded was 2009 pounds, which is more than 900 kilograms, and brought to Topsfield Fair in Massachusetts in 2012 by Ron Wallace from Rhode Island. Ron grows giant pumpkins as a hobby. People want to know _____ _____ _____ _____ _____ so big. Actually, once _____ _____ _____ _____ in growing pumpkins, growing giant pumpkins isn't so difficult because most record-breaking giant pumpkins are Atlantic Giant pumpkins or Goliath Giant pumpkins, and their seeds are readily available in the market. The next thing to remember is soil condition. Add enough amounts of fertilizer until the soil tester indicates the right value. Giant pumpkin plants require approximately 140 days to grow, and _____ _____ _____ _____ _____ growing the plant indoors first and transfer it outdoors later. The next secret key ingredient is liquid calcium because almost all fertilizers cannot be used efficiently if soluble calcium is not present in the soil. In short, if you get the right seeds and soil, you can also _____ _____ _____ with your pumpkin.

Answer Key

Answer Key

1	③	2	①	3	④	4	②	5	⑤
6	④	7	①	8	⑤	9	①	10	③
11	④	12	③	13	③	14	②	15	③
16	⑤	17	②	18	④	19	①	20	④
21	②	22	②						

문항 1 ③

Script & Dictation

M: Hey, Eunice! Did you prepare for the **field-day activities**?

W: Not yet, but the weather forecast says it'll **snow heavily all day long** on that day.

M: Oh, boy! What should we do?

W: I think we'll have to do only indoor activities.

남: 안녕, Eunice! 현장 학습 활동 준비했어?

여: 아직 안 했어. 일기예보에서 그날 종일 눈이 많이 올 거라고 하던데.

남: 정말? 그럼 어떡하지?

여: 실내 활동만 해야 하지 않을까 싶어.

해설: 현장 학습 당일에 눈이 많이 온다면 야외 활동은 하기 어려울 것이라 예상할 수 있기 때문에 정답은 ③번이다.

문항 2 ①

Script & Dictation

W: Dad, Grandma's 60th **birthday is coming** soon, isn't it?

M: Yes, it's May 2nd, a month from now.

W: Because the 60th birthday is so special, I want to **prepare a present**.

M: She'll be very happy to feel your love.

여: 아빠, 이제 곧 할머니의 60번째 생신이네요, 그렇죠?

남: 그래, 5월 2일이니 한 달 남았구나.

여: 환갑은 아주 특별하니까, 전 선물을 준비하고 싶어요.

남: 손녀의 사랑에 할머니께서 정말 기뻐하시겠는걸.

해설: 손녀로부터 환갑 기념 선물을 받으시면 할머니께서 많이 기뻐하시겠다고 말하는 것이 가장 적절한 응답이다.

문항 3 ④

Script & Dictation

M: Jennifer, what did you do last weekend?

W: I went to a **senior's hospital** to sing old pop songs. I do **volunteer work for seniors**.

M: Great! I know well you're a great singer. Do you **do it every weekend**?

W: If I don't have any other plans, I try to.

남: Jennifer, 지난 주말에 뭐했어?

여: 요양원에 가서 옛날 팝송을 불렀어. 어르신들을 위한 봉사 활동을 하거든.

남: 대단하다! 네가 노래 잘한다는 건 알고 있었어. 주말마다 하는 거야?

여: 별다른 계획이 없다면, 그러려고 노력해.

해설: 주말마다 봉사 활동을 하는지 물었으므로 이에 대한 적절한 응답은 '다른 계획이 없으면 매주 가려고 노력한다'가 되겠다.

문항 4 ②

Script & Dictation

M: There are myriads of stars in the night sky. If the star-filled **night sky fascinates you**, join the many amateur astronomers pursuing astronomy as a hobby. The David Frankel **Observatory is a suitable** place to do this. From March 1st to October 31st, it is open Tuesday through Sunday. The activities for amateur astronomers **consist of** Jupiter viewing and telescope displays. If you want, Professor Owen Wilson from University of Cunningham can guide you around the observatory. An early-bird program starting at 10 p.m. gives visitors **a chance to view** the beautiful Cunningham sky.

남: 밤하늘에는 무수한 별이 있습니다. 이렇게 별이 가득한 밤하늘에 관심이 많으시다면 취미로 다른 많은 아마추어 천문학자들과 함께 천문학을 공부해보세요. David Frankel 천문대는 이러한 활동을 하기에 적합한 곳입니다. 3월 1일에서 10월 31일 사이, 화요일부터 일요일까지 개관합니다. 아마추어 천문학자를 위해 목성 관측과 망원경 전시가 마련되어 있습니다. 희망하시는 분은 Cunningham 대학교 Owen Wilson 교수님의 천문대 안내를 받으실 수 있습니다. 밤 10시에 시작하는 얼리버드 프로그램은 방문객들에게 아름다운 Cunningham 하늘을 볼 기회를 제공합니다.

해설: 천문 활동에 관심이 있는 사람들에게 천문대에서 제공하는 프로그램을 소개하고 있는 내용이므로 '천문대 관측 프로그램 공지'가 남자가 하는 말의 목적이다.

문항 5 ⑤

Script & Dictation

W: Joss, I have **something to tell you about** your homework–writing in your English diary.

M: What's that, Ms. Palicki?

W: Your English diary is not just for writing the sequence of events that happen to you each day. You are supposed to **write on a specific theme** and present supporting ideas or your thoughts or your experiences.

M: Okay, should I be more specific when I write in my diary?

W: Yes.

M: But there's **nothing special on each day**. I just go to school and go back home, do some homework and watch TV.

W: What about **writing about your favorite** TV program? You can think about the jobs of the people who made that program and the stage sets, etc.

M: Okay, I'll make sure to **put them in** my second draft.

여: Joss, 네 영어 일기 쓰기 숙제에 관해 얘기를 좀 하고 싶구나.

남: 어떤 얘기요, Palicki 선생님?

여: 영어 일기의 목적은 그날 일어난 일을 그냥 순서대로 쓰는 것이 아니란다. 구체적인 주제에 관해 쓰고, 뒷받침하는 견해나 생각, 또는 경험을 보여줘야 하는 거야.

남: 알겠습니다. 그러니까 더 구체적으로 일기를 써야 한다는 말씀이시죠?

여: 그렇지.

남: 하지만, 매일 특별하다고 할 게 없는 걸요. 그냥 학교 갔다 집에 오고, 숙제 좀 하고, TV 보고 그러는데요.

여: 네가 좋아하는 TV 프로그램에 대해 써보는 건 어때? 그 프로그램을 만드는 사람들의 직업과 무대 장치 등에 대해 생각해 보는 거야.

남: 네, 두 번째 일기에는 그런 내용으로 써 볼게요.

해설: 여자는 남자에게 일기를 쓸 때 단순히 일어난 일을 순서대로 나열하기보다는 구체적인 주제를 가지고 써 보라고 이야기하고 있다.

문항 6 ④

Script & Dictation

W: Hello, students. I'm Doctor Elly Kim. I'm here to talk to you about bad breath today. What do you feel when your friend has bad breath? Whenever he talks, you sometimes **hold your breath**, I think. Does he brush regularly and still have bad breath? If so, it's a kind of big deal. You should **urge him to see** a doctor. Sometimes, bad breath can mean some serious health problems. It's not really common, but it could be chronic liver disease, diabetes, or stomach failure. After gargling, if his **bad breath won't disappear** and it continues for more than several days, he should consult a doctor and make sure it is not **caused by a serious disease**.

여: 학생 여러분 안녕하세요. 저는 의사인 Elly Kim이라고 해요. 저는 오늘 입 냄새에 대해서 이야기하려고 나왔어요. 여러분은 친구의 입 냄새가 심하면 기분이 어떤가요? 그 친구가 말할 때마다 여러분은 아마도 숨을 참고 있지 않을까 싶은데요. 친구가 규칙적으로 양치질을 하는데도 입 냄새가 나나요? 그럼 큰 문제인데요. 꼭 병원에 가보라고 충고하셔야 합니다. 입 냄새가 난다는 것은 건강에 심각한 문제가 있다는 뜻일 때도 있거든요. 자주 발생하는 일은 아니지만, 입 냄새는 만성 간 질환, 당뇨 또는 위장 장애일 수도 있지요. 가글링 후에도 입 냄새가 가시지 않고 며칠 동안 지속된다면 병원에 가서 심각한 병이 아닌지 확인해 봐야 합니다.

해설: 여자는 매일 양치질을 잘해도 입 냄새가 난다는 것은 건강의 적신호이므로, 병원에 가보는 것이 좋다고 설명하고 있다.

문항 7 ①

Script & Dictation

M: Granny, why are you growing **these kinds of veggies**?

W: When seeing these little creatures growing, I feel full of energy.

M: What do you usually do for them?

W: **Watering**, **weeding**, **moving** into another pot, and so on.

M: Are those plants edible?

W: Yes. It's all organic and **pesticide-free produce**. I'm so happy to give you fresh salad from the garden.

M: That's so nice. I **feel healthier**. I'll eat a lot, Granny.

W: Okay, and someday you can have your own garden. What would you want to grow?

M: My favorite: eggplants. And, your favorite: chili peppers, too.

W: How sweet you are! Probably, you can **water the chili peppers** now.

M: I'd love to.

남: 할머니, 왜 이런 채소들을 기르시는 거예요?

여: 이 작은 생명체들이 자라는 것을 보고 있으면, 활기가 느껴지거든.

남: 채소 기르실 때 보통 어떻게 하시는데요?

여: 물 주고, 김매고, 다른 화분에 옮겨심기도 하고 그러지.

남: 저 식물들은 먹을 수 있는 것들인가요?

여: 그럼, 모두 무농약 유기농 농산물이야. 텃밭에서 기른 걸로 너에게 신선한 샐러드를 만들어 줄 수 있어서 할머니는 참 기쁘단다.

남: 정말 좋아요. 더 건강해지는 것 같아요. 많이 먹을게요, 할머니.

여: 그래, 언젠가는 너도 네 텃밭을 가꿀 수 있을 거야. 뭘 기르고 싶니?

남: 제가 좋아하는 가지요. 그리고 할머니가 좋아하시는 고추도요.

여: 우리 손자 착하기도 하지! 지금 한번 고추에 물을 주어보렴.

남: 좋아요.

해설: 텃밭을 가꾸는 할머니와 손자의 대화 내용이다. 여자는 텃밭을 가꾸면서 활기를 느끼고, 또 직접 기른 채소로 샐러드도 만들 수 있다며 텃밭 가꾸기의 장점을 설명하고 있다.

문항 8 ⑤

Script & Dictation

M: Hello, Ms. Liman.

W: Hi, Tom. Thank you for coming.

M: I appreciate **your accepting this interview**. This time your focus seems to be on the eternal cycle of **birth, death, and rebirth**.

W: You're right. It was my first time working with samsara.

M: How did you like it?

W: It was very interesting and creative. I have studied a lot about **Buddhism for this film** and I am sure everyone will love it.

M: Sounds great. Where did you **get the inspiration** for this?

W: It is from my neighbor, who runs a flower shop. She has an interesting view of life. I have had a lot of conversations with her and I **came up with this theme**.

M: I see. Would you do me a favor?

W: Sure, anything.

M: Could you pose in front of your poster? I'd like to include your photo in the newspaper article.

남: Liman 씨, 안녕하세요.

여: 안녕하세요, Tom. 와주셔서 감사합니다.

남: 이번 인터뷰에 응해주셔서 감사합니다. 이번에는 탄생과 죽음, 환생이라는 윤회에 초점을 맞추신 것 같은데요.

여: 맞습니다. 처음으로 윤회에 관해 다뤘습니다.

남: 어떠셨나요?

여: 매우 재미있고 창의적인 작업이었습니다. 이 영화를 위해 불교에 관해 많이 연구해두었거든요. 많이들 좋아해 주실 거라 확신합니다.

남: 기대되네요. 어디서 영감을 얻으셨나요?

여: 꽃가게를 운영하는 이웃에게서요. 그녀는 삶에 대한 흥미로운 관점을 가지고 있습니다. 그녀와 많은 이야기를 나누다가 이 주제를 생각해내게 됐죠.

남: 그렇군요. 부탁 하나 드려도 될까요?

여: 물론이죠.

남: 포스터 앞에서 포즈를 좀 취해주시겠어요? 신문기사에 사진도 함께 게재하고 싶어서요.

해설: '인터뷰에 응해주셔서 감사하다'는 말과 'film'이라는 단어로 보아 영화에 관한 인터뷰임을 알 수 있다. 영화의 주제 및 영화를 만들게 된 배경 등에 대한 질문과 답변이 오고 가는 것으로 보아 정답은 ⑤번이다.

문항 9 ①

Script & Dictation

M: Excuse me. Is there a gas station near here?

W: Yes. There is one near Aran Bank.

M: I'm new to this area. I have no idea where Aran Bank is, either. Can you tell me how to get there?

W: Oh, yes. First, **go down this street** until you reach the second intersection.

M: Go down this street until I **arrive at the second intersection**.

W: Yes. Then, make **a left turn there**.

M: All right, and then?

W: Keep going until you see Aran Bank on your right.

M: Aran Bank? Then, where is the gas station? You said it's near the bank.

W: Yes. It's not far from the bank. **Pass the bank and turn right** at the intersection. The oil station is **on your left**.

M: I think I can get there without any difficulty. Thanks for your help.

W: You're welcome.

남: 실례합니다. 이 근처에 주유소가 있나요?

여: 네. 아란 은행 근처에 하나 있어요.

남: 이쪽은 처음이라 아란 은행이 어디에 있는 건지도 역시 모르는데요, 어떻게 가는 건지 설명해주시겠어요?

여: 그럼요. 먼저 두 번째 교차로가 나올 때까지 이 길을 따라 쭉 가세요.

남: 두 번째 교차로가 나올 때까지 이 길을 따라 쭉 가고요.

여: 네. 그런 다음 거기서 좌회전하세요.

남: 알겠습니다. 그리고 나서는요?

여: 오른쪽에 아란 은행이 나올 때까지 계속 가세요.

남: 아란 은행요? 그럼 주유소는 어디 있는 건가요? 은행 근처에 있다고 하셨잖아요.

여: 맞아요. 은행에서 별로 안 멀어요. 은행을 지나 교차로에서 우회전하시면 왼쪽에 주유소가 있을 거예요.

남: 어려움 없이 갈 수 있을 것 같네요. 도와주셔서 감사합니다.

여: 천만에요.

해설: 현재 위치에서부터 선을 긋는다고 생각하며 문제를 푼다. 두 번째 교차로까지 직진 후 좌회전하여 오른쪽에 있는 아란 은행을 지나서 나오는 또 다른 교차로에서 우회전했을 때 왼쪽에 있는 건물이 주유소이다.

문항 10 ③

Script & Dictation

M: Hi, Naomi! I need to buy some books for my presentation next Wednesday.

W: You mean the **presentation for world history**?

M: Yes, I picked the subject of genocide.

W: That sounds very interesting. But, why are you **going to the bookstore**?

M: You mean why I don't search on the Internet? I know the Internet is so convenient and has so much information, but I need **the book the teacher recommended**.

W: Sometimes, we can use books more properly than websites. But, **have you been to** the National Assembly Library?

M: No, not yet.

W: There are millions of books, and anyone can **borrow up to ten**. So I think you can get more information from there.

M: I should go there right away.

남: 안녕, Naomi! 나 다음 주 수요일 발표 때문에 책을 좀 사야 해.

여: 세계사 발표 말이지?

남: 응. 대학살을 주제로 골랐어.

여: 정말 흥미롭겠는데? 그런데 왜 서점을 가니?

남: 왜 인터넷에서 안 찾느냐는 말이지? 인터넷이 정말 편리하고 정보도 진짜 많다는 거야 나도 알지. 그런데 선생님께서 추천해주신 책이 필요하거든.

여: 웹사이트보다 책이 더 적절하게 활용될 때도 있긴 하지. 그런데 너 국회 도서관은 가봤니?

남: 아니, 아직.

여: 거기에는 수 백 만권의 책이 있고, 아무나 10권까지 빌려볼 수 있어. 그러니 거기서 정보를 더 많이 얻을 수 있을 거야.

남: 당장 가봐야겠다.

해설: 남자가 세계사 발표 준비를 위해 책을 사러 서점에 가야 한다고 하자 여자는 많은 양의 도서를 보유하고 있는 국회 도서관에서 책들을 빌려 볼 수 있다는 정보를 주었다. 이에 남자가 바로 가봐야겠다고 했으므로 정답은 ③번이다.

문항 11 ④

Script & Dictation

W: Hey, Daniel. I'm planning to **hold a surprise party** for Scarlett this Sunday.

M: Sounds fun! Who is coming to the party?

W: I'm thinking about inviting our tennis club members. Is that okay with you?

M: Why not? What about her brother, Steven?

W: Of course, he is **a key figure** in the party. Please call him and explain our plan. I'll **text the message to** my tennis club members.

M: Sure thing, and where are we going to **throw the party**?

W: Our favorite, Chris's Diner. I've booked it already.

M: Great! Scarlett likes it there without doubt. She's **so into Italian cuisine**.

W: Okay, I'll prepare a gift and write a card.

M: And write my name on it too, please.

여: 안녕, Daniel. 이번 주 일요일에 Scarlett을 위한 깜짝 파티를 열 계획이야.

남: 재미있겠다! 파티에 누가 오니?

여: 우리 테니스 클럽 회원들을 초대할까 하는데 괜찮겠니?

남: 물론이지! Scarlett의 오빠 Steven은 어때?

여: 당연히 초대해야지, 파티에서 중요한 인물인걸. Steven에게 전화해서 우리 계획을 좀 설명해 줘. 나는 테니스 클럽 회원들에게 문자 메시지 보낼게.

남: 알겠어. 그런데 우리 어디서 파티하는 거야?

여: 우리가 가장 좋아하는 Chris's Diner지. 내가 이미 예약해 뒀어.

남: 좋은데! Scarlett이 거기는 당연히 좋아하지. 이탈리아 요리 정말 좋아하잖아.

여: 그럼 내가 선물 준비하고 카드 쓸게.

남: 내 이름도 같이 써줘.

해설: Scarlett을 위한 깜짝 파티를 열 식당을 예약하고, 참석자들에게 문자를 보내고, 선물과 카드를 준비하는 일은 여자가 맡았다. 남자는 Steven에게 전화해서 파티에 관해 설명해주면 된다.

문항 12 ③

Script & Dictation

M: Hello, Ms. Oliver. As you know, we chose **new songs to perform** for this Maduro Contest.

W: Yeah, I heard that all the club members liked them very much. Were there any problems?

M: Yes, the problem is our **rival team has chosen** the same songs. They're the winners from last year.

W: You mean Kitsilano Secondary School?

M: Yes. I happened to **hear that news from** some people's conversation at a coffee house near the school.

W: So, you're saying **we need to change** our songs, right?

M: Yes. We haven't practiced yet, so we can still change and **increase our chances of winning**.

W: I see. I'll talk about it with the president of our club and call a meeting.

M: Thank you.

남: 안녕하세요, Oliver 선생님. 아시다시피, 저희가 이번 Maduro 대회에서 연주할 새로운 곡들을 선정했잖아요.

여: 그래, 클럽 회원들 모두 곡들을 굉장히 좋아했다고 들었단다. 무슨 문제 있니?

남: 네, 저희 경쟁팀이 같은 곡들을 골랐거든요. 작년에 우승한 그 팀이요.

여: Kitsilano 중등학교 말이구나?

남: 네. 학교 근처 커피숍에서 어떤 사람들이 말하는 걸 우연히 들었어요.

여: 그러니까 우리가 곡들을 바꿔야 한다는 거지?

남: 네, 아직 연습을 안 했으니까 지금이라도 곡을 바꾸면 우승할 확률을 높일 수 있을 거예요.

여: 그래 알았다. 클럽 회장과 이야기해 보고 회의를 소집할게.

남: 감사합니다.

해설: 대회에 출전하는 클럽의 일원인 남자가 우연히 경쟁팀도 자신이 속한 클럽과 같은 곡들을 선정했다는 것을 알게 되어 선생님인 여자에게 다른 곡으로 바꾸자는 제안을 하고 있으므로 정답은 ③번이다.

문항 13 ③

Script & Dictation

M: Natalie, how is the Manni Pilates Center you're attending?

W: That place is really nice, you know. The instructors are **really qualified for** teaching and consulting about health.

M: That's good. How much is the monthly tuition fee?

W: $100 a month. That's a little **on the expensive side**, but they have many kinds of physiotherapy exercise tools. They used to use them for patients getting physical therapy.

M: You know, I have **chronic low-back pain**, so it could be very helpful. Does it have a parking lot?

W: Yes, but **it's pretty small**. It's not really far from here. Why not walk there to help you warm-up?

M: I think I can walk around two bus stops. What about after class? Are there clean shower stalls?

W: They have **newly renovated shower stalls**, and the fee is included in the tuition.

M: Sounds good.

남: Natalie, 네가 다니는 Manni 필라테스 센터 어때?

여: 정말 괜찮은 거 같아. 강사들이 정말 잘 가르치고 건강 상담에도 일가견이 있어.

남: 괜찮다. 한 달 수업료는 얼마야?

여: 한 달에 100달러야. 약간 비싼 측면이 있지만, 물리치료 운동기구들을 많이 갖춰놓고 있거든. 예전에 환자들 물리치료에 사용했었대.

남: 요통이 있는데 도움이 많이 되겠는걸. 주차장은 있어?

여: 있는데 꽤 작아. 여기서 별로 안 먼데 준비 운동 삼아 걸어 다니는 건 어때?

남: 버스로 두 정류장 정도 거리라면 걸어 다녀도 될 것 같긴 하다. 수업 후에는 어때? 샤워실은 깨끗해?

여: 새로 수리한 샤워실이 있고, 이용료는 수업 비용에 포함되어 있어.

남: 좋은데.

해설: 작은 규모의 주차장, 비싼 강습 비용, 실력 있는 강사, 새로 수리한 샤워 시설에 관해서 언급했지만, 강습 시간은 언급하지 않았다.

문항 14 ②

Script & Dictation

W: May I help you, sir?

M: Yes. I bought this yellow tie here yesterday. I'd like to **exchange it for** another one.

W: Do you have the receipt?

M: Yes. Here you are.

W: You bought it for $250. Okay, **which one would you like to** exchange it for?

M: I like this blue-striped one.

W: That's $300. It's $50 **more expensive than** the previous one. Is that okay?

M: That's fine, but I saw a 10% discount sign in the show window. Does the **discount apply to this tie** as well?

W: Oh, yes. We've just started a regular bargain sale from today. You're so lucky. With the discount, that'll be $270.

M: That is nice. I already paid $250.

W: Right, you can just **pay the difference**, $20.

M: Okay. Here's my credit card.

여: 도와드릴까요?

남: 네, 어제 여기서 이 노란색 넥타이를 샀는데 다른 걸로 교환하고 싶어요.

여: 영수증 있으세요?

남: 네, 여기 있습니다.

여: 250달러에 사셨네요. 그럼, 어떤 걸로 교환하시겠습니까?

남: 이 파란 줄무늬가 좋겠습니다.

여: 그건 300달러로 전에 구매하신 것보다 50달러 더 비싼데 괜찮으시겠어요?

남: 괜찮습니다. 그런데 쇼윈도에서 10% 할인 표시를 봤는데요, 이 넥타이에도 적용되는 건가요?

여: 아, 네. 오늘 막 정기세일을 시작했습니다. 운이 좋으시네요. 할인하면 270달러입니다.

남: 좋네요. 제가 이미 250달러 냈었죠.

여: 네, 차액인 20달러만 내시면 됩니다.

남: 네, 여기 제 신용카드요.

해설: 남자는 250달러에 산 넥타이를 300달러짜리로 교환하려고 한다. 그런데 10% 할인이 적용되어 실제 가격은 270달러가 된다. 남자가 이미 250달러를 냈으므로 20달러만 더 내면 된다.

문항 15 ③

Script & Dictation

W: Welcome to Tuesday's breakfast meeting. This will be our tenth discussion since last March. **Let me brief you** on the schedule before we start. Today, we are going to discuss the subject "Myths: Restoring Lost Imaginings". Please double check your name tag on your seat. Where your name tag is shows **which group you are in** for today. After the discussion, one member from each group will **make a short speech**. Next week, our subject will be "The Next Generation Office Environment". We have prepared and distributed some reading materials on that topic, so don't forget to **take them with you**. After the speeches, breakfast will be served. You can choose between Korean and Western style breakfasts. Let the waiter or waitress **know your preference**. Now, enjoy your discussion!

여: 화요 조찬 모임에 오신 것을 환영합니다. 지난 3월 이후 10번째로 맞게 된 토론이네요. 시작하기 전에 우선 일정을 간략하게 알려드리겠습니다. 오늘 우리는 '신화: 잃어버린 상상을 되찾다'라는 주제로 토론하겠습니다. 좌석의 여러분 이름표를 다시 확인해 주시기 바랍니다. 여러분의 이름표가 있는 자리가 바로 오늘 여러분이 속한 조가 되겠습니다. 토론 후 조원 한 명이 나와 짧은 발표를 하게 됩니다. 다음주 주제는 '차세대 사무 환경'입니다. 해당 주제에 관한 읽기 자료를 준비하여 나누어 드렸으니, 잊지 말고 가져가시기 바랍니다. 발표 후, 아침 식사가 제공됩니다. 한식과 양식 중에서 선택하실 수 있으며, 종업원에게 어떤 것을 드실지 말씀하시면 됩니다. 즐거운 토론 되세요!

해설: 여자는 이름표가 있는 자리가 오늘 토론을 하게 될 조 자리이므로 이름표를 다시 확인해달라고 했다. 따라서 참가자 마음대로 조를 정할 수 있다고 한 ③번이 듣기 내용과 일치하지 않는다.

문항 16 ⑤

Script & Dictation

M: I'm so happy to tell you this news. A newly-created arts space, the Gallery Jung, will be opening **within the old city hall building**. The gallery will provide a good opportunity for many young artists to **exhibit their work for free**. Individual and group exhibition applications are welcome from not only professionals **but also amateur artists and students** in art departments. The gallery will be officially opened on April 18th, and a ceramic exhibition will show the works of a famous artisan of pottery, Sunho Lee **from the opening day**, April 18th, to April 26th. Applications to exhibit are **available from April 2nd**. For further information, please contact the Culture and Arts Department of Portsmouth City at 1464-2648 or visit our website www.portsmouthart.com.

남: 이 소식을 전하게 되어 기쁩니다. 신축 예술 공간인 갤러리 정이 옛 시청 청사 내에 개관합니다. 이 갤러리는 많은 젊은 예술가들에게 무료로 작품을 전시할 좋은 기회를 제공할 것입니다. 개인 전시와 공동 전시 신청은 전문가들뿐만 아니라 아마추어 예술가와 예술 전공 학생들도 할 수 있습니다. 갤러리 공식 개관일은 4월 18일입니다. 유명한 이선호 도자기 장인의 작품이 개관일인 4월 18일부터 4월 26일까지 도자기 전시회를 통해 선보여집니다. 전시 신청은 4월 2일부터 가능합니다. 더 자세한 정보를 알아보시려면 Portsmouth시 문화 예술 부서 연락처인 1464-2648번으로 연락하시거나, 저희 웹사이트인 www.portsmouthart.com에서 확인하세요.

해설: 4월 2일부터 전시 신청이 가능하다고 했고, 개관일은 4월 18일이므로 정답은 ⑤번이다.

문항 17 ②

Script & Dictation

M: Hi, Yuna. What are you looking for?

W: Oh, hi Michael! I'm **looking for a scale**.

M: Then take a look at this chart. This shows information about scales.

W: Oh, thank you. Hmm... I **cannot afford to buy** anything over $25. In fact, I don't think a scale should be that expensive.

M: Yeah, I agree with you.

W: And I don't want **one that is too dark**.

M: I know what you mean. Then I think there are two options.

W: Right. Oh, Borad is a Japanese company. I don't want to buy anything **made in a foreign country**. If it breaks, there could be a problem.

M: You're right. Then **this one would be** our answer.

W: Yes. Let's go and get one.

남: 안녕, 연아야. 뭐 찾고 있니?

여: 안녕, Michael! 나 체중계 좀 찾고 있어.

남: 그러면 이 도표를 좀 봐. 체중계들에 관한 정보가 나와 있어.

여: 고마워, 음… 난 25달러 이상인 것은 못 살 것 같아. 사실, 체중계가 그렇게 비싸야 할 필요도 없다고 생각하고.

남: 응, 내 생각도 그래.

여: 그리고 색깔이 너무 어두운 것도 별로야.

남: 무슨 말인지 알겠어. 그럼 후보가 2개구나.

여: 그러게. 아, Borad는 일본 회사구나. 외제품은 안 사고 싶은데. 고장 나면 문제가 생길 거야.

남: 맞아. 그러면 답이 나왔네.

여: 그래. 이제 사러 가보자.

해설: 가격이 25달러 이하인 밝은 색깔의 체중계는 ②번과 ④번이지만 여자가 외제품은 고장 시 문제가 많을 것 같아 선호하지 않는다고 했으므로 정답은 ②번이다.

문항 18 ④

Script & Dictation

M: Jennifer, what are you going to do this vacation?

W: I want to go on **a trip to Paris**.

M: What a romantic city!

W: Have you been there?

M: Yeah, I went there around five months ago **to visit the museum**.

W: You mean Pompidou Centre? That **must have been terrific**.

M: Absolutely, it was beautiful. There were many **masterpieces full of inspiration**.

W: Oh, I'm eager to go soon.

M: **I can recommend** some beautiful places for you to visit.

W: Thank you, Jake. That'd be great.

M: I'll send you an email with the information after work.

남: Jennifer, 이번 휴가에 뭐할 거야?

여: 난 파리로 여행 가고 싶어.

남: 낭만적인 도시지!

여: 거기 가본 적 있어?

남: 응, 다섯 달쯤 전에 가서 박물관 관람했어.

여: Pompidou 센터 말하는 거야? 정말 좋았겠다.

남: 정말 좋았어. 아름답더라. 영감으로 가득한 명작들이 많았어.

여: 빨리 가보고 싶다.

남: 방문해 볼 아름다운 장소들 추천해줄 수 있는데.

여: 고마워, Jake. 그래 주면 좋겠어.

남: 일 끝나면 이메일로 정보 보내줄게.

해설: 여자는 남자가 프랑스에 갔을 때 방문하면 좋을 예쁜 명소들을 추천해주기를 희망하고 있으므로 해당 정보를 이메일로 보내주겠다고 하는 것이 가장 적절한 응답이다.

문항 19 ①

Script & Dictation

W: Keunwoo. I haven't seen you in ages. How have you been?

M: Really good. Believe it or not, I **translated a book** eight months ago.

W: Really? What kind of book? I know you're so good at English.

M: Maybe **you've heard of it**. It's *The Innovation of Cancer*.

W: Did you really translate that book? I read it twice! In fact, my aunt has liver cancer.

M: Oh, poor her. I'm sorry to hear that.

W: No, it's okay. She will be better soon. She **had successful surgery**. Anyhow, I heard the book is a bestseller, right?

M: Yeah, in the **US online bookstore**.

W: What are you working on now?

M: I'm translating **a movie directed by** Yoonkyung Cho.

W: That's very nice. You are on a roll!

여: 근우야, 이게 얼마 만이니. 어떻게 지냈어?

남: 아주 잘 지냈어. 나 사실 8개월 전에 책 하나를 번역했어.

여: 정말? 무슨 책? 네가 영어 잘하는 거 알고는 있었어.

남: 어쩌면 들어봤을지도 모르겠다. '암의 혁신'이라는 책이야.

여: 진짜 네가 그 책을 번역했어? 나 두 번이나 읽었어! 사실 이모가 간암에 걸리셨거든.

남: 이모님 힘드시겠다. 어쩜 좋으니.

여: 아니야, 괜찮아. 곧 좋아지실 거야. 수술이 잘됐거든. 그런데 그 책 베스트셀러라고 들었어, 맞지?

남: 응, 미국 온라인 서점에서.

여: 지금 하고 있는 건 뭐야?

남: 조윤경 감독의 영화를 번역 중이야.

여: 정말 멋지다. 승승장구하는구나!

해설: 남자는 유명한 책을 번역했고, 현재는 영화를 번역하는 중이므로 잘되었다고 축하해주는 말인 ①번이 가장 적절한 응답이다.

문항 20 ④

Script & Dictation

W: Joanne is taking **a linguistics class this semester**. On the first day of the class, Ms. DeJesus, her linguistics teacher, said that every student should choose a foreign language they wanted to learn. And she also wanted the students to submit a brief introduction about the language before the start of the next class. Joanne understood what she had to do. However, on that day, she came to class forgetting **what she was supposed to do**. After class, Ms. DeJesus advised her to **manage her schedule**, adding that it's helpful to make a habit of **marking down activities** in her day planner. Joanne **made up her mind** to follow Ms. DeJesus's advice. In this situation, what would Joanne most likely say to Ms. DeJesus?

* Joanne: _I'll try to write down a to-do list in my planner._

여: Joanne은 이번 학기에 언어학 강의를 듣고 있다. 수업 첫날, DeJesus 언어학 교수는 학생들에게 배우고 싶은 외국어를 하나씩 선정하라고 했다. 그리고 다음 수업 시작 전에 해당 언어에 관한 간략한 소개서를 제출하라고 했다. Joanne은 자신이 무엇을 해야 하는지 알고 있었지만, 수업 당일에 해야 할 일을 잊은 채로 오고 말았다. 수업 후에 DeJesus 교수는 Joanne에게 일정 관리를 할 것을 조언하며 일일 계획표에 활동을 기록하는 습관을 들이는 것이 도움될 거라 덧붙였다. Joanne은 DeJesus 교수의 조언을 따르기로 했다. 이 상황에서 Joanne은 DeJesus 교수에게 뭐라고 말할까?

* Joanne: _일정표에 해야 할 일 목록을 쓰도록 노력할게요._

해설: 교수는 해야 할 과제를 잊은 학생에게 할 일을 기록하는 습관을 기르라는 조언을 했다. 학생이 해당 조언을 따르기로 했으므로, 교수의 말에 수긍하는 응답인 ④번이 가장 적절한 응답이 되겠다.

문항 21 ②

문항 22 ②

Script & Dictation

M: One of the world's oldest vaccines now has a new use. BCG is an 80-year-old **vaccine designed to treat** tuberculosis. But it has now been found effective in treating long-term type 1 diabetes, which is on the rise worldwide. BCG has long been administered to children in developing countries to guard against tuberculosis. But in a recent clinical trial, researchers at Harvard Medical School found the vaccine was also able to **increase insulin production** in patients with type 1 diabetes. Dr. Denise Faustman, the lead researcher, says the team was able to cure type 1 diabetes in mice. And she said in a small clinical trial, the **results in humans were also promising**. What they saw was that even with two very tiny doses of vaccine, four weeks apart, they could start to see the **killing of the bad immune cells**. Also, to our astonishment the pancreas started making small amounts of insulin again. Type 1 diabetes destroys insulin-producing cells. People who have the disease must constantly monitor and manage their blood glucose level. She expects that **identifying the correct dose** of BCG will be the major challenge in producing a sustained result for type 1 diabetes patients.

남: 세계에서 가장 오래된 백신 중 하나가 이제는 새로운 용도로 사용되고 있습니다. BCG는 결핵 치료를 위해 만들어진 80년 역사를 지닌 백신인데요. 그러나 지금은 전 세계적으로 증가하고 있는 만성 제1형 당뇨병 치료에도 효과가 있는 것으로 밝혀졌습니다. 개발 도상국에서 오랫동안 결핵 예방을 위해 어린이들에게 투여되어 온 BCG는 최근 하버드 의과 대학 연구원들이 시행한 임상 시험 결과, 제1형 당뇨병 환자들의 인슐린 생성을 증가시킬 수 있다는 것이 발견됐습니다. 수석 연구원인 Denise Faustman 박사는 쥐를 대상으로 한 실험에서 제1형 당뇨병 치료에 성공했다고 말했으며, 소규모 임상 시험에서 인간을 대상으로 한 결과 역시 좋았다고 덧붙였습니다. 연구원들은 4주간의 격차를 두고 아주 소량의 백신을 2회 투여한 결과, 망가진 면역 세포들이 파괴되는 것을 확인하였으며, 놀랍게도 췌장에서 적은 양의 인슐린이 다시 생성되기 시작하는 것을 발견했습니다. 제1형 당뇨병은 인슐린을 생성하는 세포가 파괴되는 질환으로 환자들은 지속해서 혈당 수치를 확인하고 관리해야 합니다. Faustman 박사는 적정 BCG 투여량을 알아내는 것이 제1형 당뇨병 환자들을 대상으로 일관된 결과를 도출하는 데 있어 주요 과제일 것으로 내다보고 있습니다.

해설: 21. 결핵 예방 백신인 BCG가 특정 유형의 당뇨병 치료에도 도움이 된다는 임상 시험 결과가 소개되고 있으므로 ②번이 정답이다. **22.** 백신 하나로 두 가지 질병을 치료할 수 있으므로 '일거양득'의 의미를 담고 있는 ②번이 정답이다.

1	⑤	2	①	3	③	4	④	5	③
6	④	7	①	8	⑤	9	①	10	①
11	①	12	②	13	②	14	③	15	⑤
16	④	17	④	18	①	19	⑤	20	⑤
21	⑤	22	③							

문항 1 ⑤

Script & Dictation

W: I'm afraid **you're not allowed** to check out any books until next Wednesday.

M: Oh, no! But Ms. Hong, I really need this book for my chemistry lab report.

W: Why didn't you notice that you have **overdue books**?

M: I forgot them completely. I should have checked the due dates.

여: 미안한데 다음 주 수요일까지는 도서 대출이 안 되겠는걸.

남: 안 돼요! 홍 선생님, 저 화학 실험 보고서 쓰는데 이 책이 꼭 필요해요.

여: 연체 도서 있는 걸 왜 몰랐니?

남: 완전히 잊고 있었어요. 대출 기간을 확인했어야 했는데.

해설: 연체 도서가 있는지를 왜 알지 못했는지 이유를 묻고 있으므로 완전히 잊고 있었다고 대답하는 ⑤번이 적절한 응답이다.

문항 2 ①

Script & Dictation

M: Jihye, did you buy this new TV?

W: Yes. Don't you remember **I said we needed** a better one with a full HD screen?

M: Yes, but I can't believe you bought it on your own **without letting me know**.

W: Didn't you say it was okay?

남: 지혜야, TV 새로 산 거야?

여: 응, 내가 화면이 풀 HD인 더 좋은 거 필요하다고 말했던 거 기억 안 나?

남: 기억나는데 그래도 어쩜 나한테 말도 안 하고 혼자 사니?

여: 그래도 된다고 하지 않았어?

해설: 어째서 자신과 상의도 없이 새 TV를 샀느냐는 남자의 질문에 대한 적절한 응답은 그래도 된다고 말하지 않았냐고 반문하는 ①번이다.

문항 3 ③

Script & Dictation

W: Are you going to **throw away** those plastic bottles?

M: No. I'm **sorting plastic bottles** to choose the ones I can reuse.

W: Sounds great. What is your plan for them? Anything in mind?

M: I'm thinking of making some toys for my son out of them.

여: 저 플라스틱병들 버릴 거야?

남: 아니, 재사용할 수 있는 거 골라내려고 정리 중이야.

여: 좋은 생각이다. 그걸로 뭘 할 계획이야? 생각해둔 거라도 있어?

남: 이걸로 아들 장난감 만들까 생각 중이야.

해설: 플라스틱병들을 어떻게 재활용할 것인지에 대해 물었으므로 병들로 장난감을 만들겠다고 한 ③번이 정답이다.

문항 4 ④

Script & Dictation

W: Hi, I'm Paula Patton. Did you enjoy lunch? I'm pretty sure you guys will say 'yes'. Then what do you think of the school cafeteria? Are you satisfied with all of its food? Are you happy enough with the service? I'm not sure you will say 'yes' about this. These days, I've heard that many of us are complaining about the **poor facilities** and service. I heard an **unpleasant episode about** the crew's service. We students are speaking, but do you think the school is listening? I'm so sure that our school already has a **bad reputation** for its cafeteria. But, why do they remain spectators? For the students, the school should make the cafeteria better.

여: 안녕하세요, 저는 Paula Patton입니다. 점심 맛있게 드셨나요? 여러분이 당연히 '네'라고 대답하실 것 같은데요, 그럼 학교 식당에 대해선 어떻게 생각하시나요? 음식들 모두 만족스러운 수준인가요? 서비스도 만족스러우시고요? 여전히 '네'라고 하실지 잘 모르겠네요. 저는 요새 우리 중 다수가 학교 식당의 낙후된 시설과 서비스에 대해 불만이 있다고 들었습니다. 직원 서비스와 관련된 불쾌한 사건에 대해서도 들었고요. 그런데 학생인 우리가 하는 이야기들에 학교가 귀 기울이고 있다고 생각하시나요? 학교 식당에 대한 평판은 이미 좋지 않다고 확신합니다. 그런데도 왜 가만히 있는 걸까요? 학교는 학생들을 위해 학교 식당을 개선해야 합니다.

해설: 여자는 학교 식당에 대해 학생들이 불만을 느끼고 있다고 지적하며, 따라서 학교가 학생들의 의견을 반영하여 학교 식당을 개선해야 한다고 주장하고 있다.

문항 5 ③

Script & Dictation

W: Oh, Hyunsun, it's too loud. Do you usually listen to music at this volume with your earphones on?

M: Sure thing. It **feels so free**.

W: But you know, it's not good for your ears.

M: Yeah, but there's no problem **with my hearing**.

W: That's good. But, loud music with earphones on is dangerous.

M: What do you mean?

W: Some people get lost in music and stop paying attention to what's going on around them. For instance, one of my friends, Sachi, got into a car accident last year.

M: Oh, that could be dangerous. I should be more careful.

W: Also, I saw on the TV news that people using earphones can be **the targets of crime**.

M: Uh oh. I really should be more careful then.

여: 현선아, 소리가 너무 커. 평소에 이어폰으로 음악 들을 때 이렇게 크게 듣니?

남: 그럼. 기분이 확 풀리거든.

여: 하지만 귀에는 좋지 않은걸.

남: 그렇긴 한데 내 청력에는 문제없어.

여: 다행이네. 그래도 이어폰 끼고 음악 크게 듣는 건 위험해.

남: 무슨 뜻이야?

여: 음악에 너무 빠지게 되는 나머지 주변에서 무슨 일이 일어나는지 잘 모르게 되는 사람들도 있단 말이야. 내 친구 중에 Sachi 라는 애는 작년에 그러다가 교통사고를 당했어.

남: 그건 위험할 수 있겠다. 나도 더 조심해야겠어.

여: 그리고 TV 뉴스에서 봤는데 이어폰을 사용하는 사람들은 범죄의 대상이 될 수도 있대.

남: 이런. 그렇다면 더더욱 조심해야겠다.

해설: 이어폰을 끼고 음악을 크게 들으면 청력에 손상을 끼칠 수 있고, 또 주변을 인지하지 못해 사고를 당하거나, 범죄의 대상이 될 수 있는 등 여러 가지로 위험하니 주의해야 한다는 것이 여자가 하는 말의 요지이므로 정답은 ③번이다.

문항 6 ④

Script & Dictation

W: Robert, did you wash this laundry?

M: Yeah, Mom.

W: Well, it doesn't look clean.

M: I didn't think so, either. It's not really white, so I washed it several times.

W: If you want to have white towels, underwear, and socks, you should **boil the laundry**.

M: You know what, I already did that. I thought you didn't want me to do it that way, so I didn't tell you.

W: Why **wouldn't I like it**? If you have boiled it already, you should put salt in the water while doing laundry.

M: Really? I'm curious if that really helps.

W: Trust me, son. A teaspoon of salt **per liter of water**.

M: Oh, that's very funny. But I'll try it next time.

여: Robert, 이 빨래 네가 했니?

남: 네, 엄마.

여: 글쎄, 깨끗해 보이지 않는구나.

남: 그러게요. 그다지 하얗지 않아서 몇 번 빨았어요.

여: 수건, 속옷, 양말을 하얗게 하려면 삶아야 해.

남: 벌써 그렇게 했죠. 제가 그렇게 하면 별로 안 좋아하실 것 같아서 말씀 안 드렸어요.

여: 엄마가 안 좋아할 이유가 어딨겠니? 벌써 삶았다면, 빨래 도중 물에 소금을 넣으면 돼.

남: 정말요? 진짜 도움이 되는지 궁금해지는데요?

여: 엄마를 믿어보렴. 물 1리터 당 소금 한 찻숟가락이야.

남: 정말 신기하네요. 다음에 그렇게 해 볼게요.

해설: 몇 번 삶아도 세탁물이 하얘지지 않는다는 아들의 말에 엄마가 세탁 중 소금을 넣으면 된다는 정보를 주고 있다.

문항 7 ①

Script & Dictation

W: Hi, Brandon. What are you reading? Anything new?

M: Hi, Lisa. I'm reading my smart-phone bill. It cost me more than 100,000 won this month.

W: What? Why was it so expensive?

M: Last month, I bought a new smart phone.

W: Ahh, so **the monthly divide** for the smart phone is included in your bill.

M: Yes. And also the data usage allotment is included. It's much more expensive than my 2G cell phone.

W: That's true. When I used a 2G cell phone, I selected a 'pay as you go' program, and I paid **an average of** $20 a month.

M: If there is something similar to a 'pay as you go' program for data usage, I'd definitely **go for that**.

여: 안녕, Brandon. 뭐 보고 있니? 뭐 새로운 것 있어?

남: 안녕, Lisa. 내 스마트폰 요금 청구서 보고 있어. 이번 달에 10만 원 넘게 나왔어.

여: 뭐? 왜 그렇게 많이 나왔어?

남: 지난달에 새 스마트폰 샀거든.

여: 그래서 월별 분할 납부금이 청구서에 포함되었구나.

남: 응. 그리고 데이터 사용 요금도. 2G 휴대폰보다 훨씬 비싸.

여: 정말 그래. 2G 휴대폰 사용했을 때는 선불 요금제를 선택해서 한 달에 평균 20달러 정도씩 냈는데.

남: 데이터 사용에 대해서도 선불 요금제 같은 게 있다면 꼭 그걸로 하고 싶어.

해설: 스마트폰을 새로 샀더니 월별 납부금과 데이터 사용으로 인해 2G 휴대폰보다 요금이 더 많이 나온다고 이야기하고 있다.

문항 8 ⑤

Script & Dictation

M: Hi, Emily. Finally, you're going on a business trip to Tokyo the day after tomorrow, aren't you?

W: Yes, but I really wish **the trip were canceled**.

M: What? Why? You said you were excited about this trip because you could visit your dream city.

W: I was, but not anymore. **As soon as I get there**, I have to give a presentation in a big meeting, and I am really nervous.

M: Don't worry so much. You're one of the best presenters in this field.

W: It's really kind of you to say so, but I have to do it in Japanese. I'm afraid I might mess up.

M: Try to be yourself when you are giving the presentation, **instead of being nervous**. Imagine you're in Tokyo on vacation.

W: Well, I'm not sure I can.

남: 안녕, Emily. 드디어 내일모레 도쿄로 출장 가는구나, 그렇지?

여: 응, 그런데 그 출장 정말 취소되면 좋겠어.

남: 뭐? 왜? 네가 꿈에 그리던 도시에 갈 수 있게 되어서 신 난다고 했었잖아.

여: 그랬었지. 그런데 더는 아니야. 난 거기 가자마자 큰 회의에서 발표해야 하거든. 정말 긴장돼.

남: 너무 걱정하지 마. 네가 이 분야에서 발표를 제일 잘하는 사람 중 한 명이잖아.

여: 그렇게 얘기해줘서 정말 고맙다. 하지만 난 그걸 일본어로 발표해야 하거든. 망칠까 봐 두려워.

남: 발표할 때 긴장하지 말고 네 평소 모습을 보여주도록 해 봐. 도쿄에 휴가 왔다고 상상하면서 말이야.

여: 글쎄, 그렇게 할 수 있을지 모르겠네.

해설: 일본어로 발표하는 것에 대해 염려하고 걱정하고 있으므로 정답은 ⑤번이다.

문항 9 ①

Script & Dictation

W: Welcome back home, Lucas!

M: Home, sweet home, Mom. I'm so happy to be back here. The Italian homestay parents were really good people, but I missed you and Dad so much.

W: Anyhow, you've got your **diploma of Vocal Music** from Italy. I'm so proud of you. Anyway, what do you think of this room? I rearranged some things yesterday.

M: Oh, is this the new laptop for me?

W: I said you'd get one. It's a **graduation gift** from your grandparents.

M: Ah, yes. I'll call them.

W: Do you like the photos on the board? I found some while cleaning your room, so I pinned them up.

M: I love them. Did you change my chair?

W: It looks like a new one, but **I just repainted it**.

M: Wow, that's cool. I feel sleepy seeing my own bed. Mom, where is my photo with the frame?

W: Oh, it's under the bed. Its leg was broken the other day.

여: 드디어 집에 돌아왔구나, Lucas!

남: 집에 와서 좋아요, 엄마. 돌아와서 정말 기뻐요. 이탈리아 홈스테이 부모님도 좋으신 분들이었지만 엄마랑 아빠가 진짜 보고 싶었어요.

여: 그래도 이탈리아에서 성악 학위를 땄잖아. 엄마는 네가 정말 자랑스러워. 그나저나 이 방 어때? 어제 이것저것 배치를 좀 바꿔봤는데.

남: 와, 이게 제 새 노트북이에요?

여: 하나 생길 거라고 했잖아. 할아버지와 할머니가 주시는 졸업 선물이란다.

남: 아, 네. 전화 드려야겠어요.

여: 판자에 걸린 사진들은 맘에 드니? 네 방 청소하다가 몇 장 발견해서 핀으로 꽂아봤는데.

남: 진짜 좋아요. 제 의자 바꾸셨어요?

여: 새것처럼 보이지만, 엄마가 페인트칠만 다시 한 거야.

남: 와, 멋져요. 침대를 보니 자고 싶네요. 엄마, 액자에 낀 사진은 어디 있어요?

여: 아, 침대 밑에 있어. 요전에 액자 다리가 부러졌어.

해설: 마지막에 액자는 다리가 부러져서 침대 밑에 넣어두었다고 했으므로 ①번이 정답이다.

문항 10 ①

Script & Dictation

M: Hanhee, did you hear there's a 'Dream Concert' at the World Cup Stadium tomorrow? A lot of famous singers will be singing. Why don't you **come with me**?

W: My schedule is hectic these days as I'm trying to **complete my article**. The deadline is this weekend. I have to go to the library to search for more information.

M: I think I can help you search for information on the Internet.

W: Really? But, **even if you help me**, I should go to the library. I also have to make a list of questionnaires to ask to potential customers.

M: Do you mean questionnaires for the library users? If so, then I can make the list. I took a class on library and information last semester.

W: Sounds wonderful. **I'll get the lunch bill**. Let's go.

남: 한희야, 내일 월드컵 경기장에서 '드림 콘서트'한다는 거 들었어? 유명한 가수들이 많이 나와서 노래한대. 나랑 같이 안 갈래?

여: 나 요새 기사 완성하느라 일정이 빡빡해. 이번 주말이 마감이거든. 도서관 가서 정보도 더 찾아봐야 해.

남: 인터넷으로 정보 찾는 거 도와줄 수 있을 것 같은데.

여: 정말? 하지만 네가 도와준다고 해도 도서관에 가야 해. 잠재고객에게 질문할 설문지 목록도 만들어야 하고.

남: 도서관 이용자들 설문지 말이니? 그거라면 내가 목록 만들어 줄 수 있어. 지난 학기에 도서관 정보에 관한 수업 들었거든.

여: 정말 잘됐는걸. 내가 점심 살게. 가자.

해설: 일이 많아서 함께 콘서트에 가지 못할 것 같은 여자에게 남자가 설문지를 작성해 줄 수 있다고 제안하자 여자가 반기고 있다. 따라서 정답은 ①번이다.

문항 11 ①

Script & Dictation

M: Long time no see, Ms. Jung. I thought I might meet you at this forum.

W: Oh, Mr. Song. How have you been? **Were we supposed to meet**?

M: No, I don't have your personal contact information, so I looked for you.

W: What can I do for you?

M: Our school is planning to hold an English speech contest. We **have been selected** to be a special school in English. So, our teachers are **full of passion**.

W: It could be a great opportunity for not only teaching speech strategy but also managing English projects of expertise.

M: If **you are available**, we want to have you as a judge of the contest. There will be three judges: a native professor teaching phonology, an English teacher from Seyoung Girls' High School, and you, I hope.

W: It should be no problem, but let me check my schedule first.

M: Of course. The contest **will be held** on the 26th of September.

남: 오랜만이에요, 정 선생님. 이번 포럼에서 선생님을 뵐 수 있지 않을까 생각했어요.

여: 어머, 송 선생님. 어떻게 지내셨어요? 우리 만나기로 되어 있었나요?

남: 아니요, 선생님의 개인 연락처를 몰라서 선생님을 찾고 있었거든요.

여: 제가 도울 일이라도?

남: 저희 학교가 영어 말하기 대회를 개최할 계획이에요. 영어 특성화 학교로 선정되었거든요. 그래서 선생님들 열의가 대단합니다.

여: 말하기 전략을 가르치는 것뿐만 아니라 전문성 있는 영어 프로젝트를 다루기에 정말 좋은 기회일 수 있겠네요.

남: 괜찮으시면 선생님을 대회 심사위원으로 모시고 싶은데요. 세 분의 심사위원을 모시려고 하는데 음운론을 가르치시는 원어민 교수님, 세영 여자고등학교의 영어 선생님과 함께 선생님이 해 주셨으면 해서요.

여: 문제없을 것 같은데 먼저 제 일정을 확인해 볼게요.

남: 물론이죠. 대회일은 9월 26일입니다.

해설: 남자는 여자에게 본인의 학교에서 개최하는 영어 말하기 대회에 심사위원으로 참석해 달라고 부탁하고 있다. 따라서 정답은 ①번이다.

문항 12 ②

Script & Dictation

W: Ryan? I thought you would be in Europe by now.

M: Hi, Penny. I was planning to go, but I canceled the tickets to Europe.

W: Why? You were really **looking forward to** this trip.

M: I was, but you know what? Sometimes in life, **unexpected but important** things happen.

W: What's that? **What made you** give up your dream trip?

M: Do you know Dr. Dave, the physics professor? He gave me the chance to be one of his staff in his lab. Since I got so excited and thought it would be the most important chance in my life, I just canceled the trip.

W: I am really happy for you! So, how's it going?

M: **So far, so good**.

여: Ryan? 지금쯤이면 유럽에 있을 거로 생각했는데요.

남: 안녕하세요, Penny. 그럴 계획이었는데 유럽 가는 표를 취소했어요.

여: 왜요? 이번 여행 엄청나게 기대했었잖아요.

남: 그랬죠. 그런데 말이에요, 때론 살면서 예상치 못했지만 중요한 일들이 생기는 법이잖아요.

여: 그게 뭔데요? 무슨 일 때문에 꿈꾸던 여행을 포기하게 됐나요?

남: 물리학 교수님이신 Dave 박사님 알죠? 박사님께서 저에게 실험실 연구원이 될 기회를 주셨거든요. 무척 기뻤어요. 그리고 제 인생에서 가장 중요한 기회일 거란 생각에 여행을 취소했죠.

여: 진짜 잘되었네요! 그래서 어떻게 되고 있나요?

남: 지금까지는 좋아요.

해설: 남자는 실험실 구성원 자리를 얻게 되었고, 자신의 인생에서 매우 중요한 기회가 될 거란 생각에 여행을 취소하게 되었다고 말했다. 따라서 정답은 ②번이다.

문항 13 ②

Script & Dictation

[Telephone rings.]

W: First Courier Services. How may I help you?

M: I'd like to have a small **package delivered**.

W: Where to?

M: To 444-448 Brighton Road.

W: Where's **the pick-up from**?

M: 11, Leeds Avenue, Worcester.

W: Okay. What does **your parcel contain**?

M: There are four books.

W: All right. A mailman will call you **in half an hour** and come to pick it up. Did you pack it?

M: Yes, I did. How much will it be to Brighton Road?

W: It will cost $17, and your books **will be delivered** by 5 o'clock this afternoon.

M: Do you have a cheaper service?

W: We charge $20 for that kind of parcel, but we have a special discount for shipping books right now. So the total is $17.

M: I see. I'll pay with my credit card.

[전화 벨 소리]

여: First Courier Services입니다. 무엇을 도와드릴까요?

남: 작은 소포를 배달시키고 싶은데요.

여: 어디로 보내시죠?

남: Brighton Road 444-448번지요.

여: 물건 발송지는요?

남: Worcester의 Leeds Avenue 11번지입니다.

여: 알겠습니다. 소포 내용물은 무엇인가요?

남: 책 4권입니다.

여: 알겠습니다. 배달원이 30분 후 전화 드리고 물건을 받으러 갈 겁니다. 포장은 하셨나요?

남: 네, 포장했습니다. Brighton Road까지 배송비가 얼마인가요?

여: 17달러이고 책은 오늘 오후 5시까지 배송될 겁니다.

남: 더 싼 방법도 있나요?

여: 그런 종류의 물건 배송비가 원래 20달러인데 도서 품목은 특별 할인하고 있습니다. 그래서 총 17달러입니다.

남: 그렇군요. 신용카드로 결제하겠습니다.

해설: 소포 발송지와 배송지 주소 모두 언급되었고, 내용물이 책이라는 것과 오후 5시까지 배송될 것이라는 배송 예정 시간에 관한 정보도 나왔지만, 소포를 보내는 남자의 이름은 언급되지 않았다. 따라서 ②번이 정답이다.

문항 14 ③

Script & Dictation

M: What are you looking at, Daeun?

W: Dad, check this necklace out. **Isn't it gorgeous?**

M: You're shopping online? It's really pretty. Is it your mom's birthday present?

W: Yes. Actually, I saw this at the department store this afternoon. But it's 10% cheaper online.

M: Do they sell it for $120 at the mall? You're **so smart not to buy** it at the mall but surf the Internet instead.

W: I'm buying this. Oh, something's wrong.

M: What?

W: I thought the delivery charge was included. They charge an extra $10.

M: Let me see. But that's still $2 cheaper than at the department store.

W: You're right. I'll just **have to do it.** Oh, look at this. I can have this cute card and **free gift wrapping.**

남: 다은아, 뭐보고 있어?

여: 아빠, 이 목걸이 좀 보세요. 진짜 예쁘죠?

남: 온라인 쇼핑하고 있구나. 진짜 예쁘네. 엄마 생신 선물이니?

여: 네. 사실은, 오늘 오후에 백화점에서 이걸 봤거든요. 그런데 온라인에서 10% 더 싸요.

남: 이게 매장에선 120달러니? 매장에서 안 사고 인터넷으로 알아보다니 우리 딸 참 똑똑하네.

여: 이거 사야겠어요. 어, 이럼 안 되는데.

남: 왜?

여: 배송비 포함이라고 생각했는데 10달러 더 내야 해요.

남: 어디 보자. 하지만 여전히 백화점보다 2달러 더 싸구나.

여: 그러네요. 그냥 온라인으로 사야겠어요. 이거 보세요. 이 귀여운 카드도 받을 수 있고, 무료 선물 포장도 되네요.

해설: 온라인 가격은 매장 가격 120달러에서 10% 할인된 가격이므로 108달러이다. 그러나 온라인으로 구매 시 배송료 10달러를 따로 내야 하므로 이를 더하면 총 118달러이다. 따라서 정답은 ③번이다.

문항 15 ⑤

Script & Dictation

M: Athletes, may I have your attention please? Princes Park has **decided to hold** a mini-marathons event on September 20th. These mini-marathons **consist of** three categories: a 10-km run, 15-km run and 20-km run. The top three finishers in each category will be awarded. If you register by the last day of July, you will receive a T-shirt sponsored by Newhaven Sports Club. There will be no **on-site registration** on the day of the race, so make sure to sign up before the due date. On that day, you will receive your entry number label and **a small piece of equipment** that can record your running time automatically, along with your T-shirt. For more specific information, please visit our website or the Princes Park office in person. Thank you.

남: 선수 여러분, 주목해 주시겠습니까? Princes 공원에서 9월 20일 미니 마라톤 이벤트를 개최합니다. 미니 마라톤은 10km, 15km, 20km 달리기, 이렇게 세 카테고리로 구분되어 있습니다. 카테고리별로 상위 3위 안에 드는 완주자들에게는 상이 수여됩니다. 7월 마지막 날까지 등록하시면 Newhaven 스포츠 클럽에서 후원하는 티셔츠를 받으실 수 있습니다. 경기 당일 현장 등록은 불가능하니 마감일 전까지 꼭 등록해주시기 바랍니다. 경기 당일에 참가 번호표와 달리기 시간을 자동으로 기록하는 소형기기, 그리고 티셔츠가 제공됩니다. 더 자세한 정보를 보시려면 저희 웹사이트, 또는 직접 Princes 공원 사무실을 방문해 주시기 바랍니다. 감사합니다.

해설: 공지 후반부에서 경기 당일에 달리기 기록을 재는 소형기기와 함께 참가 번호표와 티셔츠가 제공된다고 언급했다.

문항 16 ④

Script & Dictation

[Recording Voice]

W: This is Chaeyoung Lim, the tenant of the apartment in Sindorim-dong. I'm calling to inform you of the problems I'm **struggling with** in your apartment. Your apartment is **completely furnished** with the latest appliances, but the refrigerator door is broken. I'm improvising by pushing a box against it to keep it shut. The broken tile in the balcony needs to be replaced. The window frame was also broken, so I've put up **a piece of** cardboard to keep out the rain and snow. The bathtub is clogged and the sink has a few leaks. I don't know how long I can survive under these conditions. I'm waiting for you to call back **as soon as you hear** this message. Bye.

[음성녹음]

여: 신도림동 아파트 세입자 임채영입니다. 세 주신 아파트에서 여러 가지 문제를 겪고 있어서 전화 드렸어요. 아파트에 최신 전자제품들이 갖춰져 있기는 한데 냉장고 문이 고장 났습니다. 임시방편으로 상자로 막아서 문을 닫아 놓고 있습니다. 발코니에 부서진 타일도 교체해야 하고요. 창틀도 고장나서 비와 눈이 들이치는 걸 막기 위해 판지를 덧대놨습니다. 욕조는 막혔고 싱크대에선 물이 새고요. 이런 상태로 얼마나 더 오래 버틸 수 있을지 모르겠네요. 이 메시지 들으시는 대로 전화 주시기를 기다리고 있겠습니다. 안녕히 계세요.

해설: 타일 문제가 있는 장소는 샤워실이 아닌 발코니이므로 정답은 ④번이다.

문항 17 ④

Script & Dictation

W: My new clothes need washing. They have become too dirty.

M: Do you have a favorite laundry?

W: No. Can you **recommend one**?

M: If you do an online search, there's a list of laundries in this town. Let's see. Do you need dry cleaning?

W: Yes. And I think it shouldn't be **too far from here**.

M: Cape Street takes about an hour to get to from here. Glory Avenue is in this area. It'll probably take about 20 minutes to get there. How about the price? Chapman **is cheaper** than Smith. But I heard Smith has **good customer service**.

W: I think price is more important. Thanks for your help.

여: 새 옷을 좀 세탁해야겠어. 너무 더러워졌어.

남: 잘 가는 세탁소 있어?

여: 아니, 하나 추천해줄래?

남: 온라인 검색해 보면 이 동네 세탁소 목록이 있을 거야. 어디 보자. 드라이클리닝 필요해?

여: 응, 그리고 여기서 안 멀었으면 좋겠어.

남: Cape Street는 여기서 가는 데 한 시간 걸려. Glory Avenue는 이 부근에 있고. 가는데 아마 20분쯤 걸릴 거야. 가격은 어때? Chapman이 Smith보다 더 싸. 하지만 Smith의 소비자 서비스가 좋다고 들었어.

여: 난 가격이 더 중요한 것 같아. 도와줘서 고마워.

해설: 여자는 가깝고 저렴한 세탁소를 선호한다. Cape Street보다 Glory Avenue가 더 가까운데 그곳에 있는 세탁소인 Chapman과 Smith 중 세탁 가격이 더 저렴한 곳은 Chapman이므로 ④번이 정답이다.

문항 18 ①

Script & Dictation

W: Hey, Jinkyu! Do you **commute by bicycle**?

M: Hi, Yura. Yes, to lose weight, I commute by bike and **work out at the gym**.

W: I've also worked out at the gym and taken the Pilates class. But my weight is the same, and I can't feel any change in my body shape.

M: You haven't lost any weight at all?

W: No. I also ride a bike along the beach on weekends, and I am careful about my diet.

M: How long have you been doing all that?

W: Well, **it's been over** a month, I guess.

M: You have done a great job. But it's a little too soon to expect a noticeable body change.

W: Really? But I should have lost **at least** one or two kilograms I think.

M: <u>To get in shape, you should have persistence.</u>

여: 진규 씨, 안녕하세요? 자전거로 출퇴근하시는 거예요?

남: 안녕하세요, 유라 씨. 네, 살 빼려고 자전거로 출퇴근하고 헬스클럽에서 운동도 해요.

여: 저도 헬스클럽에서 운동하고 필라테스 수업도 들어왔는데 몸무게도 그대로이고 체형에도 아무 변화가 없는 것 같아요.

남: 체중이 전혀 줄지 않았다고요?

여: 네. 주말에는 해변을 따라 자전거도 타고, 식단에도 신경을 쓰는데 말이죠.

남: 그렇게 한지 얼마나 됐어요?

여: 음, 한 달 좀 넘은 것 같아요.

남: 잘하고 계시는데 뚜렷한 몸의 변화를 기대하기엔 아직 좀 이른 기간이네요.

여: 그런가요? 적어도 1 내지 2 킬로그램은 줄었어야 한다고 생각하는데요.

남: <u>몸매를 만들려면 끈기가 있어야 해요.</u>

해설: 남자는 여자가 운동한 기간에 비해 큰 변화를 기대하고 있다고 생각하므로 끈기가 필요하다고 조언하는 내용인 ①번이 가장 적절한 응답이 되겠다.

문항 19 ⑤

Script & Dictation

M: Mom, I think I need to change my glasses.

W: Why? Has something happened?

M: No, just my **vision is blurry** these days.

W: Oh, can't you read the words on the board?

M: I can read them, but sometimes the light seems dim.

W: You don't have any plans today, do you? Let's have your eyes checked at the clinic.

M: Yes. I'll **book an appointment**.

W: Good. Now go wash your hands. And Minjun, you should **stop doing things** that harm your eyes.

M: What do you mean?

W: On the school bus, don't use your mobile phone and don't read books. I think those **harm your vision**.

M: But, Mom, I would be **so bored**.

W: If you want to protect your eyes, stop doing it while on the bus.

남: 엄마, 저 안경 바꿔야 할 거 같아요.

여: 왜? 무슨 일 있었니?

남: 아뇨, 그냥 요즘 시야가 흐려서요.

여: 칠판 글씨가 안 보이니?

남: 보이기는 하는데, 가끔 흐릿해요.

여: 오늘 별다른 일 없지? 병원 가서 시력 검사해 보자.

남: 네, 제가 예약할게요.

여: 그래. 이제 가서 손 씻으렴. 그리고 민준아, 눈에 나쁜 것은 안 하는 것이 좋아.

남: 무슨 말씀이세요?

여: 통학버스에서 휴대폰 보거나 책 읽지 마. 시력 나빠질 수 있으니까.

남: 하지만 심심할텐데요, 엄마.

여: 시력을 보호하고 싶으면 버스에서 그런 건 그만하렴.

해설: 여자는 버스에서 휴대폰을 보거나 책을 읽는 것으로 남자의 시력이 나빠질 수 있다고 생각하고 있으므로 심심하더라도 시력 보호를 위해 하지 말라고 충고하는 말이 가장 적절하다.

문항 20 ⑤

Script & Dictation

M: Marielle and Andy are seniors at university. They are preparing their **essays for graduation**. They have lots of experiments, surveys, and summaries. From the beginning of this month, sometimes they stay **whole days and nights** at the lab. Today, Marielle wants some rest, so she **decides to go home** for a comfortable sleep .When she says good-bye to Andy, suddenly it starts raining cats and dogs. She doesn't have an umbrella, but Andy has a big one. Also, Andy's car is parked in the **basement parking lot** of the same building. So, Andy doesn't mind lending her his umbrella. In this situation, what would Andy most likely say to Marielle?

* Andy: Marielle, you can take my umbrella. If I were free, I would give you a ride.

남: Marielle과 Andy는 대학교 졸업반으로 졸업 과제물을 준비하고 있습니다. 실험, 조사, 그리고 요약할 것이 많아 이번 달 초부터는 실험실에서 종일 지낼 때도 있습니다. Marielle 은 오늘 좀 쉬고 싶어 집에 가서 편히 자기로 결정합니다. Andy에게 인사를 하는데 갑자기 비가 억수같이 쏟아지기 시작합니다. Marielle에게는 우산이 없지만 Andy에게는 큰 우산이 하나 있습니다. 또 Andy의 차는 같은 건물 지하 주차장에 주차되어 있습니다. 따라서 Andy는 Marielle이

우산을 빌려 가도 상관없습니다. 이런 상황에서 Andy는 Marielle에게 뭐라고 말할까요?

* Andy: Marielle, 내 우산 가져가. 내가 시간이 된다면 태워다 줄 수도 있을 텐데.

해설: Andy에게 우산이 있으므로 Marielle에게 빌려줄 수 있다. 또 지하에 주차된 차로 데려다 줄 수 있지만 Andy는 계속 실험실에 있어야 하므로 그럴 수 없다. 따라서 ⑤번이 이런 상황에 할 수 있는 가장 적절한 말이다.

문항 21 ⑤
문항 22 ③

Script & Dictation

W: Thank you for being here on time, everyone. The first item on the agenda from last week's meeting was the fact we should **supplement our personnel** to meet growing needs. So we will have Mia Foster with us from next week. Ms. Foster is joining Preacher Insurance to **fill our open position** in customer service. Her first day will be Wednesday, June 20th. Ms. Foster has worked for many years in customer service, and we are delighted to welcome her to the Preacher team. She will **take part in** employee welcoming activities for her first couple of weeks on the job. Ms. Foster's new employee mentor is Nick Holmes, so if you have questions for or need to meet with Ms. Foster, you can talk with Mr. Holmes before she begins. Ms. Foster will work closely with the customers. She will work in the west wing. **Take a moment** to stop by and welcome her to the company. This will **strengthen our new working relationship** and improve job efficiency. Next, tell us what is second on the agenda, Henry.

여: 모두 제시간에 와주셔서 고맙습니다. 지난주 회의의 첫 번째 안건은 그 필요성이 점점 증대됨에 따라 인력을 충원해야 한다는 것이었습니다. 그래서 다음 주부터 Mia Foster 씨가 출근하게 되었습니다. Foster 씨가 합류함으로써 Preacher Insurance 소비자서비스 부분의 공석을 채우게 될 것입니다. 첫 출근일은 6월 20일 수요일입니다. Foster 씨는 수년간 소비자서비스 분야에서 근무해 왔습니다. Preacher 팀에서 Foster 씨를 맞이하게 되어 기쁘게 생각합니다. 근무 첫 몇 주간은 사원 환영 활동에 참여할 것입니다. Foster 씨의 신규 사원 멘토는 Nick Holmes 씨로 Foster 씨에게 질문이 있거나, Foster 씨를 만나셔야 하는 분은 Foster 씨 출근 전, Holmes 씨와 상의하시면 됩니다. Foster 씨는 고객들과 긴밀히 협력할 것입니다. 그녀는 서관에서 근무할 예정입니다. 잠시 들러 입사를 환영해 주시기 바랍니다. 이는 우리의 새로운 업무 관계를 돈독하게 해 줄 것이며, 업무 효율성도 증대시킬 것입니다. 다음으로 두 번째 안건은 무엇인지 말씀해주세요, Henry 씨.

해설: 21. 지난 회의 안건에 따라 회사에 합류하게 된 신규 입사자를 경력, 출근일, 근무 부서 및 위치, 이끌어 줄 멘토 등의 정보를 가지고 소개하고 있다. **22.** 잠깐 시간을 내어 신규 입사자에게 들러 환영의 인사를 하라고는 했지만, 환영 파티에 대한 언급은 없었다.

1	⑤	2	②	3	⑤	4	③	5	④
6	①	7	④	8	③	9	⑤	10	②
11	④	12	⑤	13	③	14	④	15	⑤
16	④	17	③	18	②	19	②	20	①
21	③	22	①						

문항 1 ⑤

Script & Dictation

W: Danny, why **were you absent** yesterday?

M: My mom was so sick that I **had to take care of** her. My dad's out of town at the moment.

W: I was so worried about you. Is she all right now?

M: Yes, she is okay. And now my sister's looking after her.

여: Danny, 너 어제 왜 결석했니?

남: 엄마가 매우 편찮으셔서 돌봐드려야 했어. 아빠는 지금 타지에 계시거든.

여: 네 걱정 많이 했어. 어머니 지금은 괜찮으셔?

남: 응, 괜찮으셔. 지금은 여동생이 간호하고 있어.

해설: 친구의 편찮으신 어머니가 어떠신지 상태를 묻고 있으므로 ⑤번이 가장 적절한 응답이다.

문항 2 ②

Script & Dictation

M: Hi, Christina. Are you in this camp?

W: Thank God, Hyungbum. You're here. It's **so happy to see you** here.

M: **I'm here with** Kenny. Anyhow, what made you join this camp?

W: My brother, Tom, strongly recommended it.

남: 안녕, Christina. 너도 이 캠프에 참가하니?

여: 형범아, 네가 여기 있다니 어찌나 다행인지. 만나게 돼서 정말 기뻐.

남: 나는 Kenny랑 같이 왔어. 그나저나, 어떻게 이 캠프에 참가하게 됐어?

여: 우리 오빠 Tom이 적극적으로 추천했어.

해설: 남자는 여자에게 캠프에 참가하게 된 계기를 묻고 있다. 이에 가장 적절한 응답은 ②번이 되겠다.

문항 3 ⑤

Script & Dictation

W: You **look so tired**, Greg. Are you coming back from your football club?

M: Yes. **I've been practicing** a lot of free kicks for the competition.

W: Oh, have you been **chosen to compete**?

M: Yes, I think the competition will help me become a better kicker.

여: 많이 피곤해 보인다, Greg. 축구팀에 있다가 오는 길이야?

남: 응. 시합 때문에 프리킥 연습을 많이 하고 있어.

여: 시합 나가는데 뽑힌 거야?

남: 응, 시합을 통해 축구를 더 잘하는 선수가 될 수 있을 것 같아.

해설: 시합에 출전하게 되었는지 아닌지를 밝히고 있고, 이를 통해 좋은 선수로 성장해 나갈 수 있을 것 같다고 대답하는 ⑤번이 가장 적절한 응답이다.

문항 4 ③

Script & Dictation

M: Good evening. This is **an emergency announcement** for those who came to the book signing in the Cornwell Book Center. It was supposed to be held by the best-seller author Virginia Madsen at four o'clock. However, **due to a traffic accident**, Ms. Madsen will not be arriving here today. So the book signing is postponed indefinitely. We **apologize for the inconvenience** to those who have been waiting. Also, we hope Ms. Madsen will be safe. The 2014 Magazine Fair is being held at the Main Hall. There are new magazines and journals there. Please visit the magazine fair while you're here. We're sorry to have to deliver this kind of message and thank you for your understanding.

남: 안녕하세요. Cornwell Book Center 책 사인회에 오신 분들께 긴급 안내 말씀드립니다. Virginia Madsen 베스트셀러 작가의 책 사인회가 4시로 예정되어 있었으나, 교통사고가 나서 Madsen 씨가 오늘 못 오시게 되었습니다. 따라서 책 사인회가 무기한 연기되었음을 알려드립니다. 기다리신 분들께 불편을 끼쳐 죄송합니다. 아울러 Madsen 씨가 무사하시길 기원합니다. 중앙 홀에서 열리고 있는 2014 잡지 박람회에 신간 잡지와 저널들이 있습니다. 계시는 동안 잡지 박람회도 방문해주세요. 이런 소식 전하게 되어 죄송하며, 양해해 주셔서 감사합니다.

해설: 책 사인회가 예정된 작가에게 교통사고가 나는 바람에 사인회가 취소되었다고 참석자들에게 공지하고 있다. 공지 후, 진행 중인 잡지 박람회 홍보를 덧붙이긴 하였으나 이것이 안내의 주요 목적은 아니므로 정답은 ③번이다.

문항 5 ④

Script & Dictation

M: Mom, I got an A⁺ on the English test today.

W: You really did a good job. I have to **stand by my word**. What do you want to have?

M: I want to have a smart phone.

W: Honey, you changed your new cell phone just three months ago.

M: But, Mom, **all of my classmates** have smart phones except Shane and me.

W: Billy, your phone doesn't have any problems and the function of a phone is to send and receive calls.

M: These days a cell phone is for more than just making phone calls. I can access the Internet anytime, communicate with all of my friends, and study with some specific apps.

W: Smart phones **might be convenient**, but you can easily waste time with them **because of those extra features**.

남: 엄마, 저 오늘 영어 시험에서 A⁺ 받았어요.

여: 정말 잘했구나. 엄마가 한 약속 지켜야겠네. 뭐 갖고 싶니?

남: 스마트폰을 가지고 싶어요.

여: 휴대폰 바꾼 지 이제 겨우 석 달 됐잖아.

남: 그렇긴 한데요, 우리 반에서 저랑 Shane만 빼고 다 스마트폰 가지고 있단 말이에요.

여: Billy, 네 휴대폰에 무슨 문제가 있는 것도 아니고, 전화기야 원래 전화 걸고 받는 거잖니.

남: 요새는 휴대폰으로 단순히 전화만 하는 게 아니에요. 언제든지 인터넷에 접속할 수 있고, 친구들하고 연락 주고받고, 또 어떤 앱들로는 공부도 할 수 있단 말이에요.

여: 스마트폰이 편리할지도 모르지. 그렇지만 그런 부가 기능들 때문에 쉽게 시간 낭비할 수가 있어.

해설: 여자는 전화기가 통화 기능에 이상이 없으면 되므로 멀쩡한 휴대폰을 스마트폰으로 바꿀 필요는 없다고 말하고 있다. 또한 여러 부가 기능이 달린 스마트폰을 사용하다가 시간을 낭비할 수도 있다고 언급하고 있다. 따라서 ④번이 여자가 주장하고자 하는 바를 잘 나타내는 정답이다.

문항 6 ①

Script & Dictation

W: How do you feel when **a long chilly winter** has ended and spring has arrived? To some of you, just the thought of it probably makes your heart flutter. Changing weather can influence what we can do and where we can go, but it can also **play an important role** in affecting how we feel. In cold and rainy weather, people are often **more irritable**, **less interested** in their work, and feel less energetic. On the other hand, in warm, sunny weather, people usually have more energy, feel happier, work better, and seem to be **full of life**. You probably see happier faces in summer than you do in winter, right?

여: 길고 추운 겨울이 지나고 봄이 왔을 때 여러분은 어떤 느낌이 드시나요? 아마 그런 생각만으로도 가슴이 떨리는 분들이 계실 것 같은데요. 날씨 변화는 우리가 무엇을 하고, 어디에 갈 수 있는지에 영향을 미치기도 하지만 우리의 기분에 영향을 주는 중요한 역할을 하기도 합니다. 날씨가 춥고, 비가 오면 사람들은 더 짜증을 내고, 일에 대한 의욕이 적어지며 덜 활동적이게 될 때가 많습니다. 반면, 날씨가 따뜻하고 화창하면 사람들은 더욱 활동적이고, 더 행복해하며, 일도 더 잘하고 활기가 넘치는 것처럼 보입니다. 아마도 겨울보다는 여름에 사람들의 표정이 더 행복한 걸 보셨을 거예요, 그렇죠?

해설: 여자가 날씨가 춥고 궂을 때에 사람들이 짜증을 더 내고, 따뜻하고 맑을 때는 활기를 띤다고 설명한 이유는 사람의 감정이 날씨에 영향을 받는다는 것을 말하기 위함이다. 따라서 정답은 ①번이다.

문항 7 ④

Script & Dictation

W: Jeremy, here's **an invitation to** my daughter's first birthday party. Will you be able to come?

M: Sure. You must be working very hard to prepare the party.

W: No. There are **a number of party planners** who specialize in a baby's first birthday party.

M: That sounds interesting. What do they prepare for the party?

W: They prepare everything for the party!

M: Wow, that **must be quite expensive.**

W: Yes, indeed. People tend to have fewer babies nowadays, so they spend lots of money on babycare. So, the babycare business is one of the fastest growing businesses in Korea.

M: Very interesting. But it's quite strange to me. It sounds like a baby's first birthday party in Korea has **become pretty commercialized**.

여: Jeremy, 여기 우리 딸 돌잔치 초대장이에요. 올 수 있어요?

남: 그럼요. 잔치 준비에 여념이 없으시겠어요.

여: 그렇진 않아요. 돌잔치 전문 파티 기획업자들이 많거든요.

남: 흥미롭네요. 뭘 준비해 주는데요?

여: 잔치에 필요한 모든 걸 다 준비해주죠!

남: 와, 그럼 꽤 비싸겠는데요?

여: 네, 정말 그래요. 요새는 아이들을 적게 낳는 추세라서 육아에 돈을 많이 쓰거든요. 그래서 육아 사업은 한국에서 가장 빠르게 성장하고 있는 사업 중 하나죠.

남: 정말 흥미롭군요. 하지만 이상하기도 해요. 한국의 돌잔치는 많이 상업화된 것 같네요.

해설: 여자와 남자는 높은 비용을 들여 파티 기획업체를 통해 아이들의 돌잔치를 하는 한국의 상업화된 돌잔치 추세에 관해 이야기하고 있다.

문항 8 ③

Script & Dictation

M: Mom, how far is Aunt Kelly's house from here?

W: It's **about an hour and half** away.

M: I'm dying to see her.

W: Which do you miss more, your aunt or your aunt's food?

M: Actually, both, but I really miss Aunt Kelly's delicious home-made cakes and cookies.

W: I called her last night, and she said that she would **do some baking**. She's baking a chocolate cake for you now.

M: That's wonderful! I **can't wait to taste it**. I'm really happy that we're spending this holiday there with her.

W: Same here. Oh, one more thing. Her dog had ten little puppies yesterday.

M: Ten puppies? I'm sure it's going to be a great holiday!

남: 엄마, 여기서 Kelly 이모네 집까지 얼마나 멀어요?

여: 한 시간 반 정도 걸릴 거야.

남: 이모 정말 보고 싶어요.

여: 이모가 그리운 거니, 아니면 이모의 음식이 그리운 거니?

남: 사실 둘 다인데, Kelly 이모가 직접 만드시는 맛있는 케이크랑 쿠키가 진짜 그리워요.

여: 엄마가 어젯밤에 이모에게 전화했더니 이것저것 만들어 놓겠다고 하던걸. 지금은 널 위해 초콜릿 케이크를 만들고 있을 거야.

남: 정말 신 나요! 빨리 가서 먹고 싶어요. 이번 휴가를 이모와 같이 보내게 되어서 참 좋아요.

여: 나도 그래. 참, 소식이 하나 더 있어. 이모네 개가 어제 강아지 열 마리를 낳았대.

남: 열 마리요? 이번 휴가는 정말 재밌을 것 같아요!

해설: 남자는 이모가 만든 케이크에 대한 기대와 새로 태어난 강아지들 소식에 한껏 들뜨고 신이 난 상태이다.

문항 9 ⑤

Script & Dictation

M: Hi, Hyerin. What photo **are you putting** in the frame?

W: Hi, Brad. It's our family trip photo.

M: Let me see it. The tent looks so nice.

W: Yeah. My dad likes to go camping, so we travel once or twice a month.

M: So your dad bought a great tent.

W: Yeah, my mom can't sleep in **an uncomfortable site**.

M: What did you eat?

W: We had fish that my dad caught.

M: Camping, fishing, **preparing a nice tent** for family, playing the guitar... You have an excellent dad.

W: Yes. I love him so much. Look at this. Have you ever eaten sausages cooked like this? They're amazing.

M: I know your mom is an excellent cook.

남: 안녕, 혜린아. 무슨 사진을 액자에 넣는 거야?

여: 안녕, Brad. 우리 가족 여행사진이야.

남: 어디 보자. 텐트 멋있다.

여: 응. 아빠가 캠핑을 좋아하셔서 매달 한두 번씩 여행가.

남: 그래서 아버님께서 좋은 텐트를 사셨구나.

여: 맞아. 엄마도 불편한 곳에선 못 주무시기도 하고.

남: 뭐 먹었어?

여: 아빠가 잡아주신 생선 먹었어.

남: 캠핑에, 낚시에, 가족을 위한 좋은 텐트 준비에 기타 연주까지… 아버님 참 멋지시다.

여: 맞아. 난 우리 아빠가 참 좋아. 이것 좀 봐. 이렇게 요리한 소시지 먹어 본 적 있니? 진짜 맛있어.

남: 너희 어머님이 요리를 정말 잘하시지.

해설: 그림 상에서 남자가 연주하고 있는 악기는 기타가 아니라 하모니카 이므로 ⑤번이 정답이다.

문항 10 ②

Script & Dictation

W: I'm supposed to take a trip to Sapporo next week.

M: Did you **make reservations for** the place you are staying at?

W: I'm working on it. I'm considering a small hotel. But it's not easy to find the right one.

M: Do you want me to help you?

W: No, **I can handle it**. I'd like to choose the place on my own.

M: Just tell me what I can do for you.

W: Okay, **why don't you** rent a car for me?

M: Sure. No problem. What kind of vehicle do you want?

W: The same kind as I have now, **if possible**. I want a vehicle that I'm used to.

M: I know what you mean.

여: 나 다음 주에 삿포로로 여행 가기로 되어 있어.

남: 숙소는 예약했어?

여: 지금 하는 중이야. 작은 호텔에 묵을까 생각 중인데 적당한 곳 찾기가 쉽지 않네.

남: 내가 도와줄까?

여: 아니야. 내가 할 수 있어. 나 스스로 찾아보고 싶어.

남: 내가 해줄 것 있으면 말만 해.

여: 그러면, 차 좀 대신 빌려 줄래?

남: 그럼, 문제없어. 어떤 종류의 차를 원하니?

여: 가능하면 지금 내 차량 같은 걸로. 익숙한 차를 탔으면 해서.

남: 무슨 말인지 알겠어.

해설: 여자는 숙소는 스스로 예약하겠다고 했지만, 남자에게 대신 차를 빌려 달라고 부탁했다.

문항 11 ④

Script & Dictation

[Telephone rings.]

W: Hello? Do Be Publishing House, Rachel Kim speaking.

M: Hello, Rachel. This is Jacob Anderson.

W: Hello, Doctor Anderson. Did you get the documents?

M: What do you mean?

W: I **sent your documents to** your office. You left them here yesterday in the meeting room.

M: Did I? I hadn't even **noticed it** yet. Thank you so much.

W: My pleasure. And what can I do for you today? Do you have any questions about the thesis?

M: I was wondering if there will be some copies left after you publish my thesis. I'd like to send some **to my colleagues abroad**.

W: How many copies do you need?

M: Around forty.

W: We will send them to your colleagues directly from our company.

M: **I really appreciate that.**

[전화 벨 소리]

여: 여보세요? Do Be 출판사의 Rachel Kim입니다.

남: 안녕하세요, Rachel. Jacob Anderson입니다.

여: 안녕하세요, Anderson 박사님? 서류는 받으셨어요?

남: 서류라니요?

여: 박사님 사무실로 서류 보내드렸어요. 어제 여기 회의실에 두고 가셨더라고요.

남: 그랬나요? 여태 몰랐네요. 정말 감사합니다.

여: 별말씀을요. 오늘은 어떻게 도와드릴까요? 논문에 관해 질문이라도 있으신지요?

남: 논문 출간 후에 몇 권 남는 게 있을까 궁금해서요. 외국에 있는 동료들에게 좀 보내려고요.

여: 몇 권 필요하세요?

남: 한 40권 정도요.

여: 저희 회사에서 박사님 동료분들께 바로 보내드릴게요.

남: 그래 주시면 정말 고맙고요.

해설: 출간될 논문을 외국에 있는 동료들에게 보내고 싶어 출판사에 몇 권 정도 남을지 문의하는 남자에게 여자가 직접 외국으로 보내주겠다고 제안했고, 이에 남자는 제안을 받아들이며 고마워했다. 따라서 정답은 ④번이다.

문항 12 ⑤

Script & Dictation

M: What are you listening to, Sunny?

W: I'm listening to John Urban's latest album. **I'm hooked on** all of his songs.

M: I was really hoping he'd visit Korea on tour, but it seems unlikely for the time being.

W: Why is that?

M: I heard that he **was forced to cancel** two tours due to a vocal-cord injury.

W: In John's case, with his latest album, he put a horrible strain on his voice. I read in an article that he practiced songs for eight hours per day.

M: He's amazing. Singers usually have a lack of sleep, a poor diet, and drinking and smoking habits. That's terrible **on their vocal cords,** I guess.

W: It's possible to get a quick operation on the vocal cords. I think many singers **have undergone throat surgery.**

남: 뭐 듣고 있어, Sunny?

여: John Urban의 최신 앨범 듣고 있어. 그의 모든 노래에 푹 빠졌어.

남: 순회공연 때 한국에도 오기를 정말 바랐었는데. 당분간은 힘들 것 같네.

여: 왜?

남: 성대 부상으로 순회공연 일정 두 개를 취소해야 했었대.

여: John의 경우 새 앨범 준비하면서 목에 큰 부담을 줬어. 기사에서 읽었는데 하루에 8시간씩 노래 연습을 했대.

남: 정말 대단하다. 가수들은 보통 수면 시간도 부족하고, 밥도 제대로 못 먹고 음주에 흡연하는 습관도 있던데. 그런 게 성대에는 정말 안 좋을 거 같아.

여: 시간이 얼마 안 걸리는 성대 수술도 가능할 거야. 목 수술한 가수들도 많을걸.

해설: 남자와 여자가 이야기하고 있는 가수는 성대 부상으로 공연 일정을 취소했고, 새 앨범을 준비하면서 하루에 8시간씩 노래를 연습했다고 했으므로 ⑤번이 정답이다.

문항 13 ③

Script & Dictation

W: Dan, **your voice is hoarse** today. Did you catch a cold?

M: No, I'm perfectly fine. It's just my voice.

W: Hmm... Let me see. Did you practice **giving a speech** for a school campaign?

M: Nope, it **has to do with** my family.

W: Oh, I got it! Your family had a good time singing together!

M: No. Actually, my mom opened a cosmetics store yesterday.

W: Okay, but what does that have to do with your voice? What did you do at the store?

M: I helped her with the opening sale. I distributed flyers to people, continuously shouting **to advertise the shop.**

W: You're such a nice son. So, was it successful?

M: Yes. We had quite successful sales. It cost me my voice, though.

여: Dan, 너 오늘 목소리가 쉬었어. 감기 걸렸니?

남: 아니, 나 멀쩡해. 그냥 목소리만 쉬었어.

여: 음, 가만 보자… 학교 캠페인 때문에 연설 연습했어?

남: 아니. 가족들 때문에 그래.

여: 아, 알았다! 가족들과 노래하면서 즐거운 시간을 보낸 거구나!

남: 아니, 사실은 엄마가 어제 화장품 가게를 여셨거든.

여: 그랬구나. 그런데 그게 네 목소리랑 무슨 상관이 있다는 거야? 가게에서 무슨 일을 했길래?

남: 개업 판매를 도와드렸어. 사람들에게 전단 나눠주면서 가게 홍보하느라 계속 소리 질렀거든.

여: 착한 아들이네. 그래, 홍보는 성공적이었니?

남: 응, 매상이 꽤 좋았어. 덕분에 내 목소리는 쉬었지만.

해설: 남자는 남자의 어머니가 운영을 시작한 매장을 큰 소리로 홍보하느라 목이 쉬었다고 설명했다.

문항 14 ④

Script & Dictation

W: Welcome to DEF Mart. How can I help you?

M: I would like to buy that **pair of sneakers** over there. Is there any discount for a display item?

W: Yes, we give a 20% **discount off the regular price**.

M: Then, how much is the list price?

W: It's originally $170.

M: Wow, that's so expensive. What about the jogging shoes?

W: The blue ones are $100, and the blue ones with silver lining are $130.

M: **I would like** the first sneakers.

W: Okay. Anything else?

M: Hold on. I have a coupon from this store. Can I use it?

W: Let me see. You could have gotten a 10% discount, but **it is expired**.

M: Oh, okay.

여: 어서 오세요, DEF 마트입니다. 무엇을 도와드릴까요?

남: 저기 있는 스니커즈 운동화 사려고 하는데요. 진열 상품 할인은 안 하나요?

여: 네, 정가에서 20% 할인 판매 중입니다.

남: 그럼 원래 얼마인데요?

여: 정가 170달러입니다.

남: 와, 정말 비싸네요. 조깅화는 얼마인가요?

여: 파란색은 100달러이고, 은색 줄이 들어간 파란색 신발은 130달러입니다.

남: 제일 처음 스니커즈 운동화가 좋겠네요.

여: 알겠습니다. 더 필요하신 것은요?

남: 잠시만요. 이 매장 쿠폰 있는데 사용할 수 있을까요?

여: 확인 좀 해볼게요. 10% 할인 받으실 수 있었는데 사용 기한이 지났네요.

남: 아, 알겠습니다.

해설: 남자는 여러 종류의 신발 가격에 대해 물었지만 결국 제일 처음 물어봤던 스니커즈 운동화를 사기로 했다. 정가 170달러에서 20% 할인 판매되고 있으므로 남자가 내야 할 금액은 170달러에서 34달러를 뺀 136달러이다.

문항 15 ⑤

Script & Dictation

W: You may have seen a white whale on TV, in an animated movie, or at a zoo. It is called a Beluga or Belukha whale. It's white like snow and is a sleek, streamlined, aquatic mammal. During breeding season, approximately two hundred Belugas **swim around in shoals**. It's found in and around the Arctic areas of Canada and Greenland. Some people continually get confused about the difference between belugas and dolphins. Dolphins have **cone-shaped teeth** and a curved dorsal fin, while belugas have flat teeth and a **triangular dorsal fin**. Belugas sing like canaries, but each dolphin learns from its mom its own signature whistle. Also, belugas are generally **smaller than their counterparts**.

여: 여러분은 TV, 애니메이션 영화, 또는 동물원에서 하얀 고래를 보신 적이 있을 거예요. 이는 "Beluga" 또는 "Belukha"라고 불리는 흰돌고래입니다. 눈처럼 하얗고, 매끈한 유선형의 수생 포유류죠. 번식 기간에는 약 200여 마리의 흰돌고래가 무리를 지어 헤엄칩니다. 이는 캐나다와 그린란드의 북극 지역 및 그 부근에서 목격됩니다. 흰돌고래와 돌고래를 번번이 헷갈리는 분들도 있습니다. 돌고래의 이빨은 원뿔 모양이고 등지느러미는 곡선 모양이지만, 흰돌고래는 이빨이 평평하고 등지느러미는 삼각형 모양입니다. 흰돌고래는 카나리아 같은 소리를 내지만, 돌고래들은 어미로부터 저마다의 특징이 있는 휘파람 소리를 배웁니다. 또한 흰돌고래는 대개 그 비교 대상인 돌고래보다 작습니다.

해설: 흰돌고래와 돌고래의 차이점을 설명하는 제일 마지막 부분에 개체마다 특유의 휘파람 소리를 내는 것은 흰돌고래가 아닌 돌고래라고 언급하고 있다.

문항 16 ④

Script & Dictation

M: The Creation Science Camp is a **traditional occasion** for all high school students who are into science. This camp will be held in the Brighton Expo Park from the 1st to 10th of March. Participants will enjoy **various science experiments and field trips** during the event. There is no fee for the camp because our supporting electronic company, Canjin, will help financially. Students who want to join must register on the Canjin Internet registration site, starting from today. Only the first one hundred students who have **a recommendation letter** from their science teacher can participate. Your science teacher can visit www.canjin.com and **download the document**. We expect the science lovers among our high school students to be highly interested in this camp.

남: 창조과학캠프는 과학에 관심이 많은 모든 고등학생을 위한 전통적인 행사입니다. 이 캠프는 3월 1일부터 10일까지 Brighton 엑스포 공원에서 열릴 예정입니다. 행사기간 동안 참가자들은 다양한 과학 실험과 현장 학습의 기회를 누릴 수 있습니다. 후원 업체인 Canjin 전자 회사에서 재정적인 도움을 줄 것이기 때문에 캠프 참가 비용은 없습니다. 참가를 희망하는 학생들은 오늘부터 Canjin 인터넷 등록 사이트에서 등록해야 합니다. 과학 선생님의 추천서가 있는 선착순 100명의 학생만이 참여할 수 있습니다. 여러분의 과학 선생님은 www.canjin.com에 접속하여 서류를 내려받을 수 있습니다. 과학을 좋아하는 고등학생들이 캠프에 많은 관심을 기울여주길 기대합니다.

해설: 남자는 후반부에 과학 성적 증명서가 아니라 과학 선생님의 추천서가 있는 선착순 100명의 학생만이 캠프에 참여할 수 있다고 안내했다. 따라서 ④번이 정답이다.

문항 17 ③

Script & Dictation

M: Let's **keep the process going**. We need to book our rooms.

W: All right. The Chicago options. Well, I surfed the Internet and wrote down some choices.

M: Oh, it's a guesthouse list. What do you prefer?

W: **Actually I don't care** where we stay in Chicago. I just picked places with lots of rooms because there are six of us.

M: Good idea. I really want to have breakfast. It could be much better for our trips.

W: Okay, what about the location?

M: Probably downtown is convenient to go anywhere, but I think near the beach would be nice.

W: Then, what about the price?

M: I don't expect it to be expensive. But **the less** we spend, **the more** opportunities we can have to do what we want.

남: 우리 하던 거 계속하자. 숙소 예약해야 해.

여: 그래. 시카고는 어떤지 보자. 인터넷 검색으로 몇 군데 적어 봤어.

남: 숙박시설 목록이구나. 선호하는 곳 있어?

여: 사실 난 시카고에선 어디서 숙박하든 상관없어. 그냥 우리가 6명이라서 객실이 많은 곳들로 골라본 거야.

남: 잘했어. 난 아침은 꼭 먹고 싶은데. 그래야 여행하기 훨씬 더 좋을 거야.

여: 좋아. 위치는?

남: 아마도 시내에 있어야 움직이기 편하겠지만, 해변 근처도 괜찮을 것 같아.

여: 비용은?

남: 비쌀 것 같지는 않아. 하지만 아낄수록 우리가 하고 싶은 걸 할 기회가 더 많아지겠지.

해설: 우선 남자는 아침 식사가 제공되는 곳을 선택하고자 했기 때문에 ②번과 ④번은 제외된다. 숙소의 위치는 시내 또는 해변을 선호하므로 ⑤번도 제외된다. 숙박비를 아껴야 한다고 했으므로 나머지 ①번과 ③번 중 숙박비가 더 싼 ③번이 정답이다.

문항 18 ②

Script & Dictation

W: Hello, Yongjae, come on in.

M: I'm here because of my essay, Ms. Han.

W: I've already read yours.

M: Would you **give me your evaluation**?

W: Well, it's **good on the whole**, but there's one thing to point out. I think you're good at structuring an essay, but yours is short of supporting ideas.

M: You mean, things that support the topic sentence?

W: Exactly. **Adequate supporting ideas** help your readers accept what you're saying. This subject is very original, but your supporting ideas are kind of old-fashioned. Can you think differently and **revise it that way**?

M: Sure. I'll make my essay more persuasive.

여: 안녕, 용재야. 어서 와.

남: 제 에세이 때문에 왔어요, 한 선생님.

여: 이미 네 거 읽었단다.

남: 평가해 주시겠어요?

여: 전반적으로 좋은데 한 가지 지적할 것이 있어. 네가 에세이 구조는 잘 잡는 것 같지만 뒷받침하는 생각들은 부족해.

남: 주제문을 지지하는 것들 말씀이시죠?

여: 그렇지. 뒷받침하는 견해들이 충분해야 독자들이 네가 하고자 하는 말을 받아들이는 데 도움이 된단다. 주제는 매우 독창적이지만 뒷받침하는 개념들이 좀 진부해. 생각을 좀 다르게 해서 그 방향으로 수정해 볼 수 있겠니?

남: 그럼요. 에세이를 좀 더 설득력 있게 만들어보겠습니다.

해설: 선생인 여자는 제자인 남자가 쓴 에세이가 구조는 잘 잡혀 있으나 뒷받침하는 견해들이 부족하고, 진부한 편이라고 지적하며, 뒷받침하는 내용이 많아야 독자들이 에세이에 동의하게 된다고 설명했다. 따라서 여자가 언급한 사항들을 반영하여 에세이를 설득력 있게 써 보겠다고 하는 것이 흐름 상 가장 적절한 응답이 되겠다.

문항 19 ②

Script & Dictation

W: Hi, Rupert. Did you enjoy the new movie yesterday? How was it?

M: It was great, but I didn't really enjoy it that much.

W: What do you mean?

M: I really **wanted to focus on** the movie, but I argued with a man sitting in front of me.

W: What happened?

M: During the movie, he didn't **turn off his mobile phone**, which had a big screen. His phone kept getting messages and bothering everyone.

W: You mean it made sounds constantly? That's terrible.

M: No sounds, actually. But **I couldn't concentrate on** the movie because of the light. You know, the phone light looks really bright in the dark theater.

W: That **could be really annoying**. So what did you do?

M: I complained, but he didn't switch it off.

여: 안녕, Rupert. 어제 신작 영화 본 거 재미있었니? 어땠어?

남: 재미는 있었는데 그다지 즐겁지는 않았어.

여: 무슨 말이야?

남: 정말 영화에 집중하고 싶었는데 앞에 앉은 남자랑 싸웠지 뭐야.

여: 무슨 일 있었어?

남: 그 사람이 영화 내내 휴대폰을 안 끄는 거야, 화면도 큰 거였는데. 메시지가 계속 와서 다들 짜증이 났었지.

여: 그럼 계속 소리가 났다는 거야? 너무한걸.

남: 아니, 사실 소리는 안 났어. 그렇지만 빛 때문에 영화에 집중할 수 없었어. 어두운 극장에서는 휴대폰 조명이 진짜 밝잖아.

여: 정말 짜증 났겠다. 그래서 어떻게 했어?

남: 항의했는데도, 그 사람이 끄질 않더라고.

해설: 여자는 남자에게 극장에서 휴대폰을 끄지 않고 계속 메시지를 받아 그 조명 때문에 다른 관객들에게 피해를 준 사람에게 어떻게 대응했는지 묻고 있다. 따라서 정답은 ②번이다.

문항 20 ①

Script & Dictation

W: Logan has a date with his girlfriend, Jessie, and now it's time to go home. They **decide to take the bus**. As usual, Logan is going to escort her home. But Jessie realizes that the bus stop is **crowded with people**. Logan must feel tired and sleepy because he played soccer before the date. She thinks if they take a bus, they will have to stand and **wait for a long time**. Suddenly, Jessie remembers that her father is near there, so she wants her father **to drive Logan and her home**. In this situation, what would Jessie most likely say to Logan?

* Jessie: _How about calling my father to pick us up?_

여: Logan은 여자친구 Jessie와 데이트를 하고 이제 집에 가려고 한다. 둘은 버스를 타기로 하고, 보통 때처럼 Logan이 Jessie를 집까지 데려다 주려고 한다. 하지만 Jessie는 버스 정류장이 사람들로 혼잡한 것을 알게 된다. Logan은 데이트 전에 축구를 했기 때문에 분명 피곤하고 졸릴 터였다. Jessie는 그들이 버스를 타면 서서 가야 하고, 또 오랜 시간 기다려야 할 거라고 생각한다. 문득 Jessie는 아버지가 근처에 계시다는 것을 기억하게 된다. Jessie는 아버지가 자신과 Logan을 집까지 차로 데려다 주길 바란다. 이 상황에서 Jessie가 Logan에게 할 수 있는 말로 가장 적당한 것은 무엇일까?

* Jessie: _우리 아버지에게 전화해서 데리러 와 달라고 하는 건 어떨까?_

해설: Jessie는 버스에 사람이 많을 것이고, Logan이 분명히 피곤할 거라 예상하고 있다. 마침 Jessie 아버지가 근처에 계시니 차로 자신들을 데리러 와 달라고 부탁하는 것이 어떨지 Logan에게 먼저 의향을 묻는 ①번이 이 상황에서 가장 적절한 말이다.

문항 21 ③

문항 22 ①

Script & Dictation

W: Jake. What are you reading? You **look so focused** on it.

M: Hi, Helen! It's a post about ancient Chinese. Look here! These are pictures of the dolls that Chinese children played with.

W: The dolls were made of stone and clay, right?

M: Yes. According to this post, ivory and ceramics were also used.

W: Those **must have belonged to** rich people. Ivory has always been valuable.

M: Exactly. They were for the royal family in China. Playing with marbles was also quite popular, especially with the children of the Chinese royal family. I think marbles were valuable, too.

W: Why do all the photos show dolls with soldiers' features?

M: That's an interesting point. The kings of the age, I guess, wanted to protect their honor and wealth, so they needed many soldiers. **That could be reflected** in their choice of dolls and other routine things.

W: **That makes sense**. Have you heard about what "Cupak" is? It says here that it's the name of a game that was widely popular with ancient Chinese children.

M: Yeah, I already read that part. The player would hit a small piece of wood with a bat while the wood was in the air. Sounds like baseball or cricket.

W: Interesting! I think I should read that article myself.

여: Jake. 뭐 읽고 있어? 정말 열중하고 있구나.

남: 안녕, Helen! 고대의 중국인에 관한 글을 읽고 있어. 여기 봐! 중국 아이들이 가지고 놀던 인형 사진들이 있어.

여: 인형이 돌과 찰흙으로 만들어진 거지?

남: 응. 이 글에 따르면, 상아와 도자기도 사용됐대.

여: 그럼 분명 부유한 사람들 것이었겠구나. 상아는 언제나 귀한 거였잖아.

남: 정확해. 중국 왕실을 위한 거였어. 구슬 가지고 노는 것도 꽤 인기가 있었대. 특히 중국 왕실의 아이들에게 말이야. 구슬도 귀한 거였나 봐.

여: 왜 모든 사진 속 인형들이 병사의 모습을 하고 있지?

남: 재미있는 지적이야. 그 시대의 왕들은 부와 명예를 지키고 싶었던 게 아닐까 생각해. 그래서 많은 병사가 필요했던 거지. 그것이 인형과 다른 일상적인 것들을 고르는데 반영됐을 거야.

여: 말 되네. 너 "Cupak"이 뭔지 들어본 적 있어? 여기 보니 고대 중국 아이들에게 널리 인기 있던 놀이의 이름이래.

남: 응, 그 부분은 벌써 읽었어. 방망이로 공중에 뜬 작은 나무 조각을 치는 거야. 야구나 크리켓 같지.

여: 재밌는데! 나도 기사를 읽어봐야겠다.

해설: 21. 고대 중국에서 사용된 장난감들의 소재와 인형들이 병사의 모습을 한 배경, 또 아이들이 하던 "Cupak"이라는 놀이에 관해 이야기하고 있으므로 정답은 ③번이다. **22.** 돌과 찰흙, 상아와 도자기는 언급되었지만 ①번인 짚은 언급되지 않았다.

수능 7일 전 대학수학능력평가 대비 영어영역 듣기[B형]

1	⑤	2	③	3	②	4	④	5	①
6	③	7	④	8	②	9	②	10	④
11	①	12	⑤	13	②	14	①	15	①
16	②	17	②	18	③	19	②	20	④
21	②	22	④						

문항 1 ⑤

Script & Dictation

W: Inkyu, I'm terribly sorry. I'm late.

M: Clare! **I've been waiting for** you for almost an hour!

W: I'm so sorry. The meeting **took longer than I expected**.

M: _Why didn't you call me? I was so worried._

여: 인규야, 정말 미안해. 내가 늦었지.

남: Clare! 나 거의 1시간이나 기다렸어!

여: 정말 미안해. 회의가 생각보다 오래 걸렸어.

남: 왜 전화 안 했어? 많이 걱정했단 말이야.

해설: 약속 시각보다 한 시간 늦게 나타나 미안하다고 말하는 친구에 대한 적절한 응답은 ⑤번이다.

문항 2 ③

Script & Dictation

W: Where did you buy this smart-phone case? How much did you pay for it?

M: I bought it **at the US online shopping mall**. It was $25.

W: Really? I paid $50 **for the same thing**.

M: Well, but I paid the shipping charge, also.

여: 이 스마트폰 케이스 어디서 샀어? 얼마 주고 산 거야?

남: 미국 온라인 쇼핑몰에서 샀어. 25달러야.

여: 정말? 나 똑같은 거 50달러 주고 샀는데.

남: 그런데 나는 배송료도 냈지.

해설: 같은 제품을 남자는 외국 온라인 구매 사이트에서 25달러에 샀으나, 여자는 50달러에 구매한 상황이다. 이에 대해 남자가 저렴하게 사긴 했으나 배송료는 따로 더 냈어야 했다고 응답해야 대화의 흐름이 자연스럽다.

문항 3 ②

Script & Dictation

M: The final is over! I feel so relieved.

W: Yeah, **a load is off my mind**. What about going window shopping in Churchill Square?

M: I'd love to, but I'm going to **see my dentist for braces**, first.

W: All right then, maybe next time.

남: 기말시험 끝났다! 어찌나 다행인지.

여: 그래, 한시름 놓인다. 윈도 쇼핑하러 Churchill Square 안 갈래?

남: 그러고 싶은데 교정기 때문에 치과에 먼저 가야 해서.

여: 그래, 그럼 다음에 가던가 하자.

해설: 보기 중 치과에 가야 해서 함께 윈도 쇼핑을 가지 못한다는 친구에게 할 수 있는 가장 적절한 말은 다음에 같이 가자는 것이다.

문항 4 ④

Script & Dictation

M: Good morning, residents of McKibben Apartments. This is John Platt, the manager **of the property management office**, speaking. As the bulletin on each elevator has said, the **expanding new workout facilities** will start to move in around noon. The women's association of the apartment community has already bought the equipment, and it's going to be placed **in the expanded**

area to create the second gym. For more details, please visit our apartments' web community or the office in person. Thank you for your cooperation.

남: McKibben 아파트 주민 여러분, 좋은 아침입니다. 저는 아파트 관리사무소 매니저인 John Platt입니다. 각 엘리베이터 게시판을 통해 안내해드렸듯이, 확장용 새 운동 시설들이 정오쯤부터 들어올 예정입니다. 아파트 부녀회에서 이미 시설 구매를 했으며, 확장 공간에 배치하여 두 번째 체육관을 만들 예정입니다. 더 자세한 내용을 알고 싶으신 분은 아파트 웹 커뮤니티, 또는 사무실을 직접 방문해 주세요. 협조해 주셔서 감사합니다.

해설: 신규 운동 기구들을 들여와 아파트 체육 시설을 확충하게 되었음을 알리는 공지사항이므로 ④번이 정답이다.

문항 5 ①

Script & Dictation

W: Officer Ploddy. Thanks for coming.

M: You're welcome. After reading your opinion on the Internet, I thought I should come here earlier.

W: Thank you. Here is the road **I mentioned**. Traffic signs and signals are fine, but there are so many security risks.

M: You're right. We had one incident last month, in which we lost a 12-year-old girl from an illegal U-turn. It was **a real tragedy**.

W: Yes, it was so sad. But, there are some drivers still doing illegal U-turns every day. We need to **come up with a way** to stop this.

M: On this kind of road, a surveillance camera is needed. Nowadays, they're installed **not only for** speed and parking traps **but also for** security reasons.

W: That would be good. I think we need to raise awareness that U-turns here are illegal and very dangerous.

여: Ploddy 경관님. 와 주셔서 감사합니다.

남: 천만에요. 인터넷에 올리신 의견을 읽고 나서 더 일찍 와 봐야 겠다고 생각했습니다.

여: 고맙습니다. 여기가 바로 제가 말한 도로입니다. 교통 표지와 신호등은 양호하지만, 안전 문제가 정말 많습니다.

남: 맞습니다. 지난달에는 12세 소녀가 불법 유턴에 목숨을 잃는 매우 비극적인 사고가 있었습니다.

여: 네, 정말 슬펐어요. 그런데도 아직 불법 유턴을 하는 경우가 매일 발생하고 있습니다. 이를 막을 방법이 필요합니다.

남: 이런 종류의 도로에는 감시 카메라가 있어야 해요. 요새는 속도 및 주차 위반 단속 구역에 뿐만 아니라 안전상의 이유로도 카메라를 설치하죠.

여: 그게 좋겠네요. 이곳에서의 유턴은 불법이고 매우 위험하다는 인식을 높여야 할 것 같습니다.

해설: 속도나 주차 위반뿐만 아니라 불법 유턴 단속을 위해서라도, 즉 교통 법규 위반 사항을 단속하려면 감시 카메라가 필요하다는 것이 남자의 주장이다.

문항 6 ③

Script & Dictation

W: Nowadays, many people only think about having **a job that pays well**, a big house, an expensive car, and fashionable clothes, etc. **They spend all their lives working** to achieve these goals. But there are some people who give their time and energy to help those who can't help themselves. These volunteers do so without receiving any payment. They help the poor, the hopeless, the sick, and the dying, and they never look for anything in return. Volunteers may work in their own town or city or may even travel to another country or continent in order to help **those who need it most**. It's these volunteers, who often work in dangerous and difficult situations, that **deserve great reward** for their selfless acts.

여: 요즘 돈 잘 버는 직업, 큰 집, 비싼 차, 유행하는 옷 등과 같은 것만을 생각하는 사람들이 많습니다. 그러한 목표를 이루기 위해 일하는 데 인생을 바치는 이들이죠. 하지만 혼자 힘으로는 살 수 없는 이들을 돕기 위해 시간과 힘을 쏟는 사람들도 있습니다. 이러한 자원봉사자들은 아무런 대가도 받지 않고 그런 활동을 합니다. 가난하고, 희망 없고, 아프거나, 죽어가는 사람들을 돕지만, 그에 대한 보답으로는 아무것도 바라지 않는 사람들이죠. 자원봉사자들은 거주하는 동네나 도시에서 일하거나, 다른 나라 또는 다른 대륙에까지 건너가 도움을 절실히 필요로 하는 이들을 돕습니다. 위험하고 어려운 상황에서 일할 때도 많은 이와 같은 자원봉사자들의 이타적인 활동이야말로 큰 보답을 받아야 마땅합니다.

해설: 여자는 아무런 대가도 바라지 않고 시간을 할애하여 자원봉사하는 사람들을 높이 평가하고 있다. 따라서 정답은 ③번이다.

문항 7 ④

Script & Dictation

M: How many toys did you buy for your son?

W: My son Jeremy is four now. He always wants to have **toys advertised on TV**. But, you should know, it's not good for children to buy those fancy toys.

M: Really? There are so many items with pretty colors and cute cartoon characters.

W: They look beautiful, but they are **suppressing kids' creativity**. For our children, just some colored crayons and white paper is good. A few colored wood blocks can be fun, too. With around three hundred blocks, they can make anything they want.

M: Oh, that's really impressive. Sometimes, my daughter **comes up with** very creative ideas when she plays with her blocks.

W: Yeah, simple things can spark creativity.

남: 아들에게 장난감을 몇 개나 사줬나요?

여: 우리 아들 Jeremy는 4살인데요, 항상 TV에서 광고하는 장난감을 갖고 싶어해요. 하지만 아이들에게 그런 비싼 장난감들을 사주는 건 좋지 않다는 걸 아셔야 해요.

남: 그런가요? 색깔도 예쁘고, 귀여운 만화 캐릭터가 있는 장난감들이 많던데요.

여: 예쁘긴 하지만 아이들의 창의력을 억제하거든요. 우리 아이들에겐 색깔 크레용과 흰 종이만 있어도 좋습니다. 색깔이 들어간 나무 블록 몇 개만 있어도 재미있을 수 있고요. 블록 한 300개만 있으면 아이들은 원하는 것은 다 만들어낼 수 있거든요.

남: 그것참 인상적이네요. 우리 딸도 블록 가지고 놀다 정말 창의적인 발상을 할 때가 있어요.

여: 그렇죠. 단순한 것들이 창의력을 유발할 수 있답니다.

해설: 겉보기에 예쁘고 비싼 장난감 보다 단순한 소재들이 오히려 아이들의 창의력 계발에 더 좋다는 이야기를 하고 있다.

문항 8 ②

Script & Dictation

[Cell phone rings.]

W: Hello, Mr. Roger. So did you **make a decision** on which one to choose?

M: Yes. My wife and I like the one on 5th Avenue.

W: Oh, the three-story house with five bedrooms? You have made the perfect decision. It's **one of the best ones** that we could suggest now.

M: It's **a bit over our budget**. But we decided on it because it has a lovely backyard. I think my children will be happy to play there.

W: Yes, the yard is unbelievable. You are going to be happy having the yard.

M: Exactly. Is it possible to grow some vegetables in the yard? Could you ask the owner about it?

W: Sure. I've been **dealing with her properties** for many years, and she never minds how the tenants use the yard.

M: That sounds good. Then I'm ready to sign the lease.

[휴대폰 벨 소리]

여: 안녕하세요, Roger씨. 어떤 걸로 하실지 결정하셨나요?

남: 네. 아내와 저는 5번가에 있는 게 마음에 드네요.

여: 방 5개짜리 3층 집 말씀이시죠? 탁월하신 선택입니다. 저희가 현재 제안 드릴 수 있는 가장 괜찮은 집들 중 하나죠.

남: 우리 예산을 조금 초과하지만 예쁜 뒷마당 때문에 거기로 결정했어요. 우리 아이들이 거기서 놀면 좋아할 것 같네요.

여: 맞아요. 정말 멋진 뜰이죠. 뜰이 있어서 좋으실 거예요.

남: 그러니까요. 거기에 채소를 좀 길러도 될까요? 집 주인분께 여쭤봐 주시겠어요?

여: 물론이죠. 그분 부동산을 몇 년째 봐 드리고 있는데, 입주하시는 분들이 뜰을 어떤 용도로 쓰시든지 별로 상관하지 않으시긴 해요.

남: 다행이네요. 그럼 임대 계약서에 서명만 하면 되겠네요.

해설: 남자는 여자에게 세 들어갈 집의 집주인에게 뒤뜰에 채소를 심을 수 있는지 물어 봐달라고 부탁했다. 그러자 여자가 집주인의 부동산을 수년간 맡아왔다고 말하는 것으로 보아 정답은 ②번이다.

문항 9 ②

Script & Dictation

M: I'm your tour guide, Hajin. Before boarding, **let me tell you briefly** about our trip. We are going to visit four cities in the western US. After a 13-hour flight, we'll arrive in San Francisco, where you can **have great seafood** and enjoy curved hills. Next, we'll go to Las Vegas, Sin City. You can be a millionaire or **go broke**. It could be a lot of fun, but I suggest you only gamble a little. Next, we can experience the combination of Mexican and American culture in San Diego. San Diego is **very close to Mexico**, so you can experience Mexican influence everywhere. And last but not least is Los Angeles. It's so hard to explain. So much fun, so much activity, and so much variety.

남: 저는 여러분의 여행 가이드 하진입니다. 탑승 전 간단하게 이번 여행에 관해 설명하겠습니다. 미 서부 4개 도시를 방문할 예정입니다. 13시간 비행 후, 샌프란시스코에 도착하여 맛있는 해산물을 드실 수 있고 구불구불한 언덕길을 감상하실 수 있습니다. 그 후 '죄의 도시'라는 애칭으로 불리는 라스베이거스로 이동합니다. 라스베이거스에서는 엄청난 부자도 될 수 있지만 또 돈을 다 잃을 수도 있죠. 정말 재밌겠지만, 도박은 조금만 하시길 당부드립니다. 다음으로 멕시코와 미국 문화의 조화를 경험할 수 있는 샌디에이고로 갑니다. 샌디에이고는 멕시코와 아주 가깝기 때문에 도시 전체에서 멕시코적인 향취를 경험하게 될 것입니다. 마지막으로 앞서 방문한 도시들만큼이나 중요한 로스앤젤레스입니다. 이곳을 설명하기란 참 어렵죠. 엄청난 재미와 다양한 활동, 각양각색의 것들로 가득한 곳입니다.

해설: 멕시코는 세 번째로 방문할 샌디에이고를 설명할 때 그곳과 가깝다는 사실이 언급되었을 뿐 실제로 가지는 않는다. 샌디에이고 다음으로 방문할 곳은 로스앤젤레스이므로 정답은 ②번이다.

문항 10 ④

Script & Dictation

M: Christina, what are you looking at?

W: It's a letter from a girl in the second grade of Leeds Elementary School where you work.

M: Oh! There are some photos, and what's this? A bag of instant coffee?

W: Yes, near the school, there's a crosswalk that **doesn't really seem safe**. So I patrol the area every morning.

M: **Is it a kind of** thank-you gift?

W: Yes, it is. She saved her pocket money for this.

M: Oh, she is so kind and cute. But I also want to do something for that cute girl.

W: Right. So I'll **write a letter back**.

M: She deserves to be praised. I'll call the principal of the school.

W: That's a great idea. She will **get some praise** from her teachers.

남: Christina, 뭐 보고 있어요?

여: 당신이 근무하고 있는 Leeds 초등학교 2학년 여학생이 쓴 편지요.

남: 아! 사진도 있네요. 그리고 이건 뭐예요? 즉석커피 한 상자네요?

여: 네, 학교 근처에 그다지 안전하지 않은 건널목이 있어요. 그래서 매일 아침 그 부근 순찰을 하거든요.

남: 그럼 이건 감사의 선물 같은 거예요?

여: 맞아요. 학생이 이거 사려고 용돈을 모았대요.

남: 귀엽고 착하기도 하지. 나도 그 귀여운 학생을 위해 뭔가 해 주고 싶네요.

여: 그래요. 나도 답장을 쓰려고요.

남: 그 학생은 칭찬받아야 해요. 내가 학교 교장 선생님께 전화 할게요.

여: 좋은 생각이에요. 학교 선생님들께 칭찬받겠는걸요.

해설: 학교 주변을 순찰하는 여자에게 편지와 선물로 감사 인사를 한 어린 학생이 기특하여 남자는 학교 교장에게 전화하여 그 사실을 알리려 하고 있다.

문항 11 ①

Script & Dictation

M: Hi, Eunmi. I booked the camp site for this weekend.

W: God, is it this weekend? I'd love to go, but I can't. I have to prepare my presentation by Monday.

M: What? Did you forget our plans?

W: No, it's just that **I'm in trouble with** my boss, so he gave me a lot of files, I guess.

M: What are they? Can you go camping if I help you to **finish preparing and completing them**?

W: Absolutely. By tomorrow, I have to organize and re-categorize **a bunch of files** about statements of profit and loss from the last quarter. Would you type these paragraphs on the word documents?

M: Sure thing. After that?

W: I don't know. I could do with coffee. How about you?

M: No, I'm okay. I'll **go get one** for you.

W: That's sweet of you. Thanks!

남: 안녕, 은미야. 이번 주말에 갈 캠핑장 예약했어.

여: 어머, 그게 이번 주말이야? 가고 싶은데 못 갈 것 같아. 월요일 까지 발표 준비해야 해.

남: 뭐라고? 우리 계획 잊고 있었던 거야?

여: 아니, 그게 아니라 상사와 문제가 좀 있는데 그래서 그런지 나한테 파일들을 엄청나게 많이 주지 뭐야.

남: 어떤 파일들인데? 내가 파일들 준비하고 마무리하는 거 도와주면 캠핑 갈 수 있겠어?

여: 물론이야. 내일까지 지난 분기 손익계산서 파일 뭉치를 정리 하고 재분류해야 해. 이 단락들을 워드 문서에 좀 입력해줄래?

남: 문제없어. 그다음엔?

여: 잘 모르겠네. 커피가 있어야 할 것 같아. 너는?

남: 아니, 난 괜찮아. 내가 가져다줄게.

여: 그래 준다면 고마워!

문항 12 ⑤

Script & Dictation

W: Long time no see. Why do you miss so many tennis lessons?

M: **I've been busy preparing for** a promotion.

W: So did you get promoted?

M: No, I didn't.

W: Really? I'm sorry to hear that. You will **get another chance** in the future. Cheer up. By the way, will you be able to play tennis with us again?

M: I'm afraid I can't.

W: Why not? We really need you. You are **the ace of our club**, and we have a tournament next week.

M: I know. But I really need some time to get myself together. **It is really tough** to accept the result.

W: I'm sorry. I don't know what to say.

여: 오랜만이에요. 테니스 수업 왜 그렇게 많이 빠지시는 거예요?

남: 승진 준비에 바빴어요.

여: 승진하셨어요?

남: 아니요, 못 했어요.

여: 그런가요? 유감이네요. 다음에 기회가 또 올 거예요. 기운 내세요. 그나저나 그럼 다시 우리와 함께 테니스 할 수 있나요?

남: 미안한데, 안 될 것 같아요.

여: 왜요? 당신이 꼭 필요한데. 당신이 우리 클럽 에이스인데 다음 주에 토너먼트가 있어요.

남: 알아요. 그런데 마음을 추스를 시간이 필요해서요. 승진 결과를 받아들이기가 정말 힘드네요.

여: 유감이네요. 뭐라고 위로의 말을 드려야 할지.

문항 13 ②

Script & Dictation

M: Although you already know it, **I'd like to mention** a few things, again.

W: Okay.

M: Woody has to finish his homework before dinner.

W: Absolutely, I'll help him to finish it.

M: In the refrigerator, there's pasta and salad I made. Warm up the pasta in the microwave. Please check whether Woody eats his cucumber or not. **He's picky sometimes.**

W: No problem.

M: After dinner, computer games **are allowed for** just one hour. No more, never!

W: Absolutely.

M: I think I'll come back around that time, but **if I can't make it** at eight thirty, Woody should take a shower.

W: Okay, it's not really hard. I've been excited to spend time with him.

M: Thanks.

남: 이미 알고 계시지만, 몇 가지 다시 당부하려고요.

여: 좋아요.

남: Woody는 저녁 식사 전에 숙제를 끝내야 해요.

여: 물론이에요, 숙제 제가 도울게요.

남: 냉장고에 제가 만든 파스타와 샐러드가 있어요. 파스타는 전자레인지에 데워주세요. Woody가 오이도 잘 먹는지 봐 주시고요. 가끔 가릴 때도 있거든요.

여: 걱정하지 마세요.

남: 저녁 먹고 컴퓨터 게임은 딱 1시간만 할 수 있어요. 그 이상은 절대 안 됩니다!

여: 물론입니다.

남: 제가 그때쯤이면 돌아오겠지만, 혹시 못 오면 8시 30분에 Woody가 샤워할 수 있게 해 주세요.

여: 알겠습니다. 별로 어렵지 않네요. Woody랑 시간을 보내게 되어 신 나네요.

남: 고맙습니다.

문항 14 ①

Script & Dictation

M: May I help you? We're having an **off-season sale**.

W: I'm looking for a windbreaker jacket. Can I have a look around?

M: Yes. The windbreaker corner is here. Take your time.

W: Let me see... **This hooded jacket** looks nice. How much is it?

M: It's $200. But it's not part of the sale.

W: I see. It must be a new arrival, then.

M: Yes. What about **something to keep you warm**?

W: Oh, this trench coat is so chic. How much is it?

M: It's $400. But it's 20 percent off now.

W: The price of the trench coat is quite attractive. But I **prefer the windbreaker**. I'll take it.

M: All right, if you have a membership card, you can get an additional 10 percent discount.

W: That's great. Here's my card.

남: 제가 도와드릴까요? 저희가 지금 비수기 세일 중이에요.

여: 바람막이 재킷을 찾고 있어요. 좀 둘러봐도 될까요?

남: 네, 바람막이 재킷은 이쪽에 있습니다. 천천히 둘러보세요.

여: 어디 보자… 이 모자 달린 재킷 멋있네요. 얼마죠?

남: 200달러입니다. 그런데 세일 품목은 아니에요.

여: 그렇군요. 신상품인가 보네요.

남: 맞아요. 보온이 되는 종류는 어떠세요?

여: 오, 이 트렌치코트 정말 세련됐네요. 얼마죠?

남: 400달러지만 지금 20퍼센트 할인해 판매하고 있어요.

여: 가격이 꽤 괜찮네요. 그래도 바람막이 재킷이 더 좋겠어요. 그걸로 하겠습니다.

남: 알겠습니다. 회원 카드가 있으면 10퍼센트 추가 할인받으실 수 있는데요.

여: 그거 잘됐네요. 여기 제 카드요.

해설: 여자가 구매하기로 한 바람막이 재킷은 200달러이고, 세일 항목에서는 제외되었다. 그러나 여자에게 10% 추가 할인되는 회원 카드가 있으므로 내야 할 실제 가격은 180달러이다.

문항 15 ①

Script & Dictation

M: Valley Point Resort provides so many activities to our guests **on a daily basis.** Do your friends want to do something more than scuba diving or sunbathing? Does your family seek thrills beyond just camping? Then why don't you recommend trying wild boar hunting or bungee jumping off our suspension bridge? Valley Point Resort **is filled with** so much fun all around that we guarantee you leave us relaxed and refreshed. If your child is under seven, we will take care of him or her while you relax. We are located around the most beautiful scenery in the world. Don't forget you can enjoy a wonderful summer vacation with **the crystal clear waters** of Valley Point Resort, which is **free for everyone.**

남: Valley Point 리조트는 손님 여러분께 매일 정말 다양한 활동을 선보입니다. 스쿠버 다이빙이나 일광욕 말고 다른 것을 하고 싶어하는 친구분들이 계신가요? 가족이 단순히 캠핑하는 것 이상의 짜릿함을 찾고 계신가요? 그렇다면 멧돼지 사냥이나 현수교 번지 점프를 추천해 보시는 건 어떠세요? Valley Point 리조트에서는 어디를 가시든 곳곳이 재미로 꽉 차 있습니다. 손님 여러분은 확실히 편안하고 상쾌한 모습으로 저희를 떠나시게 될 것입니다. 7세 이하의 자녀가 있는 분들이 편히 쉬실 수 있도록 저희가 자녀분을 돌봐드리겠습니다. 저희는 세계에서 가장 아름다운 경치를 자랑하는 곳에 자리 잡고 있습니다. 모두에게 무료로 개방되는 Valley Point 리조트의 수정처럼 맑은 물과 함께 멋진 여름휴가를 보낼 수 있다는 것 잊지 마세요.

해설: 남자는 리조트를 홍보하고 있다. 초반에 매일 다양한 활동을 제공한다고 했으므로 '주 단위'로 프로그램이 바뀐다고 한 ①번이 남자의 말과 일치하지 않는다.

문항 16 ②

Script & Dictation

W: The Boston branch of Lancer Airline **is seeking ground crew members** with at least three years' experience. Anyone aged twenty eight and over with eligible experience and qualifications can **apply for this position.** If you can speak Spanish or Portuguese, you'll be more welcomed because the Boston branch has many Latin customers. But it's not **an essential skill.** If you are chosen for this job, you'll work three days per week. But the date and work time are flexible **depending on the flight schedules.** You'll be paid $5,000 per month. All meals during working days, major insurance, and accommodation in Boston will be provided. Applications will be accepted until December 26th. Thank you **in advance** for your interest in the position.

여: Lancer 항공사 Boston 지점에서 최소 3년 경력의 지상 근무자를 모집합니다. 적합한 경험과 자격을 갖춘 28세 이상이신 분들은 누구나 이 자리에 지원 가능합니다. Boston 지점에 라틴계 손님들이 많은 관계로 스페인어 또는 포르투갈어가 가능한 분을 더 우대하지만, 필수 요건은 아닙니다. 합격하시면 주 3일 근무입니다. 근무 날짜와 시간은 그러나 비행 일정에 따라 변동이 있을 수 있습니다. 급여는 월 5천 달러이며, 근무일 식사, 주요 보험, Boston 내 숙소가 제공될 것입니다. 지원서는 12월 26일까지 받습니다. 본 직무에 관한 여러분의 관심에 미리 감사의 말씀 드립니다.

해설: 광고 초반 여자는 경력이 최소 3년인 직원을 모집하고 있다고 했으므로 신입이 지원할 수 있다고 한 ②번이 일치하지 않는 내용이다.

문항 17 ③

Script & Dictation

W: Honey, what are you looking at? Is it a brochure?

M: It's about different **rental water purifiers.**

W: I heard they make it really **easy and convenient** to make hot water and ice.

M: Right. Do you want to get one?

W: I think Sean would like to have one. He always eats ice **after his workout.**

M: I think they're good for making coffee early in the morning.

W: Right, it would be good for you, too. How much do they cost?

M: Hmm... I think under $30 per month is suitable. Do we need a double filter?

W: That could be nice, but it increases the cost.

M: **Take a look at** the chart, then.

W: This one should be perfect for us.

여: 여보, 뭐 보고 있어요? 광고 책자인가요?

남: 임대 정수기들에 관한 거예요.

여: 온수랑 얼음 만들기가 정말 쉽고 편리하다고 들었어요.

남: 맞아요. 하나 할까요?

여: 하나 있으면 Sean이 좋아할 것 같아요. 운동 후 항상 얼음을 먹으니까.

남: 아침 일찍 커피 만들기도 좋을 것 같네요.

여: 그러게요, 당신에게도 좋겠네요. 임대료가 얼마예요?

남: 흠… 한 달에 30달러 아래인 것이 적당할 것 같은데요. 이중 필터가 필요할까요?

여: 있으면 좋겠지만, 그럼 비용이 더 들잖아요.

남: 그럼 표를 좀 봐요.

여: 우리한텐 이게 좋겠는데요.

해설: 온수 기능과 얼음 만들기 기능이 있으면서 한 달 임대료가 30달러 아래인 정수기는 ③번이다.

문항 18 ③

Script & Dictation

W: Jemin, let's have salad.

M: Oh, Mom. What's this?

W: **On the top of** the plate? They are raisins.

M: They look like pupae. I won't eat this, never, ever.

W: Honey, they're not pupae. They're raisins. They **have a chewy texture** and are very sweet.

M: Nope. I hate the shape and color. **Do I have to** eat this, Mom? I can be strong and healthy without this disgusting food.

W: Jemin, don't be so picky. If you eat these raisins, you may change your mind. I am sure **you will like them**.

M: Okay, Mom. I'll try.

여: 제민아, 샐러드 먹자.

남: 엄마, 이게 뭐예요?

여: 접시 제일 위에 있는 거 말이니? 건포도란다.

남: 번데기처럼 생겼잖아요. 절대 안 먹어요, 절대로요.

여: 아들아, 번데기가 아니라 건포도래도. 쫄깃하고 정말 달아.

남: 안 먹을래요. 모양이랑 색깔이 싫어요. 이거 꼭 먹어야 해요, 엄마? 이렇게 징그러운 음식 안 먹어도 튼튼하고 건강해질 수 있잖아요.

여: 제민아, 까탈 부리지 마. 건포도를 먹어보면 생각이 달라질 거다. 분명 좋아하게 될 거야.

남: 알겠어요, 엄마. 먹어볼게요.

해설: 건포도를 먹지 않으려는 아들과 아들이 편식하지 않도록 설득하는 엄마의 대화로, 한번 시도해 보라는 엄마의 제안에 수긍하는 모습을 보이는 ③번이 흐름 상 가장 적절한 응답이다.

문항 19 ②

Script & Dictation

[Cell phone rings.]

M: Are you ready to go to see the baseball game?

W: Hey, Young. It is only 2 o'clock. Didn't you say it starts at 6?

M: Yes, I did, but we have to get there early because we haven't bought tickets yet.

W: Why don't you use your **pre-reservation tickets**?

M: They're not available to book reservations on the same day as the game. **I should have booked them** yesterday. Sorry.

W: No problem. Then let's get tickets in advance, and before the game, let's look around the baseball shop.

M: That sounds nice. Do you think the **tickets will be sold out**?

W: Sure, nowadays baseball is really popular.

M: Yes, it seems everyone is going to the games these days. So, do you want to buy something?

W: I'd like to buy a summer jersey of the Bears. I'll get my favorite player's name **stitched on it**, too. Let's meet at Gate 3 at the station.

M: You mean at the station near the stadium?

W: No, I mean the station where we've always met before.

[휴대폰 벨 소리]

남: 야구 경기 보러 갈 준비 됐어?

여: 안녕, 영아. 아직 2시밖에 안 됐는데. 6시에 시작한다고 하지 않았니?

남: 응, 그런데 아직 표를 안 사서 우리 일찍 가야 해.

여: 사전 예약 표 사용하지 그래?

남: 경기 당일에는 예약을 못 하게 되어 있어. 어제 해야 했는데, 미안해.

여: 괜찮아. 그럼 표 미리 산 다음에 경기 시작 전에 야구용품 상점 둘러보자.

남: 좋은 생각이야. 표가 매진될까?

여: 당연하지. 요새 야구 정말 인기 많잖아.

남: 맞아. 요새는 야구 경기 안 가는 사람이 없는 거 같아. 그래, 뭐 살 거라도 있어?

여: Bears의 하계 셔츠 사고 싶어. 내가 제일 좋아하는 선수 이름도 새겨 넣어야지. 역 3번 출구에서 만나자.

남: 경기장 근처 역 말하는 거지?

여: 아니, 우리가 전에 항상 만났던 그 역 말이야.

해설: 어느 역에서 만나는 건지 확인하는 질문을 하고 있다. 실제로 만날 역에 대한 정보가 포함된 응답은 ②번이다.

문항 20 ④

Script & Dictation

M: Grace has a son, Anthony, and **is worried about** his health all the time. He's a senior in high school, and he is studying for the university entrance exam. She thinks that **he's obsessed with** his grades. She sees him studying for such a long time at his desk without any breaks. She never worries about his grades, but Anthony is **always dwelling on** his bad grades or failures. He looks so exhausted and stressed, too. Plus, his nose bleeds before breakfast. Grace thinks he needs to rest and take some dietary supplements. So she suggests he should **take a break** for a while. In this situation, what would Grace most likely say to Anthony?

* Grace: You need to take time off. <u>There's nothing more important than your health.</u>

남: Grace에게는 아들 Anthony가 있는데 그녀는 항상 아들의 건강을 걱정합니다. Anthony는 고등학교 졸업반이라 대학 입학시험을 위해 공부 중입니다. Grace는 아들이 성적에 집착한다고 생각합니다. Anthony는 쉬지도 않고 책상 앞에서 오랜 시간 공부하는 모습을 보입니다. Grace는 아들의 성적에 대해 고민해 본 적이 없지만, Anthony는 항상 성적이 안 좋거나 실패한 것에 대해 깊이 생각합니다. 너무 지치고 스트레스받은 것처럼 보이기도 하고요. 심지어 아침 먹기 전에 코피까지 흘립니다. Grace는 Anthony가 휴식을 취하고 영양제도 먹어야 한다고 생각합니다. 그래서 아들에게 좀 쉬어야 한다고 제안합니다. 이러한 상황에서 Grace가 Anthony에게 할 수 있는 말로 가장 적당한 것은 무엇일까요?

* Grace: 넌 좀 쉬어야 해. <u>건강보다 중요한 건 아무것도 없단다.</u>

해설: 여자는 아들이 공부에만 열중할 것이 아니라 쉬면서 건강도 챙겨야 한다고 생각하고 있다. 따라서 무엇보다도 건강이 중요하다고 말하며 쉴 것을 제안하는 ④번이 가장 적절한 말이다.

문항 21 ②
문항 22 ④

Script & Dictation

W: Typhoon Maemi was the strongest typhoon of 2003 and still stands as one of **the worst recorded typhoons** to hit the Korean peninsula. Though it developed slowly from a tropical atmospheric pressure to a typhoon, it became a destructive typhoon near Sakishima Islands with 910 hectopascals of pressure at its center, with maximum wind speed hitting 55m/s. When it passed through Okinawa, **wind speeds were recorded at** 74.1m/s. After that, it headed north and passed through Jeju Island on the 12th of September, and at 8:30 p.m. on the same day it arrived in Goseong-gun, Gyeongsangnam-do and **caused devastating damage**. When it landed on the Korean peninsula, its central pressure and maximum wind speed had decreased a little to 950 hectopascals and 40m/s, but it was still one of the strongest typhoons to ever hit Korea. Typhoon Maemi was downgraded to an extra-tropical cyclone near Hokkaido on the 14th of September and then disappeared. After Typhoon Maemi occurred, the name 'Maemi' has **no longer been used** for typhoons because of the extensive damage it caused. Instead, 'Mujigae' **has taken its place**.

여: 태풍 매미는 2003년에 발생한 가장 강력한 태풍이었으며, 한반도를 강타한 최악의 태풍 중 하나로 여전히 기록되고 있습니다. 열대성 저기압에서 태풍으로 발달하는 속도가 느렸음에도 사키시마 제도 부근에서는 중심 기압 910 헥토파스칼에 최대 풍속은 초속 55미터에 달하는 파괴적인

태풍이 되었습니다. 오키나와를 통과할 때의 풍속은 초속 74.1미터를 기록하였습니다. 그 후 매미는 북상하여 9월 12일 제주도를 통과하였고, 같은 날 밤 8시 30분에 경상남도 고성군에 상륙, 엄청난 피해를 줬습니다. 한반도에 상륙했을 때 매미의 중심 기압과 최대 풍속은 각각 950헥토파스칼과 초속 40미터로 그 위력이 약간 감소했음에도 여전히 한국을 강타한 가장 강력한 태풍 중 하나였습니다. 태풍 매미는 9월 14일 홋카이도 부근에서 온대저기압으로 세력이 약화되어 소멸했습니다. 태풍 매미 발생 후, 그것이 일으킨 피해가 막대했기 때문에 '매미'는 태풍 이름으로 더는 사용되지 않고 있으며, '무지개'라는 이름을 대신 사용하게 됐습니다.

해설: 21. 여자는 초반부에 태풍 매미가 열대성 저기압에서 태풍으로 천천히 발달하였음에도 엄청난 위력의 태풍이 되었다고 설명했으므로 ②번이 정답이다. **22.** 피해를 많이 준 태풍이었기에 '매미'라는 이름은 더는 사용하지 않고 '무지개'라는 이름으로 대체했다고 언급되었으므로 ④번이 정답이다.

수능 6일 전 대학수학능력평가 대비 영어영역 듣기(B형)

1	⑤	2	②	3	④	4	④	5	④
6	①	7	④	8	①	9	②	10	②
11	①	12	④	13	⑤	14	②	15	③
16	③	17	⑤	18	⑤	19	①	20	①
21	④	22	③						

문항 1 ⑤

Script & Dictation

M: Excuse me. May I **take pictures** in this gallery?

W: No, taking photos **is not allowed**.

M: What about if I **turn off** the flash?

W: <u>No exceptions. Any photos are strictly prohibited.</u>

남: 실례합니다. 이 미술관에서 사진 찍어도 될까요?

여: 안 됩니다. 사진 촬영 불가입니다.

남: 플래시를 꺼도 안 될까요?

여: <u>예외 사항은 없습니다. 사진은 엄격히 금지하고 있습니다.</u>

해설: 사진 촬영이 안 된다는 말에 남자가 플래시를 끄는 조건으로도 안 되는지 질문한 상황이다. 이에 예외는 없다고 대답하는 것이 가장 적절한 응답이다.

문항 2 ②

Script & Dictation

W: Mr. Cruise, can I **sign up for** your spring vacation class?

M: Oh, it's already full.

W: But I really need to take your class **for graduation**. Could you increase the number of students?

M: <u>I'm sorry, but I don't have the authority to do that.</u>

여: Cruise 선생님, 선생님이 하시는 봄방학 수업에 등록할 수 있을까요?

남: 이미 다 찼는데.

여: 하지만 졸업하려면 선생님 수업을 꼭 들어야 하는데요. 수강 인원 늘려주시면 안 될까요?

남: <u>미안하지만 나한테 그렇게 할 수 있는 권한이 없구나.</u>

해설: 학생이 선생에게 수업을 들을 수 있는 학생 정원 수를 늘려줄 수 없는지 물어보고 있다. 따라서 본인이 그것을 해줄 수 있는지를 알려주는 대답인 ②번이 정답이다.

문항 3 ④

Script & Dictation

M: Irene, what happened? Didn't you say that you would be in San Diego this week?

W: I canceled my holidays **due to some new research**.

M: That's too bad. I know how much you were **looking forward to the trip**.

W: <u>That's okay. I can go soon after I finish this task.</u>

남: Irene, 어떻게 된 거예요? 이번 주에 샌디에이고 간다고 하지 않았어요?

여: 새 연구 때문에 휴가를 취소했어요.

남: 너무 안타깝네요. 여행 정말 고대하고 있었잖아요.

여: 괜찮아요. 이번 작업 끝나면 곧 갈 수 있어요.

해설: 업무 때문에 휴가를 취소한 여자에게 남자가 안타까움을 표현하고 있다. 이에 대한 가장 적절한 응답은 다음에 갈 수 있으니 괜찮다고 하는 ④번이 되겠다.

문항 4 ④

Script & Dictation

M: What are you doing for your health? Are you **taking nutritional supplements** every day? What about hiking? Did you know hiking is very **beneficial for your health**? Some think hiking is just walking around in nature. That's not wrong, but hiking is great for your health. The more you walk, **the healthier you will become**. Additionally, hiking is an outdoor activity in natural environments, often in mountainous or other scenic terrain. **When going hiking**, you can put all your focus on what you're doing: your stride, your arms swinging, your breath, the sounds of an awakening neighborhood, or the sounds of bushes, wind, and birds.

남: 여러분은 건강을 위해 무엇을 하고 계시나요? 매일 영양제를 드시나요? 하이킹도 하시나요? 하이킹이 건강에 매우 유익하다는 거 알고 계셨나요? 어떤 분들은 하이킹이 단순히 자연 속을 걸어 다니는 거로 생각하기도 하죠. 틀린 말은 아니지만 하이킹은 건강에 무척 좋습니다. 더 많이 걸을수록 더 건강해질 거예요. 덧붙여 하이킹은 주로 산악 지형 또는 경관이 빼어난 지형과 같은 자연환경에서 하는 야외 활동입니다. 하이킹을 가게 되면 여러분이 하는 활동에 전적으로 집중할

수 있게 됩니다. 여러분의 발걸음, 팔의 흔들림, 호흡, 주변이 잠에서 깨어나는 소리, 또는 덤불과 바람, 새 소리 같은 것들 말이죠.

해설: 남자는 건강을 위해 할 수 있는 활동 중에서 하이킹을 소개하고 있다.

문항 5 ④

Script & Dictation

M: My daughter, Kathy, has started to learn English, so I want some interesting books in English.

W: Well, I think she **may be learning phonics** now.

M: Yes. She is just **singing and listening to** CDs and repeating them.

W: That is a good way! I think there's no need to buy English books yet. Just have fun with her **while listening to CDs** and following them.

M: But, I think reading books is important, too.

W: All babies learn their own language by listening to and speaking with their parents and babysitters. Reading is the next step.

남: 제 딸 Kathy가 영어를 배우기 시작해서 영어로 된 재미있는 책들이 있었으면 해요.

여: 지금 파닉스 배우는 중일 것 같은데요.

남: 맞아요. 노래하고, CD 듣는 걸 반복하고 있어요.

여: 좋은 방법이에요! 아직은 영어책 살 필요가 없을 것 같네요. 그냥 따님과 함께 즐겁게 CD 들으며 따라 해 보세요.

남: 하지만 책 읽는 것도 중요하다고 생각하는데요.

여: 아기들은 모두 부모 그리고 아기 돌보미가 하는 말을 듣고, 그들과 함께 말하는 것을 통해 언어를 배우죠. 읽는 건 그다음 단계랍니다.

해설: 영어를 학습할 때 읽는 것이 중요하지 않으냐는 남자의 의견에 여자는 듣고, 말하는 학습이 선행되어야 한다고 설명하고 있다. 따라서 정답은 ④번이다.

문항 6 ①

Script & Dictation

M: I'm Dwayne Johnson. As you know, we do an annual survey on the 100 most **influential people** in this city. The person **on top of this list** has always been a successful politician or entrepreneur. However, this year's person on top was a surprise to many. Students have selected Brett Ratner, an instructor talking about vision and the future. He has **offered free instruction** for college students about a positive survival strategy for these difficult times. Opportunities for employment are getting scarcer. Brett said that in this economic recession, the youth are in a plight to find jobs, to get married, and to have children. He's been preparing some special strategies for these people. Now, it's time to meet this person who **gives the youth hope** for a bright future.

남: 저는 Dwayne Johnson입니다. 여러분도 아시다시피, 매년 이 도시에서 가장 영향력 있는 인물 100인에 관한 설문조사가 진행되죠. 설문에서 1위를 차지하는 인물은 언제나 성공한 정치인이거나 사업가였습니다. 그러나 올해 1위를 차지한 분은 많은 이들을 놀라게 했는데요. 학생들은 비전과 미래에 관해 이야기하는 Brett Ratner 강사님을 1위로 꼽았습니다. Brett Ratner 강사님은 대학생들을 대상으로 이 힘든 시기 속 긍정적인 생존 전략에 관해 무료 강연을 해오고 있습니다. 취업의 기회는 점점 드물어지고 있죠. Brett 강사님은 이처럼 경제가 침체된 상황에서 젊은이들이 직업을 구하고, 결혼하고, 자녀를 낳는 데 있어 어려움을 겪고 있다고 말했습니다. Brett 강사님은 이러한 이들을 위해 특별한 전략을 준비했는데요. 젊은이들에게 밝은 미래에 대한 희망을 제시하는 그분을 지금 만나보시죠.

해설: 중반부까지는 영향력 있는 인물 설문조사에서 1위를 차지한 강사에 관해 이야기하고 있는 것처럼 보이나 마지막에 이제 그 인물을 만나볼 시간이라고 말한 것으로 보아, 강연이 있기 전 강연자가 누구인지 소개하는 상황임을 알 수 있다.

문항 7 ④

Script & Dictation

M: Hi, Linda. What's up?

W: I'm **reading an article** about a young lady who yelled at an old woman on the subway.

M: I heard that story, too. They were arguing over a subway seat.

W: That's right. The young lady sat in a senior's seat. And the old woman scolded her about that.

M: So she yelled at **a senior citizen**?

W: Yes. That happens frequently on the subway.

M: Why don't they simply increase the number of senior's seats on the subway?

W: I don't think that should be a solution. **That kind of separation** between the young and senior citizens could make the situation worse.

M: You're right. Finding a fundamental **way to resolve the conflict** between the young and the old is more critical than any other physical measures in order to make the subway experience more pleasant for all of us.

W: You can say that again.

남: 안녕, Linda. 별일 없니?

여: 지하철에서 젊은 아가씨가 나이 드신 여성분께 소리를 질렀다는 기사 읽고 있어.

남: 나도 그 얘기 들었어. 지하철 자리 때문에 다투고 있었다는데.

여: 맞아. 젊은 아가씨가 노약자석에 앉아 있었대. 그래서 나이 드신 여자분이 혼을 냈고.

남: 그것 때문에 어르신에게 소리를 질렀다고?

여: 응. 지하철에서 그런 일 자주 일어나잖아.

남: 그냥 지하철 노약자석을 늘리면 안 되나?

여: 그게 해결책이어서는 안 된다고 생각해. 그런 식으로 젊은 사람들과 어르신들을 갈라놓으면 상황이 더 악화될 수 있어.

남: 네 말이 맞다. 우리가 모두 쾌적하게 지하철을 타기 위해서는 신구 세대 간 갈등을 해결할 근본적인 방법을 찾는 것이 다른 어떤 물리적 조치보다 더 중요하겠구나.

여: 정말 그래.

해설: 남자와 여자는 대화 후반부에 물리적인 해결 방법보다는 신세대와 구세대 간 갈등을 해결하는 근본적인 방법을 찾는 것이 더 중요하다는데 서로 동의하고 있다. 따라서 정답은 ④번이다.

문항 8 ①

Script & Dictation

M: Hi, Sally. I'm so sorry I'm late. The **traffic was too heavy**.

W: You know it's rush hour. You should have hurried.

M: You're right. I'm sorry. How much time is left?

W: About five minutes. Let's go inside. The train is already here.

M: Wait! Can I go buy some snacks? I haven't eaten anything yet. It **won't take too long**.

W: There's **a snack bar on board**. You can get snacks there.

M: Sounds great. **By the way**, your bag looks very heavy. What did you pack?

W: Some books and music to help relax on the train.

M: You seem to know how to enjoy traveling. Did you get the tickets?

W: Sure, I have them in my wallet. We have to go to Gate 1. I think we should hurry.

남: 안녕, Sally. 늦어서 정말 미안해. 길이 너무 막혔어.

여: 혼잡한 시간대인 거 알면 서둘렀어야지.

남: 네 말이 맞아. 미안해. 시간 얼마나 남았어?

여: 5분 정도. 안으로 들어가자. 기차 이미 여기 와 있어.

남: 잠깐만! 나 간식 좀 사도 돼? 아직 아무것도 안 먹었거든. 오래 안 걸릴 거야.

여: 기차 안에도 간이식당 있어. 거기서 간식 사면 돼.

남: 좋은 생각이야. 그런데 네 가방 많이 무거워 보인다. 뭘 싼 거니?

여: 기차에서 쉴 때 도움이 될 책이랑 음악.

남: 여행을 즐길 줄 아는 것 같다. 표는 샀어?

여: 물론이지, 지갑 안에 있어. 1번 게이트로 가야 해. 서두르자.

해설: 핵심 단어는 역시 'train'이다. 또한 출발 시각까지 5분밖에 안 남아 게이트로 서둘러 가야 한다고 하는 것으로 보아 두 사람이 지금 기차역에 있음을 알 수 있다.

문항 9 ②

Script & Dictation

M: Oh, it's Jun and Minseo in the photo. Where have you and Jun been today?

W: We saw the musical *Cloud Candy*. It's a hit among the children of Jun's age.

M: Are those the main characters behind Jun and Minseo?

W: Yes, they are. They are two **cats wearing raincoats**. When they eat cloud candy, they can fly. So the siblings—the two cats—fly around their town and help people in need.

M: That sounds interesting. What are Jun and Minseo eating, by the way?

W: After the musical, the actors and actresses came down from the stage and **distributed cloud candy** to the children in attendance.

M: But, candy is not good for Jun's teeth.

W: Right. So I said **with a serious face**, "Jun, if you fly away, I will be so sad. And it's going to be very difficult to find you once you are gone!"

M: **You're such a liar**.

W: So, Jun ate a small piece of bagel.

남: 준과 민서 사진이군요. 오늘 준이랑 어디 갔다 온 거예요?

여: '구름 사탕'이라는 뮤지컬 봤어요. 준 또래 아이들에게 인기가 많은 뮤지컬이죠.

남: 준이랑 민서 뒤에 있는 게 주인공들이에요?

여: 맞아요. 우비를 입은 고양이가 둘이죠. 구름 사탕을 먹으면 하늘을 날아요. 그래서 이 두 형제 고양이는 마을을 날아다니며 어려움에 처한 이들을 도와줘요.

남: 재밌겠는데요. 그나저나 아이들이 먹고 있는 게 뭐예요?

여: 뮤지컬이 끝나고 배우들이 무대에서 내려와 관람 온 아이들에게 구름 사탕을 나눠줬어요.

남: 그렇지만 사탕은 준의 치아에 안 좋잖아요.

여: 맞아요. 그래서 제가 심각한 얼굴로 "준이가 날아가 버리면 엄마는 정말 슬플 거야. 준이가 없어지고 나면 찾기도 엄청나게 힘들 테고!"라고 했죠.

남: 이런 거짓말쟁이.

여: 그래서 준이는 베이글 조각만 조금 먹은 거예요.

해설: 뮤지컬의 주인공들은 두 고양이 형제이다. 따라서 개가 그려진 ②번이 정답이다.

문항 10 ②

Script & Dictation

W: I can't see anything **on my mobile phone screen**.

M: You mean, nothing is coming on the screen?

W: Nothing at all. I'll have to send it to the service center.

M: How long have you been using it?

W: Almost three years.

M: Quite a long time. I think **it's time to change it** for a new one.

W: Well, sometimes, my telecommunication firm calls me to change my phone.

M: **Let me pick** a suitable one for you. These days, smart appliances are in.

W: Now that you mention it, let's go phone shopping. **I don't know anything** about smart phones. I should see what's available.

여: 내 휴대폰 화면에 아무것도 안 보여.

남: 화면에 아무것도 안 뜬다는 거야?

여: 전혀 아무것도. 서비스 센터에 보내야겠어.

남: 그 휴대폰 쓴지 얼마나 됐어?

여: 거의 3년.

남: 꽤 오래 썼구나. 그럼 새 걸로 바꿀 때도 된 것 같은데.

여: 이동통신사에서 바꾸라고 전화 올 때도 있어.

남: 내가 적합한 걸로 하나 골라줄게. 요즘은 스마트 장비가 유행이니까.

여: 말 나온 김에 그럼 휴대폰 사러 같이 가자. 스마트폰에 대해서는 아무것도 몰라서. 어떤 걸 쓰면 좋을지 봐야겠어.

해설: 여자의 오래된 휴대폰이 고장 나자 남자는 새 휴대폰 고르는 걸 도와주겠다고 제안했다. 그러자 여자는 바로 휴대폰을 보러 가자고 했으므로 ②번이 정답이다.

문항 11 ①

Script & Dictation

W: Oh, **what a cute puppy**! Jake, where did you get it?

M: My friend, Jihye, is on vacation. She went to Guam for ten days.

W: So you are taking care of her dog during her vacation?

M: Yes. Is it okay, Mom?

W: Well... You **should have asked me in advance**.

M: Sorry. It's really cute, so I had no time to think about anything else.

W: Yeah, it's really sweet, but I'm worried about your grandmother. She doesn't like having pets inside the house.

M: **That's the point**. I want to ask you to convince Granny.

W: Oh, Jake, that could be hard.

M: Mom, please! Granny listens to you even more than to me. I'll do the dishes and **mow the lawn** the whole ten days.

W: That's a good deal.

여: 강아지 참 귀엽구나! 어디서 난 거니, Jake?

남: 제 친구 지혜가 휴가로 열흘 동안 괌에 갔어요.

여: 그래서 휴가 동안 네가 대신 봐주기로 한 거야?

남: 네. 그래도 돼요, 엄마?

여: 글쎄다. 미리 물어봤어야지.

남: 죄송해요. 정말 귀여워서 다른 생각할 시간이 없었어요.

여: 그래, 정말 예쁘긴 하다만 할머니 때문에 걱정이구나. 집안에 애완동물 들이는 걸 안 좋아하시잖니.

남: 그거 때문에 그러는데요. 엄마가 할머니 좀 설득시켜 주세요.

여: 어려울 거야, Jake.

남: 부탁이에요, 엄마! 할머니는 저보다는 엄마 말씀을 더 잘 들어주시잖아요. 열흘 동안 제가 설거지도 하고 잔디도 깎을게요.

여: 그거 괜찮네.

해설: 아들이 엄마에게 열흘 동안 친구의 개를 돌볼 수 있도록 집 안에서 애완동물 키우는 걸 싫어하시는 할머니에게 잘 말씀 드려달라고 부탁하고 있다.

문항 12 ④

Script & Dictation

M: Hi, Catherine. Where is everyone? Is the class canceled?

W: No. Class will begin at 11:30 a.m. today.

M: No way! I didn't know that. **How come** you and everyone else knew about it except me?

W: I guess you didn't attend the last class. The professor said that since he would be late today because of his seminar, he would change the class time.

M: I **definitely attended** the last class, but I didn't hear that. When did he say that?

W: He said it at the beginning of class.

M: That's why I didn't hear him say it. I arrived late last time **because I overslept**. Well, what made you come here so early?

W: I have to finish my report that's due today. **I have been working on it** here for almost three hours.

남: 안녕, Catherine. 다들 어디 있어? 오늘 강의 취소된 거야?

여: 아니. 오늘 강의는 오전 11시 30분 시작이야.

남: 그럴 리가! 나 몰랐는데. 어떻게 나 빼고 다 알고 있는 거지?

여: 지난 시간에 결석해서 그런 거 아니야? 교수님께서 세미나 때문에 오늘 늦으실 거라 강의 시간 변경한다고 하셨어.

남: 나 지난 시간에 강의 들어왔단 말이야. 그런 얘기 들은 적이 없는데. 언제 말씀하신 거야?

여: 강의 시작하실 때.

남: 그래서 못 들었구나. 늦잠 자서 지난 시간에 지각했거든. 그런데 넌 여기 왜 일찍 온 거야?

여: 마감이 오늘인 보고서 끝내야 해서. 여기서 거의 3시간째 작업하고 있었어.

해설: 남자는 지난 강의 때 지각을 했기 때문에 강의 초반 교수가 이번 주 강의 시간을 늦추겠다고 말한 것을 듣지 못해 원래 강의 시간대로 일찍 도착한 상황이다.

문항 13 ⑤

Script & Dictation

M: Hyerin, did you finish your homework? You should **finish it by Thursday**.

W: I've already finished and submitted it this morning. I really want to have A this term.

M: Then you can go to the party tonight?

W: What party? You mean Aunt Jane's **baby shower**?

M: Yes, your mom and I prepared some gorgeous baby products. Don't you want to check them out?

W: **I'm eager to see them** and want to hug the little prince, but I'm afraid I can't go.

M: What's wrong? Do you want to study more to try to get the scholarship this term?

W: No, Dad. I should attend **the club meeting** to organize a festival in the fall. I couldn't make it for last week, so the members are mad at me.

M: Oh, that's not a good situation. Were you absent from the meeting **because of homework**?

W: Yes, that's right. I should go there tonight to apologize and to contribute my ideas.

M: I see. I hope you're not in trouble, honey.

남: 혜린아, 숙제 끝냈어? 목요일까지 끝내야 하잖니.

여: 이미 끝내서 오늘 아침에 제출했어요. 이번 학기엔 꼭 A 받고 싶어요.

남: 그러면 오늘 밤에 파티 갈 수 있니?

여: 무슨 파티요? Jane 이모의 출산 축하 파티요?

남: 그래, 엄마랑 내가 멋진 아기용품을 준비했단다. 보고 싶지 않니?

여: 아기용품도 정말 보고 싶고, 아기 왕자님도 안아보고 싶지만 그럴 수가 없어요.

남: 무슨 일 있니? 이번 학기 장학금을 위해 더 공부하고 싶은 거니?

여: 아니요, 아빠. 전 가을에 있을 축제 준비 때문에 동아리 모임에 가야 해요. 지난주에 못 가서 동아리원들이 제게 화나 있어요.

남: 좋은 상황이 아니구나. 숙제하느라 모임에 안 갔던 거야?

여: 네, 맞아요. 오늘 저녁에 가서 동아리원들에게 사과하고 의견을 나눠봐야 겠어요.

남: 알겠다. 문제가 없었으면 좋겠구나.

해설: 여자는 숙제는 다 했지만 숙제하느라 가지 못했던 동아리 모임에 참석해야 하기 때문에 출산 축하 파티에 가지 못하는 상황이다.

문항 14 ②

Script & Dictation

W: Okay, thank you for your explanation. So, I have **decided to register** for this program. How much is the monthly fee?

M: It costs $50 a month.

W: That's not so cheap. It's just thirty minutes a day.

M: It **could be longer** if you add **warm-up and cooling-down** times.

W: You're right, but is there any discount?

M: If you pay for three months, we offer 10% off the total fee for the class.

W: That's good. Anything else?

M: I recommend that course. We have 30% off for six months and 50% off for a year.

W: That's good. Ah, do **I have to pay** for using the parking lot?

M: Yes, you do. But only if you stay over two hours. And then it's only $2 a day.

W: Okay, I don't think I'll need it then. I'll pay the three-month fee as you suggested.

M: Okay. Please **fill in this form** first.

여: 알겠습니다. 설명해 주셔서 감사합니다. 이 프로그램에 등록할게요. 한 달 수강료가 얼마인가요?

남: 한 달에 50달러입니다.

여: 그렇게 싸진 않네요. 하루에 딱 30분인데.

남: 준비 운동과 마무리 운동 시간을 더하면 더 길어지죠.

여: 그렇긴 하네요. 그래도 할인 안 되나요?

남: 3개월 치를 결제하시면 총 수강료에서 10% 할인해 드립니다.

여: 좋네요. 다른 건 없나요?

남: 그 과정 추천해 드려요. 6개월 등록하시면 30%, 1년 등록하시면 50% 할인해 드립니다.

여: 괜찮네요. 아, 주차장 이용 요금도 내야 하나요?

남: 그렇습니다. 하지만 2시간 이상 주차하실 때만 해당합니다. 그리고 하루에 2달러밖에 안 해요.

여: 알겠습니다. 저에겐 필요 없는 것 같네요. 말씀하셨던 3개월 수강료 낼게요.

남: 알겠습니다. 이 양식부터 작성해 주세요.

해설: 한 달 수강료가 50달러인 프로그램의 3개월 치 수강료를 내는 상황이다. 3개월 등록 시 총 수강료에서 10% 할인된다고 했으므로 여자는 150달러에서 15달러를 뺀 135달러를 내야 한다.

문항 15 ③

Script & Dictation

M: I'm here to announce a forest-experience program for young children in Mount Dorking. **The objective of** the program is to allow kids, by appealing to their five senses, **to commune with** nature. The program is open to families with children younger than seven years. The program runs from July 15th to August 25th, from 10 a.m. to 4 p.m. You can register **by phone or in person** when using the Mount Dorking facilities. Please note that the program schedule might change or be canceled, **depending on weather conditions**. If you have any questions, please call our toll-free number: 094-973-1853.

남: 어린아이들을 위한 Dorking 산의 숲 체험 프로그램에 관해 알려드리고자 이 자리에 나왔습니다. 프로그램의 목적은 아이들이 오감을 통해 자연과 교감하게 하는 것에 있습니다. 프로그램은 7세 이하의 어린이가 있는 가족들에게 개방되며, 7월 15일부터 8월 25일까지, 오전 10시에서 오후 4시 사이에 운영됩니다. 전화로, 또는 Dorking 산 시설물을 이용하실 때 직접 등록하실 수 있습니다. 프로그램 일정은 기상 상태에 따라 변경 또는 취소될 수 있다는 점 유의하시기 바랍니다. 궁금하신 점은 무료 전화 094-973-1853으로 문의해 주세요.

해설: 숲 체험 프로그램은 7세 이하의 자녀가 있는 가족이 이용할 수 있다고 했으므로 '7세 이상'이라고 한 ③번이 내용과 일치하지 않는다.

문항 16 ③

Script & Dictation

W: The Republic of Benin is one of the African countries located on the Gulf of Guinea bordered by Nigeria.

It became a protectorate in 1851. **French colonialists** constructed the Dahomey colony in Benin, and then Dahomey was incorporated into West Africa in 1904. After it **became independent** as the Republic of Dahomey in 1960, the country changed its name to the Republic of Benin in 1975. Benin still uses French **as an official language**, though it also has its own local language. The Beninese economy has maintained **an annual growth rate** of about four percent each year, but its GDP is only around $1,500, so it is still one of the poorest countries in the world.

여: 베냉공화국은 아프리카 국가 중 하나로 기니만에 자리 잡고 있으며, 나이지리아와 접해있다. 1851년 피보호국이 되었다. 프랑스 식민주의자들이 베냉에 다호메이 식민지를 건설하였으며, 그 후 1904년 다호메이는 서아프리카에 편입되었다. 1960년 다호메이 공화국으로 독립한 이후, 1975년 국가명을 베냉공화국으로 바꿨다. 토착어가 있음에도 베냉은 여전히 불어를 공용어로 사용하고 있다. 베냉의 경제는 매년 약 4%의 연간 성장률을 유지하고 있으나, GDP는 약 1,500달러에 불과해 여전히 세계에서 가장 가난한 국가 중 하나이다.

해설: 토착어가 있음에도 여전히 프랑스어를 국가 공용어로 사용하고 있다고 했으므로 ③번이 정답이다.

문항 17 ⑤

Script & Dictation

M: Hello, ma'am. How can I help you?

W: I'm looking for an apartment near here. I don't know much about this area.

M: Okay, I can help you. Here, Main is **great to live on**. How many people will be living in the apartment?

W: Four: my husband and I and our two daughters. So, we'd like two or three rooms.

M: And do you have **any preferences about floors**?

W: Not too high, not too low, I think the 10th through 20th would be nice.

M: What about the 7th or 9th floor?

W: Not too bad. Do you have anything good?

M: Yeah, you have three choices. **How much rent** are you looking to pay?

W: Oh, under $400 per month would be okay.

M: Then we have one apartment that's **right for you**. Let's go see it.

남: 안녕하세요, 손님. 무엇을 도와드릴까요?

여: 이 근처 아파트를 좀 보려고요. 이 지역은 제가 잘 몰라서요.

남: 그러시군요, 제가 도와드리겠습니다. 여기, Main 쪽이 참 살기 좋죠. 가족 몇 분이 사실 건가요?

여: 남편과 저, 딸 둘 이렇게 네 명이요. 그래서 방 두세 개짜리 아파트를 희망합니다.

남: 선호하시는 층도 있나요?

여: 너무 높지도, 낮지도 않았으면 해요. 10층에서 20층 사이가 괜찮을 거 같은데요.

남: 7층이나 9층은 어떠세요?

여: 나쁘진 않아요. 괜찮은 집 있나요?

남: 네, 세 군데가 있네요. 집세는 얼마 정도로 생각하고 있으신 지요?

여: 한 달에 400달러 아래면 좋을 것 같아요.

남: 그럼 손님께 맞는 아파트가 하나 있습니다. 가서 한번 보시죠.

해설: 방이 두세 개이면서 7층에서 20층 사이에 있는 집세 400달러 이하의 아파트는 ⑤번이다.

문항 18 ⑤

Script & Dictation

W: Well, I'm **pretty impressed**. What made you start making these?

M: Several years ago, my son, Rubin, was in an accident and lost his legs. I've made all the renovations by myself so my son could move around more easily in the house.

W: I think it **must have required** a lot of skills. How did you learn them?

M: I went to a school to learn cabinetmaking and electrical wiring. My wife, Jihyun, joined me there later to learn plumbing.

W: What kinds of changes did you make in your house?

M: We widened the entrance hall and made a big bathroom for my son. We wanted him to **feel comfortable and independent** in our house.

W: So what are you working on now?

M: My son enjoys making furniture, so we're changing the garage into a workshop.

여: 음, 정말 인상적이군요. 이런 걸 만들게 되신 계기가 무엇인가요?

남: 몇 해 전에 제 아들 Rubin이 사고로 다리를 잃었어요. 아들이 집 안에서 더 쉽게 움직일 수 있도록 혼자서 모든 걸 개조했습니다.

여: 많은 기술이 필요했을 것 같은데요, 어떻게 배우셨나요?

남: 가구 제작과 배선을 배울 수 있는 학교에 들어갔습니다. 나중엔 제 아내 지현도 그곳에서 저와 함께 배관을 배웠고요.

여: 집에 어떤 변화를 주셨나요?

남: 아들을 위해 현관 로비를 넓히고 큰 욕실을 지었어요. 아들이 집에서 편안함을 느끼고 독립적일 수 있기를 바랐죠.

여: 그럼 지금은 어떤 작업 중이세요?

남: 아들이 가구 만드는 걸 좋아해서 차고를 작업장으로 바꾸고 있어요.

해설: 여자는 사고로 다리를 잃은 아들의 편의를 위해 직접 건축 관련 기술을 배워 집을 개조한 남자와 이야기하고 있다. 따라서 현재는 어떤 작업을 하고 있는지에 대한 적절한 응답은 집과 관련하여 어떤 건축 일을 하고 있는지에 대해 언급하는 ⑤번이 되겠다.

문항 19 ①

Script & Dictation

M: Hi, Dawon. What brought you here?

W: Mr. Kim, here's my English speaking contest **script you assigned**. Thank you again for extending the deadline for me.

M: Don't mention it. You were in hospital then. I always think health comes before anything else. How are you now?

W: I feel much better. Thanks for asking. And I'm more confident about my script now than I was the last time.

M: What do you mean?

W: For this task, I didn't need to use the **automatic translation feature** on my computer. I could just write what I wanted to say.

M: I know your English has improved a lot.

W: This is all thanks to you. I have **gained a lot of confidence** in English.

M: It's **so sweet of you** to say so.

W: But, I may have made some mistakes in this script, I think.

M: Don't worry. I will work on it and correct any mistakes.

남: 안녕, 다원아. 여긴 어쩐 일이니?

여: 김 선생님, 저한테 내주신 영어 말하기 대회 대본 여기 있습니다. 마감 기한을 늦춰주셔서 다시 한 번 감사해요.

남: 당연하지. 너 병원에 있었잖니. 난 항상 건강보다 중요한 것은 없다고 생각해. 지금은 어떠니?

여: 훨씬 좋아요. 물어봐 주셔서 감사합니다. 그리고 지난번보다 제 대본에 더 자신 있고요.

남: 그게 무슨 얘기야?

여: 이번에 작업하면서 컴퓨터의 자동 번역 기능을 쓸 필요가 없었어요. 하고 싶은 말을 그냥 바로 쓸 수 있었거든요.

남: 네 영어 실력이 많이 향상된 거 알고 있어.

여: 다 선생님 덕분입니다. 영어에 자신감이 많이 붙었어요.

남: 그렇게 말해주니 고맙구나.

여: 하지만 대본에 실수가 있을지도 몰라요.

남: 걱정하지 마. 선생님이 보고 실수를 바로 잡아줄게.

해설: 학생이 선생에게 직접 작성한 영어 말하기 대본을 제출하고 있다. 학생은 영어에 대한 자신감이 생겼지만, 대화 마지막에 대본에 실수가 있을지도 모른다고 언급했으므로 그 부분은 자신이 봐주겠다고 하는 것이 선생이 할 수 있는 가장 적절한 응답이다.

문항 20 ①

Script & Dictation

W: Juhee visits her cousin Kenny's home. While she's talking to him, she sees an old digital camera on the floor and a new one on his desk. Kenny tells her he needs a lighter **camera with a larger memory** to handle more photography for his job. He says he bought the brand-new digital camera last week, and that he's going to **dump the old one** tomorrow. Juhee thinks the old one still works well. And she remembers that her brother John needs a digital camera **for his latest survey**. She thinks throwing the old camera away is wasteful, and she wants to **send it to John**. In this situation, what would Juhee most likely say to Kenny?

* Juhee: <u>Can I have the old one for John?</u>

여: 주희는 사촌 Kenny의 집을 방문 중이다. Kenny와 이야기하는 중에 주희는 오래된 디지털카메라는 바닥에, 새것은 책상에 있는 걸 보게 된다. Kenny는 직업상 더 가볍고, 더 많이 찍을 수 있는 메모리 용량이 더 큰 카메라가 필요하다고 얘기한다. 그래서 지난주에 새 디지털카메라를 샀고, 오래된 것은 내일 버릴 거라고 한다. 주희가 보기에 오래된 카메라도 여전히 잘 작동되는 것 같다. 또 남동생 John이 최근 조사를 하는데 디지털카메라가 있어야 한다는 것이 생각난다. 주희는 오래된 카메라를 버리는 건 낭비라고 생각하고 그것을 John에게 보내고 싶어한다. 이러한 상황에서 주희는 Kenny에게 뭐라고 말할 것 같은가?

* 주희: <u>오래된 건 John에게 주게 내가 가져도 될까?</u>

해설: 이젠 Kenny에게 쓸모가 없어진 오래된 카메라를 주희는 동생 John에게 주고 싶어하는 상황이므로 그래도 될지 허락을 구하는 것이 가장 적절한 말이 되겠다.

문항 21 ④
문항 22 ③

Script & Dictation

M: Sepaktakraw is one of the most popular sports in Southeast Asia. Sepaktakraw is **a compound word** combining Sepak from Bahasa Malaysia and Takraw from Thai, and it means 'kick the ball with the foot.' It is a kind of kick volleyball that is native to the Malay-Thai peninsula. Sepaktakraw differs from volleyball in its use of a rattan ball. It is made of synthetic fiber or soft durable material **for the purpose of** softening the impact when players touch the ball. Three players are **on each team**. The players are allowed to touch the ball only with their knees, feet, chests, and heads. Any team that **lets the ball touch the ground** in their court gives one point to the opponent. When a team reaches 15 points, it wins a 'set'. A match is won when a team wins three sets. The net is 1.55 meters high, so martial-arts-like kicks are frequently observed to **send the ball into** the opponent's court. These spectacular actions have helped make this sport popular around the world. Now, more than 120 countries worldwide enjoy Sepaktakraw.

남: 세팍타크로는 동남아시아에서 가장 인기 있는 운동 경기 중 하나입니다. 세팍타크로(Sepaktakraw)란 말레이시아어 '세팍(Sepak)'과 태국어 '타크로(Takraw)'가 합쳐진 합성어로서 '발로 공을 차다'란 뜻입니다. 이것은 말레이-타이 반도에서 기원한 일종의 발로 하는 배구죠. 세팍타크로는 라탄 공을 사용한다는 점에서 배구와 다릅니다. 라탄 공은 선수들이 공을 다룰 때 충격을 완화하기 위한 목적으로 합성 섬유나, 부드럽고 내구성 있는 소재로 만들어집니다. 3명의 선수가 한 팀입니다. 선수들은 무릎, 발, 가슴, 그리고 머리로만 공을 칠 수 있습니다. 자기 팀 코트 바닥에 공을 떨어뜨린 팀이 상대에게 1점을 줍니다. 한 팀이 15점을 얻으면 한 '세트'를 이기게 됩니다. 3세트를 이기는 팀이 경기에서 이깁니다. 네트의 높이가 1.55미터이기에 상대 코트에 공을 보내기 위한 무술 같은 킥 동작이 자주 선보여집니다. 이처럼 화려한 동작들 덕분에 세팍타크로는 전 세계적으로 인기입니다. 현재 세계 120개국 이상에서 세팍타크로를 즐기고 있습니다.

해설: 21. 중반부에 선수가 받을 충격을 완화하기 위해 합성 섬유를 공의 재질로 사용한다고 했으므로 ④번이 내용과 일치하지 않는다.
22. 세팍타크로가 인기가 많은 이유는 후반부에 언급되었다. 멋진 무술 동작과 같은 발동작을 선보이기 때문에 전 세계적으로 인기 있다고 했으므로 정답은 ③번이다.

수능 5일 전 대학수학능력평가 대비 영어영역 듣기(B형)

1	①	2	①	3	⑤	4	①	5	④
6	①	7	③	8	①	9	③	10	⑤
11	②	12	④	13	③	14	⑤	15	②
16	④	17	③	18	①	19	③	20	②
21	②	22	③						

문항 1 ①

Script & Dictation

W: Donghyun, **how about volunteering** at the St. Patrick's Day festival with me?

M: That **sounds interesting**. I'm in.

W: Also, we can enjoy Irish dance performances in the free time.

M: <u>Excellent. That serves two ends.</u>

여: 동현아, 나랑 성패트릭데이 축제에서 봉사활동 하는 거 어때?
남: 재미있겠다. 나 할래.
여: 게다가 자유 시간에는 아일랜드 춤 공연도 감상할 수 있어.
남: <u>멋진걸. 일거양득이네.</u>

해설: 봉사활동을 하면서 춤 공연도 볼 수 있으므로 두 가지 좋은 점이 있다는 의미를 담고 있는 ①번이 정답이다.

문항 2 ④

Script & Dictation

W: Honey, **have you seen** the car key on the table?

M: No, I haven't. But I saw you had it when you **entered the house** this morning.

W: I know, but I can't find it anywhere in the house.

M: <u>I'll help you look for it. It must be around here somewhere.</u>

여: 여보, 탁자 위에 차 키 못 봤어요?

남: 아니요, 못 봤어요. 하지만 오늘 아침 당신이 집에 들어올 때 가지고 있는 건 봤는데요.

여: 알아요, 그런데 집 어디서도 못 찾겠네요.

남: 내가 찾는 걸 도와줄게요. 분명히 이 주변 어딘가에 있을 거예요.

해설: 여자가 집에 가지고 들어온 것이 분명한 키를 못 찾는 상황이므로 주위 어딘가에 있을 테니 같이 찾아보자고 하는 것이 가장 적절한 응답이다.

문항 3 ⑤

Script & Dictation

M: Cathy, what do you read? You **are so focused**.

W: I'm reading *Les Miserables*. I like it, but it's a little difficult to read.

M: **What about seeing** the musical instead? When I saw that performance, I was so impressed.

W: Me, too. After seeing the musical, I started reading.

남: Cathy, 뭐 읽고 있어? 완전히 열중하고 있구나.

여: '레미제라블' 읽고 있어. 재미는 있는데 읽기 좀 어려워.

남: 대신에 뮤지컬을 보는 건 어때? 나 공연 봤는데 정말 감명 깊었어.

여: 나도 그랬어. 뮤지컬 보고 나서 책 읽기 시작한 거야.

해설: 책으로 읽는 '레미제라블'이 어렵다고 하는 여자에게 남자는 뮤지컬을 보라고 제안한다. 이러한 제안에 여자도 공연을 본 적이 있으며, 그러고 나서 책을 읽기 시작했다고 대답하는 것이 가장 적절한 전개가 되겠다.

문항 4 ①

Script & Dictation

M: Hello, I'm Justin Reardon, and I'm here to speak about the city's plan to build a shopping center at Bradley Park. As you know, Bradley Park is a wonderful place for every citizen to relax. Whenever I go there, I can see children playing together and families **resting on** the grass or under the trees. We have two huge shopping centers in the neighborhood already. When another shopping center is built, you **won't be able to** see these peaceful scenes anymore. Instead, every weekend, the park **will be crowded with** cars. Do you think it'll improve our quality of life? Absolutely not!

남: 안녕하세요, 저는 Justin Reardon이라고 합니다. Bradley 공원에 쇼핑센터를 짓기로 한 도시 계획에 관해 말씀드리려고 이 자리에 나왔습니다. 여러분도 아시다시피 Bradley 공원은 시민 모두가 편히 쉴 수 있는 멋진 공간입니다. 그곳에 갈 때마다 저는 아이들이 함께 놀고, 가족들이 잔디나 나무 아래에서 쉬는 모습을 볼 수 있습니다. 동네에 대형 쇼핑센터가 이미 두 군데나 있습니다. 하나를 더 지으면 이런 평화로운 광경들을 더는 못 보게 될 것입니다. 대신 공원은 주말마다 차들로 혼잡해지겠지요. 그것이 우리 삶의 질을 높이는 것일까요? 절대 그렇지 않습니다!

해설: 남자는 쇼핑센터 준공 계획을 반대할 목적으로 시민들이 편히 쉴 수 있는 공간에 쇼핑센터를 지으면 평화로운 모습은 사라지고 혼잡해질 것이라는 이유를 들어 자신의 의견을 피력하고 있다.

문항 5 ④

Script & Dictation

W: What are you looking at, Robert?

M: I'm checking **the reservation for** my trip to Detroit next week.

W: Oh, you are finally going to the motor show.

M: Yeah, I've always been **eager to visit** the show. I'm so excited that I can see and touch my dream cars in person.

W: Great for you. So, did you book your flight and hotel?

M: Flight? Yes. A long time ago. But no hotel yet. I'm thinking of searching for one when I get there.

W: You'd better not do that. Due to the motor show, there are plenty of people. Hotels won't **have enough vacancies**, I think.

M: You mean there might not be an empty room?

W: Right. Search for accommodations right now, and there could be a discount for **early bird travelers**.

M: What?

W: Some hotels give discounts if you book in advance.

M: That's good to know. Thanks.

여: 뭐 보고 있어, Robert?

남: 다음 주 디트로이트 여행을 위해 예약한 거 확인하고 있어.

여: 아, 드디어 모터쇼에 가는구나.

남: 맞아. 난 항상 그 쇼에 정말 가보고 싶었지. 내가 꿈꿔왔던 차들을 직접 보고 만질 수 있게 되어 진짜 신 나.

여: 참 잘 됐다. 그래, 비행편이랑 호텔 예약은 했니?

남: 비행편? 응. 오래전에 했지. 그런데 호텔은 아직 안 했어. 디트로이트 가서 알아볼까 생각 중이야.

여: 그렇게는 하지 않는 게 좋을 것 같아. 모터쇼 때문에 사람들이 엄청나게 많을 거야. 그럼 호텔에 남는 객실도 충분히 없을 텐데.

남: 그러니까 빈방이 없을 것 같단 말이니?

여: 응. 지금 당장 숙박 시설 찾아봐. 부지런한 여행객들은 할인을 받을 수도 있어.

남: 뭐?

여: 일찍 예약하면 숙박비를 할인해주는 호텔들이 있거든.

남: 좋은 정보인걸. 고마워.

해설: 여행 목적지에 도착하면 숙박시설을 알아보려는 남자에게 여자는 사람들이 많아 남는 객실이 없을 수도 있고, 또 일찍 예약하면 할인해주는 호텔도 있으니 미리 알아보는 것이 좋을 거라 조언해주고 있다.

문항 6 ①

Script & Dictation

M: I was scolded by Mr. Gwen for **spelling errors** again.

W: Again? Why didn't you check the report more closely?

M: I reviewed it again and again, but he still found some mistakes. I think he hates me, and he just looks really carefully for my mistakes.

W: Why do you think that?

M: My first year here, I made a big spelling mistake in a very important meeting presentation. Since then, I think, he has had **a fixed image** of me.

W: Oh, that's too bad. I think you need to meet Mr. Gwen and talk to him about that. You can't **keep going on** like this, can you?

M: You're right. I should talk to him about **how stressed out** I am from this.

남: 철자법을 틀려서 Gwen 씨에게 또 한 소리 들었어.

여: 또? 왜 더 세심하게 보고서를 확인하지 않았니?

남: 확인하고 또 확인했는데도 여전히 몇 개씩 찾아낸다니까. 날 싫어하는 것 같아. 그냥 기를 쓰고 내가 실수한 걸 찾으니.

여: 왜 그렇게 생각해?

남: 여기 입사한 첫해, 아주 중요한 회의 프레젠테이션에서 철자에 큰 실수를 했어. 내 생각엔 그 이후로 나에 대해 고정된 이미지를 갖게 된 것 같아.

여: 정말 속상하겠네. Gwen 씨를 만나서 그에 관해 얘기할 필요가 있을 것 같아. 계속 이럴 순 없지 않겠어?

남: 네 말이 맞아. 내가 이걸로 얼마나 스트레스받는지 그에게 말해야겠어.

해설: 대화 후반부에서 여자는 남자에게 심리적인 부담을 주는 상대와 직접 그에 관해 이야기를 해보는 것이 좋겠다고 조언하고 있으므로 ①번이 정답이다.

문항 7 ③

Script & Dictation

W: There is a very interesting article about **the multitasking paradox**.

M: Multitasking? You mean somebody doing a number of jobs at the same time? Isn't that what most companies want from their employees?

W: That's right. But the interesting thing is that multitasking is **counterproductive**. They followed the timelines of two workers, one who changed focus relatively few times and one who constantly shifted between activities.

M: So the one who shifted **more frequently** had less productive results?

W: That's right. It showed that the worker who shifted less frequently between activities spent only 40 minutes on **unproductive tasks** compared to 5 hours on unproductive tasks for the worker who shifted more frequently.

M: Wow, so the paradox of multitasking means that while somebody is shifting between tasks, that person becomes unfocused and unproductive.

여: 멀티 태스킹의 역설에 대한 매우 흥미로운 기사가 있어.

남: 멀티 태스킹? 누군가가 동시에 많은 작업을 수행하는 거 말이니? 그게 대부분의 회사에서 직원들한테 원하는 거 아니야?

여: 맞아. 그런데 재미있는 게 멀티 태스킹이 비생산적이라는 거야. 집중 대상을 비교적 적은 횟수로 바꾼 사람과 계속해서 활동을 바꾼 사람, 이렇게 일하는 두 사람의 시간표를 따라가 봤어.

남: 그랬더니 하는 일을 더 자주 바꾼 사람의 결과가 덜 생산적이었던 거구나?

여: 맞아. 활동을 자주 바꾸지 않은 사람은 생산성이 낮은 작업을 하는데 40분밖에 안 걸렸던 것에 비해 자주 바꿨던 사람은 5시간이 걸렸대.

남: 우아, 멀티 태스킹의 역설은 그러니까 작업 사이를 왔다 갔다 하는 사람은 덜 집중하게 되고 생산성도 낮아진다는 얘기구나.

해설: 여자와 남자는 기사를 통해 생산적인 업무 방식이라 여겨졌던 멀티 태스킹이 사실은 비생산적인 활동이었음을 알게 되었다. 따라서 정답은 ③번이다.

문항 8 ①

Script & Dictation

M: Why is the line so long here?

W: It is because this shop is very popular. **Not only do they roast** their own beans but they also have the best teas.

M: I see. Oh, the interior looks very special. It looks like a traditional Korean house.

W: It was not a shop at first, but originally a traditional Korean house. They just **changed it for** the business.

M: Hmm, that's interesting. By the way, the garden over there is so beautiful!

W: Yes, it is. They also **grow their own herbs** in their garden by themselves.

M: That's awesome. Do they **provide visitors with** those rooms, too? If so, it would be a really special experience.

W: No, unfortunately, they don't. They just sell drinks.

M: That's a shame.

남: 여기 줄이 왜 이렇게 길어?

여: 인기가 정말 많은 가게라서 그래. 콩을 직접 볶을 뿐만 아니라 차도 최상품이거든.

남: 그렇구나. 오, 실내장식이 굉장히 특별해 보인다. 한국 전통 가옥처럼 생겼어.

여: 여기 처음엔 가게가 아니었어. 원래는 한국 전통 가옥이었는데 사업을 하려고 이렇게 바꾼 거야.

남: 음, 흥미롭군. 그나저나, 저기 정원이 참 아름답다!

여: 맞아. 정원에서 직접 허브도 기른대.

남: 멋지다. 방문객에게 저 방들도 제공해 주는 건가? 그렇다면 정말 특별한 경험이 될 텐데.

여: 아쉽지만 그렇지는 않아. 그냥 음료만 팔아.

남: 아쉽네.

문항 9 ③

Script & Dictation

W: Welcome, everybody! I'm Professor Emily Choi, and **I'll be teaching** you Introduction to Music History. I'll let you know the location of the music hall where we have class this semester. On entering the main gate, you can choose paths going in three directions. Please take the one on the right and follow it until you see **the first intersection**. Take a left and you can see the engineering college first. But **keep going**. Then, you can see a building with a big swimming pool on the first floor. The building **behind that one** is the music hall. Also, if you want to see me in person visit me in my office from 9 to 11 a.m. every Tuesday. If you go **straight from the gate**, you can see a statue. The building to the left of the statue is my office building. Find me on the second floor.

여: 모두 환영합니다! 저는 여러분에게 음악사 입문을 가르치게 될 Emily Choi 교수입니다. 이번 학기 수업 장소인 음악강당이 어디 있는지 알려드릴게요. 정문으로 들어오면 길이 세 방향으로 나 있습니다. 오른쪽 길을 따라 오다가 첫 번째 사거리에서 좌회전 하면 제일 먼저 공과대학이 보일 겁니다. 계속 가세요. 가다 보면 1층에 큰 수영장이 있는 건물이 보일 거예요. 그 건물 뒤에 있는 건물이 바로 음악강당입니다. 또한 저를 직접 만나고 싶은 학생은 매주 화요일 오전 9시에서 11시 사이에 제 사무실로 오세요. 정문에서 직진하시면 동상이 하나 보일 텐데요. 동상 왼쪽에 있는 건물이 제 사무실 건물입니다. 사무실은 2층에 있어요.

해설: 정문에서 제일 오른쪽 길을 따라가다가 좌회전 하면 차례로 공과대학과 수영장 건물이 보인다고 했다. 수영장 건물 뒤에 있는 건물이 음악강당 이라고 했으므로 정답은 ③번이다.

문항 10 ⑤

Script & Dictation

W: So, how are you feeling, Steve?

M: I thought I'd get better, but I feel **worse than before**.

W: That's too bad. You are scheduled to give a presentation at work on Friday, right?

M: Yeah, so I have to be better by then. I thought I had the flu, but the doctor said it was just a bad cold. He gave me some cold medicine, but it doesn't seem to help.

W: You know, my **mom is really into** this herbal tea, and she and I use it for colds. Would you like to try it?

M: No thanks.

W: Come on! **Give it a try**. Drink it four times a day, and, believe me, it works. I can bring more to you after work, if you want.

M: Well, I guess it wouldn't hurt to **give it a shot** since nothing else seems to be doing the job.

W: Great. I'll **come by your place** at 7:30. See you then.

여: 그래 몸은 좀 어때, Steve?

남: 좀 나아질 거로 생각했는데, 전보다 더 안 좋은 거 같아.

여: 정말 안됐구나. 금요일에 회사에서 발표하기로 되어있지 않아?

남: 응, 그래서 그때까지 괜찮아져야 해. 나는 내가 독감에 걸린 줄 알았는데 의사 말로는 그냥 감기가 심한 거래. 감기약을 줬는데 도움이 되는 것 같지 않아.

여: 우리 엄마가 이 허브차에 관심이 많으신데 엄마와 나는 감기약으로 쓰거든. 너도 한번 마셔볼래?

남: 아니, 사양할게.

여: 그러지 말고! 한번 해 봐. 하루에 네 잔 마시면 진짜 효과 있다니까. 원하면 퇴근 후에 더 가져다줄게.

남: 그래, 지금으로선 잘 듣는 약이 없는 것 같으니 시도해서 나쁠 건 없겠구나.

여: 잘 생각했어. 7시 30분에 너희 집으로 갈게. 그때 보자.

해설: 감기약이 효과가 없다는 남자에게 여자는 허브차를 추천했고, 남자가 한번 마셔보겠다고 하자 남자의 집으로 직접 가져다주겠다고 말했다. 따라서 정답은 ⑤번이다.

문항 11 ②

Script & Dictation

[Telephone rings.]

M: Hello?

W: Good afternoon. I'm calling from Songhyung Zoo. **Do you have any time** to talk?

M: I guess so. What can I do for you?

W: Songhyung Zoo **wants to purchase** two chimpanzees from Africa. As you know, chimpanzees live far from here, so the shipment is very expensive.

M: Yes, I've heard about it.

W: Also, we want to buy one male and one female and **let them breed**.

M: I think that's a great idea. But why are you calling me?

W: Because the price is so high, we're asking people who have visited our zoo to send us money to **help pay for them**. Can you help us?

M: That sounds good, but I'll have to give it some more thought.

[전화 벨 소리]

남: 여보세요?

여: 안녕하세요. 송형 동물원입니다. 통화 괜찮으신지요?

남: 네, 그런 거 같은데 무슨 일이시죠?

여: 저희 송형 동물원에서는 아프리카에서 침팬지 두 마리를 사려고 합니다. 아시다시피 침팬지가 여기서 먼 곳에 살고 있어서 운송비가 매우 비싸잖아요.

남: 네, 그 얘기 들었어요.

여: 또 수컷과 암컷 한 마리씩 사서 교배시키려고 하거든요.

남: 참 좋은 생각인 것 같네요. 그런데 왜 저에게 전화하셨나요?

여: 그러니까, 비용이 매우 많이 들기 때문에 저희 동물원을 방문하셨던 분들께 비용을 댈 수 있도록 돈을 좀 보내주십사 하고 부탁하고 있습니다. 도와주시겠어요?

남: 좋은 것 같은데 생각을 좀 더 해 볼게요.

해설: 동물을 사들이려고 하는 동물원에서 동물원 방문객에게 기부를 요청하고 있으므로 ②번이 정답이다.

문항 12 ④

Script & Dictation

W: Hello, I'm Carla Jones from Dowon F&B Company.

M: Ms. Jones, so what is this visit about?

W: I'm a salesperson **in this district**, and I am the one who designed and developed the Blue Shoes.

M: The Blue Shoes! Wow! They're really popular **among young people** these days.

W: I'm pleased to hear that. Now that you mention it, I'm here **to do a survey** on the Blue Shoes. Could you give me a hand with that?

M: Sure. How can I help you?

W: Could you **fill out this questionnaire**? We'd like to know how shop owners feel about the Blue Shoes.

M: Okay. Would you like to have some tea while I'm **working on it**?

W: That's really nice of you.

여: 안녕하세요, 도원 F&B사의 Carla Jones입니다.

남: Jones 씨, 무슨 일로 오셨나요?

여: 제가 이 지역 영업 사원이자 Blue Shoes를 기획, 개발한 사람입니다.

남: Blue Shoes요! 와! 요새 젊은 사람들 사이에서 인기가 대단해요!

여: 반가운 소식이네요. 그 얘기가 나와서 말인데, Blue Shoes에 관해 설문 조사를 하려고 온 거예요. 저 좀 도와주실 수 있나요?

남: 물론이죠. 어떻게 도와 드릴까요?

여: 이 설문지 좀 작성해주시겠어요? 점주들이 Blue Shoes에 대해 어떻게 생각하고 계시는지 알고 싶습니다.

남: 알겠습니다. 제가 작성하는 동안 차라도 드시겠어요?

여: 정말 친절하시네요.

해설: 여자는 대화 중반부에 Blue Shoes라는 상품에 대한 매장주들의 의견을 듣고자 설문 조사를 하고 싶다고 말하고 있다. 따라서 ④번이 정답이다.

문항 13 ③

Script & Dictation

W: Greg, here is the report that you wrote **about our curriculum**. You did a good job. It's so helpful for our school.

M: Thank you, Kate. I worked hard on it.

W: I think it's one of the best, but there are some minor problems.

M: Could you explain what kind of problems it has?

W: It is **well-organized**, and has good content, but there are a few errors in the analyzing graph. Accuracy is important in figures. I marked the **mistaken numbers** in red.

M: During the time I was writing and analyzing the figures, I got LASIK surgery. So I had blurry vision. I **should have rechecked them**.

W: But you still did great work. Just fix that part.

M: Okay, I'll go and correct right away what you've pointed out.

여: Greg, 우리 교육과정에 관해 네가 쓴 보고서 여기 있어. 잘 썼더라. 학교에 많은 도움이 될 거야.

남: 고마워, Kate. 열심히 작업했어.

여: 가장 잘 쓴 것들 중 하나라 생각해. 그런데 사소한 문제점들이 좀 있어.

남: 어떤 문제들이 있는지 설명해줄래?

여: 잘 정리되어 있고, 내용도 좋은데 도표 분석에 몇 가지 오류가 있어. 수치는 정확성이 중요해. 잘못된 숫자들은 내가 빨간색으로 표시했어.

남: 수치 작성하고 분석하던 당시에 라식 수술을 받아서 시야가 흐릿했어. 다시 확인했어야 하는 건데.

여: 그래도 정말 잘했어. 그 부분만 고쳐봐.

남: 그래. 가서 네가 지적한 부분 바로 고칠게.

해설: 여자는 남자의 보고서가 전반적으로 훌륭하지만, 대화 중간에 도표의 수치가 정확하지 않아 그 부분을 표시해놨다고 언급했다. 따라서 정답은 ③번이다.

문항 14 ⑤

Script & Dictation

M: Hayun, how's your part-time job?

W: It's good, James.

M: Can I ask **how much you get paid** an hour?

W: The pay went up last month. I get $15 an hour.

M: Wow, that's really good. Did the Labor Department increase minimum wage or did your boss increase the pay rate?

W: **I don't care either way**. I'm satisfied with the position and pay now.

M: Great for you! How many days do you work?

W: Around twelve a month. I work on every Friday, Saturday, and Sunday.

M: How many hours do you work a day?

W: I have to work eight hours **except lunch time**.

M: You work quite long. What about lunch?

W: The company doesn't cover it, but usually my boss or senior colleagues take care of me. So, I **seldom spend money** on lunch.

M: It couldn't be better.

남: 하윤아, 아르바이트 어때?

여: 좋아, James.

남: 시급 얼마인지 물어봐도 돼?

여: 지난달에 올랐어. 시간당 15달러야.

남: 와, 정말 괜찮다. 노동부에서 최저임금을 올린 거니, 아니면 너희 사장님이 시급을 올려준 거니?

여: 뭐든 상관없어. 지금 자리랑 시급에 만족해.

남: 잘 된 일이구나! 며칠 일해?

여: 한 달에 12일 정도. 매주 금요일, 토요일, 일요일에 일해.

남: 하루에 몇 시간 일해?

여: 점심시간 제외하고 8시간 일해야 해.

남: 꽤 오래 일하는구나. 점심은 어떻게 하고?

여: 회사에서 제공해주진 않는데 보통 사장님이나 선배들이 챙겨주셔. 그래서 점심값이 거의 안 들어.

남: 최곤데.

해설: 여자는 시급 15달러인 아르바이트를 하루에 8시간씩 한 달에 12일 하고 있으므로 계산하면 총 1,440달러이다.

문항 15 ②

Script & Dictation

W: Khone Falls is one of the longest waterfalls in the world. **It is located in** the southern part of Laos and runs through the border between Laos and Cambodia. It is **in the main stream** of the Mekong River, which is also one of the longest rivers in the world. Though Khone Falls is only 21-meters high, its length is more than 10 kilometers because it **consists of a number of** small falls such as Khong Phapheng Falls and Somphamit Falls. Approximately 11,000 tons per second of water flow through these waterfalls **in normal seasons** and more than 40,000 tons per second in the rainy season.

여: 코네 폭포는 세계에서 가장 긴 폭포 중 하나이다. 라오스 남부에 자리 잡고 있으며, 라오스와 캄보디아 국경 사이를 흐른다. 코네 폭포는 메콩 강의 본류에 있는데 메콩 강 역시 세계에서 가장 긴 강 중 하나이다. 코네 폭포는 높이가 21미터에 불과하지만, 그 길이는 10킬로미터 이상에 달한다. 이는 콩 파펭 폭포, 솜파밋 폭포와 같은 많은 소규모 폭포들로 이루어져 있기 때문이다. 이 폭포들을 통해 평수기에는 초당 약 1만 1천 톤의 물이 흐르며, 우기에는 초당 4만 톤 이상이 방류된다.

해설: 코네 폭포는 라오스 북부가 아닌 남부에 자리 잡고 있다고 했으므로 ②번이 일치하지 않는 내용이다.

문항 16 ④

Script & Dictation

M: On this Wednesday evening, students will get together for a lecture about **how to prepare for** job interviews. The lecture will **take place** in the auditorium and last about an hour. We expect that most seniors will participate. Interested **sophomores and juniors** will be there as well, so we cannot guarantee enough seats for everyone. Therefore, at 6 o'clock on the nose, we will close the doors. Latecomers can go to the library and watch the lecture on TV screens there. After the lecture, students will have **the opportunity to consult with** experts one-on-one. These consultations, however, are only open to seniors. The lecturer will be Jieun Kim, the HR manager from KW recruiting company.

남: 이번 수요일 저녁, 학생들이 함께 모여 면접 준비 방법에 관한 강연을 듣게 될 것입니다. 강연은 강당에서 약 1시간 정도 진행될 것입니다. 4학년 학생 대부분이 참여할 것으로 예상하고 있습니다. 관심 있는 2, 3학년 학생들도 올 것이기에 좌석이 충분하지 않을 수도 있습니다. 따라서 6시 정각이 되면 강당 문을 닫겠습니다. 늦게 오는 학생들은 도서관에 가시면 그곳에 마련된 TV 스크린으로 강연을 시청할 수 있습니다. 강연이 끝나면 학생들에게 전문가와 1대1 상담을 받을 기회가 주어질 것입니다. 상담은 그러나 4학년만을 대상으로 합니다. 강연자는 김지은 KW 채용사 인사부 관리자입니다.

해설: 전문가와의 개별 상담은 희망 학생들이 다 받을 수 있는 것이 아니라 4학년 학생들만 받을 수 있다고 했으므로 정답은 ④번이다.

문항 17 ④

Script & Dictation

W: Hello. Surin Hotel. How can I help you?

M: I'd like to **reserve a room** for two people on the 25th of September. Are you all booked that night?

W: Well, no... We do have **one suite available** and the view of the city is great. It's $250, plus 10% tax.

M: That's too expensive. What about either on the 24th or the 26th?

W: Well, would you like a smoking or a non-smoking room?

M: Non-smoking, please.

W: Okay, we do have **a few rooms available** on the 24th. The view is not good, though. And **we're full** on the 26th.

M: Well, how much is **the non-smoking room** on the 24th?

W: $100, plus 10% room tax.

M: Okay, great. My name is Dominic Burgi. B-U-R-G-I.

여: 안녕하세요, Surin 호텔입니다. 무엇을 도와드릴까요?

남: 9월 25일에 2인용 객실 하나 예약하려고 하는데요. 그날 예약 다 찼나요?

여: 아니요, 멋진 도시 풍광을 감상하실 수 있는 스위트룸 이용 가능하십니다. 250달러이고 10% 세금이 가산됩니다.

남: 너무 비싼데요. 24일이나 26일은요?

여: 흡연실과 금연실 중 어디를 원하시는지요?

남: 금연실요.

여: 네, 24일에 투숙 가능하신 객실이 몇 개 있습니다. 그런데 전망이 좋은 편은 아니에요. 그리고 26일엔 객실이 모두 찼고요.

남: 24일 금연실 숙박료가 얼마인가요?

여: 100달러에 객실 세금 10% 가산됩니다.

남: 네, 그게 좋겠네요. 제 이름은 Dominic Burgi입니다. B-U-R-G-I요.

해설: 24일에 예약할 수 있는 객실은 전망이 좋지 않다고 언급했으므로 ④번의 'great view'라는 설명은 잘못된 것이다.

문항 18 ①

Script & Dictation

M: Hello, I'm back. Ami, any messages for me?

W: Yes, Mr. Min. There were **a couple of calls** from Ms. Yang, the human resources consultant, about an hour ago.

M: Why did she call?

W: She asked to **reschedule the meeting** to tomorrow morning.

M: Don't I have the breakfast meeting with JAU MBA members?

W: That's **the day after tomorrow**, Friday morning, sir. You're not scheduled for anything tomorrow morning.

M: Oh, yeah. Where is the MBA meeting?

W: The 48th floor of the Sussex Hotel.

M: I got it. I remember that place. Ami, call the leader of the marketing team and ask him if it's okay to change the meeting time to tomorrow morning. **If he is fine** with it, please call Ms. Yang and tell her that we have confirmed the change.

W: Yeah, and you are also **free for Friday evening**.

M: No, I should go to my son's soccer game that evening.

W: Then, you don't have free time this week.

남: 나 돌아왔어요. Ami 씨, 나한테 온 메시지 있나요?

여: 네, 민 선생님. 인사부 자문 위원이신 양 선생님께서 1시간 전에 몇 번 전화하셨어요.

남: 왜 전화하셨지?

여: 회의 시간을 내일 오전으로 재조정해도 되는지 여쭤보셨어요.

남: JAU MBA 사람들과 조찬 회의 있지 않나요?

여: 그건 내일모레 금요일 아침입니다, 선생님. 내일 아침엔 일정이 비어있습니다.

남: 그렇군요. MBA 회의 장소가 어디였죠?

여: Sussex 호텔 48층입니다.

남: 알았어요. 어딘지 기억나네요. Ami 씨, 마케팅 팀장님께 전화해서 내일 오전으로 회의 시간 변경해도 되는지 물어봐 주세요. 괜찮다고 하시면 양 선생님께 전화해서 시간 변경이 확정됐다고 알려 주세요.

여: 알겠습니다. 그리고 선생님 금요일 저녁에도 일정 없으세요.

남: 아니요, 있어요. 그날 저녁엔 아들 축구 경기에 가야 해요.

여: 그럼 이번 주에 비는 시간이 없으시네요.

해설: 내일모레가 금요일인 것으로 보아 오늘은 수요일이다. 남자는 양 선생님과의 회의를 목요일 오전으로 변경할 것이고, 금요일 오전에는 다른 조찬 회의가 있으며, 저녁에는 아들의 축구 경기에 가야 하는 바쁜 상황이므로 보기에서 가장 적절한 답은 ①번이다.

Script & Dictation

M: Hyeyoung, do you have plans for after college?

W: I'm thinking about going to England to study flowers.

M: That sounds great. **Would that be for** graduate school?

W: No, it's a course in a private school. What about you?

M: I think I'm going to change my major.

W: Oh, Peter. You're already a senior. I don't think it's a good idea.

M: But I believe it's **not too late to think about** what I really want to do since it's still before graduation.

W: You're majoring in technical engineering. That could **get you a job** more easily than other majors.

M: I know, but I'd like to study veterinary science. I want to be Schweitzer for animals.

W: I think **you had better meet** your student adviser.

M: Before that, I have to persuade my parents.

W: Don't your parents like the idea?

M: No, they're opposed to my plan.

남: 혜영아, 대학 졸업 후 계획이 어떻게 돼?

여: 영국에 가서 화훼 공부를 할까 생각 중이야.

남: 멋지다. 대학원 과정인 거야?

여: 아니, 사립학교 과정이야. 너는?

남: 난 전공을 바꿔야 할까 봐.

여: Peter, 너 벌써 졸업반이잖아. 좋은 생각이 아닌 것 같아.

남: 하지만 아직 졸업 전이니까 내가 진짜 뭘 원하는지 생각해 보는 것도 늦지 않은 것 같은데.

여: 너 기술 공학 전공이잖아. 다른 전공보다 취직하기 쉬울 수 있어.

남: 아는데, 나 수의학 공부하고 싶어. 동물들의 슈바이처가 되고 싶거든.

여: 학생 상담사를 만나보는 게 좋을 거 같아.

남: 그 전에 부모님을 설득해야 해.

여: 부모님께서 좋아하지 않으셔?

남: 응, 내 계획을 반대하셔.

해설: 여자는 남자의 부모가 전공을 변경하려는 남자의 계획을 좋아하지 않느냐고 물었다. 남자가 이미 부모님을 설득해야 한다고 언급했으므로 그의 부모가 반대하고 있다는 내용이 나와야 흐름이 자연스럽다.

문항 20 ⑤

Script & Dictation

W: A farmer wished to buy a strong horse and **wanted to make sure that** it was the right one before he bought it. He told the owner that he'd like to try out the horse for a day, and the owner agreed. The farmer took the horse home and **put it in the field** with his other horses. The next day, the new horse **stayed away from** the strong horses and sat beside the laziest and weakest one. Seeing this, the farmer decided not to buy the horse and **took it back to** its owner. Its owner asked how he knew it was not good in just one day. In this situation, what would the farmer most likely say to the owner?

* Farmer: _Birds of a feather flock together._

여: 한 농부가 튼튼한 말을 사려고 했다. 말을 사기 전, 제대로 된 말인지 확인하고 싶었던 농부는 말 주인에게 하루 동안 말을 평가해 보고 싶다고 했고, 말 주인은 이를 허락했다. 농부는 말을 데리고 집으로 돌아와 그의 다른 말들이 있는 사육장에 들여 놓았다. 다음 날, 새 말은 튼튼한 말들 사이에서 떨어져 제일 게으르고 약한 말 옆에 앉아있었다. 이를 본 농부는 말을 사지 않기로 하고 주인에게 다시 가져갔다. 주인은 어떻게 하루 만에 좋은 말이 아닌지 알 수 있느냐고 물었다. 이런 상황에서 농부는 주인에게 뭐라고 말할 것 같은가?

* 농부: _끼리끼리 모이는 법이거든요._

해설: 농부는 새로 들이려고 하는 말이 튼튼한 말과 게으르고 약한 말 중 어느 무리에 속하는지를 보고 좋은 말인지 아닌지를 판단했으므로 비슷한 성향이 있는 것끼리 어울린다는 속담인 ⑤번이 이 상황에 가장 어울리는 말이 되겠다.

문항 21 ②
문항 22 ③

Script & Dictation

M: Helen, have you listened to Mr. Porter's lecture this week? It was great!

W: Yes. It was really insightful. I **was really impressed with** how companies try to ease their competitiveness in the market.

M: Companies used to avoid the problems caused by other competing companies in the marketplace. But the focus of this lecture was how companies have to make their own competition environment. Basically, most companies now **implement strategies** to make it difficult for other companies to step into the same business.

W: That way, the company can enjoy its strength in that business for a long time without competition.

M: I was also impressed with the five competitive forces that reflect the intensity of industry competition and profitability. When companies choose a business **they are willing to** start with, these five forces are something they must consider in advance.

W: That's right. Among them, I think entry wall is the most important thing because it will make the company more profitable once it starts **establishing its name value** in the market.

M: I agree with you. Anyway, this lecture totally changed my way of thinking and broadened my point of view.

남: Helen, 이번 주 Porter 교수님 강의 들었니? 무척 좋았어!

여: 응, 정말 통찰력 있는 강의였어. 기업들이 시장에서 어떻게 경쟁을 줄이려고 하는지가 참 인상적이었어.

남: 회사들은 시장에서 다른 경쟁사들로 인해 발생하는 문제를 피하려 하곤 했지. 하지만 강의의 초점은 기업이 어떻게 스스로 경쟁 환경을 만들어야 하는가였어. 기본적으로 대부분의 회사들은 이제 다른 기업들이 같은 사업에 진입하기 어렵게 만드는 전략을 쓰고 있어.

여: 그렇게 함으로써 기업은 해당 사업에서 경쟁 없이 오랫동안 이점을 누릴 수 있어.

남: 산업 경쟁의 강도와 수익성을 반영하는 5대 경쟁 요인도 인상적이었어. 회사가 벌이려는 사업을 결정할 때, 이 다섯 가지 요소는 미리 생각해 놔야해.

여: 맞아. 난 그중에 진입 장벽이 가장 중요하다고 생각해. 기업이 일단 시장에서 지명도를 형성하면 더 많은 수익을 창출할 수 있게 하니까.

남: 나도 동의해. 어쨌든 이번 강의로 내 사고방식도 완전히 바뀌었고, 시야도 넓어졌어.

해설: 21. 남자와 여자의 대화 내용에 의하면, 강의의 초점은 '기업이 사업을 할 때 어떻게 경쟁하는지'에 관한 것이었으며, 이를 반영하는 전략 경쟁 요인에 관한 내용도 함께 소개되었다. 따라서 두 사람이 들은 강의의 제목으로 가장 적절한 것은 ②번이다. **22.** 대화 후반부에 여자는 기업이 지명도를 갖게 되면 더 많은 수익을 창출할 수 있게 해준다는 측면에서 진입 장벽이 가장 중요한 요소인 것 같다고 언급했다.

수능 4일 전 대학수학능력평가 대비 영어영역 듣기(B형)

1	①	2	④	3	②	4	②	5	④
6	⑤	7	①	8	③	9	③	10	②
11	②	12	④	13	⑤	14	③	15	⑤
16	③	17	④	18	①	19	②	20	④
21	④	22	③						

문항 1 ①

Script & Dictation

M: Sandra, what did you do last Saturday? I **saw you going** somewhere.

W: Did you? I was **on the way to** the 'House of Love'.

M: The organization for orphans? For volunteer work?

W: Yes, I went there to read books for the kids.

남: Sandra, 지난 토요일에 뭐 했어? 네가 어디 가고 있는 거 봤는데.

여: 그랬어? 나 '사랑의 집' 가는 길이었어.

남: 고아원 말이니? 봉사활동 한 거야?

여: 응, 아이들에게 책 읽어주러 간 거야.

해설: 남자가 여자에게 봉사활동 하러 고아원에 간 것인지 묻고 있으므로 그곳에서 어떤 활동을 했는지 설명하는 ①번이 가장 적절한 응답이다.

문항 2 ④

Script & Dictation

W: Jason Park, I'm afraid you are not allowed to borrow any DVDs now.

M: What? I need these movies. I have **a plan to watch** them tonight with my friends. Why can't I borrow them?

W: You have **three items overdue**.

M: Oh, no! I should have checked the due date.

여: Jason Park, 죄송하지만 지금은 DVD를 대여해드릴 수 없겠는데요.

남: 네? 이 영화들 빌려야 하는데. 오늘 밤 친구들이랑 같이 보기로 했거든요. 왜 못 빌리나요?

여: 세 개가 연체됐어요.

남: 오, 이런! 반납 기한을 확인했어야 하는데.

해설: 연체된 DVD가 있어 대여하지 못하는 상황이다. 반환 날짜를 확인하지 않은 것을 후회하는 내용의 ④번이 가장 적절한 응답이 되겠다.

문항 3 ②

Script & Dictation

M: Jiyoung, **will you be able to** help me with my English after dinner?

W: Why not? Let's meet in the language lab.

M: Okay. **Should I bring** my electronic dictionary?

W: We don't need it. Just bring your textbook.

남: 지영아, 저녁 먹고 나 영어 공부하는 것 좀 도와줄 수 있니?

여: 그거 좋지. 어학실에서 만나자.

남: 그래. 내 전자사전 가지고 와야 할까?

여: 필요 없어. 그냥 교과서만 가져와.

해설: 영어 공부를 위해 전자사전은 필요 없고, 교과서만 가져오면 된다고 하는 것이 흐름 상 가장 자연스러운 대답이다.

문항 4 ②

Script & Dictation

W: Attention, please. Last Wednesday, the school board, **along with the principal** and teachers, decided to revise some library rules to **meet the needs** of the students. First, the number of books you can borrow will increase from 4 to 5, and you can have them for 2 weeks, not just 1 week. Also, since most students come to school on Saturdays, our library will be open then from now on. But, **due to issues** related to managing library personnel, only the reading room and the discussion room will be open. Its opening hours are from 9 a.m. to 7 p.m. I'm sure we'll use the library more effectively and comfortably even on Saturdays. These new rules will **take effect** from this coming Wednesday.

여: 주목해주세요. 지난 수요일, 교장 선생님 휘하 선생님들과 함께 교육 위원회에서는 학생들의 요구 사항을 충족하고자 도서관 규정을 개정하기로 했습니다. 먼저 대출 가능한 도서 수는 4권에서 5권으로 늘릴 것이고 대출 기간은 1주가 아닌 2주로 변경됩니다. 또한, 학생들 대부분이 토요일에도 등교하므로 이제부터는 토요일에도 개방할 예정입니다. 그러나 도서관 직원 관리 문제로 열람실과 토론실만 개방합니다. 개방 시간은 오전 9시에서 오후 7시까지입니다. 토요일에도 도서관을 더 효율적이고 편하게 사용하게 될 거라 확신합니다. 새 규정들은 오는 수요일부터 적용됩니다.

해설: 초반부에 이미 도서관 이용 규정이 변경되었음을 언급하였다. 그 이후 내용은 바뀐 도서관 이용 규정을 상세하게 설명하고 있는 것이므로 정답은 ②번이다.

문항 5 ④

Script & Dictation

M: Jennifer, **our sales figures** this month have dropped considerably.

W: You're right. And a new Chinese restaurant just opened nearby. We are **in big trouble**.

M: But I don't have any good ideas to get our customers back.

W: I've thought about it. What about focusing on our special dishes?

M: You mean dishes we serve that other restaurants don't?

W: Exactly, focusing on and professionalizing that will save us.

M: Which dishes did you **have in mind**?

W: Of course, our best-sellers: curries.

M: Okay, then I'll promote our restaurant more.

W: Yeah, I'll use SNS for ads. You can check out the flyers. **We've got leftovers** from our last advertising campaign.

M: Okay. Let's do it.

남: Jennifer, 이번 달 매출액이 상당히 줄었어요.

여: 당신 말이 맞아요. 게다가 근처에 새 중국 식당도 문을 열었고요. 큰일이에요.

남: 그런데 저에겐 고객들의 마음을 돌릴 묘안이 없어요.

여: 제가 생각해 봤는데요, 우리 특선 요리에 집중하는 건 어떨까요?

남: 다른 식당에서는 하지 않는 요리 말이에요?

여: 그렇죠. 특선 요리에 집중하고 그걸 전문화하면 잘 될 거예요.

남: 생각해 둔 요리 있어요?

여: 당연히 제일 잘 나가는 카레죠.

남: 좋아요, 그럼 전 식당 홍보를 더 할게요.

여: 그래요, 전 SNS를 광고 수단으로 활용해볼게요. 전단을 좀 확인해 봐요. 지난번 광고 활동 때 남은 게 있어요.

남: 그래요. 해 봅시다.

해설: 여자는 매출을 늘리는 방법으로 제일 잘 팔리는 특선 요리인 카레에 집중해 보자고 제안하였다.

문항 6 ⑤

Script & Dictation

M: Good morning, students. I'm Daniel Minahan, your vice-principal. Today after lunch, we're going to **participate in** emergency drills to prepare for a possible major blackout. This afternoon, the drills will take place **throughout the country**. When the siren goes off at 2 p.m., all of you should act according to your homeroom teachers' instructions. **This drill will last** for about fifteen minutes. I ask all students of Timothy High School for your **active participation and support**. Thank you for your attention.

남: 안녕하세요, 학생 여러분. Daniel Minahan 교감입니다. 우리 학교는 오늘 점심시간 이후에 대규모 정전에 대비하는 비상 훈련에 참여합니다. 오늘 오후 전국적으로 비상 훈련이 시행될 예정입니다. 오후 2시에 사이렌이 울리면 모두 담임 선생님들의 지시 하에 움직이기 바랍니다. 이번 훈련은 약 15분가량 진행됩니다. Timothy 고등학교 학생 모두의 적극적인 참여와 협조 부탁합니다. 경청해주셔서 감사합니다.

해설: 정전 사태에 대비하기 위해 실시하는 비상 훈련에 관해 안내하고 있다.

문항 7 ①

Script & Dictation

W: Jason, are you listening to Queen?

M: Did I interrupt you?

W: No. That's okay. But are you okay **with that loud volume**?

M: I know. But if I listen to the music quietly, I can't enjoy the music properly. This drum and guitar.

W: **You can say that again.** How about buying new earphones? Nowadays, there are a number of earphones with noise-canceling technology. With those earphones, you can enjoy the music **without increasing the volume**.

M: Well, yes. But it sounds a bit expensive.

W: It's better to spend some money now rather than to have **ringing in your ears** later.

M: You're right. I'm going to buy new earphones this Saturday. Let's go together.

W: Okay. I know some good models.

여: Jason, 너 Queen 음악 듣고 있니?

남: 내가 방해됐니?

여: 아니, 괜찮아. 그런데 그렇게 크게 들어도 괜찮아?

남: 나도 아는데, 그래도 음악을 조용히 들으면 제대로 감상할 수 없어서. 이 드럼과 기타 소리 말이야.

여: 네 말이 맞아. 그러면 새 이어폰을 사는 게 어때? 요새는 잡음 제거 기술이 적용된 이어폰들도 있는데. 소리를 키우지 않고도 음악을 감상할 수 있을 거야.

남: 그렇긴 하겠지만 좀 비쌀 것 같은데.

여: 지금 어느 정도 돈을 쓰는 게 나중에 이명이 생기는 것보다 나을걸.

남: 네 말이 맞다. 이번 토요일에 새 이어폰 사야겠어. 같이 가자.

여: 그래. 내가 좋은 모델들을 좀 알아.

해설: 여자는 남자에게 잡음을 막아주는 이어폰을 살 것을 권유하면서 음악을 크게 들으면 청력에 이상이 올 수도 있다고 충고한다. 이에 남자도 수긍하면서 조금 비싸더라도 잡음 제거가 되는 새 이어폰을 사겠다고 했으므로 ①번이 정답이다.

문항 8 ③

Script & Dictation

M: I'm terribly sorry to keep you waiting for so long.

W: I was getting really **worried about you**, David. What happened?

M: My parents went out tonight, so a babysitter for my little brother **was supposed to come**. But she arrived late.

W: I see. By the way, where's Amy?

M: Oh, she said she couldn't be with us today because she had to go to the airport to see her elder sister off.

W: Oh, no! I can't borrow books here **for a while** because of unpaid overdue charges. Besides, she has the book list we need to refer to for that report!

M: Well, I can check out the books instead. And why don't we ask her to give us the list and collect the data ourselves? She can type it up and **make the presentation** for us.

W: That sounds good. Let's start checking the reference books here.

M: Right. Okay.

남: 오래 기다리게 해서 진짜 미안해.

여: 정말 걱정했단 말이야, David. 무슨 일이야?

남: 오늘 저녁에 부모님이 외출하셔서 남동생 봐줄 베이비시터가 오기로 했는데 늦게 왔지 뭐야.

여: 그랬구나. 그런데 Amy는 어딨어?

남: 아, Amy는 언니 배웅하느라 공항에 가야해서 오늘 못 온다고 했어.

여: 그럼 안 되는데! 나 연체료 안 내서 한동안 여기선 책 못 빌린단 말이야. 게다가 보고서 쓰는 데 참고해야 할 도서 목록도 Amy한테 있고.

남: 책은 내가 대신 대출할 수 있어. 그리고 Amy한테 목록 달라고 해서 우리가 직접 데이터를 모으면 어때? Amy는 타이핑하고 발표하면 될 것 같은데.

여: 좋은 생각이야. 여기서 참고 도서 확인해 보자.

남: 그래, 좋아.

해설: '연체료', '대출' 등의 표현이 등장하는 것으로 보아 두 사람이 현재 도서관에 있음을 알 수 있다.

문항 9 ③

Script & Dictation

[Cell phone rings.]

W: Hello.

M: Hi, Ms. Hong. How is my campaign poster going?

W: Mr. Kensary. It's almost finished. I put **your revised photo** in the center and the election slogan at the bottom of the poster.

M: That's good. What about the candidate number?

W: It's **on the top left side**. And I drew our party logo in the background. You'll like it.

M: Okay, good. What photo did you put in?

W: You prefer the one without glasses, but the image consultant, Ms. Timothy insists on the one with glasses.

M: So, you followed her, right?

W: Yes, I did. It looks **more intelligent**.

M: I think she would be right. That's why she's a professional. Thank you.

W: This is going to be really nice. I think there's **nothing left to improve**.

M: Thank you for your effort, again.

W: My pleasure.

[휴대폰 벨 소리]

여: 여보세요.

남: 안녕하세요, 홍 선생님. 제 캠페인 포스터는 어떻게 되어가고 있나요?

여: Kensary 후보님, 거의 끝나갑니다. 포스터 중앙에는 수정된 사진을, 맨 아래에는 선거 표어를 배치했어요.

남: 좋군요. 후보자 기호는요?

여: 좌측 상단에 넣었습니다. 그리고 배경에는 우리 정당의 로고를 그려 넣었습니다. 후보님도 좋아하실 거예요.

남: 알겠습니다, 좋습니다. 어떤 사진을 넣었나요?

여: 후보님은 안경 안 쓴 사진을 더 좋아하셨지만, 이미지 컨설턴트 Timothy 씨께서 안경 쓴 사진을 고집하셔서요.

남: 그래서 그분의 의견을 들으신 거죠?

여: 네, 그랬습니다. 그 사진이 더 지적으로 보이세요.

남: Timothy 씨 말이 맞을 거예요. 그러니 그분이 전문가겠죠. 고마워요.

여: 정말 근사할 거예요. 더 개선할 것도 없어 보이고요.

남: 수고해줘서 다시 한 번 고마워요.

여: 별말씀을요.

해설: 이미지 컨설턴트의 조언에 따라 포스터에는 더 지적으로 보이는 안경 쓴 사진을 사용했다고 했으므로 ③번이 정답이다.

문항 10 ②

Script & Dictation

M: **Why didn't you dress up** for the musical?

W: I'm sorry. I remember you mentioned it a few days ago, but it slipped my mind. So I forgot to call the babysitter. Why don't you just go by yourself?

M: I hate going to **that kind of place** without you. And these tickets cost a bundle. I really don't want to waste them.

W: Well, there must be someone else who'd like to go.

M: Who am I going to call? It's pretty short notice.

W: Well, **let me think**. What about Kyungmin?

M: Kyungmin's out of town.

W: Hmm. I'm trying to remember who likes musicals. What about Byunghyun?

M: Well... We don't **have much in common**.

W: Give him a call. I think he might be free because he quit his job not long ago.

M: It's really short notice, but... All right.

남: 뮤지컬 보러 가는데 왜 옷을 안 차려입었어요?

여: 미안해요. 며칠 전에 당신이 얘기한 거 기억하고 있다가 그만 깜박했어요. 그래서 베이비시터 부르는 걸 잊어버렸어요. 당신 혼자 가지 그래요?

남: 당신 없이 그런 데 가는 건 싫어요. 그리고 이 표들 비싸단 말이에요. 정말 낭비하고 싶지 않아요.

여: 음, 가고 싶어할 사람이 분명 있을 텐데.

남: 누구한테 전화해요? 이렇게 촉박하게 말이에요.

여: 음, 어디 보자. 경민 씨는 어때요?

남: 출장 중이에요.

여: 흠. 뮤지컬 좋아하는 사람이 누구더라. 병현 씨는요?

남: 글쎄요… 공통점이 많지 않아서.

여: 전화해 봐요. 얼마 전에 일을 그만둬서 시간이 될지도 몰라요.

남: 정말 급하게 얘기하는 거라… 알았어요.

해설: 대화 후반부 여자는 남자에게 그의 친구에게 전화해 보라고 제안한다. 이에 남자는 시간이 너무 촉박하지만 그래도 해 보겠다고 말했으므로 정답은 ②번이다.

문항 11 ②

Script & Dictation

[Telephone rings.]

W: Hi, Billy. This is Serena. I'm calling you to see if you know someone who can **advise me on** portrait rights.

M: Portrait rights? Is there a problem with your photo exhibition?

W: No, not really. **I'm planning to** publish a book using exhibited photos.

M: Do you want to know if you have to pay portrait rights fees or not?

W: Exactly, and more information.

M: Then, I know the perfect person for that. One of my friends, Chloe, **wrote an article about** portrait right protection.

W: That's perfect. So, can I have her phone number or email address?

M: Sure. But first **I should check with** her whether she can help you or not. Don't worry, she's generous and will be happy to help. But I think it's polite to ask first.

W: You're right. I'll wait for your call.

[전화 벨 소리]

여: 안녕, Billy. 나 Serena야. 혹시 초상권에 대해 자문해 줄 수 있는 사람 아는지 궁금해서 전화했어.

남: 초상권? 네 사진전에 무슨 문제라도 있는 거야?

여: 아니, 그렇지 않아. 전시된 사진들을 활용해서 책을 출간할 계획이거든.

남: 초상권 사용료를 내야 하는지 궁금한 거구나?

여: 맞아. 그리고 정보도 더 필요하고.

남: 그렇다면 내가 적임자를 알고 있지. 내 친구 중에 Chloe라고 있는데 초상권 보호에 관한 기사를 썼어.

여: 정말 좋은데. 전화번호나 이메일 주소 좀 알 수 있을까?

남: 그럼. 하지만 널 도와줄 수 있는지부터 확인해야 할 것 같아. 마음씨 좋은 친구라 기꺼이 도와줄 테니 걱정하지 마. 그래도 먼저 물어보는 게 예의인 것 같아.

여: 네 말이 맞아. 전화 기다리고 있을게.

해설: 여자는 남자의 친구 중, 자신이 궁금해하던 초상권 문제에 관해 잘 알고 있는 사람이 있다고 듣고 연락처를 달라고 했으므로 ②번이 정답이다.

문항 12 ④

Script & Dictation

M: Shanon, what are you doing here? Why didn't you go home?

W: Well, I don't want to go home early.

M: Why not?

W: Do you remember my family just **moved into a new place**?

M: Yes. You said your apartment building has **a view of the river**.

W: Right, the view is great.

M: Then what is the problem? Why do you stay out late?

W: The problem is it is located in the middle of downtown. So, many cars **come and go** at the time I finish school.

M: So that's why you stay here at the library till late.

W: Yes. It's much better to be here reading than to go home early **in the heavy traffic**.

남: Shanon, 여기서 뭐 해? 왜 집에 안 갔어?

여: 그게, 집에 일찍 가고 싶지 않아.

남: 왜?

여: 우리 가족이 얼마 전에 새집으로 이사한 거 기억나?

남: 그럼. 아파트 건물에서 강이 보인다고 했잖아.

여: 맞아, 전망은 참 좋아.

남: 그러면 뭐가 문젠데? 왜 늦게까지 밖에 있어?

여: 문제는 위치가 시내 한복판이라는 거야. 하교 시간에 차가 너무 많이 다녀.

남: 그래서 늦게까지 도서관에 있는 거구나.

여: 응. 차 막히는데 집에 일찍 가려고 하는 것보다 여기서 책 읽는 게 훨씬 더 낫거든.

해설: 대화 중간 여자는 집이 시내에 있어 차들이 많이 오간다고 했고, 마지막에 다시 교통 체증을 겪으며 집에 가는 것보다 늦게까지 도서관에 남아있는 게 낫다고 말했다. 따라서 정답은 ④번이다.

문항 13 ⑤

Script & Dictation

W: So, what's your usual day like? You always seem so busy.

M: I usually get up around 5 a.m. I **have to leave home** at twenty to seven so I can catch a bus at 7 o'clock.

W: And what time do you get to work?

M: The subway **takes about** an hour to get there, but the station is right in front of my office.

W: So, when do you work on your website? You said one time that **you run it** at home?

M: Well, my wife and I often watch TV or talk until 10 o'clock. She then often reads while I work on my site, and I sometimes **stay up** until the early hours of the morning, but I try to finish everything by one.

여: 평상시 일과가 어떻게 되나요? 항상 바빠 보이시던데.

남: 저는 보통 새벽 5시쯤 일어나요. 7시 버스를 타기 위해 6시 40분에 집을 나서야 해요.

여: 몇 시에 직장에 도착하시나요?

남: 직장까지 지하철로 1시간 정도 걸려요. 그런데 사무실 바로 앞에 역이 있죠.

여: 그럼 웹사이트 작업은 언제 하세요? 이전에 집에서 운영하신다고 말씀하지 않으셨나요?

남: 아내와 저는 10시까지 TV를 보거나 얘기할 때가 많아요. 그리고 나서 아내는 주로 책을 읽고, 저는 웹사이트 작업을 하죠. 저는 이른 새벽까지 안 잘 때도 있는데 1시까지는 다 마무리하려고 노력해요.

해설: 남자는 자신이 웹사이트 작업을 할 때 독서를 하는 것은 그의 아내라고 얘기했다. 또한, 그의 독서 시간은 언급되지 않았으므로 정답은 ⑤번이다.

문항 14 ③

Script & Dictation

W: Good morning, Mr. Choi. Thank you for coming every day.

M: Hello. **As usual**, I'd like to have a cup of iced coffee, please.

W: Sure, no onion bagel for you this morning?

M: No, thanks. Oh, **add an extra shot**, please.

W: All right. It's $3.60, and the shot is ¢40. And here is your coffee.

M: Thank you. Is this that new French-roast coffee?

W: That's right. Do you like it?

M: I can smell the aroma of the freshly-brewed coffee. Do you sell these beans?

W: We sell the coffee **in limited quantities**. They were originally $3 per ounce, but now we're offering them at a 10-percent discount.

M: That's great! I'll take twenty ounces.

W: All right. Let me **put them in a bag**.

M: How much is the total of my iced coffee and the beans?

여: 좋은 아침이에요, 최 선생님. 매일 와 주셔서 감사합니다.

남: 안녕하세요. 평소처럼 아이스 커피 한 잔 부탁해요.

여: 알겠습니다. 오늘 아침엔 양파 베이글은 필요 없으신가요?

남: 네, 괜찮습니다. 아, 그리고 샷 추가해 주세요.

여: 알겠습니다. 3.6달러에 샷 추가는 40센트입니다. 여기 커피 나왔습니다.

남: 고마워요. 이게 그 새로 나온 프렌치 로스트 커피인가요?

여: 맞아요. 맘에 드시나요?

남: 방금 내린 커피 향이 나네요. 이 원두 파는 거예요?

여: 한정 수량을 판매하고 있습니다. 원래 온스 당 3달러인데 지금은 10% 할인 판매하고 있어요.

남: 그거 좋네요! 20온스어치 살게요.

여: 알겠습니다. 봉지에 담아드릴게요.

남: 아이스 커피와 원두 다 해서 얼마인가요?

해설: 원래 가격이 3.6달러인 아이스 커피에 40센트짜리 샷을 추가했으므로 4달러이다. 온스 당 3달러인 원두를 20온스 구매하면 60달러이지만 10% 할인을 받아 54달러가 됐다. 따라서 아이스 커피 가격에 원두 가격을 더하면 총 58달러이다.

문항 15 ⑤

Script & Dictation

W: Have you ever heard about beta-carotene? As people become more and more interested in health and well-being, **the media coverage** of beta-carotene keeps increasing. Beta-carotene is a nutrient that activates Vitamin A in the liver and intestine. Appropriate beta-carotene levels keep our bodies **from developing cancer**, adult diseases, arthritis, etc. As an antioxidant, it maintains smooth skin and health and prevents free radicals. Carrots are one food high in beta-carotene. Many people **consume carrots raw** or drink them in juice, but it's much better for the body to consume them after cooking. Because beta-carotene is **oil soluble**, carrots cooked in oil allow for much higher vitamin absorption.

여: 베타카로틴에 대해 들어본 적 있나요? 건강과 웰빙에 대한 사람들의 관심이 점점 늘어나면서 매체에서도 베타카로틴에 대해 다루는 경우가 많아졌습니다. 베타카로틴은 간과 장에서 비타민 A를 활성화하는 영양소입니다. 적정 수준의 베타카로틴은 우리 몸에서 암, 성인병, 관절염 등이 발병하는 것을 막습니다. 항산화제로서 매끈한 피부와 건강을 유지하게 해주기도 하며, 활성산소를 예방합니다. 당근은 베타카로틴 함량이 높은 식품입니다. 당근을 날로 먹거나, 주스로 마시는

분들이 많지만 조리해서 먹는 것이 몸에는 훨씬 더 좋습니다. 베타카로틴은 지용성이므로 기름으로 당근을 조리하면 비타민 흡수율도 훨씬 높아집니다.

해설: 당근을 날것으로 먹을 때와 주스로 마실 때 중 어느 것이 몸에 더 좋은지가 언급된 것이 아니라, 이 두 가지 경우보다 조리해서 먹을 때 더 좋다고 했으므로 ⑤번이 정답이다.

문항 16 ③

Script & Dictation

M: As people love coffee more and more, the preference in various coffee beans has been **attracting much more attention**. Coffee was first found in Ethiopia, and it still grows wild there throughout the country. In fact, coffee is **the backbone of** the Ethiopian economy, making up more than half of total exports. In the whole country, there are over 320,000 small farms. Among the various beans growing in Ethiopia, Yirgacheffe has become popular **all over the world**. All Yirgacheffe beans grow wild as well. The coffee brewed from these beans is ranked as a great and refined coffee. Yirgacheffe beans are described as soft with a strong floral aroma, sweet and sour taste, and sweetness like chocolate.

남: 사람들이 점점 더 커피를 좋아하게 되면서 다양한 원두에 대한 애호 역시 훨씬 더 많은 관심을 끌게 되었다. 커피는 에티오피아에서 최초로 발견되었으며, 여전히 나라 전역의 야생에서 자란다. 사실 커피는 에티오피아 경제의 근간으로 전체 수출품의 절반 이상을 차지한다. 전국적으로 32만 개가 넘는 소규모 농장이 있다. 에티오피아에서 자라는 많은 원두 중, 예가체프가 전 세계적으로 인기다. 모든 예가체프 원두 역시 야생에서 자란다. 이 콩으로 우려낸 커피는 훌륭하고 세련된 커피로 평가받는다. 예가체프 원두는 꽃향기가 강하게 나는 부드러우면서도 달고 신 맛과 초콜릿 같은 달콤함으로 묘사된다.

해설: 중반부에 에티오피아의 수출품 중 절반 이상이 커피이기 때문에 커피가 나라 경제의 근간이라는 내용이 언급된다. 따라서 ③번이 정답이다.

문항 17 ④

Script & Dictation

M: I'm looking for a bag. But, in fact, I've never shopped **at an online store** before, so I'm very confused.

W: I'll help you. It's not that difficult.

M: Thank you.

W: First of all, what price range are you looking at? There seems to be **an infinite variety**.

M: Around $500 through $700.

W: Is it for a special birthday?

M: It is for our 40th wedding anniversary.

W: Congratulations! **What about the color?**

M: I think my wife has many black and brown bags, so she might appreciate something unique.

W: Then, how about this one? It's a pink bag **with four inner pockets**. What do you think?

M: It's gorgeous! I'll take it.

W: Okay, click here and type in your credit card number.

남: 가방을 찾고 있어요. 그런데 사실 온라인 매장에선 사 본 적이 없어서 뭐가 뭔지 하나도 모르겠네요.

여: 제가 도와드릴게요. 그렇게 어렵지 않아요.

남: 고마워요.

여: 먼저 가격대를 어느 정도로 생각하고 계세요? 종류가 정말 다양한데.

남: 한 500달러에서 700달러 정도 생각하고 있어요.

여: 특별한 생일을 위한 선물인가 봐요?

남: 저희 결혼 40주년 기념 선물입니다.

여: 축하드려요! 색깔은 어떤 걸로 하시겠어요?

남: 아내에게 검은색과 갈색 가방이 많아서 뭔가 독특한 걸 좋아할 것 같기도 하네요.

여: 그럼 이건 어떠세요? 안주머니가 네 개 있는 분홍색 가방이에요. 어떠세요?

남: 예쁘네요! 이걸로 사야겠어요.

여: 그럼 여기를 클릭하셔서 신용 카드 번호 입력하세요.

해설: 500달러에서 700달러 사이의 가격대에 있는 안주머니가 4개 달린 분홍색 가방은 ④번이다.

문항 18 ①

Script & Dictation

W: Sungmo, wow, what's this? Did you buy a **state-of-the-art** mobile phone?

M: My mom bought it for me yesterday. Doesn't it look cool?

W: Can I see it a little? Wow, it feels nice. How do I **get to the camera**?

M: Just push the button on the side of the phone.

W: **The picture quality** is really good. You already have so many apps.

M: Yes. In fact, yesterday I didn't do anything but download the applications.

W: Did your mom let you do that?

M: At first, she was **okay with it**, but then she yelled at me in the end. I spent almost 10 hours focusing on the new phone.

W: Don't you think that's too much?

M: <u>Not really, it was the first day. I won't spend so much time on it anymore.</u>

여: 성모야, 와, 이게 뭐야? 최신 기종 휴대폰 산 거야?

남: 어제 엄마가 사주셨어. 멋지지 않니?

여: 내가 좀 봐도 될까? 와, 좋은데. 카메라는 어떻게 켜?

남: 그냥 휴대폰 옆에 있는 버튼 누르면 돼.

여: 사진 화질도 진짜 좋다. 벌써 앱이 많구나.

남: 응. 사실 어제 아무것도 안 하고 애플리케이션 다운만 받았지.

여: 너희 어머니가 그걸 그냥 두셨단 말이야?

남: 처음엔 괜찮으셨는데 결국엔 나한테 소리를 지르셨지. 새 휴대폰에만 거의 10시간 정도 신경 쓰고 있었거든.

여: 그건 너무 심하다고 생각하지 않아?

남: <u>글쎄 뭐, 첫날이었잖아. 더는 그렇게 오래 안 할 거야.</u>

해설: 새 휴대폰을 산 남자가 하루에 10시간 넘게 휴대폰에만 신경을 썼다고 하자 여자가 너무 심한 거 아니냐고 물었다. 이에 휴대폰을 산 첫날이었기 때문에 그랬던 것이지 앞으로는 그렇지 않을 거라고 대답하는 것이 대화의 흐름 상 가장 적절한 응답이 되겠다.

문항 19 ②

Script & Dictation

M: Saeko, I heard you went to the baseball park yesterday. How was it?

W: It was one of the best days of my life.

M: The game ended **as a called game**. It's good for your team, but I think, fans in the ball park were not very excited.

W: The game was okay, but **something really special** happened after the game.

M: What do you mean?

W: I got Dahyun Song's autograph. I still **can't believe it**!

M: How did you get it?

W: After the game, I dropped by a snack bar near the ball park to get something to drink, and I saw him **sitting at the corner**!

M: Really? What was he doing there?

W: He was having a bottle of water after the game.

M: So, you got his autograph there?

W: <u>Yes. I got it on my uniform!</u>

남: Saeko, 어제 야구장 갔다 왔다고 들었어. 어땠어?

여: 내 인생 최고의 날이었지.

남: 콜드 게임으로 끝났잖아. 네가 응원하는 팀에겐 좋은 일이 지만 야구장에 온 팬들은 별로 안 신 났을 것 같은데.

여: 경기는 괜찮았는데, 경기 끝난 후에 정말 특별한 일이 있었지.

남: 무슨 말이야?

여: 나 송다현 선수 사인받았어. 아직도 안 믿어져!

남: 어떻게 받은 거야?

여: 경기 후에 뭐 좀 마시러 경기장 근처 매점에 갔는데 송다현 선수가 구석에 있는 걸 앉아 있는 걸 본 거야!

남: 정말? 그 선수는 거기서 뭐 하고 있었어?

여: 경기 끝나고 물 마시고 있더라고.

남: 그래서 거기서 사인받은 거구나?

여: <u>응. 내 유니폼에다 받았어!</u>

해설: 줄곧 야구선수의 사인을 받았다는 이야기를 하고 있으므로 이와 관련된 응답이 나와야 대화의 흐름이 자연스럽다.

문항 20 ④

Script & Dictation

M: Ryan is a middle school student. He gets good grades in every subject except in Korean. He decides to **consult with** his Korean teacher, Mr. Murphy, about the matter. Although he is a Canadian, Ryan studies Korean really hard. So he speaks Korean very fluently **like a native speaker**. However, the problem is that he never **pays attention to** his Korean spelling. Mr. Murphy figures out that Ryan's problem is that he knows how to read sentences but **makes spelling errors** on written tests. Mr. Murphy wants to tell Ryan that correct spelling is another important factor, especially in Korean. In this situation, what would Mr. Murphy most likely say to Ryan?

* Mr. Murphy: <u>You should make an effort to reduce mistakes in your spelling</u>.

남: Ryan은 중학생으로 한국어 빼고 모든 과목의 성적이 좋습니다. Ryan은 한국어 선생님인 Murphy 선생님에게 그 문제에 대해 상담을 받기로 합니다. Ryan은 캐나다인이지만 한국어 공부를 아주 열심히 하기 때문에 한국어가 모국어인 사람처럼 매우 유창하게 한국어를 합니다. 그러나 문제는 Ryan이 한국어 맞춤법에 전혀 주의를 기울이지 않는다는 것입니다. Murphy 선생님은 Ryan의 문제가 문장을 읽는 방법은 알지만, 필기시험을 보면 맞춤법 실수를 한다는 데 있는 걸 알아차립니다. Murphy 선생님은 Ryan에게 올바른 맞춤법 사용은 특히 한국어에서 중요한 또 다른 요소라고 말해주고 싶습니다. 이러한 상황에서 Murphy 선생님이 Ryan에게 할 수 있는 말로 가장 적당한 것은 무엇일까요?

* Murphy 선생님: <u>맞춤법 실수를 줄이도록 노력해야 한단다</u>.

해설: 한국어를 공부 중인 Ryan의 문제는 맞춤법 실수가 잦다는 것이므로 맞춤법에 신경을 쓰도록 조언하는 것이 이 상황에 가장 적절한 말이다.

문항 21 ④
문항 22 ③

Script & Dictation

W: Dave, what did you do last weekend?

M: I **participated in** a writer's lecture about effective communication skills.

W: That sounds great. So what are some important factors in effective communication?

M: It is quite difficult to define in just a few words, but **being assertive** is definitely one of the most important things in the communication.

W: But being assertive can easily fall into being aggressive. Once your partner **gets upset with your attitude**, communication ends and you cannot achieve your goal.

M: I know. So being assertive without slipping over the line into being passive or aggressive is the key, but it's also **a real challenge**.

W: Then, how can we become assertive without being passive or aggressive?

M: The writer said it is better to use "I messages" instead of "You messages" because people often receive "You messages" as blaming. For example, say "I am really disappointed that we lost the bidding" instead of saying "You didn't try hard enough to win the bidding."

W: I see. That means finger-pointing behavior easily **falls into aggressiveness**. Right?

M: Right. Also, phrases like "Yes, I understand that", "I can see why you think that", "Yes, I think I've got your point", and "You may be right" can deflect criticism.

W: I will use them when I have to criticize.

M: Remember that avoiding criticism cannot help. When criticism is necessary, you have to do it; just try to be sensitive when you do.

여: Dave, 지난 주말에 뭐했어?

남: 효과적인 의사소통 기술에 관한 어떤 작가의 강연에 참석했어.

여: 멋지다. 효과적인 의사소통에 있어서 중요한 요소들엔 뭐가 있어?

남: 몇 가지 단어로만 정의 내리는 건 좀 어렵겠지만, 확실히 자신감 있는 것이 의사소통에 있어서 가장 중요한 것 중 하나야.

여: 하지만 자신감 있다는 건 자칫하면 공격적인 게 될 수도 있잖아. 태도 때문에 상대방 마음이 상하면 의사소통은 끝나버리고, 얻고자 하는 것을 얻을 수 없게 된다고.

남: 맞아. 그래서 수동적이거나 공격적인 성향으로 치우치지 않고 자신감 있는 것이 핵심이야. 하지만 진짜 어려운 일이지.

여: 그렇다면 어떻게 해야 수동적이거나 공격적이지 않고, 자신감 있을 수 있는 건데?

남: 작가 말로는 '너는'이라는 말 대신 '나는'이라는 말을 사용하는 것이 더 좋다고 해. 사람들이 '너는'이란 말을 비난으로 받아들이는 경우가 많으니까. 예를 들어, '너는 입찰을 따내기 위해 충분히 노력하지 않았어.'라고 말하기보단 '나는 우리가 입찰을 따내지 못해서 정말 실망했어.'라고 말하는 거지.

여: 그렇구나. 그러니까 지적하는 행동이 자칫하면 공격적인 게 될 수 있는 거란 말이지?

남: 맞아. 또 '그래, 이해해', '네가 왜 그렇게 생각하는지 알 거 같아', '그래, 네 말뜻 잘 알겠어', '네 말이 맞을지도 몰라'와 같은 표현으로 비난을 피할 수 있지.

여: 비판해야 할 때 그런 표현들을 사용해 봐야겠어.

남: 비판을 피하는 것은 도움이 안 된다는 것을 기억해. 비판해야 할 때는 해야지. 하지만 그럴 땐 세심해져야겠지.

해설: 21. 대화 초반, 남자는 효과적인 의사소통 기술에 관한 강의를 듣고 왔다고 언급하였다. 그리고 나서 공격적 또는 수동적으로 보이거나, 남을 비난하는 것처럼 보이지 않는 의사소통 방식에 관해 다양한 표현 예시를 들어 대화를 이어가고 있으므로 정답은 ④번이다. **22.** 남자는 상대방을 비난한다는 오해의 소지 없이 말하는 방법으로 '너는'이라고 말하는 대신 '나는'이라고 표현해야 한다는 것을 언급했다. 이러한 측면에서 이야기의 초점이 내가 아닌 상대방에 가 있는 ③번은 비판의 말로 적절하지 않다.

1	④	2	⑤	3	④	4	②	5	②
6	③	7	⑤	8	④	9	⑤	10	②
11	④	12	⑤	13	①	14	④	15	③
16	①	17	③	18	③	19	①	20	③
21	③	22	⑤							

문항 1 ④

Script & Dictation

W: Leon, I'd like to start **my own business**.

M: What kind of business are you interested in?

W: Something to do with sports, but I'm not sure if I should open a sports equipment store or **establish a sports agency**.

M: It seems the latter one is more suitable for you.

여: Leon, 전 제 사업을 시작하고 싶어요.

남: 어떤 종류의 사업에 관심 있는데요?

여: 스포츠와 관련된 거요. 그런데 스포츠용품 판매장을 열지, 아니면 스포츠 대행사를 설립해야 할지 잘 모르겠네요.

남: 후자가 당신에게 더 어울릴 것 같네요.

해설: 스포츠 관련 사업을 하고 싶은데 어떤 걸 해야 할지 모르겠다고 고민하는 여자에게 언급한 사업들 중 하나를 골라 그것이 더 잘 어울릴 것 같다고 말하는 ④번이 적절한 응답이다.

문항 2 ⑤

Script & Dictation

M: I want to go to Italy next semester. **Have you been there** before?

W: I've been to Rome and Venice for summer vacation. Why do you want to go?

M: I'm interested in the language. But I don't know **what to do** to learn it.

W: Look for some language program on the Internet, first.

남: 다음 학기에 이탈리아 가고 싶다. 넌 가본 적 있니?

여: 여름방학 때 로마랑 베니스 가봤어. 왜 가고 싶은데?

남: 이탈리아어에 관심이 있거든. 그런데 배우려면 어떻게 해야 하는지는 모르겠어.

여: 먼저 인터넷으로 언어 프로그램을 찾아보렴.

해설: 남자는 이탈리아어에 관심이 많아 이탈리아에 가고 싶다고 했으나 언어를 배우기 위해서는 뭘 해야 할지 모르겠다고 하는 상황이다. 따라서 언어 공부와 관련하여 도움이 될 만한 조언을 해주는 것이 자연스러운 응답이 되겠다.

문항 3 ④

Script & Dictation

W: Jinsu, I heard you play the drums very well.

M: Not really. **I've just been practicing** as a kind of hobby.

W: Do you have **any plans to join** a band or anything like that?

M: That would be too stressful. I just play to relax.

여: 진수야, 너 드럼 굉장히 잘 친다고 들었어.

남: 그렇지도 않아. 그냥 취미로 연습하고 있어.

여: 밴드에 가입한다거나 할 계획은 없어?

남: 그럼 너무 스트레스받을 것 같아서. 난 그냥 긴장을 풀려고 연주하는 거야.

해설: 남자는 취미 삼아 드럼을 치고 있다고 말했다. 따라서 밴드 가입에 대한 생각을 물었을 때 적절한 답변은 그러면 드럼 치는 것이 큰 부담이 될 것 같다고 말하는 ④번이 되겠다.

문항 4 ②

Script & Dictation

W: Hello, Luke students. I'm Laura Dern, **a junior** in the Department of German Language and Literature. It has already been a month since you entered Luke College **as freshmen**. How's everything going? Is it as exciting as you expected? If not, why don't you join the college's theater group? The club has a 40-year-old tradition, and it is one of the most popular clubs among students. If you **become a member** of the club, you'll make friends with many other members, and you can perform in a play every semester. I'm sure it'll make your college life **more rewarding**. Even if you're only interested in watching plays, join our theater group. You can also discuss your favorite plays.

여: 안녕하세요, Luke 학생 여러분. 저는 독어독문학과 3학년에 재학 중인 Laura Dern입니다. 여러분이 Luke 대학교 신입생으로 입학한 지도 벌써 한 달이 되었네요. 어떠세요? 생각한 것 만큼 재미있나요? 그렇지 않다면 우리 대학 연극 동아리에 가입해 보는 건 어때요? 40년 전통의 연극 동아리는 학생들에게 인기 많은 동아리 중 하나랍니다. 동아리 회원이 되면 다른 동아리 회원들과 친구도 될 수 있고, 매 학기 연극 공연도 할 수 있어요. 여러분의 대학 생활을 더 보람 있게 만드는 활동이 될 거라 확신합니다. 연극 관람에만 관심이 있어도 저희 연극 동아리에 가입해 보세요. 여러분이 좋아하는 연극에 관해 토론도 할 수 있답니다.

해설: 독일어가 전공인 여자가 대학교 1학년 학생들을 대상으로 연극 동아리를 소개하면서 가입을 권유하고 있다.

문항 5 ②

Script & Dictation

W: Kevin! What is this **wrapping paper**?

M: What? Ah, I ate a hamburger.

W: I told you lots of times, Kevin. Fast food is **bad for you**.

M: I know, Mom. But you kind of promised.

W: What do you mean?

M: You said if I got an A⁺ on the math exam, you'd **grant my wish**.

W: Did you get an A⁺ in math?

M: Yes, so I bought and ate the hamburger. I love hamburgers.

W: You **did a great job** on the exam. But, you should have called and asked me about the hamburger, first.

M: I'm sorry, Mom. But I was really hungry.

W: Okay, but again, fast food is not healthy. You should try not to eat it so often.

여: Kevin! 이 포장지는 뭐니?

남: 네? 아, 제가 햄버거 먹었거든요.

여: 엄마가 여러 번 말했잖니, Kevin. 패스트 푸드는 안 좋다고 말이야.

남: 저도 아는데요, 그런데 엄마가 약속하셨잖아요.

여: 무슨 말이니?

남: 제가 수학 시험에서 A⁺ 받으면 소원 들어주신다고 했잖아요.

여: 수학에서 A⁺ 받은 거야?

남: 네, 그래서 햄버거를 사 먹었어요. 햄버거가 정말 좋아요.

여: 시험은 정말 잘 쳤구나. 그렇지만 먼저 엄마한테 전화해서 햄버거 사 먹어도 되는지 물어봤어야지.

남: 죄송해요, 엄마. 하지만 정말 배고팠거든요.

여: 알았어. 그래도 다시 한 번 말하지만 패스트 푸드는 건강에 안 좋아. 너무 자주 먹진 않도록 노력해.

해설: 대화 초반부에 여자는 패스트 푸드는 좋지 않다고 언급했고, 대화 마지막 부분에서 이를 다시 한 번 더 강조하면서 될 수 있으면 자주 먹지 말라고 말했다.

문항 6 ③

Script & Dictation

M: Hi, how are the wedding preparations going?

W: They're going well, thanks. I'm going to buy furniture this weekend.

M: Are you going to buy it in **an offline shop**?

W: Well, I am planning to have a look in some offline shops first. Then, if I see anything I like, I will try to find something **similar at online stores**. I'll go for the cheapest offer.

M: That's a brilliant idea. But be careful with online shopping. You should research the online seller before you give them your credit card information.

W: Of course. I always **check out the reliability** of the company first.

M: Also, using credit cards can be safer than transferring money.

W: You're right. Online shopping is one good way to buy cheap products, but people should always keep in mind that **they can be cheated**.

남: 안녕, 결혼 준비는 어떻게 돼가?

여: 잘 돼가고 있어, 고마워. 이번 주말에 가구를 사려고.

남: 오프라인 매장에서 살 거야?

여: 먼저 오프라인 매장에서 한번 살펴볼 계획이야. 그러고 나서 맘에 드는 게 있으면 그것과 비슷한 것을 온라인 매장에서 찾아보려고. 제일 싼 걸로 살 거야.

남: 정말 좋은 생각이다. 하지만 온라인 쇼핑할 때 조심해. 네 신용카드 정보를 건네기 전에 온라인 판매자에 대해 좀 더 알아봐야 해.

여: 물론이지. 난 항상 믿을만한 회사인지부터 확인하는걸.

남: 그리고 신용카드 사용하는 게 돈을 이체하는 것보다 안전해.

여: 네 말이 맞아. 온라인 쇼핑은 물건을 값싸게 구매할 수 있는 좋은 방법이지만 사람들은 항상 사기당할 수도 있다는 걸 명심해야 해.

해설: 여자가 가구를 가격 비교를 하여 온라인 매장에서 저렴한 것으로 구매하겠다고 하자, 남자는 온라인 매장 이용 시 유의할 점들을 언급한다. 이에 여자도 사기를 당할 수도 있음을 명심해야 한다면서 남자의 말에 동의하고 있으므로 정답은 ③번이다.

문항 7 ⑤

Script & Dictation

M: Maria, I heard **a beeping sound** just now. Can you step on the brake lightly?

W: Okay. Is that enough?

M: A little bit harder. Okay. There it is. When did you last change the brake pads?

W: I don't know. I haven't actually changed the brake pads for a few years.

M: Usually, people **replace their brake pads** every 25,000 kilometers. Otherwise, you could have a serious car accident, especially when you **are driving downhill**.

W: Really? I didn't know that.

M: Oh, boy. Not only brake pads. There are a number of things you should periodically check in the car.

W: For example?

M: Engine oil level, timing belt, tire air pressure... There are many of them. I think it's better to go to the garage to check the brake pads. Then we can get some information about **a periodic check list** for a car.

W: That sounds great.

남: Maria, 방금 삐 소리가 들렸는데. 브레이크 살짝 밟아볼래?

여: 알았어. 이 정도면 됐어?

남: 조금만 더 세게. 좋아. 그거였네. 마지막으로 브레이크 패드 교체한 게 언제야?

여: 모르겠는데. 사실 교체 안 한 지 몇 년 됐어.

남: 보통은 2만 5천 킬로미터 주행할 때마다 교체하는데. 안 그러면 심각한 차 사고가 날 수도 있어. 특히 내리막길 운전하다 말이야.

여: 정말? 몰랐어.

남: 오, 이런. 브레이크 패드뿐만이 아니라고. 차 내부엔 정기적으로 점검해야 할 것들이 많아.

여: 예를 들면?

남: 엔진 오일 수준, 타이밍 벨트, 타이어 공기압… 확인할 게 많아. 브레이크 패드 점검하러 정비소 가 보는 게 좋을 거 같아. 그럼 자동차 정기 점검 목록에 관한 정보도 좀 얻을 수 있을 거야.

여: 좋아.

해설: 몇 년 동안 브레이크 패드를 교체하지 않았다는 여자의 말에 남자는 주기적인 자동차 점검의 중요성에 대해 설명하며 정비소에 가는 것이 좋을 것 같다고 했고, 여자도 이에 동의하였다.

문항 8 ④

Script & Dictation

W: Good morning. What can I help you with?

M: I'm here to ask about some information **regarding your ad** in today's paper.

W: You mean the Paris-Venice tour package?

M: That's right. **Would you give me** some more details about it?

W: Of course. This one includes tours of the Eiffel Tower and the Louvre Museum and the wonderful scenery of water city from a boat, and you can enjoy original French and Italian cuisine.

M: Sounds fascinating. How about the flight? Can I **take a non-stop flight**?

W: Of course.

M: Okay, then, how much is the package?

W: **The original price** is $3,500, but if you book it today, you can have a 25% discount.

M: That sounds great! I'd like to reserve it right away.

여: 좋은 아침이네요. 뭘 도와드릴까요?

남: 오늘 신문에 내신 광고에 대해서 물어볼 게 좀 있어서 왔습니다.

여: 파리-베니스 관광 패키지 말씀이세요?

남: 맞습니다. 좀 더 자세히 알 수 있을까요?

여: 물론이죠. 이 상품은 에펠탑과 루브르 박물관 방문, 보트에서 보는 수상 도시의 멋진 경치 관광을 포함하고 있습니다. 또 정통 프랑스 요리와 이탈리아 요리도 맛볼 수 있고요.

남: 멋지네요. 비행편은요? 직항 탈 수 있나요?

여: 물론이죠.

남: 그렇군요. 그럼, 패키지 가격은 어떻게 되나요?

여: 원래는 3,500달러인데 오늘 예약하시면 25% 할인받으실 수 있습니다.

남: 정말 괜찮은데요! 바로 예약하고 싶습니다.

해설: 신문에 게재된 외국 여행 패키지 광고를 본 남자가 광고를 낸 여행사에 직접 찾아가 직원으로부터 해당 패키지에 관한 자세한 설명을 듣고 예약을 하려고 하는 상황이다. 따라서 ④번이 정답이다.

문항 9 ⑤

Script & Dictation

[Telephone rings.]

W: Hi, Eunsik. I'm Cathy. I just called to tell you how to get to my place.

M: Oh, thanks. I can **write it down** now.

W: Do you know the fire station between Queen Street and William Avenue?

M: Yes. Oh, I can use the parking lot near the fire station, right?

W: Right. **Park there and walk out** to William Avenue. Then you'll see a crosswalk.

M: Okay, I know that area a bit. Should I **cross the road** there?

W: Yeah. Then you can see Italian Square and a fountain. Walk through the square until you get to an M-Mart on the right.

M: Okay, the M-Mart. Go on.

W: Then, you can see my place across from the M-Mart.

M: Across from the M-Mart? Which side do you mean? Across the square or beside the M-Mart building?

W: Oh, **sorry for the confusion**. Just go to the next building. That's it.

M: Okay, I got it.

[전화 벨 소리]

여: 안녕, 은식아. 나 Cathy야. 우리 집 어떻게 오는지 알려주려고 전화했어.

남: 아, 고마워. 지금 받아 적을 수 있어.

여: Queen Street와 William Avenue 사이에 있는 소방서 아니?

남: 응. 아, 소방서 근처의 주차장 이용할 수 있지?

여: 맞아. 거기 주차하고 William Avenue로 나와. 그럼 건널목이 보일 거야.

남: 알았어, 그 부근은 좀 알고 있어. 거기서 길 건너야 하니?

여: 응. 그럼 Italian 광장이랑 분수가 보일 거야. 광장을 따라 걸어 내려오다 보면 오른쪽에 M 마트가 나와.

남: M 마트란 말이지, 알았어. 계속 해 봐.

여: 그러면 M 마트 건너에 우리 집이 보일 거야.

남: M 마트 건너라고? 어느 쪽으로 말이니? 광장 건너인 거니, 아니면 M 마트 건물 옆인 거니?

여: 아, 헷갈리게 해서 미안해. 그냥 그다음 건물로 가. 그러면 돼.

남: 그래, 알았어.

해설: 소방서 근처의 주차장에 주차한 후, 건널목을 건너서 나오는 광장을 따라 가다 보면, 그림 상 위에서 아래로 내려오는 사람의 기준으로 오른쪽에 M 마트가 있다. 남자가 여자의 집이 M 마트에서 어느 방향으로 건너에 있는지를 묻자, 여자는 옆에 있는 건물이라고 했으므로 ⑤번이 정답이다.

문항 10 ②

Script & Dictation

[Telephone rings.]

W: Harvia Sauna. How can I help you?

M: I left my watch there.

W: Did you use a safe deposit box or just leave it in **a normal locker**?

M: It's not really an expensive watch, so I didn't use a safe deposit.

W: Okay, let me check... Hmm... *[Pause]* I checked our **lost-and-found box**. What color is your watch?

M: It's just white with a round-shaped face and a black strap. It's a very common kind of watch, but it has the initials "RB" on **the edge of the strap**.

W: I can see it. Right, we have your watch.

M: Oh, thank you.

W: It's my pleasure. **Would you like me** to have it delivered?

M: No, thanks. I'll stop by this evening on my way back home. Thank you so much.

[전화 벨 소리]

여: Harvia 사우나입니다. 무엇을 도와드릴까요?

남: 거기에 제 시계를 두고 왔어요.

여: 귀중품 보관함을 사용하셨나요, 아니면 일반 물품 보관함에 두셨나요?

남: 그렇게 비싼 시계가 아니라 귀중품 보관함은 사용하지 않았습니다.

여: 알겠습니다, 확인해 보죠. 흠… *[잠시 후]* 분실물 상자를 확인해 봤는데 시계가 무슨 색깔인가요?

남: 흰색에 모양이 동그란 시계입니다. 시곗줄은 검은색이고요. 아주 평범한 시계인데 시곗줄 끝에 'RB'라는 머리글자가 있어요.

여: 보입니다. 손님 시계가 여기 있네요.

남: 고맙습니다.

여: 천만에요. 배송해드릴까요?

남: 아닙니다, 괜찮습니다. 오늘 저녁 집에 가는 길에 들르겠습니다. 정말 고맙습니다.

해설: 남자는 전화 건 곳에 자신이 두고 온 시계가 있다는 것을 확인하였다. 배송 여부를 묻는 여자에게 대화 마지막에 직접 찾으러 가겠다고 말했으므로 ②번이 정답이다.

문항 11 ④

Script & Dictation

M: Okhee, what are you doing?

W: I'm writing a social science report about a **nursery facility**.

M: What is the focus of the report?

W: **According to** my survey, there are so many children near my area and some of them can't go to the nursery.

M: I heard a lot of news that there's a nursery crisis.

W: Right. I didn't expect to find that the **nurseries here are lacking**, so one mother even quit her job. On the other hand, in the country, nurseries are closing because student numbers are too low.

M: That's true. Why don't you include an interview with a couple whose children go to a nursery in the report?

W: If possible, could you **arrange a meeting with** some parents so that I could talk to them?

M: I'll ask my neighbors.

남: 옥희야, 뭐 하고 있어?

여: 보육시설에 관한 사회과학 보고서 쓰고 있어.

남: 무엇에 초점을 둔 보고서니?

여: 내 조사에 의하면 내가 사는 곳 주변에는 아이들이 정말 많은데 어린이집에 못 가는 아이들이 있어.

남: 나도 어린이집의 위기에 관한 소식을 많이 들었어.

여: 맞아. 여기 어린이집이 모자랄 거라곤 예상하지 못했어. 그래서 어떤 엄마는 직장도 그만뒀대. 반면에 시골에서는 학생 수가 너무 적어서 보육시설들이 문을 닫고 있대.

남: 맞아. 보고서에 자녀들이 어린이집에 다니는 부부의 인터뷰를 넣는 건 어때?

여: 혹시 가능하면, 내가 몇몇 부모들과 이야기해 볼 수 있게 자리 좀 만들어줄 수 있어?

남: 이웃들에게 물어볼게.

해설: 보육시설에 관한 보고서를 쓰는 여자는 대화 후반부 남자에게 보육시설에 다니는 자녀를 둔 부모들과 인터뷰 자리를 주선해달라고 부탁하고 있다. 따라서 정답은 ④번이다.

문항 12 ⑤

Script & Dictation

M: Hello, Ms. Parker? My name is Dongkyun Lim. I was a student in your drama class last year.

W: Oh, you're a student at Yerin Art Institute! You sang **on the last day** of my class!

M: Yes, that was me. I released an album though it didn't sell very well.

W: Don't be disappointed. You are young and have so much potential.

M: Thanks. I heard that you **are currently directing** the musical, *The Romantic Holiday*. I was wondering if there was **anything I could help** you with.

W: What can you do?

M: I can sing, act, and even dance. Would there be **a little role for me**?

W: Hmm, why don't you audition first? That is the best I can do.

M: I know I won't disappoint you. Thank you so much!

남: 안녕하세요, Parker 선생님? 저는 임동균입니다. 작년 선생님의 드라마 수업 들었던 학생이에요.

여: 아, 예린 예술 학교 다니던 학생이군요! 수업 마지막 날 노래도 불렀잖아요!

남: 네, 그게 저였어요. 잘 팔리진 않았지만 앨범도 냈습니다.

여: 실망하지 마요. 학생은 어리고 가능성도 많으니까.

남: 고맙습니다. 선생님께서 지금 '로맨틱 홀리데이'라는 뮤지컬 감독하고 계시다고 들었어요. 제가 도와드릴 수 있는 일은 없을지 궁금해서요.

여: 뭘 할 수 있나요?

남: 노래와 연기를 할 줄 알고, 또 춤도 출 수 있습니다. 작은 배역이라도 맡을 수 있을까요?

여: 음, 일단 오디션부터 보는 게 어때요? 그게 내가 할 수 있는 최선인데.

남: 실망하지 않으실 거예요. 정말 고맙습니다!

해설: 노래를 잘하는 남자는 뮤지컬을 감독 중인 여자에게 뮤지컬 배역을 달라고 부탁하고 있다.

문항 13 ①

Script & Dictation

[Telephone rings.]

M: Hello.

W: Hi, Roberto. It's me. **I've just checked in** to the hotel room.

M: Hey, how are you? Did you enjoy the flight?

W: It was okay. It is really nice here. The weather is cool and the wind is sweet.

M: You really like Rome, huh. I **fed your parrots** and watered the plants.

W: Thank you. Are they okay?

M: Sure, and I **picked up your clothes** from the dry cleaner's.

W: Oh, I should have done that before leaving. Thank you so much for that.

M: No problem. Also, I told our yoga teacher about your absence for two weeks. The **electric bill arrived**, but the due date is far enough away. You can cover it when you get back.

W: Sure. Once again, thanks so much for everything! You are the best!

[전화 벨소리]

남: 여보세요.

여: 안녕, Roberto. 나야. 방금 호텔 객실에 체크인했어.

남: 안녕? 비행은 즐거웠어?

여: 괜찮았어. 그리고 여기 진짜 좋아. 선선한 날씨에 바람도 상쾌해.

남: 너 정말 로마를 좋아하는구나. 네 앵무새들 먹이 주고 화분에 물 줬어.

여: 고마워. 다들 괜찮지?

남: 그럼. 그리고 세탁소에서 네 옷도 찾아다 놨어.

여: 맞다, 떠나기 전에 해야 했는데. 해 줘서 정말 고마워.

남: 천만에. 그리고 우리 요가 선생님께 너 2주 동안 빠진다고 말씀드렸어. 전기세 고지서도 왔는데 납부기한 아직 한참 남았으니까 네가 돌아와서 처리하면 될 거야.

여: 당연히 그럴게. 다 처리해 준 거 다시 한 번 고마워! 네가 최고야!

해설: 남자는 외국으로 여행을 가서 집을 비운 여자를 위해 여러 가지 일을 대신 봐주고 있다. 대화 후반부에 전기세 납부는 기한이 많이 남았기에 여자가 여행에서 돌아오면 처리할 수 있다고 말했으므로 ①번이 정답이다.

문항 14 ④

Script & Dictation

M: Good morning, ma'am. May I help you?

W: I'm from Dream and Love Kindergarten.

M: Ahh. Two hundred flowers, right?

W: Right. Which flowers **do you recommend** for this fall?

M: In fall, chrysanthemums are the most popular choice.

W: Is there **any difference in cost** between pink and yellow?

M: Not at all. They're both $3 each.

W: Then, I'll have 50 of each. **What about** this beautiful lotus?

M: Children will love it. You have a big pond, so it will be really good. They're $4 each.

W: Then I'll take 100 lotuses, too.

M: You've ordered over 100, so I can **give you a ten-percent discount** on the total price.

W: Oh! Thank you.

남: 좋은 아침입니다, 손님. 도와드릴까요?

여: '꿈과 사랑' 유치원에서 왔습니다.

남: 아, 꽃 200송이 말씀하신 분, 맞죠?

여: 맞아요. 올가을에 추천해주실 만한 꽃이 뭔가요?

남: 가을엔 국화가 가장 인기가 많죠.

여: 분홍색과 노란색은 가격 차이가 있나요?

남: 전혀요. 둘 다 송이당 3달러입니다.

여: 그럼, 각 50송이 주세요. 이 예쁜 연꽃은요?

남: 아이들이 굉장히 좋아할 거예요. 유치원에 큰 연못이 있으니 딱 좋을 겁니다. 송이당 4달러입니다.

여: 그럼, 연꽃 100송이도 살게요.

남: 100송이 이상 주문하셨기 때문에 총 구매 가격에서 10% 할인해 드리겠습니다.

여: 오! 고맙습니다.

해설: 색깔에 상관없이 송이당 가격이 3달러로 같은 국화를 분홍색과 노란색 각각 50송이씩 산다고 했으므로 300달러이고, 한 송이에 4달러인 연꽃은 100송이를 산다고 했으므로 400달러다. 따라서 총 700달러이지만 10% 할인을 해 준다고 했기 때문에 여자가 내야 할 금액은 700달러에서 70달러를 뺀 630달러이다.

Script & Dictation

M: A pike conger is **a kind of eel**. They normally reach 1.5 meters in length and sometimes reach more than 2 meters. This species is caught in deep seas. It is popular in Japan for a **traditional cuisine** named Hamo. In the past, people in China and Korea did not eat this because the fish look like snakes. So whenever they caught pike congers, they sold them to Japanese people. This eel **contains a lot of protein**, so it is also known to be a healthy food. It is especially rich in EPA and DHA, **which are reported** effective to clean blood, so eating a lot of pike conger can help prevent heart disease.

남: 갯장어는 장어의 일종이다. 길이는 보통 1.5미터에 이르지만 2미터 이상 자라는 경우도 있다. 이 종은 심해에서 잡힌다. 일본에서 갯장어는 '하모'라는 전통 요리로 인기가 많다. 과거에 중국인과 한국인은 갯장어가 뱀처럼 생겼다는 이유로 이를 먹지 않았다. 그래서 갯장어를 잡으면 일본인에게 팔았다. 갯장어는 단백질이 풍부해 건강식품으로도 알려졌다. 특히 혈액을 정화하는데 효과적인 것으로 알려진 EPA와 DHA가 많아 갯장어를 많이 먹으면 심장 질환을 예방할 수 있다.

해설: 예전에 중국과 한국에서는 사람들이 그 생김새가 뱀 같은 갯장어를 먹지 않고, 잡는 대로 일본 사람들에게 팔았다고 했으므로 ③번이 정답이다.

문항 16 ①

Script & Dictation

W: Fleur de Sel de Guérande, this is a French or Celtic sea salt that takes on a gray color. It is a coarse, granular sea salt popularized by the French. As French cuisine **gains popularity** worldwide, this gray salt is also becoming famous because it is one of the most important and basic ingredients in French cuisine. **This salt is harvested** in solar evaporation salt pans, and the harvesters deliberately **put the salt in** contact with the silt beneath it. This harvesting process may seem a bit dirty, but it is known that this process **enriches the mineral contents** of the gray salt.

여: 플뢰르 드 셀 드 게랑드는 회색을 띠는 프랑스 또는 켈트 해의 소금이다. 프랑스인들이 대중화한 알갱이가 있는 굵은 바다 소금이다. 프랑스 요리가 세계적인 인기를 얻게 됨에 따라 이 회색 소금 역시 유명해지는 중이다. 프랑스 요리에서 가장 중요하면서도 기본적인 재료이기 때문이다. 이 소금은 천일염전에서 수확되는데 수확하는 사람들은 일부러 소금을 밑에 깔린 토사와 접촉하게 한다. 이러한 수확 과정이 조금 비위생적으로 보일 수도 있겠지만 그렇게 함으로써 이 회색 소금의 미네랄 함량이 풍부해진다고 한다.

해설: 프랑스 요리의 필수 재료가 된 이유에 대해서는 언급되지 않았다. 또한 미네랄 함량이 풍부하다는 사실은 언급되었으나 염분 함량에 대한 정보는 소개되지 않았으므로 정답은 ①번이다.

문항 17 ③

Script & Dictation

W: What type of bike do you want? Will you bike **in a rugged place** or just cruise downtown or along the river?

M: For cruising is good enough for me. My girlfriend rides so well, so I want to ride with her **along the river**.

W: That sounds romantic. Actually, bikes are really fun and make your life so much easier.

M: What do you mean?

W: **When commuting**, or going to a shop or library, there are some distances that make it difficult to decide whether to take a bus or to go on foot. **For those distances**, bikes are perfect.

M: Oh, yes. I see what you mean. Do you recommend a bike with high gears?

W: Well, in your case, **just over fifteen** would be enough. Under ten is for the elderly and children.

여: 어떤 종류의 자전거를 원하세요? 길이 험한 곳에서 타실 건가요, 아니면 그냥 시내나 강가에서 쉬엄쉬엄 타실 건가요?

남: 천천히 돌아다니는 용도로도 충분해요. 제 여자친구가 자전거를 잘 타서 함께 강가로 타러 가고 싶어요.

여: 낭만적이네요. 사실 자전거 타기는 참 재미있기도 하고, 삶을 훨씬 더 편하게 해주기도 하죠.

남: 무슨 말씀이세요?

여: 통근할 때나, 아니면 가게나 도서관 같은 곳을 갈 때 버스를 타기도 그렇고 걸어가기도 좀 모호한 거리가 있잖아요. 그럴 때 자전거 타는 게 안성맞춤이죠.

남: 오, 그렇네요. 무슨 말씀인지 알겠어요. 기어가 높은 자전거를 타야 할까요?

여: 손님은 그냥 15단 이상이면 충분해요. 10단 이하는 어르신이나 아이들 용이죠.

해설: 남자는 시내나 강가에서 탈 수 있는 산책용 자전거면 충분하다고 했고, 여자가 15단 이상 기어를 추천했으므로 ③번이 정답이다.

문항 18 ③

Script & Dictation

W: What's wrong with you, Jaewon? You look down.

M: I'm in trouble, Hyunjoo. The science homework **is killing me**.

W: What, you mean for Mr. Han's class?

M: Yeah, **I'm supposed to** dissect a fish, and sketch the internal organs. I think it's too cruel. I don't want to do this assignment.

W: Jaewon, but you eat fish. Eating is much crueler, don't you think?

M: No, it's different. But when you put it like that, I think I want to **stop eating fish**.

W: Come on, Jaewon, don't be so silly! When do you **have to finish it by**?

M: By Wednesday. Do you think I can do it?

W: You can do it well, of course. Just do it.

M: Thank you. I'm so lucky to have you as a friend.

여: 무슨 일이야, 재원아? 기분이 안 좋아 보이네.

남: 나 큰일 났어, 현주야. 과학 숙제 때문에 너무 괴로워.

여: 한 선생님 수업 말이야?

남: 응, 물고기 해부해서 내장을 스케치해야 하거든. 너무 잔인한 것 같아. 이 과제 하고 싶지 않아.

여: 그렇지만 너 생선 먹잖아. 먹는 게 더 잔인한 거 아니야?

남: 아니야, 그건 달라. 하지만 네가 그렇게 말하니까 나 이제 생선도 그만 먹어야겠어.

여: 제발, 재원아, 바보 같은 소리 하지 마! 언제까지 끝내야 해?

남: 수요일까지. 내가 할 수 있을까?

여: 당연히 잘할 수 있어. 일단 해봐.

남: 고마워. 너 같은 친구가 있어 난 참 행운이야.

해설: 물고기 해부 과제를 못 하겠다고 하는 남자에게 친구인 여자는 대화 후반부에 할 수 있다며 격려해주고 있다. 따라서 이에 고맙다고 화답하는 것이 자연스러운 응답이 되겠다.

문항 19 ①

Script & Dictation

M: This apartment is located near the subway station, so it's very convenient to **get to downtown** or anywhere else.

W: Yes, you're right. And to our family, that's an important option. Especially, my daughter is a freshman in University of Aran.

M: In that case, this town is **so good for** her. Okay, look around this house.

W: How many rooms are there? We need at least three rooms and two bathrooms.

M: This is just what you need. How old are your kids?

W: My daughter is a freshman as I said, and the boy is fifteen.

M: Near here, there's a middle school. It's **a leading private school** with a long history and tradition.

W: That sounds so nice. **How long does it take** to get there?

M: Around fifteen minutes on foot.

W: This is the perfect house for us.

남: 이 아파트는 지하철역 근처에 있어서 시내나 다른 어디든 이동하기가 참 편하답니다.

여: 그러네요. 우리 가족에게는 중요한 요소랍니다. 특히 딸이 아란 대학교 1학년이거든요.

남: 그렇다면 이 동네가 따님께 정말 좋겠네요. 자, 집을 둘러 보세요.

여: 방이 몇 개나 되나요? 적어도 방 세 개에 욕실 두 개는 있어야 하는데.

남: 그렇다면 이 집이 딱 맞네요. 자녀분들이 몇 살인가요?

여: 말씀드린 것처럼 딸은 대학 신입생이고, 아들은 15살이에요.

남: 이 근처에 중학교가 있어요. 역사와 전통이 오래된 명문 사립 학교죠.

여: 정말 괜찮네요. 거기까지 가는 데 얼마나 걸리나요?

남: 도보로 15분 정도요.

여: 이 집은 우리 가족에게 정말 안성맞춤이네요.

해설: 아파트의 위치, 방과 욕실 수, 주변 시설 등 여자는 아파트의 조건에 만족하고 있다. 따라서 자신이 찾던 바로 그런 곳이라는 응답이 흐름 상 자연스럽다.

문항 20 ③

Script & Dictation

W: Yumi is driving her car to go to her mother's place. When she's almost there, a boy suddenly comes out from **between parked cars**. He is cycling with earphones on. She stops the car as soon as she can and honks at him. But he **doesn't notice anything** due to the earphones. He's not really cycling fast, but Yumi feels he's going **much faster than** any pedestrians. She is really astonished, but he doesn't know what happened. Yumi thinks about what to do. **Looking at a phone** or listening to music with earphones while riding a bike is really dangerous. So she wants to warn the boy of this dangerous behavior. In this situation, what would Yumi most likely say to the boy?

* Yumi: You must not use your earphones while cycling.

여: 유미는 어머니 집에 가려고 운전 중이다. 거의 다 도착했을 무렵, 주차된 차들 사이로 갑자기 한 소년이 나왔다. 소년은 이어폰을 낀 채 자전거를 타고 있다. 유미는 재빨리 차를 멈추고 소년을 향해 자동차 경적을 울렸다. 그러나 이어폰 때문에 소년은 미처 알아채지 못한다. 빠른 속도로 자전거를 타고 있는 건 아니지만 유미는 소년이 다른 보행자들보다 훨씬 빨리 가고 있다고 느낀다. 유미는 정말 깜짝 놀랐지만, 소년은 무슨 일이 일어났는지 모르고 있다. 유미는 어떻게 해야 할지 생각한다. 이어폰을 낀 채로 자전거를 타면서 휴대폰을 보거나 음악을 듣는 것은 정말 위험한 일이다. 따라서 유미는 소년의 이런 위험한 행동에 대해 경고하고 싶다. 이러한 상황에서 유미가 소년에게 할 수 있는 말로 가장 적당한 것은 무엇인가?

* 유미: 자전거 탈 때 이어폰을 사용하면 안 돼.

해설: 유미는 운전 중 갑자기 튀어나온 자전거에 놀란 상황이다. 그러나 자전거를 타고 있는 소년은 이어폰을 끼고 있어서 벌어진 상황에 대해 인지하지 못하고 있으므로 이를 지적하는 내용의 경고를 하는 ③번이 가장 적절한 답이다.

문항 21 ③
문항 22 ⑤

Script & Dictation

M: Finland has probably the hardest and the most challenging drivers' tests in the world. It is known to have 36 months of **mandatory driving school**, and the course includes theory and practical driving skills.

One interesting thing is that this snow-covered country requests all drivers learn how to save a car in critical situations such as spinouts, **sudden obstacles**, and flat tires. So basically, all Finns who have a driver's license are familiar with drifting a car. It is indeed not a strange thing to request such a difficult driving skill to the drivers in Finland because Finland **is also famous for** its severe weather conditions. Finland's roads are normally covered with snow and ice, so it is basically always slippery. There is a famous term describing their driving skills: the 'Scandinavian flick,' which is included in the practical driving skills learned at the driving school. The Scandinavian flick is the way Finnish people **turn their cars** on slippery roads, which is simply turning a corner by allowing the rear wheels to slide on the road. So it is no wonder Finns become champions in many driving competitions.

남: 핀란드의 운전 시험은 아마도 세계에서 가장 어렵고 까다로운 운전 시험일 것입니다. 핀란드에서는 36개월간 필수 운전 학교에 다녀야 하는 것으로 알려졌으며, 과정에는 운전 기술의 이론과 실제가 포함되어 있습니다. 한 가지 재밌는 사실은 이 눈 덮인 나라에서 모든 운전자가 스핀 아웃 (차가 회전하면서 코스를 이탈하는 현상), 갑자기 나타나는 장애물, 타이어 펑크와 같은 위태로운 상황에서 자동차를 구하는 방법을 배워야 한다는 것입니다. 그래서 운전면허가 있는 핀란드 사람이라면 누구나 자동차 드리프트에 익숙합니다. 핀란드는 날씨가 험하기로도 유명하기 때문에 핀란드의 운전자들에게 이처럼 어려운 운전 기술을 요청하는 것은 사실 그다지 이상한 일이 아닙니다. 핀란드의 도로는 보통 눈과 얼음으로 뒤덮여 있기 때문에 항상 미끄럽습니다. 핀란드 사람들의 운전 기술을 묘사하는 잘 알려진 용어가 있는데 바로 '스칸디나비안 플릭'이라는 것입니다. 운전 학교의 실제 운전 기술에도 포함된 스칸디나비안 플릭은 핀란드인들이 미끄러운 도로에서 자동차를 돌리는 방법으로, 뒷바퀴가 도로에 미끄러지도록 하여 코너를 도는 기술입니다. 그러니 많은 자동차 경주 대회의 우승자들이 핀란드 사람인 것도 놀랄 일이 아니죠.

해설: 21. 남자는 후반부에 스칸디나비안 플릭을 미끄러운 도로에서 코너를 도는 핀란드인들의 운전 기술이라고 소개했다. **22.** 중반부에 험한 날씨와 눈과 얼음 때문에 미끄러운 도로 상황에 대비하기 위해 까다롭게 운전을 배운다고 설명하고 있다.

수능 2일 전 대학수학능력평가 대비 영어영역 듣기(B형)

1	⑤	2	④	3	⑤	4	④	5	①
6	①	7	③	8	②	9	③	10	③
11	④	12	②	13	⑤	14	③	15	④
16	②	17	⑤	18	④	19	①	20	⑤
21	②	22	⑤						

문항 1 ⑤

Script & Dictation

W: Honey, did you book the tickets for the baseball game?

M: Oh, God. I **forgot about** that. I'll do it right now.

W: How could you forget that? They're **all sold out now**. Jason will be so disappointed.

M: I'm sorry. I promise we will go there next Saturday.

여: 여보, 야구 경기 표 예약했어요?

남: 오, 맙소사. 잊어버렸어요. 지금 당장 할게요.

여: 그걸 잊으면 어떡해요? 지금 다 매진됐단 말이에요. Jason이 정말 실망할 텐데.

남: 미안해요. 다음 주 토요일에는 꼭 가도록 약속할게요.

해설: 남자가 깜박 잊고 야구 표를 사지 못했고, 현재는 표가 매진되어 야구 경기를 보러 갈 수 없게 되었으므로 이에 대해 여자에게 사과하고 다음 기회를 약속하는 응답이 가장 자연스럽다.

문항 2 ④

Script & Dictation

M: It's already noon. Let's go and have lunch. I'm starving.

W: Tommy, wait. I just **need a little more time** to finish this.

M: We can work on it more after lunch. Let's **get some fresh air** for a while.

W: Then you go first. I'm supposed to prepare materials for the meeting.

남: 벌써 정오네요. 점심 먹으러 가요. 정말 배고프네요.

여: Tommy 씨, 잠깐만요. 조금만 더 있으면 이거 끝낼 수 있어요.

남: 점심 후에도 우리 그 일 더 할 수 있잖아요. 잠깐이라도 바람 쐬러 가요.

여: 그럼 먼저 가세요. 전 회의 자료 준비해야 해요.

해설: 남자는 빨리 밖에 나가기를 원하고 있지만, 여자는 해야 할 일이 남아 있다고 언급했으므로 흐름 상 ④번이 가장 적절한 응답이다.

문항 3 ⑤

Script & Dictation

M: Jina, **you're so good at** playing the flute.

W: Thanks. Do you want to try it? It's easier than you think.

M: I'd love to, but I'm not a **musically talented person**.

W: As everyone does, you just have to start as a beginner.

남: Jina, 너 플루트 연주 정말 잘한다.

여: 고마워. 너도 한번 해볼래? 생각보다 쉬워.

남: 하고는 싶지만, 난 음악엔 소질이 없어서.

여: 다들 초보자로 시작하는 거지 뭐.

해설: 악기 연주에 자신 없어 하는 남자에게 누구나 다 초보로 시작하니 한번 해 보라고 격려하는 말이 이어져야 내용상 자연스럽다.

Script & Dictation

M: Good afternoon, everyone. I'm Steve Pink, **the spokesman for** the student union, and I'm a senior in the Department of Arts Business Administration. The reason I'm standing here is to talk about the **upcoming election** for the student president. Nearly 80 percent of voters went to the polls for last year's election, one of the college's **highest turnouts** ever. This year, we have many improvements to talk about such as the school cafeteria, the beverage vending machines, and the library's facilities. Please **keep in mind that** you should vote for a better school to improve your school life. The election day is the 28th of February.

남: 좋은 오후입니다, 여러분. 저는 미술경영학 졸업반에 재학 중인 학생회 대변인 Steve Pink입니다. 곧 있을 학생회장 선거에 관해 말씀드리고자 이 자리에 섰습니다. 작년 선거 때는 투표자의 거의 80%가 투표를 했는데요, 이는 학교 사상 최고의 투표율에 속합니다. 올해는 학교 식당, 음료 자판기, 도서관 시설과 같이 개선을 논의해야 할 것들이 많습니다. 여러분의 학교생활이 개선될 수 있는 더 나은 학교를 위해 꼭 투표하셔야 함을 기억해주세요. 선거일은 2월 28일입니다.

해설: 학생회 대변인인 남자는 높았던 지난해 투표율과 더 나은 학교생활을 위해 투표권을 행사해야 한다는 이유를 들어 올해도 꼭 학생회장 투표에 참여할 것을 장려하고 있다.

Script & Dictation

M: Eva, what time are you coming home today?

W: I don't know, Dad. It **depends on** the traffic situation.

M: These days, I **am very concerned about** how late you've been coming home.

W: I have been studying at the library and coming home by subway, but it comes really late.

M: Yes, at night, **the trains run less frequently**.

W: Right. And the bus going to the subway station is usually held up by traffic.

M: I think it would be better to come home early. You can study at home, too.

W: You know I can study better at school, but I don't want you to worry about me.

M: If it's okay with your friends, you can all study at our house. And I can drive them home when you're done.

W: Thanks, Dad. I'll tell Chris and Jun about it.

남: Eva, 오늘 몇 시에 집에 오니?

여: 모르겠어요, 아빠. 교통상황에 따라 달라지겠지요.

남: 요새 집에 계속 늦게 와서 많이 걱정되는구나.

여: 요새 도서관에서 공부하고 집에 올 때 전철 타는데 정말 늦게 와요.

남: 그래, 밤에는 열차가 좀 뜸하지.

여: 맞아요. 그리고 전철역으로 가는 버스는 교통 때문에 대개 늦게 오고요.

남: 내 생각에는 집에 일찍 들어오는 게 좋겠어. 집에서도 공부할 수 있잖아.

여: 전 학교에서 공부 더 잘되는 거 아시잖아요. 하지만 아빠가 걱정하시는 건 싫어요.

남: 네 친구들만 괜찮다면 우리 집에서 공부하렴. 공부 끝나면 아빠가 친구들을 데려다 주면 되지.

여: 고마워요, 아빠. Chris와 준이에게 얘기해 볼게요.

해설: 남자는 학교 도서관에서 공부하고 집에 늦게 돌아오는 딸을 걱정하고 있다. 아빠로서 딸이 일찍 귀가해야 안심할 수 있기에 친구들과 함께 집에서 공부해도 된다는 제안을 하고 있으므로 정답은 ①번이다.

Script & Dictation

W: Everyone here has seen football or baseball games. Suppose a player makes a final touchdown or a batter hits a home run **in the bottom of** the ninth inning. What is about to happen? **The crowd goes crazy** and the stadium bursts with the sound of wild cheering, right? Then the player and teammates will be more motivated and try to do a better job. Likewise, I think **that kind of atmosphere** should be formed when you are at work, home, or school. It's a well known fact that when people **get credit and praise**, they will try their hardest. Rewarding one's efforts could be the best motivation.

여: 여기 계신 분들 모두 미식축구나 야구 경기 본 적 있으실 거예요. 어떤 선수가 마지막 터치다운을 하거나, 아니면 9회 말에 홈런을 쳤다고 생각해 보세요. 어떤 일이 벌어질까요? 관중들이 열광하여 경기장은 열렬한 응원소리로 떠나갈 듯하겠죠? 그럼 그 선수와 팀 동료들은 더욱 동기부여가 되어 더 잘하려고 노력하게 될 것입니다. 마찬가지로 저는 여러분이 직장, 집, 또는 학교에 있을 때에도 그러한 분위기가 조성되어야 한다고 생각합니다. 사람들이 인정과 칭찬을 받을 때 최선을 다한다는 건 잘 알려진 사실입니다. 노력을 보상해주는 것이야말로 가장 훌륭한 동기부여가 될 수 있습니다.

해설: 사람들은 칭찬과 인정을 받을 때 동기부여가 되어 더 잘하려고 노력한다는 내용을 스포츠 경기와 선수들을 소재로 들어 설명하고 있다.

Script & Dictation

M: Jihye, what pictures are you looking at?

W: It's about the Bilon people. These pictures are about their wedding ceremony.

M: Who is the bride?

W: The bride is the one **covered with white cloth**. Nobody can see her. She looks like a ghost, doesn't she?

M: Yes. Also, it looks like a modern bridal veil. Does that originate from the Bilon people?

W: That sounds right, but I don't know **if that's true or not**.

M: What about the paintings? What are they for?

W: It's a sand painting. Making a sand painting on the ground is part of the ritual. They believe the marks of the painting can **allow the couple to** have many children.

M: I like the designs, and they use a lot of white.

W: White means a new beginning.

M: Really? **That suits** a wedding ceremony.

남: 지혜야, 무슨 사진을 보고 있니?

여: Bilon 부족이야. 이건 그들의 결혼식 사진들이고.

남: 누가 신부니?

여: 신부는 흰 천에 싸여있어. 아무도 신부를 볼 수 없지. 유령처럼 보이지 않니?

남: 그러네. 또 요새 면사포 같기도 해. Bilon 부족에게서 유래된 건가?

여: 그럴듯한데, 사실인지 아닌지는 모르겠네.

남: 이 그림들은? 왜 있는 거지?

여: 이건 모래 그림이야. 땅에 모래 그림을 그리는 게 의식의 일부이지. 그림에 있는 표식들이 부부가 자식들을 많이 낳게 해 준다고 믿는대.

남: 디자인 맘에 든다. 그리고 흰색을 많이 쓰는구나.

여: 흰색이 새 출발을 의미하거든.

남: 정말? 결혼식과 잘 어울리는구나.

해설: 대화 초반 Bilon 부족의 결혼식 사진을 보고 있다고 언급하면서 신부의 모습, 모래 그림을 그리는 의식 등 부족의 결혼 문화를 소개하고 있으므로 정답은 ③번이다.

문항8 ②

Script & Dictation

M: Sunny, hurry up! Everyone has already **reached the top**.

W: I'm doing my best. Just go ahead.

M: We can get fresh air and appreciate the fascinating scenery up there.

W: [Pause] Wow! It's really nice! It is definitely **worth coming up** here!

M: I told you so. Look! The water is clean and has an unbelievably beautiful color.

W: It really is beautiful! Hey, look! Seagulls!

M: Quick! Give me some chips. Do you know what happens if we throw some food to them? They'll catch and eat it.

W: I am not sure if it is permitted for us to feed them, though.

M: It's okay. As you can see, other people are feeding them, too.

W: All right. Here you are, but you should be careful **not to fall into** the ocean.

M: Where are you going? You don't want to try feeding them?

W: No, thanks. I'll just **go inside the cabin**. I think I'm getting seasick. I have to sit down and rest for a while.

M: Oh, really? Then I'll come with you.

남: Sunny, 빨리! 다들 벌써 위에 도착했단 말이야.

여: 열심히 가는 중이야. 너 먼저 가.

남: 올라가면 신선한 바람도 쐬고, 멋진 경치도 감상할 수 있어.

여: [잠시 후] 와! 진짜 멋지다! 정말 올라와 볼 만한걸!

남: 내가 그렇다고 했잖아. 봐봐! 물이 깨끗하고 색깔도 정말 아름답다.

여: 정말 예쁘다! 봐봐! 갈매기야!

남: 빨리! 나한테 과자 좀 줘봐. 갈매기에게 먹을 걸 던져주면 어떻게 되게? 받아서 먹는대.

여: 그런데 먹을 걸 줘도 되는지 모르겠다.

남: 괜찮아. 보면 다른 사람들도 주고 있잖아.

여: 알았어. 여기 있어. 그런데 바다에 안 빠지게 조심해.

남: 어디 가? 먹이 안 줄 거야?

여: 아니, 괜찮아. 그냥 선실에 들어가 있으려고. 뱃멀미 하는 것 같아서. 앉아서 좀 쉬어야겠어.

남: 정말? 그럼 나도 같이 갈게.

해설: 대화에는 'seagulls', 'cabin', 'seasick' 등과 같은 단어가 등장하고 있다. 또한 남자가 바다에 빠질까 봐 걱정하는 여자의 말로 미루어 보아 두 사람이 배 위에 있음을 알 수 있다.

문항9 ③

Script & Dictation

M: Congratulations! You finally **got admitted to** Harvard!

W: Thank you. Are you coming to my **farewell party** on Saturday?

M: Sure, I am planning to. I don't know where your new home is, though.

W: Do you know where Hove High School is?

M: Yes, it's **on the corner** of Jason and Victoria, isn't it?

W: Yeah, from there, continue on Victoria and take a right at Robson. Go one block and you'll see the statue in the middle of the intersection. Do you follow me so far?

M: Yes. Please go on.

W: Turn left when you see the statue. That's Kansas Street. **Go one block** on Kansas until you reach another intersection. Turn right, and it will be on your left.

M: Thanks for the directions. I'll see you there.

남: 축하해! 드디어 하버드에 합격했구나!

여: 고마워. 토요일 내 작별 파티에 올 거지?

남: 그럼. 가려고 해. 그런데 너희 새집이 어딘지 모르겠어.

여: Hove 고등학교 어디 있는 줄 알아?

남: 응, Jason 가와 Victoria 가가 만나는 모퉁이에 있는 거 아니니?

여: 맞아. 거기서 Victoria 가를 따라 가다가 Robson 가에서 우회전 하는 거야. 한 블록 가면 교차로 중앙에 있는 동상이 보일 거야. 여기까지 이해했지?

남: 응. 계속해봐.

여: 동상이 보이면 좌회전해. 그러면 Kansas 가가 나와. 또 다른 교차로가 나올 때까지 Kansas 가를 따라 한 블록 가는 거야. 거기서 우회전하면 왼쪽에 우리 집이 있어.

남: 길 알려줘서 고마워. 파티 때 보자.

해설: Victoria 가와 Robson 가가 만나는 곳에서 우회전 하여 한 블록 가면 교차로 한가운데 있는 조각상이 보인다. 거기서 다시 좌회전하여 Kansas 가로 나오운 후 한 블록 더 가면 또 다른 교차로가 나오는데 거기서 우회전 후 왼쪽에 있는 건물인 ③번이 여자의 집이다.

문항 10 ③

Script & Dictation

M: Sally, there's a sign that says "Cherry Blossom Festival" over there. Wow! There are a lot of cars.

W: Yeah, parking will be **a big challenge**.

M: We should park somewhere and grab a cup of coffee.

W: Oh, the "**Lot Is Full**" sign is out on all these parking lots.

M: I hope we can find a parking space.

W: Hey, I think we can park in the coffee house building parking lot.

M: Great idea! You go buy the tickets. I will park and come back to you. People are lined up over there already.

W: Okay. Let's **meet at** the entrance gate.

M: All right. What kind of coffee do you want? I'm getting a latte as usual.

W: Make it two.

남: Sally, 저쪽에 '벚꽃 축제'라고 쓰여 있는 표지판이 있어. 와! 차들이 많네.

여: 그러게. 주차하는 거 정말 힘들겠는데.

남: 주차하고 커피 마셔야 하는데.

여: 주차장마다 '만차' 표시가 있네.

남: 주차 공간을 찾을 수 있으면 좋을 텐데.

여: 아, 우리 커피숍 건물 주차장에 주차할 수 있지 않을까?

남: 좋은 생각인데! 네가 가서 표를 사. 나는 주차하고 다시 올게. 사람들 저기 벌써 줄 서 있어.

여: 알았어. 입구에서 만나자.

남: 좋아. 어떤 커피 마실래? 난 평소처럼 라떼 마시려고.

여: 같은 걸로 할게.

해설: 주차할 공간이 없자 남자는 본인이 커피를 사며 커피숍 건물에 주차하겠다고 말하면서 여자에게는 표를 사라고 했다.

문항 11 ④

Script & Dictation

M: Honey, are you ready?

W: Almost done. I'm just looking for my passport.

M: I'm carrying both our passports, don't you remember?

W: Oh, right. I totally forgot that. I guess I'm too excited about our trip to Milan!

M: I know it's your **long-cherished desire** to see a fashion show in Milan. It will be at last accomplished. But, can't you hurry?

W: Okay, sorry. Do you also have our flight tickets?

M: I saved them on my cell phone.

W: That's good. And have our mail and newspapers been **taken care of**?

M: I've asked Alvin to get them while we're away.

W: Your friend Alvin? But he has become more and **more forgetful** like me. Call him again and remind him.

M: I will. And please **remind me to** call my parents.

W: No problem. I'll check the gas and electric cords. Then we can hit the road.

남: 여보, 준비됐어요?

여: 거의 다 됐어요. 내 여권 찾고 있어요.

남: 나한테 우리 두 사람 여권 다 있잖아요, 기억 안 나요?

여: 아, 그렇지. 완전히 잊고 있었어요. 밀라노 여행 때문에 너무 들떴나 봐요!

남: 밀라노에서 열리는 패션쇼 보는 게 당신의 오랜 소원인 거 나도 알아요. 드디어 소원 성취네요. 그래도 좀 서두를 수 없어요?

여: 알았어요, 미안해요. 항공권도 당신이 가지고 있어요?

남: 내 휴대폰에 저장해 뒀어요.

여: 잘했어요. 우편물이랑 신문도 처리했어요?

남: Alvin에게 우리 없는 동안 맡아달라고 부탁했어요.

여: 당신 친구 Alvin 씨요? 그 사람도 나처럼 건망증이 점점 심해지고 있는데. 전화해서 다시 한 번 알려줘요.

남: 그럴게요. 그리고 우리 부모님께 전화하는 거 나한테 다시 한 번 상기시켜줘요.

여: 알겠어요. 가스랑 전기 코드는 내가 확인할게요. 그런 다음 출발하도록 해요.

해설: 남자는 집을 비우는 사이 우편물과 신문 오는 것을 친구에게 봐달라고 부탁한 상황이다. 여자는 그 사람이 건망증이 있으므로 남자에게 다시 전화를 걸어 무엇을 해야 하는지 상기시켜야 한다고 이야기했으므로 정답은 ④번이다.

문항 12 ②

Script & Dictation

[Cell phone rings.]

W: Hello, Andrea Anderson speaking.

M: Andrea, this is Gale. Where have you been? I have been **trying to contact you** for hours.

W: Really? Sorry. Why were you calling me?

M: I found a great restaurant on 10th Avenue.

W: Wow, that's great. **Shall we go** tonight?

M: I wish we could. But while I was trying to call you, it was booked up for tonight.

W: Oh, that's too bad. **I wish I had answered** the phone. My cell phone was completely dead.

M: What happened to it?

W: Unfortunately I dropped it into the toilet. Though I was trying to save it, I failed. So I had to buy another one.

M: **That's why** you didn't answer the phone all morning.

[휴대폰 벨 소리]

여: 여보세요, Andrea Anderson입니다.

남: Andrea, 나 Gale이야. 어디 갔었어? 너한테 몇 시간 동안이나 연락했었어.

여: 정말? 미안해. 왜 전화했어?

남: 10번 가에 좋은 식당 하나 발견했거든.

여: 와, 정말 잘 됐다. 오늘 밤에 갈래?

남: 그러면 좋을 텐데 너한테 전화하는 동안 거기는 오늘 밤 예약이 다 찼어.

여: 너무 아쉬운데. 전화받을 수 있었으면 좋았을걸. 난 휴대폰 완전히 고장 났어.

남: 어쩌다가?

여: 내가 변기에 빠뜨렸지 뭐야. 살리려고 해 봤는데 실패했지. 그래서 새 휴대폰을 사야 했어.

남: 그래서 아침 내내 전화를 못 받은 거구나.

해설: 남자가 여러 번 전화하였지만, 여자는 휴대폰을 변기에 빠뜨려서 완전히 고장 나는 바람에 남자의 전화를 받지 못한 것이다.

문항 13 ⑤

Script & Dictation

W: Did you buy out the whole bookstore? One wall of the room is fully packed!

M: Yes, there are more than 800 books here.

W: Amazing! And **have you read** all these books?

M: Sure thing. I read books in the library or book stores, and if I find a book I like, I just buy it.

W: Wow, so those books seem to be entirely new. What do you **take into consideration** when you buy a book?

M: I consider who wrote the book, **what it is about** and whether its cover is unique.

W: Yeah, those are important things. Anything else?

M: I collect books from certain publishing companies.

W: Oh, you have collected books from only Random Publishing in this corner. Do you **have any connection to** the company?

M: Not at all. I just happen to like the publisher.

여: 서점 하나를 통째로 다 산 거니? 방 한쪽 벽면이 꽉 찼네!

남: 응, 여기 800권 넘게 있어.

여: 대단한데! 책들 다 읽은 거니?

남: 물론이지. 도서관이나 서점에서 책 읽다가 마음에 드는 게 있으면 구매해.

여: 그래서 책들이 완전히 새 거구나. 책 살 땐 어떤 것들을 고려하니?

남: 글쓴이가 누군지, 주제가 뭔지, 표지는 독특한지를 살펴봐.

여: 그래, 중요한 것들이지. 다른 거는?

남: 특정 출판사에서 나온 책들을 모으기도 해.

여: 이쪽에는 Random 출판사에서 나온 책들만 모아놨구나. 그 회사랑 무슨 관계라도 있니?

남: 아니, 전혀. 그냥 그 출판사가 좋아서.

해설: 책 사는 것을 좋아하는 남자는 대화 중반 책의 저자, 주제, 표지의 독특함 등을 살펴보고 책을 구매한다고 했다. 또 후반부에는 좋아하는 출판사에서 나오는 책들도 모은다고 했다. 그러나 출판연도는 언급하지 않았다.

문항 14 ③

Script & Dictation

W: Honey, let's go to the Emerson Museum today.

M: It's too far, darling. **It takes about** an hour and half. I don't want to drive that far on a Sunday.

W: You know the Kingsley Bridge **has just been completed**. Let's take the road across the bridge.

M: Was the construction done? I guess we could get to the museum in half the time, then.

W: Right. You will have to pay money to cross the bridge, though.

M: I'll check it from my smart phone. Oh, it **looks gorgeous**. We have to pay $2.

W: Every crossing makes the government $2? That's too much, I think.

M: No, it's not **an expensive toll**. The original charge is $4. $2 is for local residents like us.

W: Oh, okay. Is it based on just the car or on the number of passengers?

M: Just on the car.

여: 여보, 오늘 Emerson 박물관 가요.

남: 너무 멀어요. 1시간 30분 정도 걸린단 말이에요. 일요일에 그렇게 먼 곳까지 운전하고 싶지 않아요.

여: Kingsley 다리가 완공됐대요. 다리 건너서 가 봐요.

남: 공사 끝났어요? 박물관까지 가는 시간을 반으로 줄일 수 있겠네요, 그럼.

여: 맞아요. 그런데 다리 건널 때 통행료 내야 해요.

남: 스마트폰으로 확인해 볼게요. 다리 멋있네요. 통행료는 2달러예요.

여: 매번 다리 건널 때마다 정부에 2달러씩 낸다고요? 너무한 것 같네요.

남: 비싼 통행료는 아니에요. 원래는 4달러인데 우리 같은 지역 주민은 2달러 내는 거예요.

여: 그렇군요. 차량 기준이에요, 아니면 탑승인 수 기준이에요?

남: 차량 기준이네요.

해설: 다리가 완공되어 박물관까지 가는데 기존에 1시간 30분 (90분) 걸리던 시간이 절반으로 줄었다고 했으므로 45분이 단축된 것이고, 남자와 여자와 같은 지역 주민에게는 차량 기준으로 통행료를 2달러만 받는다고 했으므로 정답은 ③번이다.

문항 15 ④

Script & Dictation

W: **Have you ever wondered** about the accessories of the French queen, Marie Antoinette? There will be an exhibition **revealing her splendid diamonds** and fantastic accessories from August 9 to September 8 at the National Gallery. The exhibition will show the most expensive diamond in the world, some fabulous colored jewels, and the King's and Queen's crowns. It may be **the only opportunity for** you to see these priceless jewels. The exhibition will be open Tuesday through Sunday, 10 a.m. to 6 p.m. The admission fee is $10 for adults and $8 for students up to high school. There is **no discount for** groups of over 20 people.

여: 프랑스의 여왕 마리 앙투아네트의 장신구에 대해 궁금하셨던 적이 있나요? 마리 앙투아네트의 인상적인 다이아몬드와 환상적인 장신구들이 8월 9일에서 9월 8일 사이 국립 미술관 전시회를 통해 공개됩니다. 세계에서 가장 비싼 다이아몬드, 멋진 유색 보석류, 왕과 왕비의 왕관들이 전시회에서 선보여집니다. 이처럼 진귀한 보석들을 보게 될 다시없는 기회가 될 것입니다. 전시회는 화요일에서 일요일 오전 10시에서 오후 6시까지 열립니다. 성인 입장료는 10달러, 고등학생 이하 학생 입장료는 8달러입니다. 20인 이상에 대한 단체 할인은 없습니다.

해설: 안내 후반부에 20명 이상이 관람해도 단체 할인은 없다고 언급했으므로 ④번이 정답이다.

문항 16 ②

Script & Dictation

M: Have you ever heard about 'hand-foot-and-mouth disease'? If you are a parent whose baby is under five, or if you have a baby sibling, you probably have. It's a common **contagious disease** in summer and autumn for infants. It's usually a mild illness, sometimes **accompanied by** a fever. The tongue and the inside of the mouth can become reddish, and there could be some blisters in the oral cavity, on lips, hands, feet, and other parts. Most patients recover spontaneously after seven through ten days. **In severe cases**, patients will receive proper treatment. It's possible to spread this disease by saliva, nose and throat secretions, or the stool of the infected. Make sure to wash hands well after **contact with patients**.

남: '수족구병'에 대해 들어보신 적 있나요? 5세 이하의 아이가 있는 부모님 또는 어린 형제자매가 있는 분은 들어보셨을 수도 있을 겁니다. 수족구병이란 여름과 가을에 유아들에게 흔히 발생하는 전염병입니다. 가끔 열이 동반되기도 하는 가벼운 질병이죠. 혀와 입안이 빨개지고, 구강, 입술, 손, 발과 다른 부위에 물집이 생깁니다. 환자 대부분은 7일에서 10일이면 자연스럽게 회복됩니다. 심각한 경우에는 적절한 치료를 받아야 합니다. 감염자의 침, 코와 목의 분비물 또는 대변으로 전염될 수 있습니다. 환자와 접촉 후에는 반드시 손을 잘 씻도록 해야 합니다.

해설: 증상으로 가끔 열이 난다고 했으므로 고열을 동반하는 경우가 대부분이라는 ②번이 일치하지 않는 내용이다.

문항 17 ⑤

Script & Dictation

[Telephone rings.]

W: Hello, Facilities Management Team. This is Jungeun Bae speaking.

M: Hello, this is Cooper. **I'm calling to** reserve the Dante board room next week.

W: Are you going to have a presentation?

M: Yeah, I will need a projector system and some refreshments during the meeting.

W: Don't worry. What time would you prefer? Morning or afternoon?

M: Afternoon **would be better** for us.

W: Then, three days are available. Monday, Wednesday, or Thursday.

M: Monday's so busy for everyone. I'd like to book Wednesday afternoon.

W: Okay. Oh, sorry! On Wednesday, **we're scheduled** to clean all the air conditioning system in the whole building.

M: Oh, you're right. I'll book **the only day left**, then.

[전화 벨 소리]

여: 여보세요, 시설 관리팀 배정은입니다.

남: 안녕하세요, Cooper입니다. 다음 주에 Dante 회의실 예약하려고 전화했습니다.

여: 발표 있으신가요?

남: 네. 회의 때 프로젝터 시스템과 간식도 필요합니다.

여: 걱정하지 마세요. 오전과 오후 중 어느 시간대가 좋으세요?

남: 오후가 더 좋을 것 같아요.

여: 그렇다면 월, 수, 목 이렇게 세 요일이 가능합니다.

남: 월요일은 모두 바쁘니 수요일 오후로 예약할게요.

여: 알겠습니다. 어, 죄송해요! 수요일엔 건물 전체 에어컨 시스템을 청소하기로 되어 있네요.

남: 아, 그러네요. 그럼 남은 요일로 예약해야죠, 뭐.

해설: 회의실을 예약하려는 남자는 오후 시간을 선호한다고 말했다. 월요일은 모두 바빠서 수요일로 예약하려 했으나 그날엔 건물 에어컨 청소가 예정되어 있기 때문에 남아 있는 요일인 목요일 오후가 최종적으로 예약한 날과 시간이 되겠다.

문항 18 ④

Script & Dictation

M: Woojin, where did you get this cute little kitty?

W: I adopted him from an animal shelter **where I volunteer**. His name is Nabi.

M: You did a good thing. I heard that some people abandon their pets when they go on vacation in the summer just because **there's no one** to take care of them.

W: I am so mad at those people. And that's why I volunteer at the animal shelter.

M: Those poor animals, they all **deserve to be loved**. And you're such a good person.

W: I just do it since I like it.

M: **I'd love to** volunteer, too. How can I do it?

W: It is not difficult. You can visit the website and follow the directions there.

남: 우진아, 이 귀여운 새끼 고양이 어디서 데려온 거야?

여: 자원봉사하는 동물 보호소에서 입양했어. 이름은 나비야.

남: 좋은 일 했구나. 여름휴가 때 돌봐줄 사람이 없다는 이유로 애완동물을 버리는 사람들도 있다고 들었어.

여: 그런 사람들 때문에 화가 나. 그래서 동물 보호소에서 봉사활동 하는 거야.

남: 그 불쌍한 동물들도 다 사랑받을 자격이 있는데 말이야. 넌 정말 좋은 아이야.

여: 좋아서 하는 일인 걸 뭐.

남: 나도 자원봉사하고 싶은데. 어떻게 하면 되는 거야?

여: 어렵지 않아. 웹사이트 들어가서 지시사항을 따르면 돼.

해설: 대화 마지막 남자는 여자에게 어떻게 하면 동물 보호소 자원봉사를 할 수 있는지 물었으므로 그 방법을 알려주는 대답인 ④번이 가장 자연스러운 응답이다.

문항 19 ①

Script & Dictation

[Telephone rings.]

M: Dawa Travel Agency. How may I help you?

W: Hi, I'm calling to **book a package tour** to Guam. There are 4 people including me, and we'd like to leave on July 5th.

M: Sure. And **for how long**?

W: We're going to stay for 5 nights. Which hotels are available?

M: **I'd like to recommend** the Balijian Hotel. It's located near a beautiful beach and is well known for its great seafood.

W: Sounds lovely.

M: Oh, and I've just found out that they are having a special promotion. You will get a free round of golf on Monday.

W: That's great! What is the **promotion for**?

M: They're celebrating their 10th anniversary.

[전화 벨 소리]

남: 다와 여행사입니다. 무엇을 도와드릴까요?

여: 안녕하세요, 괌 패키지 투어 예약하려고 전화했습니다. 저까지 4명이고, 7월 5일에 출발하고 싶습니다.

남: 알겠습니다. 투어 기간은요?

여: 5박 있을 예정이에요. 어떤 호텔들이 투숙 가능한가요?

남: Balijian 호텔을 추천해드리고 싶네요. 아름다운 해변 근처에 자리 잡고 있고 훌륭한 해산물 요리로 유명한 곳입니다.

여: 근사하네요.

남: 아, 방금 알게 됐는데 특별 프로모션도 있네요. 월요일에 골프 한 게임 무료로 치실 수 있게 됐어요.

여: 좋네요! 프로모션은 왜 하는 거죠?

남: 10주년을 기념하는 중이라네요.

해설: 남자가 여자에게 숙박지로 추천하는 호텔에서 무료 골프 프로모션을 하고 있다. 여자가 프로모션을 하는 이유를 궁금해하고 있으므로 호텔 10주년을 기념하는 프로모션이라고 대답하는 것이 흐름 상 자연스럽다.

문항 20 ⑤

Script & Dictation

M: Mark is a freshman at Ruffalo Secondary School. As the new semester starts, all the clubs in the school are **recruiting new members**. There are various clubs and Mark **is very interested in** the drawing club called 'Terminals'. Mark is having **a conversation with** his counselor. He asks her whether he should join the club or not. Mark wants to be an engineer, so he thinks the drawing club is not really helpful for his university entrance. But, the teacher doesn't agree with him since he has joined a lot of **engineering-related activities** already. In this situation, what would the teacher most likely say to Mark?

* Teacher: Choose what you like, not what you have to do.

남: Mark는 Ruffalo 중등학교 신입생이다. 새 학기가 시작되면서 교내 모든 동아리가 새 동아리원을 모집하는 중이다. 다양한 동아리 가운데 Mark는 'Terminals'라는 그림 그리기 동아리에 큰 관심이 있다. Mark는 지금 상담 선생님과 이야기를 나누는 중이다. Mark는 선생님께 동아리에 들어야 할지 말지 물어본다. Mark는 엔지니어가 되고 싶은데 그림 그리기 동아리가 대학 입학에는 별 도움이 되지 못한다고 생각한다. 그러나 선생님은 Mark와 생각이 다르다. Mark는 이미 엔지니어링과 관련된 활동에 많이 참여하고 있기 때문이다. 이러한 상황에서 선생님이 Mark에게 할 수 있는 말로 가장 적당한 것은 무엇일까?

* 선생님: 네가 해야 하는 것이 아닌 네가 좋아하는 것을 선택하렴.

해설: Mark는 장래 직업과 관련된 여러 가지 활동을 하고 있으므로 이번만큼은 좋아하는 것을 해 보는 것이 어떠냐고 얘기하는 것이 흐름 상 가장 적절한 응답이다.

문항 21 ②
문항 22 ⑤

Script & Dictation

W: Sir Robert Walpole is known to be the first prime minister of Great Britain. Although the position was not precisely 'Prime Minister' at that time since there was no law acknowledging the position of a prime minister or **no official title** for it, there is no doubt that Walpole was the first prime minister because of his influence in the cabinet. His premiership was between 1721 and 1742, when the power of the king was **gradually diminishing** and the power of the cabinet was gradually increasing. The French Revolution started in 1789, and a republic was proclaimed in 1792, so the British premiership was a little bit ahead of the rest of Europe. Walpole's **influence on the politics** of Great Britain was tremendous. He also contributed to his country's peace and prosperity. But in the year 1742, when he was in his mid-sixties, many politicians thought **an aging prime minister** could not lead a military campaign. At that time, the British military was not as strong as it had previously been, and he finally resigned after a disastrous **loss in a battle with** Spain. The town of Walpole in Massachusetts, USA was founded in the same year when he started his premiership and named after Sir Robert Walpole, and Walpole Street in Wolverhampton is also named after him.

여: Robert Walpole 경은 영국의 초대 국무총리로 알려져 있다. 당시에는 국무총리직을 인정하는 법이나, 이에 대한 정식 직함이 없었기 때문에 그의 직위는 엄밀히 말해서 '국무총리'는 아니었다. 그러나 Walpole 경이 내각이 미친 영향력을 봤을 때 그가 초대 국무총리였음은 의심의 여지가 없다. 재임 기간은 1721년에서 1742년으로, 이 시기는 왕의 권력은 점차 줄어들던 반면 내각의 권한은 점점 늘어나던 때였다. 1789년에 프랑스 혁명이 시작되어, 1792년에 공화정이 선포되었으니 영국의 총리직은 다른 유럽 지역보다 조금 앞선 것이었다. 영국 정치에 있어 Walpole 경의 영향력은 막강했다. 경은 자국의 평화와 번영에도 기여했다. 그러나 Walpole 경이 60대 중반이던 1742년, 많은 정치인들은 점점 나이 들어가는 국무총리가 군사작전을 지휘하지 못할 것으로 생각했다. 당시 영국 군대는 예전만큼 강하지 않았고, 스페인과의 전투에서 처참하게 패배한 후 Walpole 경은 결국 사임한다. 미국 매사추세츠 주에 있는 도시인 Walpole은 Robert Walpole 경이 총리직을 시작하던 해에 그의 이름을 따서 건립되었다. 울버햄프턴의 Walpole 가 역시 경의 이름을 따서 지었다.

해설: 21. 후반부에 다른 정치인들이 나이 든 Walpole 경의 군사 지휘 능력에 회의적이었고, 스페인과의 전투에서 크게 패한 후 경이 사임했다고 언급되었으므로 ②번이 정답이다. **22.** 그 당시 국무총리직을 인정하는 법이나 정식 직함은 없었으나, 영국 내각에서 막강한 영향력을 발휘했기에 영국 최초의 국무총리로 평가된다고 하였으므로 정답은 ⑤번이다.

수능 1일 전 대학수학능력평가 대비 영어영역 듣기(B형)

1	④	2	⑤	3	④	4	①	5	⑤
6	②	7	④	8	②	9	②	10	⑤
11	①	12	⑤	13	②	14	③	15	③
16	④	17	⑤	18	③	19	⑤	20	③
21	⑤	22	④						

문항 1 ④

Script & Dictation

W: You love Michael Nicolas's music. Do you know his cello **recital has just opened**?

M: Of course, I do. I've got my ticket already.

W: Me, too. I've got **a balcony seat**. What about you?

M: <u>Oh, good for you. Mine is an orchestra seat.</u>

여: 너 Michael Nicolas 음악 좋아하잖아. 그의 첼로 연주회가 막 시작된 거 아니?

남: 당연하지. 벌써 표 구했어.

여: 나도. 난 발코니 좌석인데, 너는?

남: <u>좋겠다. 나는 오케스트라 좌석이야.</u>

해설: 연주회의 어떤 좌석 표를 구했는지 물어봤으므로 답변에 좌석 종류가 언급되어야 한다. 따라서 정답은 ④번이다.

문항 2 ⑤

Script & Dictation

W: Coach, it's my turn.

M: Don't be nervous. You've practiced this program **for such a long time**.

W: Right. But there are so many **participants with great ability**.

M: <u>Don't compare yourself with those around you. Just relax.</u>

여: 코치님, 제 차례예요.

남: 긴장하지 마. 넌 오랫동안 이 프로그램을 연습해왔잖아.

여: 맞아요. 하지만 재능이 뛰어난 참가 선수들이 정말 많은 걸요.

남: <u>너 자신을 주변 사람들과 비교하지 마. 긴장 풀어.</u>

해설: 실력 있는 다른 선수들 때문에 걱정하는 선수에게 오랜 기간 연습했으니 긴장하지 말 것을 당부하는 것과 같은 맥락으로 선수를 격려하고 있는 ⑤번이 가장 적절한 응답이다.

문항 3 ④

Script & Dictation

M: Bell, my daughter is going to graduate from high school tomorrow, but I have **a big presentation**, too.

W: But it's impossible that you can do both.

M: I know. Which do you think is **more crucial**?

W: <u>Always, family affairs belong at the top of the to-do list.</u>

남: Bell, 내일이 우리 딸 고등학교 졸업식인데 나도 중요한 발표가 있어요.

여: 하지만 둘 다 할 수는 없잖아요.

남: 그러니까요. 뭐가 더 중요하다고 생각해요?

여: <u>가족 행사는 언제나 해야 할 일 목록 제일 위에 있어야죠.</u>

해설: 남자는 여자에게 가족 행사와 일 중 어느 것을 선택해야 해야 할지 물어봤으므로 이에 대한 여자의 의견을 제시한 ④번이 정답이다.

문항 4 ①

Script & Dictation

W: Hello. I'm Lisa Smith from Green Efron Company. Have you ever heard about electronic waste? It means **electronic devices** such as mobile phones, laptops, computers and televisions thrown away by people after they use them. It's said that every year more than 20 million tons of electronic devices **are thrown away**. People nowadays upgrade their electronic equipment more frequently than ever before. So electronic waste is **the fastest growing waste**, and there's not a good solution yet. Soon, it will be a more serious problem than any other kind of waste.

여: 안녕하세요. 저는 Green Efron 사의 Lisa Smith입니다. 혹시 폐전자제품이란 것에 대해 들어보셨나요? 폐전자제품이란 사람들이 사용 후 버린 휴대폰, 노트북, 컴퓨터, 텔레비전과 같은 전자기기를 말합니다. 매년 2천만 톤 이상의 전자기기가 버려진다고 합니다. 요즘 사람들은 그 어느 때보다 더 자주 전자장비를 업그레이드하죠. 그래서 폐전자제품은 가장 빠른 속도로 증가하는 폐기물이 되었지만 아직 좋은 해결책이 없습니다. 폐전자제품은 곧 그 어떤 종류의 폐기물보다 더 심각한 문제가 될 것입니다.

해설: 폐전자제품이 무엇인지 소개하면서 그것이 빠른 속도로 증가하는 폐기물이나 좋은 해결책이 없다고 설명하고 있으므로 폐전자제품의 심각성을 알리고자 하는 것이 여자의 목적이라 할 수 있다.

문항 5 ⑤

Script & Dictation

W: Honey, I think I have to go on a diet.

M: Why? You look great all the time. I've never thought of you as fat.

W: I know I'm not fat. But **the result of** my regular checkup said I'm likely to get an excessive accumulation of fat in the abdominal area.

M: That can't be right. Your belly is in fine shape.

W: Honey, it's called intra-abdominal fat accumulated obesity. In the future, when I'm in middle age, it could **cause an adult disease**.

M: All right. What are you going to do?

W: I need to be careful about my diet. I eat too many carbohydrates. I should instead eat carrots, tomatoes, and so on.

M: It could be really hard to change **all of a sudden**. Slow and steady wins the race.

W: You can say that again.

여: 여보, 나 다이어트해야 할 것 같아요.

남: 왜요? 당신은 항상 보기 좋은 걸요. 난 당신이 한 번도 뚱뚱하다 생각한 적 없어요.

여: 나도 내가 뚱뚱하지 않다는 거 알아요. 그런데 정기 검진에서 복부 쪽에 지방이 과도하게 축적될 가능성이 있다는 결과가 나왔어요.

남: 그럴 리가 없는데. 당신 배는 정상이라고요.

여: 여보, 이걸 내장지방형 비만이라고 한대요. 앞으로 내가 중년이 됐을 때 성인병을 유발할 수도 있어요.

남: 알았어요. 어떻게 할 건데요?

여: 식단을 조심해야겠어요. 난 탄수화물 식품을 너무 많이 먹어요. 대신 당근, 토마토 같은 것을 먹어야겠어요.

남: 갑자기 바꾸면 매우 힘들 수 있어요. 천천히 그리고 꾸준히 해야 성공할 수 있어요.

여: 당신 말이 맞아요.

해설: 성인병을 유발하는 내장지방형 비만 성향이 있는 여자는 식단을 조절해야 하는 상황이다. 또한 서두르지 말고 천천히 바꾸라는 남자의 조언에 동의하였으므로 ⑤번이 정답이다.

문항 6 ②

Script & Dictation

M: There's no person who hasn't worried at one time or another. It's a part of our life. We all worry about family events, **relationships with others**, financial problems, and so on. However, according to experts, worrying is not always bad. Some worry is necessary for concentrating on a problem and finding solutions or as a way to deal with a problem. Some worry is inspiring. It can **propel you to do** better work or complete tasks on time. In other cases, however, our worries can **interfere with** our problem-solving abilities. We worry so much that it prevents us from taking steps needed to solve a problem. If it continues, worrying can **take away our energy** and lead to even physical problems such as fatigue, headaches, muscle pain, or insomnia.

남: 누구나 한 번쯤은 걱정하기 마련입니다. 그것은 우리 삶의 일부입니다. 우리는 모두 가족 행사, 다른 사람들과의 관계, 재정 문제 등과 같은 것을 걱정합니다. 그러나 전문가들에 의하면 걱정하는 것이 항상 나쁜 것은 아니랍니다. 문제에 집중하고 해결책을 찾거나 문제에 대처하는 방법으로서 걱정이 필요한 때도 있다고 합니다. 자극 역할을 하는 걱정도 있고요. 걱정은 일을 더 잘하게 하거나, 제때에 일을 마칠 수 있도록 우리를 움직일 수 있습니다. 그러나 어떤 경우, 걱정은 우리의 문제 해결 능력을 방해할 수도 있습니다. 걱정을 너무 많이 하는 나머지 문제 해결에 필요한 조치를 하지 못하게 되는 것이죠. 이런 상황이 지속되면 걱정 때문에 활기를 잃고 심지어 피로, 두통, 근육통 또는 불면증과 같은 신체 문제로 이어질 수도 있습니다.

해설: 초반에는 걱정이 가지고 있는 긍정적인 효과를 소개하고 있지만, 중반 이후부터는 걱정을 너무 많이 할 때 겪게 되는 문제점에 관해서도 소개하고 있으므로 ②번이 정답이다.

문항 7 ④

Script & Dictation

M: Jane, what are you reading?

W: Hi, Taejun. I'm reading the newspaper article Mr. McBryde **handed out** yesterday.

M: I think we should spend more money on the military. Considering the situation on the Korean peninsula, we need to **build a stronger army**.

W: But I think once we **spend money on** the military to build a stronger army, then North Korea will also spend more money on their military and the tension between the two will never end.

M: You have a point, but it's quite difficult to say it's wrong to spend more money on the military when there is another country threatening us.

W: It might be a **temporary measure**, but I believe increasing military budget will make the situation worse.

남: Jane, 뭐 읽고 있어?

여: 안녕, 태준아. 어제 McBryde 선생님께서 나눠주신 신문 기사 읽고 있어.

남: 난 군대에 돈을 더 써야 한다고 생각해. 한반도 상황을 고려한다면 더 강한 군대를 만들 필요가 있어.

여: 더 강한 군대를 만들려고 돈을 쓰면 북한도 군대에 더 많은 돈을 쓸 거고, 그렇게 되면 두 나라 간의 긴장은 절대 풀리지 않을 거야.

남: 네 말도 일리가 있지만, 다른 나라가 우리를 위협하는 상황에서 군대에 돈을 더 많이 쓰는 게 잘못 됐다고 말하기는 좀 어려울 것 같은데.

여: 임시방편이 될 수는 있겠지만 군대 예산을 늘리는 건 상황을 더 악화시킬 거로 생각해.

해설: 더 강력한 군대를 만들기 위해 돈을 쓰는 것에 대해 남자는 찬성하고 있고, 여자는 반대하고 있는 것으로 보아 두 사람이 읽은 신문 기사 내용이 이를 주제로 하는 찬반양론을 다루고 있음을 유추해 볼 수 있다. 따라서 정답은 ④번이다.

문항 8 ②

Script & Dictation

W: Hi. Did you **press your call button**, sir?

M: Yes, I did. Thank you for coming so quickly.

W: My pleasure, sir. How may I help you?

M: It's a little bit cold here, so I would like to get a blanket.

W: Of course. **I'll get one** for you right away. Is there anything else you need?

M: Yes. I am a bit thirsty. Can I have something to drink?

W: Sure. We have coke and water. Which one would you prefer?

M: Just water will be fine with me.

W: Okay. It is going to be **a long flight**. You should get some sleep.

M: Good idea. Do you know when we arrive?

W: **We're scheduled to arrive** at 11 p.m., local time.

M: Thank you very much.

여: 안녕하세요. 호출 버튼 누르셨나요?

남: 네. 빨리 와주셔서 고맙습니다.

여: 별말씀을요. 어떻게 도와 드릴까요?

남: 여기가 좀 춥네요. 담요 하나 부탁합니다.

여: 물론이죠. 지금 바로 가져오겠습니다. 더 필요하신 건 없으세요?

남: 네. 목이 좀 말라요. 마실 것 좀 부탁해도 될까요?

여: 그럼요. 콜라와 물 중 어떤 것이 좋으세요?

남: 그냥 물이면 될 것 같아요.

여: 알겠습니다. 긴 비행이 될 것 같으니 잠을 좀 자 두시면 좋을 것 같네요.

남: 좋은 생각이네요. 언제 도착하는지 아세요?

여: 현지 시각으로 밤 11시에 도착 예정입니다.

남: 정말 고마워요.

해설: 담요와 음료를 부탁하는 것과 '비행시간이 길다', 그리고 '현지 시각으로 밤 11시에 도착한다'고 설명하는 것으로 볼 때 비행기 안에서 이루어지는 승무원과 탑승객의 대화임을 알 수 있다.

문항 9 ②

Script & Dictation

W: How have you been? Wow, the room is really clean and neat. I'm so glad you arranged it well for my son to concentrate on studying.

M: Thank you. Actually, I study the relationship between study performance and surroundings.

W: I like **the low bookcase**. Children can reach any books they want. And I like the globe as well. Some people think that's not really a big deal, but **I prefer children to** always be able to see the globe.

M: You're right. When they want to know something about the world, a globe can satisfy their curiosity. And there's a bulletin board on which you can see Jay's drawing. He's good at fine art.

W: Thank you. Since the clock is behind the classroom, they can't always **check the time**. It can be helpful for the class to remain focused on the lesson.

M: Right, but the door is **on the opposite side**. When someone is late for the class, every student can see.

여: 어떻게 지내셨나요? 와, 교실이 정말 깨끗하고 깔끔하네요. 저희 아들이 공부에 집중할 수 있게 교실을 잘 정돈해 주셔서 정말 기쁩니다.

남: 고맙습니다. 제가 사실 학습 수행과 환경의 관계에 관해 공부하고 있어요.

여: 책장이 낮아서 좋네요. 아이들이 읽고 싶은 책을 마음대로 꺼내 볼 수 있겠어요. 지구본도 마음에 들어요. 별거 아니라고 생각하는 사람들도 있겠지만 전 아이들이 항상 지구본을 볼 수 있는 게 더 좋아요.

남: 맞는 말씀이에요. 아이들이 세계에 대해 알고 싶은 것이 생기면 지구본이 그런 호기심을 채워줄 수 있죠. Jay의 그림을 보실 수 있는 게시판도 있습니다. Jay가 미술을 잘해요.

여: 고맙습니다. 시계가 교실 뒤에 있어서 아이들이 항상 시간 확인을 할 수는 없겠네요. 아이들이 수업에 집중하는 데 도움이 되겠어요.

남: 맞습니다. 하지만 문은 반대편에 있어요. 수업에 지각하면 학급 전체가 볼 수 있죠.

해설: 대화 마지막, 남자는 문이 교실 뒤에 있는 시계 반대편에 있다고 했다. 그러나 그림에서 문의 위치는 시계 옆이므로 ②번이 정답이다.

문항 10 ⑤

Script & Dictation

M: I want to get some information on package tours for Jeju or perhaps Hong Kong.

W: We have some very good **package tours available for** 4 days and 3 nights.

M: How much do they cost?

W: To Jeju it is $500 and to Hong Kong it is a little more.

M: Which would you recommend?

W: It depends on your company. If you intend to **take a trip** with your parents, Jeju is better, but with your friends, Hong Kong is preferable.

M: Is there **anything special** about the two areas?

W: You can visit lots of attractive natural places in Jeju, and Hong Kong is one of the most popular places for shopping. You can get any item you want **at a reasonable price**.

M: It seems both places are so attractive. I need to talk with my family, and I'll let you know later. Thank you.

남: 제주나 홍콩 패키지 투어 정보를 좀 얻고 싶은데요.

여: 3박 4일 일정의 아주 괜찮은 패키지 투어들이 있습니다.

남: 비용은 얼마나 되나요?

여: 제주는 500달러고, 홍콩은 조금 더 비싸요.

남: 어떤 걸 추천하시나요?

여: 누구와 함께 가시는지에 따라 다르죠. 부모님과 함께 가실 거라면 제주가 낫고, 친구분들과 하는 여행이라면 홍콩이 더 낫고요.

남: 두 여행지에 뭔가 특별한 점이 있을까요?

여: 제주에서는 멋진 자연 명소를 많이 방문할 수 있습니다. 홍콩은 가장 인기 있는 쇼핑 명소 중 하나이죠. 합리적인 가격에 원하는 물건을 살 수 있답니다.

남: 두 곳 모두 정말 매력적이네요. 가족과 이야기해 보고 나중에 알려드릴게요. 고맙습니다.

해설: 여행지 두 곳 모두 괜찮아서 결정할 수 없던 남자는 대화 마지막에 여자에게 가족과 함께 상의해 보겠다고 말했다. 따라서 정답은 ⑤번이다.

문항 11 ①

Script & Dictation

[Cell phone rings.]

M: Hyeyeon, I'm **out of the office** on business today. But I left my laptop at the office.

W: Didn't you say you wanted to buy the concert tickets today?

M: Yeah, you know how much **I have been waiting** for that show.

W: Of course, it's your tradition for your wedding anniversary. So you want me to book the tickets for you and Mom, right?

M: That's right, honey. Can you do it?

W: Actually, I'm shopping at the mall with Jessie. What time **should I get** the tickets?

M: It's on a first-come-first-served basis. And tickets are **available online** from 5 p.m. You should go back home by quarter before five, I think.

W: Okay, Dad.

[휴대폰 벨 소리]

남: 혜연아, 아빠가 오늘 일 때문에 외근인데, 사무실에 노트북을 두고 왔지 뭐니.

여: 오늘 콘서트 표 사고 싶다고 하지 않으셨어요?

남: 그래, 아빠가 그 쇼를 얼마나 기다렸는지 알잖니.

여: 당연하죠. 두 분 결혼기념일마다 쇼 보러 가셨잖아요. 엄마랑 아빠 표 제가 예약하면 되는 거죠?

남: 맞아, 우리 딸. 할 수 있겠니?

여: 사실 저 지금 Jessie하고 쇼핑몰에서 쇼핑하고 있어요. 표 언제 사면 돼요?

남: 선착순 예매인데 오후 5시부터 온라인으로 살 수 있어. 5시 15분 전에는 집에 가야 할 것 같구나.

여: 알았어요, 아빠.

해설: 콘서트 표를 구매할 수 없는 상황인 아빠가 딸에게 전화하여 대신 표를 사달라고 요청하고 있다.

문항 12 ⑤

Script & Dictation

M: Hey, slow down, please.

W: Oh, sorry. I **have a bad habit** of driving too fast.

M: It's a relief that you know that, but you have to try to change it. You must always be careful when you're driving.

W: I know, but it's not that easy.

M: Do you remember my friend, Samantha? She was **in a car accident** last week.

W: Really? Was she seriously injured?

M: Fortunately, she only broke one rib, and **she is recovering** now.

W: What a relief! How did she get into the accident?

M: While she was driving to work, she bumped into a car in front of hers.

W: Oh, that's terrible.

M: She told me that her car slid **due to** a lot of snow on the road from last week.

남: 속도 좀 줄여.

여: 아, 미안. 나한테 과속하는 안 좋은 습관이 있어서.

남: 알고 있다니까 다행이긴 한데, 습관을 바꾸도록 노력해야 해. 운전할 땐 항상 조심해야지.

여: 아는데 쉽지가 않네.

남: 내 친구 Samantha 기억해? 지난 주에 교통사고 당했어.

여: 진짜? 많이 다쳤어?

남: 다행히 갈비뼈 하나만 부러졌고 지금은 회복 중이야.

여: 정말 안심이다! 어쩌다 사고가 난 거야?

남: 출근길에 운전하다가 앞차랑 부딪혔어.

여: 세상에나.

남: 지난주에 온 폭설로 도로에 눈이 많아 차가 미끄러졌다고 하더라고.

해설: 대화 후반부에 남자의 친구에게 교통사고가 난 원인이 언급되었다. 도로에 쌓인 많은 눈 때문에 차가 미끄러져 사고가 났다고 설명하고 있으므로 정답은 ⑤번이다.

문항 13 ②

Script & Dictation

W: Stephen, do you usually give your daughter an allowance?

M: Yeah, I've been **giving her some allowance** since she entered elementary school.

W: How much money do you think is **suitable for** my son?

M: Well, I give my daughter five bucks a week.

W: Is it enough for her?

M: I think so. And I buy her anything she needs for school. If she needs more money, she **does some chores** around the house.

W: What does she do?

M: She washes the dishes, **vacuums the floors**, helps her brother to do his homework and sweeps out the porch.

W: She must be learning the value of work and money.

여: Stephen 씨, 따님에게 보통 용돈을 주시나요?

남: 네, 초등학교 입학한 이후로 주고 있어요.

여: 우리 아들에게는 얼마를 줘야 적당할까요?

남: 저 같은 경우 일주일에 5달러 주고 있어요.

여: 충분한가요?

남: 제 생각에는요. 학교 준비물은 제가 사 주고 있거든요. 용돈이 더 필요하면 딸애가 집안일을 하기도 해요.

여: 뭘 하는데요?

남: 설거지, 진공청소기 돌리기, 남동생 숙제 도와주기, 현관 쓸기를 해요.

여: 일과 돈의 가치를 확실히 배우겠네요.

해설: 남자는 딸이 초등학교에 입학한 후 일주일에 5달러씩 용돈을 주고 있으며, 학교 준비물은 용돈에서 해결하게 하는 것이 아니라 본인이 직접 사준다고 말했다. 또한 여러 가지 집안일을 통해 용돈을 더 벌 수 있게 하고 있다고 언급하기도 했다. 그러나 딸이 용돈을 어디에 어떻게 쓰는지는 언급하지 않았다.

문항 14 ③

Script & Dictation

W: I'd like to have a family-size hot chicken pizza to go.

M: Okay, ma'am. **We're now celebrating** our 50th anniversary and offering family-size pizzas **for the price of** large pizzas. So, that will only be $18.

W: That's great. Also, I want a mushroom pasta with cream sauce and a salad pack.

M: The pasta is $9, and the salad is $7.

W: Okay. I have a 10% discount coupon.

M: I'm afraid you can't use it as **we are having** a special promotion that gives you a bigger discount.

W: Okay. **What about** my loyalty card? I have $2 worth of discounts on my loyalty card.

M: You can use that.

여: 패밀리 사이즈 핫 치킨 피자 하나 포장해 주세요.

남: 알겠습니다. 50주년 기념으로 패밀리 사이즈 피자를 라지 피자 가격에 드리고 있어서 18달러입니다.

여: 좋네요. 버섯 크림소스 파스타랑 샐러드 팩도 살게요.

남: 파스타는 9달러, 샐러드는 7달러입니다.

여: 네. 저 10% 할인 쿠폰 있는데요.

남: 죄송하지만 사용하실 수 없어요. 할인이 더 되는 특별 프로모션 중이라서요.

여: 알겠습니다. 그럼 제 로열티 카드는요? 2달러어치 할인받을 수 있게 되어 있는데요.

남: 사용 가능합니다.

해설: 피자 가격 18달러에 파스타와 샐러드는 각각 9달러와 7달러로 총 34달러이다. 그러나 로열티 카드로 사용할 수 있는 2달러를 차감하면 32달러가 된다.

문항 15 ③

Script & Dictation

W: Herpes Zoster comes with a painful skin rash. Herpes Zoster or simply 'zona' is a viral disease caused by the zoster virus. **The earliest symptoms** of zona are simply headache and fever, which are quite non-specific, so they may result in a wrong diagnosis. Sometime later, those early symptoms **are followed** by sensational burning pain. Zona in children is commonly painless, but older people are more likely to experience severe pain for a longer period of time. Severe pain normally lasts **for a couple of** weeks, and the treatment is only to reduce the severity and duration of the pain. After the patient is up and about, the virus is still present **in a latent state** and zona may occur again.

여: 대상 포진은 고통스러운 피부의 발진을 동반합니다. 영어로 'Herpes Zoster' 또는 짧게 'zona'라고 불리는 대상 포진은 대상 포진 바이러스에 의해 발병하는 바이러스성 질환입니다. 대상

포진의 가장 초기 증상은 단순한 두통과 발열로 일반적인 증상이기에 잘못된 진단이 내려질 수도 있습니다. 시간이 지나면 이러한 초기 증상에 이어 타는 듯한 극심한 통증이 수반됩니다. 어린이들에게 나타나는 대상 포진은 대개 통증이 없으나, 어른들은 대상 포진으로 인해 더 오랫동안 심한 통증을 경험하게 될 가능성이 많습니다. 심한 통증은 보통 몇 주간 지속되며, 통증의 강도와 기간을 줄이는 것만이 유일한 치료법입니다. 환자의 상태가 호전되어도 바이러스는 여전히 잠복 상태로 존재하기 때문에 대상 포진이 다시 발병할 수도 있습니다.

해설: 아이들에게 발병하는 대상 포진은 대개 통증이 없으나, 어른들에게는 심한 통증이 나타난다고 했으므로 정답은 ③번이다.

문항 16 ④

Script & Dictation

M: Have you ever heard about natural dyeing with ocher soil? Natural dyeing uses various materials from fruits, leaves of trees and grasses, and ocher soil. Ocher soil is red-and-ocher colored, and emits far-infrared radiation. This radiation has an amazing ability to clean, decompose, detoxify, **as well as** to heal a hangover, relieve pain, purify the air, and dehumidify. This campsite allows campers to **try dyeing** every Wednesday from 9 a.m. to 4 p.m. You can try natural dyeing with ocher soil, tangerines, and bamboo charcoal. The field study fee is $5 for adults and students. If you are **in a group** with over 20 members, contact us to make a reservation and **get a discount**.

남: 황토로 하는 천연 염색에 대해 들어보신 적 있으세요? 천연 염색에는 과일, 나뭇잎, 풀, 황토에서 나오는 다양한 재료가 사용됩니다. 붉은 황갈색의 황토는 원적외선을 방출합니다. 이 원적외선에는 세정, 분해, 해독하는 기능과 더불어 숙취 해소, 통증 완화, 공기 정화, 습기 제거와 같은 놀라운 기능이 있습니다. 캠핑객 여러분께 매주 수요일 오전 9시에서 오후 4시까지 본 캠프장에서 염색을 경험해보실 기회를 드립니다. 황토, 감귤, 대나무 숯으로 천연 염색을 해보실 수 있습니다. 체험 학습비는 어른과 학생 모두 5달러입니다. 20명 이상의 단체인 경우, 예약 전화 주시면 할인해 드립니다.

해설: 매주 수요일에 천연 염색 체험을 할 수 있다고 했으므로 이번 주 수요일에만 진행된다고 한 ④번이 일치하지 않는 내용이다.

문항 17 ⑤

Script & Dictation

M: I will visit Mr. Miller, the calligrapher. **Want to join me**, Arin?

W: Sure, why not? It would be an honor to meet him. How do you know him?

M: He's my professor this semester.

W: Oh, that's fantastic. Let's see. I'm scheduled to go to the yoga class with Bella tomorrow. What about Wednesday?

I have a meeting late in the afternoon, but **I'm free** in the morning.

M: I have to study on Wednesday because I have an achievement test on Thursday. What about Thursday afternoon or Friday?

W: I'm **doing volunteer work** at the library on Thursday. I was planning to watch a movie with Mom on Friday, but I should be able to reschedule it.

M: Then, I'll **call the office** of Mr. Miller now.

남: 나 서예가 Miller 선생님 뵙기로 했는데 같이 갈래, 아린아?

여: 물론이야! 만나 뵙게 되면 영광일 거야. 선생님을 어떻게 아는 거야?

남: 이번 학기 교수님이셔.

여: 와, 굉장한걸. 어디 보자. 내일은 Bella와 요가 수업 가기로 되어 있어. 수요일은 어때? 오후 늦게 모임이 있긴 한데 아침엔 시간 괜찮아.

남: 목요일에 성취도 평가가 있어서 수요일에는 공부해야 해. 목요일 오후나 금요일은 어때?

여: 목요일에는 도서관에 봉사활동 가기로 돼 있어. 금요일엔 엄마랑 영화 볼 계획이었는데 일정을 조정할 수 있을 거야.

남: 그럼 지금 Miller 선생님 사무실에 전화할게.

해설: 화요일과 목요일에는 여자에게 다른 일이 있어서, 수요일에는 남자에게 일이 있어 선생과 만날 약속 날짜로는 부적합하다. 여자가 금요일에 계획했던 일을 조정하겠다고 했고, 남자가 바로 선생의 사무실로 전화하겠다고 했으므로 이 두 사람이 선생을 찾아갈 요일은 금요일이다.

문항 18 ③

Script & Dictation

M: Misook, what do you usually do in your free time?

W: I paint and **hang out with friends** sometimes. I'm learning about coffee, nowadays. What about you, Hyunwoo?

M: I like cooking.

W: Really? I **haven't met any man** who enjoys cooking.

M: I know not many men do, but you see, the most famous chefs and lots of cooks in famous hotels are men.

W: You're right. I don't know why I didn't **think about that**.

M: Usually, fathers don't cook, and mothers do. That's the reason. After cooking, I share my food with my friends and family. I love that moment.

W: Oh, you really **make people happy** with food.

M: I hope so. I'll call you next time for sharing.

남: 미숙아, 한가할 때 주로 뭐 해?

여: 그림 그리고, 친구들 만날 때도 있고 그래. 요새는 커피에 관해 공부하고 있어. 현우 너는?

남: 난 요리를 좋아해.

여: 정말? 요리 좋아하는 남자는 만나 본 적이 없어.

남: 그런 남자들이 별로 없긴 하지. 그런데 유명 주방장이나 많은 유명 호텔 요리사들은 보면 대개 남자들이잖아.

여: 그러네. 내가 왜 그 생각을 못 했나 모르겠네.

남: 보통 아빠들은 요리를 안 하고, 엄마들이 하니까. 그것 때문이지. 난 요리한 다음에 가족, 친구들과 나눠 먹어. 그 순간이 정말 좋아.

여: 넌 정말 음식으로 사람들을 행복하게 만드는구나.

남: 그러면 좋겠다. 다음에 나눠 먹을 때 전화할게.

해설: 남자가 음식을 만들어서 다른 사람들과 나눠 먹는 걸 좋아한다고 했으므로 다음에 음식을 하게 되면 초대하겠다고 말하는 것이 흐름 상 가장 자연스럽다.

문항 19 ⑤

Script & Dictation

M: I hope that everything is satisfactory. How was your steak?

W: Perfect. We're all very **satisfied with** our meals.

M: I'm glad to hear that. Would you care for dessert?

W: No, thank you. Just **some more water**, please.

M: Certainly, ma'am.

W: By the way, I'd like to take the rest home. Could you **wrap this up**, please?

M: Sure, no problem. Do you have our steakhouse membership card? If you do, you can get a 10% discount.

W: No, I don't. May I get a membership now? And the bill, please.

M: **I'll register** a new membership card for you. Is this all on one bill or on separate checks, ma'am?

W: All together. And I need the receipt as well.

남: 모든 게 만족스러우셨기를 바랍니다. 스테이크 어떠셨나요?

여: 완벽했어요. 우리 모두 음식이 매우 만족스러웠습니다.

남: 그러시다니 기쁘네요. 디저트 드시겠습니까?

여: 아니요, 괜찮아요. 그냥 물만 더 주세요.

남: 물론입니다.

여: 그리고 남은 음식은 집에 싸 가고 싶은데요. 포장해 주실 수 있나요?

남: 그럼요. 저희 스테이크 하우스 회원 카드 가지고 계세요? 그럼 10% 할인받으실 수 있는데요.

여: 아니요, 없습니다. 지금 하나 발급받을 수 있을까요? 그리고 계산서 부탁합니다.

남: 지금 새 회원 카드 등록해 드리겠습니다. 계산 한 번에 같이 하시겠어요, 아니면 따로 하시겠어요?

여: 전부 다 같이요. 그리고 영수증도 주세요.

해설: 여러 사람이 먹은 음식값 계산을 한꺼번에 같이 할 것인지 아니면 각자 따로 할 것인지를 묻고 있으므로 이에 대한 대답과 함께 영수증을 요청하는 ⑤번이 정답이다.

문항 20 ③

Script & Dictation

W: Natalie and Gavin are really close siblings. They went to movies and played tennis together when they were young. **As time goes by** and they grow up, they can't hang out together as much as before. Natalie gets up every morning and rides a bicycle to her office. **On the other hand**, Gavin favors after-work dining and drinking with his co-workers. Also he hardly does any exercise and is becoming more and more overweight. He recently **had a checkup** at the hospital and was told that he has a fatty liver. So, Natalie wants her brother to take care of himself and **get in shape**. In this situation, what would Natalie most likely say to Gavin?

* Natalie: You should take care of yourself. Let's play tennis after work.

여: Natalie와 Gavin은 아주 친한 남매이다. 어렸을 때는 함께 영화도 보고 테니스도 했다. 시간이 지나고 둘이 점점 커갈수록 예전만큼 함께 어울리지 못한다. Natalie는 매일 아침 일어나 사무실까지 자전거를 타고 간다. 반면 Gavin은 퇴근 후 동료들과 저녁을 먹거나 술자리 갖는 것을 좋아한다. 게다가 운동을 거의 하지 않아 점점 과체중이 되고 있다. 최근 병원에서 건강 검진을 받았는데 지방간이 있다는 이야기도 들었다. 그래서 Natalie는 동생이 자신을 스스로 관리해서 건강한 몸 상태를 유지하기를 바란다. 이러한 상황에서 Natalie는 Gavin에게 뭐라고 말할 것 같은가?

* Natalie: 너는 스스로 관리를 좀 해야 해. 퇴근하고 같이 테니스 하자.

해설: 함께 운동하던 남매였으나 Natalie는 지금도 계속 건강을 관리하고 있지만, Gavin은 체중도 늘고, 지방간이 생긴 상태이다. 이를 걱정하는 Natalie가 함께 운동하자고 제안하는 것이 흐름 상 가장 적절하다.

문항 21 ⑤
문항 22 ④

Script & Dictation

M: The heaviest pumpkin ever recorded was 2009 pounds, which is more than 900 kilograms, and brought to Topsfield Fair in Massachusetts in 2012 by Ron Wallace from Rhode Island. Ron grows giant pumpkins as a hobby. People want to know **how he grows his pumpkins** so big. Actually, once **you have some experience** in growing pumpkins, growing giant pumpkins isn't so difficult because most record-breaking giant pumpkins are Atlantic Giant pumpkins or Goliath Giant pumpkins, and their seeds are readily available in the market. The next thing to remember is soil condition. Add enough amounts of fertilizer until the soil tester indicates the right value. Giant pumpkin plants require approximately 140 days to grow, and **it is better to start** growing the plant indoors first and transfer it outdoors later. The next secret key ingredient is liquid calcium because almost all fertilizers cannot be used efficiently if soluble calcium is not present in the soil. In short, if you get the right seeds and soil, you can also **break the record** with your pumpkin.

남: 지금까지 기록된 가장 무거운 호박은 2009파운드, 즉 900 킬로그램 이상으로 로드 아일랜드의 Ron Wallace가 지난 2012년 매사추세츠의 탑스필드 품평회에서 선보인 것이었다. Ron은 취미로 초대형 호박을 키우고 있다. 사람들은 그가 어떻게 호박을 그렇게 크게 키우는지 궁금해한다. 사실 호박을 한번 길러보고 나면 초대형 호박을 기르는 것도 그다지 어려운 일은 아니다. 기록을 깨는 초대형 호박들은 대부분 애틀랜틱 자이언트 호박이거나 골리앗 자이언트 호박인데 시장에서 쉽게 이들 품종의 씨앗을 구할 수 있기 때문이다. 다음으로 기억해야 할 것은 토양의 상태이다. 토양 검사기에 적정 값이 나타날 때까지 비료를 충분히 뿌린다. 초대형 호박이 자라는 데는 약 140일 정도가 걸리는데 처음엔 실내에서 기르기 시작했다가 나중에 실외로 옮기는 것이 좋다. 그다음 비법이 되는 주재료는 액상 칼슘이다. 토양에 수용성 칼슘 성분이 없으면 거의 모든 비료가 효율적으로 사용될 수 없기 때문이다. 요약하자면, 제대로 된 씨앗과 토양만 있다면 당신이 기른 호박도 기록을 깰 수 있다.

해설: 21. 세계 기록을 갈아치우는 초대형 호박 품종들을 언급하면서 종자들은 시장에서 쉽게 구할 수 있다고 했으므로 ①번이 잘못된 내용이다. **22.** 초반부에 Ron Wallace라는 사람이 선보인 2009 파운드짜리 호박이 가장 무거운 호박으로 기록되었다고 했다.

대학수학능력평가 대비 영어영역 듣기 답안지 (B형)

수능 10일 전

문번	답안				
1	①	②	③	④	⑤
2	①	②	③	④	⑤
3	①	②	③	④	⑤
4	①	②	③	④	⑤
5	①	②	③	④	⑤
6	①	②	③	④	⑤
7	①	②	③	④	⑤
8	①	②	③	④	⑤
9	①	②	③	④	⑤
10	①	②	③	④	⑤
11	①	②	③	④	⑤
12	①	②	③	④	⑤
13	①	②	③	④	⑤
14	①	②	③	④	⑤
15	①	②	③	④	⑤
16	①	②	③	④	⑤
17	①	②	③	④	⑤
18	①	②	③	④	⑤
19	①	②	③	④	⑤
20	①	②	③	④	⑤
21	①	②	③	④	⑤
22	①	②	③	④	⑤

수능 9일 전

문번	답안				
1	①	②	③	④	⑤
2	①	②	③	④	⑤
3	①	②	③	④	⑤
4	①	②	③	④	⑤
5	①	②	③	④	⑤
6	①	②	③	④	⑤
7	①	②	③	④	⑤
8	①	②	③	④	⑤
9	①	②	③	④	⑤
10	①	②	③	④	⑤
11	①	②	③	④	⑤
12	①	②	③	④	⑤
13	①	②	③	④	⑤
14	①	②	③	④	⑤
15	①	②	③	④	⑤
16	①	②	③	④	⑤
17	①	②	③	④	⑤
18	①	②	③	④	⑤
19	①	②	③	④	⑤
20	①	②	③	④	⑤
21	①	②	③	④	⑤
22	①	②	③	④	⑤

수능 8일 전

문번	답안				
1	①	②	③	④	⑤
2	①	②	③	④	⑤
3	①	②	③	④	⑤
4	①	②	③	④	⑤
5	①	②	③	④	⑤
6	①	②	③	④	⑤
7	①	②	③	④	⑤
8	①	②	③	④	⑤
9	①	②	③	④	⑤
10	①	②	③	④	⑤
11	①	②	③	④	⑤
12	①	②	③	④	⑤
13	①	②	③	④	⑤
14	①	②	③	④	⑤
15	①	②	③	④	⑤
16	①	②	③	④	⑤
17	①	②	③	④	⑤
18	①	②	③	④	⑤
19	①	②	③	④	⑤
20	①	②	③	④	⑤
21	①	②	③	④	⑤
22	①	②	③	④	⑤

수능 7일 전

문번	답안				
1	①	②	③	④	⑤
2	①	②	③	④	⑤
3	①	②	③	④	⑤
4	①	②	③	④	⑤
5	①	②	③	④	⑤
6	①	②	③	④	⑤
7	①	②	③	④	⑤
8	①	②	③	④	⑤
9	①	②	③	④	⑤
10	①	②	③	④	⑤
11	①	②	③	④	⑤
12	①	②	③	④	⑤
13	①	②	③	④	⑤
14	①	②	③	④	⑤
15	①	②	③	④	⑤
16	①	②	③	④	⑤
17	①	②	③	④	⑤
18	①	②	③	④	⑤
19	①	②	③	④	⑤
20	①	②	③	④	⑤
21	①	②	③	④	⑤
22	①	②	③	④	⑤

수능 6일 전

문번	답안				
1	①	②	③	④	⑤
2	①	②	③	④	⑤
3	①	②	③	④	⑤
4	①	②	③	④	⑤
5	①	②	③	④	⑤
6	①	②	③	④	⑤
7	①	②	③	④	⑤
8	①	②	③	④	⑤
9	①	②	③	④	⑤
10	①	②	③	④	⑤
11	①	②	③	④	⑤
12	①	②	③	④	⑤
13	①	②	③	④	⑤
14	①	②	③	④	⑤
15	①	②	③	④	⑤
16	①	②	③	④	⑤
17	①	②	③	④	⑤
18	①	②	③	④	⑤
19	①	②	③	④	⑤
20	①	②	③	④	⑤
21	①	②	③	④	⑤
22	①	②	③	④	⑤

* 시험 시, 답안지 작성은 컴퓨터 사인펜을 사용하여야 합니다. 수정테이프 또는 개인물품 사용 불가, 감독관에게 의뢰합니다.

대학수학능력평가 대비 영어영역 듣기 답안지 (B형)

수능 5일 전 / 수능 4일 전 / 수능 3일 전 / 수능 2일 전 / 수능 1일 전

문번 / 답안 (1 2 3 4 5), 문항 1~22

* 시험 시, 답안지 작성은 컴퓨터용 사인펜을 사용하여야 합니다. 수정테이프 또는 개인물품 사용 불가, 감독관에게 의뢰합니다.